— a complete messo

God, Guns and Israel

Britain, the First World War and the Jews in the Holy Land

JILL HAMILTON

SUTTON PUBLISHING

First published in the United Kingdom in 2004 by
Sutton Publishing Limited · Phoenix Mill
Thrupp · Stroud · Gloucestershire · GL5 2BU

British Library Cataloguing in Publication Data
A catalogue record for this book is available from the British Library.

ISBN 0-7509-3323-2

To Dame Miriam

This book would not have been possible without the inspirational SOAS library in London – the largest source of printed material on all aspects of the Middle East.

Typeset in 10.5/15pt Photina MT.
Typesetting and origination by
Sutton Publishing Limited.
Printed and bound in England by
J.H. Haynes & Co. Ltd, Sparkford.

Contents

Preface v

Prologue: The Bible and the Flag vii

PART 1 THE WAR CABINET AND THE BALFOUR DECLARATION

1. War Cabinet 1

PART 2 HOW THE OLD TESTAMENT WENT FULL CIRCLE – FROM JERUSALEM TO ENGLAND AND BACK TO JERUSALEM

2. Why the Old Testament became part of the Christian Faith 17
3. Empress Helena Goes to Jerusalem 28
4. The Crusades 36
5. The Wife of Bath Goes to Jerusalem 40
6. The Bible Begins to Speak with Many Tongues 45
7. In the Footsteps of the Old Testament 55
8. Lord Shaftesbury Campaigns for a Jewish Homeland 63
9. From Jerusalem to the Crimean War 76
10. Gladstone, Lloyd George and the 'Eastern Question' 83
11. With a Spade, a Rifle and Hope 92

PART 3 FROM THE BEGINNING OF THE FIRST WORLD WAR TO THE GRANTING OF THE MANDATE

12. From Peace to War, November 1914–March 1915 102
13. In the Realm of the Pharaohs 112
14. A New Empire from Cairo to the Persian Gulf 121
15. The Jewish Legion 126
16. The Fateful Embrace in the 'Garden Suburb': the Balfour Declaration 132
17. Judah's Broken Shell 140
18. Sunrise in Jerusalem 151
19. 'If I forget thee, O Jerusalem!' 159
20. 'The Turks Must Go!' 173

21. After the Armistice with Turkey 183
22. The Peace Conference 189
23. Arab Riots Begin 194
24. Riots and a Royal Visit 202

PART 4 FROM OFFICIAL MANDATE TO STATE 1922–48
25. The Fall of Lloyd George 208
26. Orde Wingate and the Haganah 223
27. The Second World War 233
28. David and Goliath 239
29. The Culmination of 2,000 Years of Prayer and Longing 246
30. The New Army 257
Epilogue 262

Appendices
1. The Religion of Britain's Prime Ministers 265
2. Jewish Immigration to Palestine and Demographics 267
3. Ben Gurion's Declaration, 14 May 1948 268
4. Outline for a Jewish Colonization Scheme, drawn up by Lloyd George, 1903 270
5. An Example of the Diminishing Support for Lloyd George by the Nonconformists 273
6. Balfour's Plea for Zionism 273
7. Summary of the Rise of Arab Nationalism in Palestine until the time of the Mandate 274

Notes 278
Outline Map of Palestine 292
Acknowledgements 293

Preface

There is a dry wind blowing through the East, and the parched grasses wait the spark.

Greenmantle, John Buchan

The horse my father owned in Egypt carried him to the fringes of the decisive battles that wrested Palestine and Syria from the Ottoman Empire. On 1 October 1918, when only sixteen, he rode into Damascus with the Australian Light Horse hours ahead of T.E. Lawrence (Lawrence of Arabia), Prince Feisal and the colourful Arab Irregulars. Fighting in the same campaign were another 100,000 soldiers, including the 38th Royal Fusiliers, known as the Jewish Legion, the first armed Jewish battalions to fight in Palestine for 2,000 years. My father's stories and his trophies of war – a Turkish sword, binoculars, a subaltern's brass uniform buckle, a battered knife in a sheath and a heavy pair of stirrups – formed part of the backdrop to my childhood. A newly framed Islamic prayer to Allah hung in our hall and competed with my father's Roman Catholic education and the ancient Bible which had been in my mother's strict Nonconformist family in Suffolk and Norfolk since the early seventeenth century. Until they migrated to South Australia in 1850, nearly each generation boasted a Nonconformist minister.

My father's involvement, small though it was, in the downfall and break-up of the 400-year-old Ottoman Empire, prompted me to follow the progress of the new nation states which were formed in the Middle East – Syria, Lebanon, Jordan, Iraq and Israel. Tracing various strands from London to Jerusalem, from Paris and New York to Damascus and Amman, revealed the influence of the Bible on the politicians who shaped the Middle East at the beginning of the twentieth century. Repercussions from their decisions have reverberated into conflict ever since.

Researching and writing two books on the Middle East in the First World War, *First to Damascus* and *Gallipoli to Gaza*, led me to numerous books on Christian Zionists, but most have overlooked the personalities of the politicians who actually opened the door to the Jewish return. So the emphasis in what follows is on the key men in the British and American governments and the effect of the Old Testament and Nonconformity on their decisions.

Among the many aspects examined is the view that the Arabs were not opposed to Jewish settlement until the Balfour Declaration. The question is also asked why pre-war tensions in Palestine were ignored by both the War Cabinet in London and the peace conference after the First World War. Another question posed is whether the Balfour Declaration should be called the Lloyd George Declaration, as David Lloyd George had more to do with the events that led up to the formation of a Jewish homeland than Arthur Balfour.

While writing this book I had much help from Lloyd George's nephew, Dr William George, who after reading the manuscript made the following pertinent comment: 'Lloyd George started out politically in the 1890s as an ardent young Welsh nationalist. He had an awareness of what it is to be a member of a small nation with an historical sense of being dominated by a larger nation, and having been oppressed. An ancient Welsh prophecy was that the Welsh would be driven out of their land; they would lose their territory but not their language. The Brythons or ancient Welsh occupied most of the north of England up to the Scottish border. The early Welsh poem 'Gododdin' concerned the loss of territory in the region where Edinburgh now stands. This would correspond with the history of the Jews, the Exodus from Egypt. This lead on several centuries later to the conquest of Wales.

This book lays no claim to historical completeness, and much detail has been omitted. Moreover, there are several things that this book is not. It makes no attempt to cover the history either of Zionism or of Palestine, nor is it a 'drums and trumpets' history which details strings of the battles that changed the course of events. Because it covers over 2,000 years brevity has been essential.

PROLOGUE

The Bible and the Flag

And did those feet in ancient time
Walk upon England's mountains green?
And was the Holy Lamb of God
On England's pleasant pastures seen?
And did the countenance divine
Shine forth upon our clouded hills?
And was Jerusalem builded here
Among these dark satanic mills?
Bring me my bow of burning gold!
Bring me my arrow of desire!
Bring me my spear! O clouds, unfold!
Bring me my chariot of fire!
I shall not cease from mental fight:
Nor shall my sword sleep in my hand
Till we have built Jerusalem
In England's green and pleasant land.

from the preface to 'Milton', William Blake

When war broke out in Europe in 1914, few scenarios seemed as improbable as the Jews of the Diaspora regaining Palestine. Stateless since the Romans had forced them out of Jerusalem 2,000 years earlier, they prayed to 'return to Zion'. This yearning to turn the clock back was and still is expressed by the Jews in many ways. They finished the annual Passover seder and the Yom Kippur service by reciting 'Next year in Jerusalem!' and three times a day they face Jerusalem and pray. In the long interval since their exile, the hilly strip on the eastern Mediterranean, through which the River Jordan slowly winds its way,[1] had become a crumbling backwater. With low rainfall, an inhospitable terrain, no oil resources and little industry, most of the people were poor. Prospects, too, were few. Apart from increasing tourism, there was little trade other than the export of a small amount of grain, sesame seed, olives from the groves in northern Galilee and oranges from around Jaffa. Despite these drawbacks, for two millennia Palestine has enjoyed an almost universal appeal. Measuring just 290 miles long and 85 miles at its widest point, it is one of the pivotal places in history. Religious significance has made it coveted, fought over and cursed.

The birthplace of two monotheistic religions, Judaism and Christianity, and a holy place for Islam, Palestine's parched soil is sacred to three faiths, three worlds and three dissimilar ways of life. Different though these religions are, they have one thing in common, a deep respect for the Old Testament, which includes the ancient texts of the Torah, comprising the five books of Moses[2]. They also share an empathy with this land, where much of the Old Testament was written, as a place of the source of truth, the inspired Word of God.

There was nothing new in the concept of the 'Restoration of the Jews'. Since the seventeenth century there had been initiatives in England. In 1840 *The Times* even ran an editorial supporting the idea, which gained wide currency after the publication of George Eliot's novel *Daniel Deronda*. This novel concludes with the hero returning to Palestine to give 'a political existence to my people, making them a nation again'. But it is unlikely that the Jews would have been able to establish themselves in Palestine during the three decades after 1918 had it not been for David Lloyd George. Nor would they have established their official footing there without support from President Woodrow Wilson. With all the determination in the world they would not have been in a position to expand their hold on its worn-out land if they had not first had this strong backing from the British and, later, the government of the United States of America. Quite simply, Israel might never have existed.

It is always difficult to prove what elements shape a decision, but in this case a pattern emerges of politicians with Nonconformist or Evangelical backgrounds in which the Old Testament had been a major early influence. And it was these men who, through their decisions, provided the Jews with a platform, a springboard,[3] on which to rebuild their sovereignty – and thereby unwittingly laid the foundations of one of the most protracted conflicts of the twentieth century.

The motives behind the British push to create a Jewish homeland in Palestine have never been fully explained. Nor has a reason been given as to why the discussions leading up to it were never debated in the House of Commons, or whether Britain's adoption of Zionism was an incidental corollary to the main purpose of the British offensive. To decide to bring

Palestine into the British Empire was one thing; to make it also a haven for Jews was another. Despite frequent articles and letters in *The Times*, the *Sunday Times*, the *Manchester Guardian* and other newspapers in 1917, and frequent discussions with the Foreign Office and Jewish leaders, especially between the Foreign Secretary, Arthur Balfour, and Lord Rothschild, the head of the dazzling Jewish banking family and leader of the Jewish community in Britain, the final discussions took place behind the closed doors of 10 Downing Street. Here, and, occasionally, in two temporary wooden buildings in its leafy walled garden, members of the War Cabinet discussed how to create a homeland for the Jewish people. The policy was not formalized into a declaration until British guns were poised on Gaza, on the eve of the British army entering the Holy Land in November 1917 – just before the first anniversary of Lloyd George's first year as prime minister. Because this declaration bears the name of the Foreign Secretary, Balfour, it is usually his name alone which is associated with the formation of the Jewish homeland, yet, significant though his rôle was, he only took up the idea after it was accepted by Lloyd George's War Cabinet, of which he was not a member.

The thesis of this book is that the long-held Jewish dream of a homeland in Palestine became as a result of a remarkable military, political and theological confluence. This is reflected in the three words in the title, *God, Guns and Israel*: the word 'God' is a reference to the Old Testament; 'Guns' refers to the Jewish Legion, the Haganah and the wars which accelerated the establishment of the Jewish homeland, and, eventually, Israel which owed so much to American politics.

Among the many influences behind the decision of the British War Cabinet in 1917 to take the unprecedented step of forming a Jewish homeland within the British Empire, was the Bible. The following chapters could almost be the biography of the Old Testament itself. They show how its influence went full circle, from Palestine to England and back to Palestine. It was as if the pages of the Old Testament were scattered to form the sections of a temporary bridge between Britain and the Holy Land. During that brief time, became an invisible aid in helping the Jewish people fulfil their wish to achieve their almost unquenchable desire, 'the hope' for Israel, *Tikveh Yisroel*. For centuries they had been persecuted in the name of Christianity, but 1917 briefly changed all that.

While looking at the circuitous journey of the Old Testament, some unexpected facts have emerged. It played a large part in the lives of a number of British and American government officials who assisted the Jewish people in their quest to establish themselves in Palestine. A sound knowledge of the Hebrew Scriptures can be firmly placed beside gunpowder, as an ingredient that led to the momentous decisions and actions. This fits with Thomas Carlyle's hypothesis that 'the three great elements of modern civilization' were 'Gunpowder, Printing, and the Protestant Religion'.[4]

The Bible was the 'book of books' on which generation after generation of British people were brought up. Lord Macaulay, the most popular historian of the Victorian era, said that the English Bible, apart from being the core of Christianity, was the 'book which if everything else in our language should perish, would alone suffice to show the whole extent of its beauty and power'. Since the Reformation no other book in British history has been so universally read or so carefully studied.

Of the ten men who, at some stage, were members of Lloyd George's War Cabinet, seven had been raised in Nonconformist families and one, although Church of England, had come from one with a strong Evangelical leaning. Three – Lloyd George, Andrew Bonar Law and Lord Curzon – were the sons or grandsons of church ministers. Jan Christian Smuts, the Defence Minister of South Africa who joined in June 1917 as a representative of the Dominions, would have been ordained as a minister in the Dutch Reform Church in the Cape Colony had he not chosen to study at Cambridge. Arthur Henderson, the leader of the Labour Party, was such a committed Christian that he continued working as a Methodist lay preacher until his death.

A close acquaintance with the Old Testament had given more than half the members of the War Cabinet a feeling of familiarity with the Holy Land. This intimacy also predisposed them to listen sympathetically to Zionist arguments. Many of them could quote lengthy passages including the Psalms – the poetry of the Bronze Age – by heart. Like a large number of British people during the nineteenth century, and indeed the early twentieth, they came from homes where the Bible had few competitors.

Enthralled during their childhoods with stories set in Jerusalem, Jericho, Jaffa, Gaza and other places in the Old Testament some exhibited a lifelong fascination with the Holy Land, others with the Bible itself. Lloyd George said he preferred the Old Testament to the New, and once remarked that he knew the names of the towns in the Holy Land better than those on the Western Front. On another occasion he explained that he had learnt the names of the rivers, valleys and mountains of the Holy Land long before those in either Wales or England. For him and others, drawing up plans for the Jewish people to 'return' to a place which the Bible had made so familiar had a particular appeal,[5] especially as the Jews were seen not only as the 'people of the Book',[6] but as a downtrodden people and a worthwhile cause. There was also the age-old problem in Europe of anti-Semitism and the need to find a home for displaced Jewish refugees fleeing from Russia.

The fact that Nonconformists, with their drumbeats of moral discipline and self-improvement, helped to shape British politics during the last half of the reign of Queen Victoria and the early twentieth century is usually forgotten, as is any acknowledgment that ten out of the nineteen prime ministers who came to power in the twentieth century had been raised as Nonconformists. Only nine had been brought up in the Established Church, although the number is reduced to seven if Stanley Baldwin and Harold Macmillan are counted. Both Baldwin's parents were Methodists who in adult life were rebaptised into the Church of England. Macmillan, too, was partly of Nonconformist stock: his mother until her marriage was staunchly Methodist.[7] (For details of the religions of England's prime ministers see Appendix 2.)

The Russian-born lecturer in biochemistry at Manchester University, the charismatic Dr Chaim Weizmann, who became the main Zionist link with the cabinet, remarked in his autobiography on the religious sentiment and romantic idealism which brought converts to Zionism among British leaders, '. . . men like Balfour, Churchill, Lloyd George, were deeply religious, and believed in the Bible . . . to them the return of the Jewish people to Palestine was a reality, so that we Zionists represented to them a great tradition for which they had enormous respect.'[8]

With the exception of Smuts, these politicians were a mixture of Liberal, Conservative and Labour, and the majority had little in common except that they were all accustomed to simplicity rather than pomp in worship and came from backgrounds which were either Nonconformist – that is Wesleyan Methodist, Primitive Methodist, Baptist, Unitarian, Presbyterian or Congregationalist – or Anglican with strong Evangelical leanings. With two exceptions the Bible was the thread of continuity linking them together. Some were rich, others were struggling. Only one was an aristocrat; the parents of three were working class, the rest a melange of rising lower middle and middle class. Three had been born in England, two in Scotland, one in Germany, one in South Africa, one in India, one in Ireland and one in Canada. (Lloyd George was born in Manchester, but had Welsh parents and was brought up in a Welsh-speaking home in Wales.)

The religious backgrounds of these politicians would have had little effect without either the earlier precedent of the British government's attempt to form a Jewish homeland within the British Empire or the forceful arguments put forward by Jewish intellectuals. Leaders among these were Sir Herbert Samuel, who was the first Jew to become a cabinet minister in Britain, and Weizmann, who was said to be able to charm the spots off a leopard. The first practical steps towards forming a Jewish homeland had begun in the middle of the nineteenth century with Lord Shaftesbury and gathered momentum with the offer, in 1903, by the British Colonial Secretary, Joseph Chamberlain, to Theodor Herzl (1860–1904), the founder of the Zionist movement of a large part of Kenya (usually referred to as 'the Ugandan offer') which was to be called 'New Palestine'. Lloyd George, then one of the rising stars of the Liberal Party, had been closely involved in this scheme. Indeed, he was employed in a private capacity as a solicitor by the newly formed Jewish Colonial Trust in London, which chose him because as an MP he could consult the Foreign Office to find out in advance what would be acceptable for such a settlement. But after the complicated legal papers he drew up on behalf of the Zionists were presented to the British government, both sides cooled. The project itself came to nothing.

* * *

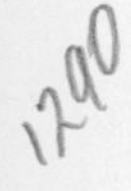

It was ironic that a Welshman, let alone the British government, made a cradle in Palestine in which the Jews could create their own state. Britain, one of the last countries in which Jewish people settled in Europe, was also the first European country which forcibly expelled Jews *en masse*. Jews had not begun migrating to the British Isles until the reign of William the Conqueror, in 1066. Then, only two centuries after they had begun to put down roots, King Edward I threw out every Jewish man, woman and child from his kingdom. Total expulsion was then unprecedented in continental Europe, but the persecution of the Jews was not. The last English with a foothold in the Holy Land had been the Crusaders. They had attacked and killed all the Jews they encountered with such ferocity that 10,000 had been killed in the first month of the First Crusade alone during the journey to Palestine. Death and destruction came also to thousands of other Jews in the Holy Land itself. Edward had become king of England in 1272 when, accompanied by his wife Eleanor of Castile and Leon, he was fighting his way unsuccessfully into Jerusalem on the eighth and last major crusade.

On his return to England in 1274, the new king's first ruthless act was a series of incursions against the Welsh, during which Llewelyn, prince of Gwynedd and Prince of Wales, was forced to surrender Criccieth Castle. Eight years after Edward's final subjugation of the Welsh in 1282, the Jews became his target. His expulsion in 1290 of every Jewish man, woman or child from the kingdom, under the pain of death, was so merciless that he could have earned the title of 'Hammer of the Jews' as well as the 'Hammer of the Scots' – the faded Latin inscription above his coffin at Westminster Abbey which reads '. . . Scotorum Malleus . . .'. All Jews left the country before the Feast of All Souls; none were formally permitted to live in England again for nearly four centuries, until the time of Oliver Cromwell.

Despite this record, it was Britain, the country which set such a cruel example of anti-Semitism in the Middle Ages, that 627 years later conquered the Holy Land and created a safe haven for the Jews under the red, white and blue British flag. Edward would have been infuriated: his descendant's army had achieved what he had failed to do in the name of England but was preparing to hand the newly conquered territory back to the Jews, the very race he had turned into exiles. To add to the poignancy, their return was made possible by Lloyd George, who had been brought up in Criccieth on the Welsh coast. The childhood home of this son of Gwynedd was less than two miles from the very castle that had borne the brunt of Edward's army.

Lloyd George's policy towards the Jews, which was the start of so much heartache to some and consolation to others, was one of the most controversial outcomes of the First World War. But despite his close involvement, in his *War Memoirs* Lloyd George gave just two reasons for 'the fount and origin' of the setting up of the Jewish homeland. The first was a reward to Weizmann for his invention of synthesizing acetone, which had been the key in maintaining a high output of explosive during the war. The second was the need to 'enlist Jewish support in neutral countries, notably in America . . .'. By implying that his initial contact with Zionism was during his term as Minister of Munitions in 1915, soon after Weizmann had started research, Lloyd George created a myth that placed the initiative with the Jews rather than with the War Cabinet or himself. He declined to mention anything about the first papers submitted to the Foreign Office for a Jewish homeland which had been drawn up by him or the fact that he had changed the direction of the war in Middle East within days of taking office. Ignoring the earlier failed invasions into Turkey on the Gallipoli peninsula in 1915 and the Siege of Kut in Mesopotamia in 1916, he had immediately intensified the British campaigns against the Turks. Until then operations beyond the Suez Canal had been essentially defensive in principle.

Ignoring the fierce reluctance on the part of the generals, Lloyd George stepped up invasions into Turkish territory. The Sinai offensive grew into the Palestine campaign and General Stanley Maude's invasion up the Tigris to Baghdad was expanded. Lloyd George's actions would later alter the map of the Middle East and make Britain the unwelcome godmother of the future states of Israel and Iraq. Indeed, Lloyd George, who inherited William Ewart Gladstone's bitter and entrenched prejudice against the Turks, would become the main player in the final act in what nineteenth-century politicians called 'the Eastern Question', which began in 1821 with the beginning of the Greek War of Independence, and developed into one of the great diplomatic preoccupations of the nineteenth century. Attitudes were complicated after the 1890s by the discovery of large deposits of oil in Mesopotamia and Iran, making covetous Western eyes gaze at Ottoman territories. But while the First World War saw Britain taking over Turkey's dominant role in the Middle East, during the Second World War the United States took over by expanding her share of Middle Eastern oil and becoming the power behind the transformation of the Jewish homeland into the state of Israel.

* * *

The First World War was not the first war to have been a watershed for the return of the Jews to Palestine: the Crimean War (1854–6) and the Boer War (1899–1902) also acted as turning-points. In each case a politician sympathetic to the Jewish people had managed to tie a few Jewish needs to British imperial interests. Just as the battles between Persia and Media against Babylonia had led the Persian King Cyrus to permit the Jews to return to Samaria and to Israel in 538 BCE, the prospect of British victory in the First World War added a new dimension to the Zionist dream and led Lloyd George, Balfour and the members of the War Cabinet to throw open the doors of the Holy Land to the Jews. Their offer was made before the Allies had conquered any of it, when the crescent moon and star flag of the sprawling Ottoman Empire was still fluttering over Syria, Palestine and Mesopotamia, as it had for four centuries. The sultan, from his palace in the Bosphorus in Constantinople, controlled a vast empire in the sands that had once included much of North Africa. In the previous fifty years his empire had shrunk considerably, but still contained ten legendary and ancient cities of the Orient: Damascus, Baghdad, Jerusalem, Gaza, Jaffa, Jericho, Bethlehem, Amman, Mecca and Medina.

The majority of British generals were 'Westerners', believing that Allied forces and effort should be concentrated in the main theatre of war, the Western Front in France and Belgium. The 'Easterners', led by Lloyd George, favoured staging smaller campaigns against the enemy's weakest points, in places such as the Balkans and the Middle East. He wanted more men and more money to be thrown into the war against Turkey. This would prove less costly in soldiers' lives, weaken the underbelly of Germany and give Britain the trump card during future negotiations when the Ottoman Empire finally collapsed and was carved up between the Great Powers. The generals did not agree. Sir Douglas Haig (of the distilling and whisky family), the dour, uncommunicative commander of the British armies in France, was opposed to any operations that might deflect British resources from the main theatre of war in France and Belgium. Lloyd George's *bête noire*, General Sir William Robertson, Chief of the Imperial Staff, had a similar attitude. This favourite of the king who looked like a gruff old sergeant-major was the only soldier in British history to rise from footman to private to field marshal.

* * *

The high-point of Nonconformity and Evangelism in politics had peaked in the years after the 1868 election with the establishment of the first unequivocally Liberal government with Gladstone as prime minister.[9] The three Liberal prime ministers of the twentieth century, Campbell-Bannerman, Asquith and Lloyd George, had been brought up as Nonconformists in lower middle-class and working-class families. Just how informal and incomplete the connection was between the Liberal Party and the Nonconformists can be seen by the fact that their two predecessors as Liberal prime ministers, Gladstone and Lord Rosebery, were Old Etonians and members of the Established Church. Gladstone had been a devout member of the Church of England (even though his Scottish father was Presbyterian and his Scottish mother had been Episcopalian until they converted after their marriage). Even so, the main supporters of the Liberals were the Nonconformist industrialists and artisans of the north of England, Scotland

and Wales. Unlike the Conservatives who had grown out of the old Tory Party, the Liberal Party was much more than just a transformed Whig party; it was a merger between Peelites, radicals and other pressure groups. This new party was now repaid in kind for the courageous support given by the Whigs for the religious and other rights of the Nonconformists since the seventeenth century.

Nonconformist opinion was significant. In a survey on one Sunday in 1851, Nonconformists claimed that about one in two of the population had attended a chapel or kirk. Even after the religious revival which had swept through Victorian England and occupied so large a part of the nation's life had begun to decline from 1880 onwards, it was very much alive. The Nonconformist conscience continued to dominate public morality, together with Temperance, Sunday observance and Gladstonian rectitude.

* * *

By the time of the First World War, Kirk, Chapel, Church and organized religion were no longer central to as many communities or families as at the end of the previous century. Religious bodies often did not have such a robust hold on their members, so when Members of Parliament came from a Nonconformist background they were often not as steeped in the Bible as their predecessors had been. The temper of the age was changing socially and economically. Now the Victorian Sabbath was giving way to the one-and-a-half day secular weekend with cycling and train excursions, motoring and motorcycling, hiking and golf competing with hymns, prayers and sermons. An investigation by the *Daily News* in London between November 1902 and November 1903 showed that out of London's population of 6.25 million, only 1.25 million attended church regularly, with the majority belonging to the lower middle class. Noticeable though the decline was, religion remained powerful in many families, particularly in rural areas where places of worship and Sunday schools had higher attendance rates. As in the nineteenth century, many children stared at maps of Bible lands and looked at life-like illustrations of shepherds in flowing white attire, biblical towns, hills, deserts, lakes, wilderness and the Dead Sea shimmering in a haze of heat. Scenes were often as real as were some biblical epics and battles from memories of flickering lantern slides on a sheet pinned up on Sunday school walls. Stories, such as the passionate tale of Samson and Delilah, had been learned in

Christian communities everywhere, from the Welsh valleys to the Gothic chapels of England's public schools, and from weatherboarded farmhouses on the plains of America to the halls of Princeton University.

The elections in January 1906 had brought 185 Nonconformists into parliament and the affinity between Nonconformists and the Liberal Party, although weakening, continued. At that time, with few exceptions, the majority of Nonconformists voted for Liberal candidates. But Nonconformists were turning increasingly towards the new Labour Party and, to a lesser degree, to the Conservatives. Because of loss of faith and social changes, along with the declining church attendance numbers, the differences between Church and Dissent were becoming less marked. Denominationalism ceased to be a determining factor in people's lives at the same time as the Liberals entered into their rapid decline.

The First World War coincided with the eve of the death of Nonconformity as a political force. In the postwar 1918 election only eighty-eight Nonconformist MPs were elected. The underlying affinity between Nonconformists and Liberals in British politics was dead. Votes were picked up by the Labour Party, which had its own Welsh Methodist base. The Liberal Party has been out of office since 1922. Lloyd George's War Cabinet was the swansong of the party and, paradoxically, also the most internationally powerful hour of Nonconformists in British politics. Palestine and Israel are the legacy.

The impact of Nonconformity stretched to the United States. A Jewish homeland would have not have become a reality without a nod from President Woodrow Wilson. The son and grandson of Presbyterian ministers, he had been steeped in Bible study as a child and was constant in his habit of reading the Bible daily throughout his life. His first wife, Ellen, was the daughter of yet another Presbyterian minister.

After the Jewish homeland was formed there were also other Nonconformists who helped make it viable. The influence peaked in May 1948 with the help of President Harry S. Truman. So dramatic was his participation that he could have been on a stage accompanied by the rousing chorus of the Hebrew slaves from Verdi's *Nabucco*. Like Lloyd George he was a Baptist. And like Lloyd George he acted as a midwife to the birth of Israel. Although not a lay preacher he had read the Bible from beginning to end five times before he was fifteen. Truman's message from the White House in Washington to the United Nations building in New York arrived within minutes of the British pulling out. It announced to the world that the United States recognized the new state of Israel and thus its survival was assured.

* * *

In Britain the Bible is no longer central to most people's lives and Christianity is usually assumed to have lost its influence on politics. But this is not the case in the United States. Here the Bible has retained its position. A staggering 86 per cent of the population in the US practise a religion. In contrast, a report in the year 2000 found that in the UK the figure is only 48 per cent.[10]

In the 1970s the United States experienced a religious revival, which accelerated the rise of Christian Zionism. Evangelical and Charismatic movements became the fastest growing branches of American Christianity. When Jimmy Carter, a Southern Baptist Sunday school teacher, became President in 1976 *Time* magazine declared that year 'the year of the Evangelical'. This trend continued to increase following the election of Ronald Reagan, a committed Christian Zionist, in 1980. Once again the Bible became a force in shaping international attitudes to Israel.

Many Evangelicals and 'religious conservatives' regard the creation of Israel in 1948 as proof that biblical prophecies are coming true.[11] Strong backing[12] is shown by both groups rallying to the cause of Israel and by voting for pro-Israel politicians.[13] Indeed, supporting Israel brings many votes from Conservative Protestants, the Moral Majority or Christian Coalition. Christian Zionists, especially the Southern Baptists and other members of the Christian Coalition of America, comprise, according to London's *Guardian* of 28 October 2002, 'between 15 and 18% of the electorate'. In contrast, the 6 million US Jews constitute only around 2.5 per cent of the American population.

Evangelical Jerry Falwell has said, 'Right at the very top of our priorities must be an unswerving commitment and devotion to the state of Israel.' Pat Robertson, another leading Evangelical, says, 'The future of this Nation (America) may be at stake, because God will bless those that bless Israel.'

Reared in the centuries-old tradition of Evangelical thought, which stresses that Jews should be restored to Zion, such men believe that the return of the Jews to their Promised Land is a fulfilment of biblical prophesies and a portent of the Second Coming of Christ (which for the Jews would be their long-awaited and only Messiah).

Support for Israel is publicized by press releases, tele-vangelists, conferences and rallies with cheer leaders, especially by the Conservative Fundamentalist Church. But such assistance is double-edged: Evangelicals also hope to convert Jews, and with slogans such as 'Jews for Jesus' try to awaken them to an acceptance of Jesus.[14] Evangelicals want every inch of the Holy Land for Israel. Some also believe that one of the preconditions for the Second Coming is for the Jewish people to return to their homeland. Others insist that Jews need to be converted first and so vigorously strive to win them over – a formidable task. The seventeenth-century English poet Andrew Marvell used the difficulty of turning Jews into Christians as a metaphor for his doubtful chance of seducing his imaginary mistress, while he used 'the flood' to refer to Noah in the Bible.

> Love you ten years before the flood,
> And you should if you please, refuse
> Till the conversion of the Jews . . .
>
> *'To His Coy Mistress', Andrew Marvell*

Conservative America continues to rally to Israel. In his book *The Right Man: The Surprise Presidency of George W. Bush,*[15] David Frum said that Evangelical Christianity sits at the core of George W. Bush's own reformed personality. According to Frum, an intellectual Jewish Canadian neo-conservative, who was with Bush for thirteen months as a speech-writer, every cabinet meeting at the White House now begins with a prayer. He stresses that Bush's confidence stems from his belief that 'the future is held in stronger hands than his own'.[16]

Bush, though brought up in Presbyterian and Episcopalian churches, has been an active Methodist since quitting alcohol and finding God in 1985. He is believed to be strongly influenced by Oswald Chambers, an obscure Scottish preacher who was born in 1874 in Aberdeen and died in Cairo in 1917. Every morning, before Bush brings his wife Laura her cup of coffee, he sits in a quiet corner to read a devotional text from Chambers' *My Utmost for His Highest*. With two million copies sold in the USA since 1991, this Christian classic has been continuously on sale in the United States since 1935 and keeps its place in the top ten titles of the religious best-seller list. The president's faith, articulated by Chambers, now permeates the White House, yet the coincidence is seldom noticed that Chambers wrote this text mostly in the Middle East, during his years at the YMCA at Zeitoun in Egypt during the First World War when he was ministering to Australian and New Zealand troops in the Palestine and Syrian campaign. It will be seen in the following pages that in contrast to Bush's overt and publicly avowed religious beliefs, the religious influence on the policy-makers in the Middle East in the First World War was indirect, understated and behind the scenes. Because this influence was not usually acknowledged there, it is seldom associated with the present Christian American religious focus. But no decisive reason has ever been given as to why Britain found it expedient to create a Jewish homeland in Palestine within the British Empire. Suggested motives are scattered throughout the text in this book and range from Lloyd George's attraction to Weizmann's saying that Palestine, like Wales, was 'a little mountainous country' to safeguarding the Suez Canal, to the protection of trade and empire, to the pre-empting of French claims in Palestine by giving an altruistic pretext for control, to the rallying of Jews worldwide to the Allied cause, especially in Bolshevik Russia and the United States.

ONE
War Cabinet

O that the Lord's salvation
Were out of Zion come,
To heal His ancient nation,
To lead His outcasts home!

How long the Holy City
Shall heathen feet profane?
Return, O Lord, in pity;
Rebuild her walls again.

Let fall Thy rod of terror;
Thy saving grace impart;
Roll back the veil of error;
Release the fettered heart.

Let Israel, home returning,
Their lost Messiah see;
Give oil of joy for mourning,
And bind Thy church to Thee.

'O That the Lord's Salvation', Charles Lyte

In 1916 millions of men in France and Belgium ate and slept, surrounded by blood and mud, in trenches and dugouts. With the rain the deep holes became mud pools, and with the snow they became iceboxes. To survive a man needed rat poison, wellington boots, sheepskin jerkins and coats. Cleanliness in these open warrens was impossible. Large rats scurried around attracted by unavoidable filth and carrion. Tins labelled 'Against Vermin in Trenches' were welcomed in the comfort parcels for these troops. Exploding shells mutilated bodies, and in some cases men completely disappeared with the blast of a shell. Horrific casualties resulted from a myriad other weapons including bullets, bombs and hand grenades. Flying pieces of skin, skulls, tongues and intestines landed on both man and earthen floors. Bloody fragments became the nourishment of rats and crows. The appalling death rate just kept climbing. No victory was in sight. Protected by barbed wire entanglements and the combined firepower of machine-guns and artillery, armies faced each other from unbroken lines of trenches. Safe movement in the open was nearly impossible. Battle lines zigzagged from the Swiss Alps along the French border, through Luxembourg, past the Belgian and Dutch borders, through mountains, valleys, hills and plains. Germany was still astride Europe. Dramatic changes were needed to alter the course of events.

In the second year of the war Lloyd George was made Minister for Munitions, with a remit to deal with the weapons crisis that was seriously affecting the performance of the army. Almost immediately he stood out as the most outstanding member of the cabinet. Cutting red tape, he appointed businessmen as well as politicians into key positions and soon guns, ammunition, shells and tin hats were pouring out of Britain's factories. Shortages caused him to ask scientists to find a synthetic substitute for two vital ingredients for explosives, acetone and cordite. Acetone, a colourless inflammable liquid, is a solvent used for many purposes, from removing nail polish and bloodstains, to being an essential ingredient in both Trinitrotoluol (TNT) and in artillery shells. Weizmann, vice-president of the English Zionist Federation (EZF), in a laboratory at the Lister Institute in Chelsea, isolated for research purposes an organism capable of transforming the starch present in maize and other cereals into acetone butyl alcohol – and Britain reached her goal of increasing the production of explosives with 'thirty thousand tons of acetone'.

Lloyd George's vigour and energy was a contrast to the seemingly stolid detachment of Prime Minister Herbert Asquith. In June 1916, when Lord Kitchener had been drowned at sea in the cruiser *Hampshire* while *en route* to Russia, Lloyd George took his place as Secretary for War but found he could not change its course. At the beginning of December 1916, for the third time, hope that the troops would be home by Christmas again evaporated. The fighting that had been going on for two years and three months showed no sign of victory on either side. Disgusted and agitated by the way the war was being run and by the attrition of the flower of British youth, Lloyd George handed in his resignation. On 5 December Asquith also resigned.

For a moment it seemed that Andrew Bonar Law would take up office, but about 130 Liberal MPs demonstrated their readiness to follow Lloyd George. King George V summoned him, along with Bonar Law, Balfour, Henderson and a few other politicians to Buckingham Palace. The die was cast when Balfour suggested to the king that he would become Foreign Secretary if Lloyd George would take on the role of prime minister. Bonar Law also said he would work under Lloyd George. Blanche Dugdale, Balfour's niece, wrote that a family letter jokingly said that Balfour and Lloyd George, despite having known each other since Lloyd George's early days in parliament, seemed to have 'fallen in love with each other at the Buckingham Palace conference'. Years later a visitor to Lloyd George's house noticed a framed photograph of Balfour on his desk.

Asquith did not go meekly. War or no war, the split within the Liberal Party caused insurmountable divisions. He refused either to join Lloyd George's cabinet or to give up the leadership of the Liberal Party. Loyal followers backed his every move. Mostly members of the higher professional classes, including financiers, merchants and lawyers, these men were a sharp contrast to Lloyd George's supporters, who were humbler in origin, mostly in small business and typical radical Nonconformists.[1] As Lloyd George wrote in his *War Memoirs*, 'The majority of the Tory Ministers in the Asquith coalition were definitely opposed to my Premiership . . . they accepted the prospect of serving under my leadership with bitter reluctance . . .'. The Asquith/Lloyd George split had disastrous repercussions for the Liberals as it provoked the radical left of centre voters to look towards the newly formed Labour Party, which, like the Liberals, also had a Welsh Methodist base and strong links with Nonconformism.

Lloyd George's accession to power was much more than a change of government. A.J.P. Taylor has described it as 'a revolution, British-style. The party magnates and the whips had been defied . . . Lloyd George was the nearest thing England has known to a Napoleon, a supreme ruler maintaining himself by individual achievement.'[2] He added later that Lloyd George 'stood alone against the best-entrenched governing class in Europe'. So great was the crisis facing Britain that Lloyd George was able to get away with exercising power in a sweeping, controversial manner. He was also the first 'man of the people to become Prime Minister', or, as he said in his *War Memoirs*, the first, other than Disraeli,[3] 'who had not passed through the Staff College of the old Universities . . .'.[4] To understand the attitude of his opponents he stressed that 'it was necessary to bear in mind that there had never before been a "ranker" raised to the Premiership'.[5] He did not assimilate the manners or accent of the upper or middle classes. Nor was he ever deferential to those who thought themselves better. In contrast, James Ramsay MacDonald, who had been born out of wedlock in a 'butt and ben' in Lossiemouth, and was soon to be Britain's first Labour prime minister, was later seduced by both the ways – and the women – of aristocratic society.

Previous occupants of 10 Downing Street who had not come from the upper strata of society had polished their manners and imitated their predecessors. Their clothes and their behaviour were constantly brushed in case a speck of dust from the northern industrial belt might settle. Take Asquith, for example. His aloofness and polish, acquired at Oxford, together with the airs and wit of his second wife, Margot Tennant,[6] usually hid the fact that he was the son of a relatively poor member of the northern middle class, a Congregationalist wool merchant who was the son of a woollen mill owner in Yorkshire. Asquith's predecessor, Sir Henry Campbell-Bannerman was also the son of a Nonconformist businessman who had started life as a draper in Glasgow and died a knight, a Tory and a Member of Parliament.

At the age of fifty-three Lloyd George showed that his religious upbringing had not been repressive.[7] His affair with his secretary Frances Stephenson, according to A.J.P. Taylor, was so flagrant that it was said that he was the first prime minister since Lord Grafton to openly live with a mistress at No. 10. (He eventually married Frances, after his wife's death in the Second World War when he was eighty and she was fifty-five.)[8]

Lloyd George's extraordinary confidence, rhetoric and wit came not from the elegant drawing-rooms of London but from draughty chapels and hastily erected platforms at Temperance meetings. His schoolteacher father had died when he was just two and he was brought up in[9] North Wales by his mother and her brother, his beloved Uncle Lloyd, a well-read village shoemaker[10] and Baptist lay preacher. After leaving school at fourteen, Lloyd George was articled to a solicitor at Porthmadog, and, like his uncle he brought passion and vigour to the chapel in Berea, Criccieth, as a fiery lay preacher. At the same time he had hung up a dignified nameplate on a door in his local village advertising his services as a solicitor and set up his first legal practice. Concern for the plight of the working man and a willingness to defend the underdog, including locals accused of breaking game laws, had given him the nickname 'the poachers' lawyer'.

Idealism and religious precepts had been ingrained in Lloyd George during his formative years. His biographer, John Grigg, described how he 'had been brought up on the Bible, and the story of the ancient Jews was as familiar to him as the history of England. He was a romantic nationalist . . . the idea of reuniting the Jewish people with the land of their forefathers appealed to him.'[11] On another occasion Lloyd George said, 'I was taught in school far more about the history of the Jews than about the history of my own land. I could tell you all the Kings of Israel. But I doubt whether I could have named half a dozen of the Kings of England and no more of the Kings of Wales.'

During Lloyd George's career as a politician, which began in 1890 when he arrived in London as the Liberal member for Caernarvon Boroughs (a constituency which he was to serve for fifty-five years), he was never afraid to say exactly what he thought. Beatrice Webb's description of him summed up his distinctive style, 'The little Welsh conjuror . . . is so pleasant and lively that official defense and personal respect fade into the atmosphere of agreeable low company . . . of a most stimulating kind – intimate camaraderie with a fellow adventurer.' Soaring to new heights at the age of forty-two when he became president of the Board of Trade and then Chancellor of the Exchequer, he made his mark as a social reformer with his highly controversial 'People's Budget', the Old Age Pensions Act and the National Health Insurance Act which later became the backbone of the welfare state. Many aristocrats, though, never forgave him for curbing the anachronistic power of the House of Lords.

The same disregard of precedent was evident when he became prime minister. Within a day of taking office Lloyd George formed his high-powered War Cabinet of five men. Asquith's War Cabinet had met weekly, but under Lloyd George's dynamic rule it would meet at least once daily[12] and liaise constantly with the War Office and the generals. Although he announced that he and the other four members of the War Cabinet would be more involved in strategy, as it turned out they managed to deal drastically with the Admiralty over convoys, but were less effective in handling the War Office and the Army. Knowing that the war would consume all his time Lloyd George arranged for the Chancellor to stand in as the Leader of the House and answer for the government in debates. Ever resourceful, when offices could not be found to house the secretariat of the new cabinet, he put up temporary huts in the garden at No. 10 behind the high walls near Horse Guards Parade. The old kitchens in the basement were used as a makeshift air-raid shelter. As the War Cabinet itself also met in the garden on occasions, it was referred to, often derisively, as 'the Garden Suburb'.[13]

Since members were few in number the cabinet could assemble quickly and make rapid decisions. But during its near three-year existence it expanded and was served by a total of ten men, representing a mixture of the three main political parties. More than half were members of families in which the Bible had been central to their childhood, and had belonged to Baptist, Methodist, Presbyterian and other Nonconformist or Evangelical denominations. The Church of England had been the established religion since the Reformation in the sixteenth century, yet Curzon was the only member of the War Cabinet who had been brought up an Anglican, and he was emphatically Low Church. Only two members of the War Cabinet were born in England; one was a lifelong abstainer and campaigner for Temperance and another had trained to be a minister in a Nonconformist church in South Africa.

In the first group to form the War Cabinet, three out of the five members were from the most humble of backgrounds and all but one had had deeply religious childhoods. As noted earlier, not only had Lloyd George once been a passionate lay preacher, but Henderson was still practising as one and Curzon and Bonar Law were both the sons of church ministers. The latter, as the new Chancellor of the Exchequer, moved in to No. 11 Downing Street, a far cry from the lonely wooden manse in which he had spent his early years. Lloyd George, appreciative of Bonar Law's backing, which had helped make him prime minister,[14] grew close to his lonely new neighbour whose wife had died earlier and whose two sons had been killed in the war. In his *War Memoirs* Lloyd George wrote, 'We had nothing in common, except a lowly origin . . . in a humble manse. . . . We had the same stern puritan upbringing. These early influences differentiated us completely from the other leading figures with whom he and I had to work . . .'.

Bonar Law's father, the Revd James Law, had migrated from Scotland to Rexton, New Brunswick (now part of Canada), where he had worked as a minister of the Free Church [of Scotland] – colloquially called the Wee Frees. Comparing Lloyd George and Bonar Law to the biblical Mary and Martha, Roy Jenkins wrote that they seemed an unlikely pair, and 'developed a compatibility of opposites, who knew they each needed the other. . . . They settled down remarkably smoothly to Mary and Martha-like roles. Mary of course had the glory, but Martha had the solid domestic position.' Jenkins also remarked on Lloyd George's 'mercurial and intuitive brilliance and Law's head-down chessboard application to problems – they were even less like each other than Law and Asquith, who at least shared a certain phlegmatism'.[15]

Unlike Winston Spencer Churchill, who felt grand enough to drop the 'Spencer' and just use one name, Lloyd George and Bonar Law both added an extra element to their names to give kudos. In Lloyd George's case it was also to acknowledge his surrogate father Uncle Lloyd. Andrew Law adopted his middle name – despite no members of his family bearing the surname 'Bonar'. At his christening he had been named after the famous Scottish Divine, Andrew A. Bonar, so his name was just Andrew Law. In 1890, ten years before Bonar Law became a Unionist Member of Parliament, his namesake, well known for his zealous conversion of the Jews to Christianity, had founded the Hebrew Christian Testimony to Israel, a mission to convert Jews in Palestine.

The trend of making the surnames of future prime ministers more euphonious began with Gladstone's father, Mr 'Gladstones', who dropped the 's'.[16] In 1872 Henry Campbell-Bannerman had added a hyphen and 'Bannerman' to his plain Campbell to fulfil the conditions of an inheritance. As Britain's first Labour prime minister used the names of both his unmarried mother and his father, and was usually known as 'Ramsay Macdonald', three prime ministers in a row were distinguished by 'improved' names.

It is hard to gauge the effect of religion on Sir Alfred Milner, that apostle of empire and High Commissioner in South Africa before, during and after the Boer War. His father, like his German grandmother, had been a Lutheran, but his mother, who died when he was fifteen, had been a member of the Church of England. The daughter of the governor of the Isle of Man and widow of an army officer killed in Ireland, she went with her two young sons to live in Bonn, where life was cheaper than in England. Here she engaged as a tutor a medical student, Charles Milner, who was half-English and half-German. He was twenty years her junior and had no money, but he quickly changed roles from teaching her children to being her husband. Alfred, the only child of this unlikely marriage, was born soon afterwards in 1854 in Giessen, in the principality of Hesse-Darmstadt, a small university town, he spent many of his formative years in London and Germany. When his father worked as a doctor in Chelsea he attended an Anglican school, and was also educated in Germany. But from the time of his luminous career at Oxford onwards, even when working in Egypt or southern Africa, his home was firmly in England.

Milner's intellectual hauteur contrasted with Henderson's simple, almost hearty straightforward ways. This Scot born in a Glasgow tenement had helped build up the Labour Party of which he was now chairman. As well as being an active member of the Wesleyan Methodist Church he was a Temperance campaigner, and delivered rousing addresses as a lay preacher on the platform of Brotherhood meetings – a movement formed to attract young men and women into Christian fellowship. In his autobiography *From Foundry to Foreign Office*[17] Henderson describes with pride that he was one of the Dissenters who were inaugurating a moral and social revolution in Britain. Brought up in Newcastle by his father, a cotton spinner, Henderson began work as an iron-moulder. Then, when he was sixteen years old, he converted from Congregationalism to Wesleyan Methodism. Inspired by the teachings of John Wesley, Henderson's sincere aim was to help the poor and make the world a fairer place. It was members like him who made the phrase that the old-style Labour supporters were 'more Methodist than Marxist' almost a cliché. In her classic book *Poverty and Compassion*[18] Gertrude Himmelfarb says that socialism was 'the embodiment of Christianity in our industrial system', pointing out that 'the generic form of Christian socialism . . . was present among all the late-Victorian socialist groups, including the most radical of them.'

Henderson helped set up the War Emergency Committee, the most effective Labour body yet formed, to look after the interests of workers in wartime by ensuring that food prices were regulated and servicemen's families received allowances. Two of its most active members were Ramsay MacDonald, who, as a pacifist, had been forced to resign from his local golf club, and the legendary socialist Sidney Webb, one of the founders of the Labour Party and the London School of Economics.

The sole old Etonian and Oxford graduate in the War Cabinet was Curzon, the former Viceroy of India, and the son of an aristocrat who was also a country vicar. His father, the Revd Alfred Nathaniel Curzon, who had unexpectedly inherited the title Lord Scarsdale from his uncle, had been the emphatically dour 'Low Church' rector of All Saints' Church on the family estate, which had belonged to the Curzon family for 700 years. Despite the neoclassical family mansion in Derbyshire, Curzon had 'spent his childhood in what was essentially a mid-Victorian parsonage'.[19] Although gifted and quick-witted, Curzon's aloofness and aristocratic disdain could sometimes make him impervious to others' points of view and suggestions. This pomposity and self-regard exposed him to satirists – as is shown by the famous rhyme:

My name is George Nathaniel Curzon,
I am a most superior person,
My cheek is pink, my hair is sleek,
I dine at Blenheim once a week.

He was also the only member of the War Cabinet to have visited the Holy Land. His biographer, Kenneth Rose, described his reaction to the historical sites of the prophets during a journey to Jerusalem in 1883: 'Brought up on the Bible, he filled notebook upon notebook during his tour of Palestine with eloquent recollections of the Old Testament.' He also quotes him as saying that the Plain of Esdraelon had produced 'the two finest bursts of poetry in Hebrew, perhaps in any tongue: the noble paeon of conquest and the most pathetic dirge of despair.' Rose also gave a description of the Sunday Curzon spent at Mount Carmel and 'reading as part of the morning service "that glorious chapter I Kings xviii . . . the most dramatic scene in Jewish history".' Like many Protestant visitors to the Church of the Holy Sepulchre in Jerusalem, Curzon voiced his disapproval of the inaccurate historical information given out by its attendants. His visit coincided with the extended stay of General Charles Gordon, better known as 'Gordon of Khartoum', but Curzon missed meeting him and never had another chance. Less than two years later Gordon was killed at Khartoum.

Insinuations that two members of the War Cabinet had had, or were both having, an affair with the same woman gave meetings a certain awkwardness. While it was common knowledge that Curzon had been the lover of Elinor Glyn, the red-headed society beauty, the 'It' girl of the Edwardian era, for years no one was ever sure about Milner's affair with her. As a political thinker and philosopher Milner was renowned for inspiring a band of disciples, known as his 'kindergarten', but less well known for being the recipient of Elinor Glyn's devotion. Elinor's diary records the pleasure listening to him reading Plato aloud to her, and sometimes he rewrote and improved a little of the prose of her romantic novels.[20] Curzon's eight-year romance with the enigmatic Elinor had started within days of his seeing her perform in a play she had written. In lieu of flowers he sent, as a token of his interest, the skin of a tiger he had shot in India, an action caricatured by the rhyme,'Would you like to sin, With Elinor Glyn on a tiger skin? Or would you prefer, With her to err, On some other fur?' In a biography of Elinor written by her grandson there is reference to an entry in her diary that describes

Milner:[21] 'I have seen him, my old friend. He loved me and he loves me still. His stern face grew soft when his eyes rested on me . . .'. But competition between the two men ceased in the second month of the War Cabinet, when Curzon married his second wife, the American widow Grace Duggan, whom he hoped would give him a son and heir.

* * *

Perhaps the name almost synonymous with the British backing of a Jewish homeland is that of Balfour. But the following pages examine whether he was as pivotal as commonly thought – whether Lloyd George was indeed the 'author of the Jewish homeland' – and whether the supremacy achieved by Britain's Middle East affair was initiated by Lloyd George or Balfour. While ministers from many departments sat through different meetings of the War Cabinet, Balfour, as Foreign Secretary, was present at 300 of 500. He might have looked like a typical upper-class country gentleman but, regular churchgoer though he was, his interest in spiritualism, psychic research, telepathy, psychic phenomena, attendances at séances where he had a flood of 'communications' from 'the other side', and his attitude to the question of survival after death made him a truly unconventional Protestant. At home in his ancestral mansion, Whittingehame, in East Lothian, he conducted family prayers for the staff every Sunday night and took his pew during services at the local Church of Scotland church. In London he attended Church of England services. Spiritualism, though, deepened his profound belief in an afterlife.

Balfour had been steeped from early childhood in the Old Testament. His father had died in 1850, when he was two years old, leaving a large estate with an ancient castle, four children and a forceful widow, Lady Blanche. Sister of a future prime minister, Lord Salisbury, and goddaughter of the Duke of Wellington, she had been a dedicated mother and a devout Presbyterian who gave her children daily Bible classes. This may not have happened if her husband, who was said to have had a violent temper and opposed her devotion to religion, had lived.[22]

Inheriting his mother's attachment to the Old Testament, Balfour later went so far as to say that Christianity had never adequately repaid the Jews for their gift of the Bible to Christianity. His biographer, Max Egremont,[23] sums up the effect of his association with the Jewish cause: 'In Weizmann he had met an inspirational articulator of a message which took him back to the stern Old Testament tenets of his mother's low church faith and the Presbyterianism of the Scottish Lowlands. . . . At the peace conference and afterwards Balfour defended the Zionist cause; and was henceforth looked upon as one of its greatest allies.' Egremont also said that Balfour believed in an afterlife and in 'both his long philosophic works there are passages of an almost mystical intensity concerning the impossibility of total intellectual comprehension or proof of the foundations of the Christian ethic. In response to the encroaching dogmatism of science, in 1879 he published *Defence of Philosophical Doubt*, a plea for intellectual liberty.' For fifty years he was at the very centre of England's social and political worlds.

Balfour's dazzling academic career had begun at Eton and continued at Cambridge where, with an aristocratic group of friends, he formed the 'Souls',[24] whose reputation is still a by-word for wit and glamour. Arriving at the university just seven years after Charles Darwin had published *On the Origin of Species*, Balfour began his quest to resolve arguments between theology and science as presented in the works of Charles Lyell, Thomas Huxley, Alfred Wallace and Darwin. Balfour retained his close friendship with two Fellows of Trinity College and in 1882 they became foundation members of the Society for Psychical Research, The most outstanding member of this group was Henry Sidgwick, later distinguished as a Fellow of Trinity College, Cambridge, who resigned his fellowship as he could not assent to the thirty-nine articles of Christian faith. He was married to Balfour's sister, Eleanor, the principal of Newnham College for eighteen years, between 1892 and 1910.

Spiritualism had become fashionable in the late nineteenth century and attracted all sorts of people, as did the Society, which was well known for specializing in clairvoyance, séances and out-of-body experiences. Balfour became its president when he was thirty-four. The Society's headquarters still proudly displays Balfour's portrait in their London offices. On the crowded shelves are the voluminous spirit speeches, *The Palm Sunday Case*,[25] put together by his great-niece, Jean Balfour, which describe his long psychic involvement with Mary Lyttelton, whom he had wanted to marry. When Mary died of typhoid fever on Palm Sunday in 1885, aged twenty-five, he gave an engagement ring to her brother to place on her hand in the coffin. Dead she may have been, but he remained in touch with her through séances for the rest of his life. To keep in contact with Mary's disembodied spirit Balfour also joined circles of spiritualists who practised 'automatic writing'. Like other spiritualists he thought that humans possess a soul capable of existing outside the body and, believing that Mary was waiting for him 'on the other side', he remained a bachelor until his dying day. For the next fifty-five years after Mary's death, Balfour spent Palm Sunday with the friends he and Mary had shared. Spiritualists believe that Mary and Balfour's younger brother Frank, who had died three years before Mary, made frequent trips to communicate with Balfour, often referring to palms, or using palm imagery in their language to mark the day of her sudden death. Sometimes the 'entities' were said to use the words of a poem by Thomas Hood as a sign that they were present.

Balfour had entered parliament as MP for Hertford in 1874, and nearly thirty years later, in 1902, when his uncle Lord Salisbury stood down as prime minister, he had handed the reins to his nephew. But Balfour, with his languid aristocratic charm and walrus moustache, had been a lacklustre prime minister, if later a brilliant elder statesman and Foreign Secretary. It is generally believed that the declaration that bears his name was entirely initiated and nurtured by him. It cannot be stressed too much that he pushed the Palestine plan as if it were his own[26] *after* the concept had been accepted as policy by Lloyd George's War Cabinet and *after* it won the tacit approval of the President of the United States. Ten years earlier, during his term as prime minister, he had seen through the 1905 Aliens Bill. This had put legal restrictions on the number of Jewish refugees coming into Britain, many of whom were desperate and impoverished victims from Eastern Europe. His change of attitude, however, was sincere, and he later said that in his fifty-year career he valued his involvement in setting up the Jewish homeland above all other achievements.

* * *

Apart from Balfour, other outsiders regularly present at the 'Garden Suburb' in Downing Street were Sir Mark Sykes and Leo Amery, who formed a two-man secretariat under Sir Maurice Hankey. They were soon joined by William Ormsby-Gore, heir to Lord Harlech. Another secretariat member, though for a very short time, was Ronald Storrs, who was later governor of Jerusalem. Hankey, Sykes and Amery were all Members of Parliament and, by chance, all dedicated Zionists. Sykes, a somewhat unconventional Roman Catholic and MP for Central Hull since 1911, had been introduced to Zionist principles by Dr Moses Gaster, a Romanian, Rabbi and religious leader of the

London Sephardi community. In 1913 Sykes succeeded his father as 6th Baronet and inherited the magnificent Sledmere estates in East Yorkshire. When war broke out his knowledge of Arabic meant that he was sent to Cairo to work in military intelligence and diplomacy, where he became co-author of the Sykes–Picot agreement of January 1916. This delineated British and French shares of territory after the presumed future break-up of the Ottoman Empire, giving France Upper Syria and the territories eastwards up to Mosul, and Britain the Holy Land and Mesopotamia. From the end of 1916 Sykes was active in the Secretariat of the War Cabinet and became almost an unofficial link between the Zionists and the government. Sykes was the only man involved in two of the three British wartime Middle East agreements.

The War Cabinet's use of the term Palestine shows a link with the Bible. Politically Palestina, the name given by the Romans to Judea after Pompey captured it in 63 BC and which had been used by them during their long reign which lasted until the seventh century, had been non-existent since Roman times. (The name is derived from the ancient Greek name Palaistina, land of the Philistines.) The name used on the atlases of the world for the Holy Land was Syria, but the British persisted in calling it Palestine, the nomenclature used in the New Testament. In the Ottoman Empire the word Palestine was neither an administrative nor a territorial division;[27] the only place the word could be found was in Bibles, Sunday school and history books. Stretching from somewhere in the Sinai Peninsula in the south to somewhere below the mountains of Lebanon in the north, Palestine had neither frontier nor legality. It was Lloyd George who turned this vague geographic area of the Holy Land into a modern state with formal boundaries. Since Roman times it had been administered as Southern Syria, and for the past four centuries, since the sixteenth century, as a hotchpotch of *sanjaks* or sub-provinces ruled by a pasha who reported back to the government both in Damascus and the Sublime Porte in Constantinople. Lloyd George told the cabinet that it would be an outrage to let the Christian holy places in Palestine fall into the hands of 'Agnostic Atheistic France'. And on another occasion he stated that it was not worth winning the Holy Land only to 'hew it in pieces before the Lord'.[28] This enthusiasm was mocked by Simon Schama in *Two Rothschilds and the Land of Israel*[29] as the 'Celtic fundamentalism and Gaelic mysticism to which the Prime Minister and Foreign Secretary were prone'.

Just three days after Lloyd George had become prime minister, Robertson[30] (no. 26174 cipher) telegraphed the Commander-in-Chief of British forces in Egypt, General Sir Archibald Murray, asking what additional troops would be required for action beyond El Arish (now near today's Egyptian/Israeli border), the ancient mud village which was the largest centre of population in the whole Sinai Peninsula. As the next large centre was none other than the desert gateway of Palestine, the ancient biblical Philistine city of Gaza, and its line of ridges from the coast to the town of Beersheba of the Seven Wells, this was a coded way of instructing the army to break through the Palestine/Egyptian border. Only the small town of Rafah stood between the British Army at El Arish and Gaza. The message concluded, 'I cannot help thinking that in view of [the] importance of achieving [a] big success on Eastern front, and the effect this will have. . . . A success is badly needed, and your operation promises well.' These new plans were a dramatic contrast to those under Asquith. A few months earlier the Imperial General Staff had informed Murray that the policy for Egypt in the immediate future must be, strategically at least, only defensive. Strategy then was only to occupy El Arish, nothing further.

But it is seldom realized that this change in direction was introduced immediately after Lloyd George's ascent to power. Cyril Falls, the official war historian and co-author with Sir George Fletcher MacMunn of *Military Operations, Egypt and Palestine*,[31] stated that '. . . Lloyd George attached great importance to the effect that the expulsion of the Turks from Jerusalem would have upon the opinion of the world'. He added that Robertson tried to give effect to the prime minister's policy, 'while maintaining the general policy that France was the main theatre of war'.

A further letter to Murray from Robertson said that his reply had been seen by the prime minister, 'who wishes you to make the maximum possible effort during the winter . . .'. Soon the Desert Mounted Corps would be sweeping up the coast to Jaffa and Jerusalem in the first British attempt to get a foothold in Palestine since the Crusades. But before they did so Murray needed to augment his 'ration strength of 150,000 British and 6,000 Indian troops, and of 13,000 Egyptian Labour Corps'. He also requested more transport, more camels, more horses.

During Lloyd George's first weeks at 10 Downing Street, troops trudged over the oldest road in the world – the vaguely marked highway connecting Africa with Asia that runs across the Sinai Desert. Since pre-biblical times, invaders – Babylonians, Assyrians, Persians, Greeks, the Roman legions, the Crusaders and Napoleon's *chasseurs* – had marched here. The present army, like those thousands of years before, were irritated by the desert's fine powdery dust, which pervaded everything. Nor were they exempt from the bitter cold of the December nights or from thirst. Even though it was the winter season when the rare rains fall the water rations were inadequate. The Turkish forces, too, also suffered, as had all the travellers who had preceded them, whether Moses in the long-drawn-out wandering, the Queen of Sheba and her luxurious train of camels, or the boy Joseph. The idea of the reconquest of Palestine was something dear to the heart of many of the British and there probably were few men in that great British army who were not touched by the idea of reaching Bethlehem and Jerusalem and seeing the illustrations from Sunday school come alive. Although the troops were not informed that they would be continuing the invasion into the heart of Palestine or Syria, rumours soon spread and spirits were raised.

Christmas Day 1916 was celebrated by British forces in El Arish, with carols and Christmas cake, just two weeks after Lloyd George had come to power. There was a feeling of general excitement about the push to Gaza. Many men knew the Old Testament well, and were familiar with the story of the hill of Alimuntar, to the south-east of Gaza, where Samson had carried the gates of the city when the Philistines tried to shut him in.

* * *

Just over a century and a half earlier, the triumphal progress of the Old Testament had reached a peak in the birth of the Evangelical movement, the arrival of the Wesley brothers and the burgeoning membership of the other Dissenting religious movements. Nonconformism was almost an attempt to return to Judaism's roots (modified, of course, by the coming of Christ and the Gospel). While the worship, simplicity and interiority of the religion of Nonconformists mirrored rabbinic Judaism in its emphasis on the centrality of the Word and the absence of imagery, the New Jerusalem, which was taken over and redirected from the early Church, was also a potent source of inspiration. Followers looked towards the Holy Land and to the time when the Old Testament, the story of the Jews in Israel, ended and the New Testament, the story of Jesus, began.

As religious history and political history are seldom researched together the names of Cleopatra and Jesus are rarely linked, yet only about sixty years and 350 miles separate Cleopatra's suicide by hugging a poisonous brown and yellow asp to her breast in 31 BCE, and Jesus' Crucifixion in Jerusalem around 30 CE. Both untimely deaths were caused by the rapid expansion of the Roman Empire and occurred when each was in their thirties. Dissimilar though the Queen of Egypt's suicide and the brutal nailing to the cross of the founder of Christianity were, they both witnessed the waning of one great civilization in the East and acted as harbingers of the rise of another. This period marked the end of the Ptolemies in Egypt and the consolidation of Roman might in the eastern Mediterranean after the defeat of Cleopatra's husband Mark Antony by his rival Octavius at Actium.

Soon after Cleopatra's death both Egypt and Palestine sank into decline. Along with its pyramids, sphinx and pharaohs, Egypt faded into a mere curiosity in Western minds.[32] Scholars did not bother to translate Egyptian hieroglyphics until the nineteenth century.[33] But Palestine, a petty territory when compared to Egypt,[34] had one export that was to ensure its fame for ever: the Hebrew Bible, which became known as the Old Testament.

This became the longest part of the most widely disseminated book ever produced,[35] the Bible. No other book in the history of mankind has had such a worldwide influence. As the early Christians initiated the practice of integrating the books which were later called the Old Testament with the Gospels into the Christian religion, they ensured that Jewish culture would have an unparalleled and enduring impact on the West and the early history of the Jews would become familiar to the Western world. Indirect though their influence was, no race, apart from the Greeks of the classical period, had such a widespread effect on other religions as the Jews. Over the next 2,000 years the Bible would affect many aspects of world civilization.

This, the 'Book of Books,' is now translated into more than 2,000 languages[36] and dialects.[37] Just how important it is can be seen by looking at the Coronation Service at Westminster Abbey in Britain in 1953. Before being anointed, the present Queen was handed a Bible which was described as 'the most valuable thing that this world affords'.

Why though was it necessary for Christianity to have kept this book which traces the long saga of the Jews and Israel? Why did the early Christians not abandon it and concentrate on the New Testament, which is, after all, the story of Jesus?[38]

TWO

Why the Old Testament became part of the Christian Faith

Life is real! Life is earnest!
And the grave is not its goal;
'Dust thou art, to dust returnest,'
Was not spoken of the soul.

'A Psalm of Life', Henry Wadsworth Longfellow [after Genesis 3:19]

If the Hebrew Bible had not been adopted as the 'Old Testament' by Christians, knowledge of its contents, and its impact, would have been small. Benjamin Disraeli, a Jewish convert who saw Christianity as 'completed Judaism', summarised how Christianity became a vehicle for making the Old Testament so well known:

> If it were not for the Church, I don't see why the Jews should be known. The Church was founded by Jews, and has been faithful to its origin. It secures their history and their literature being known to all . . . and keeps alive the memory of its public characters, and has diffused its poetry throughout the world. The Jews owe everything to the church. . . . The history of the Jews is development or it is nothing.[1]

The early Christian Church denounced both Judaism and Jews, but retained the Old Testament and wove Jewish customs and prayers into its beliefs and rituals. Repercussions of this were many, even before the two collections of writings of prophets and apostles were bound into one volume as 'the Bible'. By adopting the Old Testament, Christianity, like Judaism, gained enormous status from the authority of its antiquity and for over a century it was the only religious text used by the Christians. Jesus, a Jew, was seen as a fulfilment of the Old Testament prophecies that God would one day send a Messiah. The God of the Jews was the God of Jesus.[2] By referring to the books of the Old Testament, the authors of the New Testament demonstrated the authenticity of Christian doctrine and the divine origin of Jesus. Yet their interpretation was often different from that of the Jews.

The Jews were, and still are, waiting for the Messiah, while Christians believe he has come once and that there will be a Second Coming to fulfil God's promise to redeem mankind. For all the historical and theological closeness of the two religions, the figure of Jesus thus marks a decisive rift between Judaism and Christianity. Similarly, although Christianity retained the concept of Jewish monotheism – a single God that nobody has ever seen, and who has no form and no name – it put much emphasis on the fact that God became man and exists in three persons and one substance (the Holy Trinity). Another fundamental difference is the Christian belief that the word of God is revealed in the New Testament as well as in the Old Testament. A further, although less quantifiable, difference is that Jews are not as explicit as Christians in their belief in an afterlife – Jews do not give prominence to a life hereafter. The subject of the soul going to hell or heaven is undefined in either the Hebrew Scriptures or in the general precepts of Judaism. Descriptions of life after death in the Old Testament are few, and Judaism, which deems that individual ethical behaviour is important, does not believe that faith alone dictates whether a person automatically goes to hell or to heaven. Christians, on the other hand, offer the certainty of a life hereafter, a deeply held human need.

Christ's teachings were not divorced from what had gone before. Indeed, Jesus insisted on this. For instance, the Ten Commandments, given by God to Moses on Mt Sinai and recited in the book of Exodus in the Old Testament, are integral to both religions.[3]

With its many references to the Jewish prophets, prophecies and beliefs, the New Testament can be more fully understood with knowledge of Old Testament texts. The very basis of the Jewish faith is the Scriptures. Judaism was a religion which had been revealed by God to prophets and written down on the surface of stone tablets and copied on to papyrus. As well as giving Jews their religion these texts contained the history of their forefathers, their geography, law and philosophy. Unlike pagan religions, followers of Judaism did not always need an altar, since the Jewish God was accessible through texts with the law. David Ben-Gurion, the first prime minister of Israel, explained to a Bible study circle:

> . . . the Bible . . . has accompanied our people in all of its metamorphoses and wanderings for some 2,500 years. In the books of the Bible, for the first time in human historiography, we are given the story of the birth, growth and struggles of a nation. The writing of Hebrew history pre-dated the works of Herodotus and Thucydides and other books of history written by Greeks and Romans in days of old.[4]

* * *

Jesus' birth in Bethlehem, about the same year as Herod's death, is described in the four documents known as the Gospels. These are the sole account of the Son of God who visited earth in human form. There are no contemporary descriptions of Jesus' life – no records, no archaeological evidence. Monasteries around the Mediterranean have been combed, as have Roman records and synagogues and the copious writings of the Judean rabbis of the period. References to Jesus' life all come from a later age. Jesus himself is not mentioned anywhere outside the Gospels by name until at least a few decades after the Crucifixion. And there is a strong possibility that none of the New Testament was written before 51 CE (some say 72 CE). Only three of the supposed eight authors of the New Testament knew Jesus – Matthew, Mark and John – and some writers deny that they were eyewitnesses. Even if the authors of the Gospels had known him, the 5 per cent of the New Testament that was allegedly penned by them is the only evidence of his birth and life. Apart from the New Testament there are no other records, not even sparse ones. Every reference to Jesus in the New Testament belongs to oral tradition and most is literally second, third or fourth-hand, written down by believers who wanted to record this oral tradition before it faded away. Information came from what had been preserved by the growing number of Judeo-Christian communities. When the Dead Sea Scrolls, which had been hidden in caves at Qumran from 68 CE, were found in the 1950s, they were examined by scholars in the hope of finding a line or two about Jesus. But nothing was found. The sole reference to Jesus is an indirect remark used to identify James as 'the brother of Jesus the so-called Christ'.[5]

Some scholars have even suggested, as the Gospels were written so long after Jesus' death, that they are 'after the event' stories, and, consequently, that there had been time to manipulate accounts of events. This makes it difficult to decide exactly which of Jesus' doings, parables and sayings are authentic.

For example, the Temple was already destroyed when an apostle wrote that Jesus had foreseen its destruction.[6] The oral transmissions and the four Gospels, all independent works showing differences, fundamentally agree on basic facts but the paucity of contemporary material is so great that Christianity, like earlier creeds and other religions, has to remain mystical. Even the history by the Jewish writer Josephus Flavius is not contemporary and he was writing as a servant of Vespasian. Born after the Crucifixion, he wrote far away in Rome in the 70s and 90s. Tacitus, who was not born until 55 CE, wrote in the year 115, and was a boy of ten when Nero's persecution of the Christians took place, and he, like so many, did not once make the journey to Jerusalem.

In the decade following Jesus' death, Paul, a Jewish tent maker from Tarsus, inspired by his vision of Christ on the road to Damascus, took the new religion to Anatolia, Syria, Egypt and other places in the Mediterranean, including Rome,[7] where followers worshipped behind closed doors and were buried secretly in the catacombs. Persecution and martyrdom was a dramatic element of the early history of Jesus' followers. Possibly as many as 2,000 Christians were killed in Jerusalem itself in the early days of the new religion.

After Paul, rivalry between Judaism and Christianity escalated. Before the birth of Christianity large numbers of pagans had gone through complicated rituals in order to be accepted into the Jewish faith. Now, the Christians, with their call to the eternal life in heaven, were attracting the most converts, including rich people who endowed the Church. Slaves, too, were welcomed as converts. Those who had a miserable existence on earth found that the prospect of a continuation of life in heaven gave them hope, and they renounced the pagan Roman deities. Initially new converts had observed the Jewish laws but soon they were admitted as members, without being initiated in the Torah and other Jewish beliefs. But Jewish converts were obliged to observe dietary restrictions and had to undergo the extremely painful and unpleasant process of circumcision. Denuding the penis of the foreskin was one of the special marks of the Jew, but it was also later, as it still is, practised generally in the Syrio-Palestinian world.[8]

A hundred years after Jesus died Christianity was still a Jewish sect in Jerusalem, but abroad the strict rules of Judaism had, despite angry arguments between the apostles, been deliberately abandoned. During his lifetime Jesus' preaching had been conducted within the religious framework of Judaism. Whether or not he had intended to start a new religion, or whether he was trying to teach Jews how to be better Jews[9] is disputed by some until this day. The new beliefs, despite the ban by Rome, swept around the shores of the eastern Roman Empire.[10]

Life was dangerous for Jews and Christians alike; both became scapegoats as they struggled for political and religious survival. When fire, according to the annals of Tacitus, swept through Rome in 64 CE, Nero blamed the Christians. As a result they were crucified, burned and used as living torches. In Jerusalem two years later, Roman oppression drove the Jews into two successive revolts. An uprising at Masada on the shores of the Dead Sea in 66 CE, reached Jerusalem. Trouble had started when Caligula had announced a statue of himself was being set up in the Temple. Triumphant, the Jews threw the soldiers in the Roman garrisons out of Herod's towers and secured all of Judea and Galilee. For three years they held their ground.[11]

Nero sent Vespasian from Britain where he had suppressed the Druids[12] to quell the siege in Jerusalem. Vespasian's son, Titus, stormed the city in the summer of 70 CE. Josephus Flavius, one of Titus's prisoners was spared, then adopted by Vespasian. In Rome he recorded the siege in *The Jewish War*:

> Yet more terrible than the din were the sights that met the eye. The Temple Hill, enveloped in flames from top to bottom, appeared to be boiling up from its very roots; yet the sea of flame was nothing to the ocean of blood, or the companies of killers to the armies of killed; nowhere could the ground be seen for corpses, and the soldiers climbed over heaps of bodies as they chased the fugitives. The terrorist horde pushed the Romans back, and by a violent struggle burst through into the outer court of the Temple. . . . So fell Jerusalem in the second year of Vespasian's reign. . . . No destruction ever wrought by God or man approached the wholesale carnage of this war. . . . All the prisoners taken from beginning to end of the war totalled 97,000.

Whole families died of hunger and the dead lay unburied in the streets and, according to Joseph Flavius, a total of just over a million people died in the whole campaign.[13] Like Nebuchadnezzar six and a half centuries earlier, Titus destroyed Jerusalem. This time only a part of the Western Wall of the Temple and the three great towers of Herod's palace were left standing. During the first centuries after the Destruction of the Temple, the Jews generally went to the Western Wall of the Temple on that historic day, known as the 9th of Ab. This practice, which, with the exception of the Crusader period, continued over the centuries and, with the increase in the numbers living in Palestine and the influx of Jewish pilgrims, expanded to allow people to come at the times of other religious feasts and on the Sabbaths.

A magnificent arch in the forum in Rome is inscribed to the glory of 'Titus Caesar Vespasian, Father of His Country, who subdued the race of the Jews and destroyed their City of Jerusalem, a city which all kings, commanders and nations before him have either attacked in vain or left wholly unassailed'. The inscription fails to mention either that Masada held out for another four years or that during the siege of Jerusalem, the new Christians, although Jewish, took no part in the battles and decamped to Pella in Transjordan. Thus continued the acrimonious detachment of the Christians and the Jews. Early Christians, who were mostly Jewish, distanced and separated themselves completely from the Jewish faith, not only out of fear for their lives, but because of a developing enmity towards Judaism.

It seemed that the Jews whose numbers had been ravaged were no longer a threat to the Roman Empire, but crushed as they were they rose up again. Simon Bar Kochba, the revolutionary Jewish leader, brought his men down from the Judean hills and nearly swept the Romans from the land. For three years, the Jews held out within the walls of Jerusalem, but in 132 CE[14] the Romans again flattened the city.[15] The Emperor Hadrian, famous for the construction of the wall he built between Solway and Tyne, to separate Scotland and England, is perhaps less well known for his destruction of Jerusalem. In 134 CE this former Roman prefect of Syria and Palestine made his last journey to Jerusalem, staying to quell a huge uprising (partly caused by his own ban on circumcision which he considered inhumane). He tore down buildings, erected pagan shrines and temples on Jewish and Christian sites, and not only forbade the Jews to come within sight of the city on pain of death but obliterated all traces of the Jewish faith in Jerusalem and even changed its name to Aelia Capitolina. This time the majority of the Jews were slowly forced out of Palestine and the Diaspora began to widen. They already formed one-tenth of the population of the Roman Empire and 40 per cent of the population in Alexandria. Only a minority, who mostly led deeply religious lives, stayed in Palestine. With Jerusalem destroyed, the Christians too looked elsewhere for a centre for their religion, to Rome, and to Saint Peter, the rock of the church, as their first pope.

Countering the embarrassment that the founder of their religion had been executed under Roman law by Pontius Pilate, the Roman procurator, the

Christians pointed out that the Jews had demanded his Crucifixion. In the Gospels, the Jews are not just accused of rejecting the claims of the Son of God, but of murdering him. Matthew, who was himself a Jew (Matthew 27:25) claims that Jews in the crowd at the Crucifixion said, 'let his blood be on our heads and the heads of our children'; every Jew from then onwards could be regarded as a 'Christ-killer'.[16] In the Gospel of Saint John, the term 'Jew' is also used in a derogatory manner. The rejection of Jesus by the Jews during his lifetime was also stressed, as was the fact that he had told his disciples to take his message to the Gentiles. But it was not until the fourth century that the bigoted persecution of the Jews began. One prayer, which was not removed from the liturgy until 1959, shows the enmity of the Catholics towards the Jews. It began with the words, 'Let us pray also for the perfidious Jews . . .', and was recited in Roman Catholic churches throughout the world on Good Fridays.

Despite this acrimonious separation, and the abandonment of many[17] Jewish restrictions and practices, worship in both synagogue and church follows similar patterns.[18] One reason for this is that during the early decades of the Church's life, before it expanded with converts, every believer was Jewish. As noted earlier, not only was Jesus Jewish, but so were seven out of the eight authors of the New Testament. Although the Old Testament is central to both faiths, the Christian Church lacks the Jewish ritual that surrounds the Torah, which is kept in the Ark and is only seen when it is read to the congregation during worship.

With the exception of Greek Orthodox churches, synagogues and churches provide seats and their services centre around Bible-reading, prayers, the recital of Old Testament psalms (plus hymns in the Christian Church) and have an order of service. In both, King David's 23rd psalm is one of the most frequently heard. Hymns, many of which are based on psalms, are a relatively modern introduction into Church services. The practice was usually as in synagogues, to sing psalms during normal services.[19] Even though medieval Latin hymns abounded – Martin Luther wrote many – they did not become a regular part of the service until much later with the introduction of stirring hymns like 'O God, our Help in Ages Past' written by the Evangelical Isaac Watts at the beginning of the eighteenth century.

While Christianity adhered to the ideals of Judaism – love, prayer, repentance and an upright life[20] – practitioners seldom acknowledged that the phrase 'Thou shalt love thy neighbour as thyself' was from the Book of Leviticus (19:18). Jesus quoted it so frequently (see Matthew 19:16; 22:39;

Mark 12:31; 12:33; Luke 10:27; Romans 13:9; Galatians 5:14; James 2:8) that it became one of the familiar commands of Christianity. Nor do the words of the Lord's Prayer given by Jesus to his disciples, which petitions God to make things as they are in heaven, have an exclusively Christian content.[21] Each of its six clauses has parallels with Jewish prayers, such as the Kaddish, which is recited in synagogues and homes. Cecil Roth wrote that 'The Lord's Prayer and the Sermon on the Mount have been paralleled from the Talmud, verse for verse and phrase for phrase. The Golden Rule – "Do unto they neighbour as thou wouldst be done by" – is only a paraphrase of the recommendation of Jesus' older contemporary, Hillel, who died when the founder of Christianity was only ten years old.'[22] In the Prologue to his *History of the Jews*, Paul Johnson summed up the debt of Christianity to Judaism:

> It was not, as I had been taught to suppose, that the New Testament replaced the Old; rather, that Christianity gave a fresh interpretation to an ancient form of monotheism, gradually evolving into a different religion but carrying with it much of the moral and dogmatic theology, the liturgy, the institutions and the fundamental concepts of its forbear.

Other similarities abound. Christian baptism dates back to the symbolic bath given to new converts to Judaism that was adapted by John the Baptist. Similarly, the communion service was modelled on the Seder, the Passover Service. Temple motifs, such as cherubim, first appear in accounts of the Tabernacle built by Moses, and were adapted as decoration in churches. 'Jubilee', 'Satan', 'Paradise', 'Armageddon' 'Cherub' and numerous other words we think of as Christian are taken from the Old Testament, as are many phrases, mostly from the Proverbs of Solomon. A few examples are 'the apple of the eye', 'by the skin of his teeth', 'lick the dust' and 'the pride before the fall'.

'Hallelujah' also comes from Judaism, while the chanting of the affirmation 'Amen' at the end of prayers meaning 'so it be' appears in the Old Testament thirty times.[23] Grace, a prayer to thank the Lord for meals, is yet another custom common to both religions.[24] The light before the high altar in churches was copied from the perpetual lamp,[25] and the use of incense was mentioned in the Old Testament. In Rome it is sometimes said that the Sistine Chapel has the same dimensions (40.93 metres long by 13.41 metres wide) as the Temple of Solomon, built in the tenth century BCE.

One of the achievements of the Reformation throughout Europe was to put Protestants more directly in touch with the characters and the history of the Jews as portrayed in the Old Testament. This trend became almost startling later, among the break away Protestants (known in Britain as Free Churches Dissenters and Nonconformists) and Evangelicals, many of whom relied on the literal interpretation of the Bible. Although Roman Catholics were interested in the Holy Land, as is seen by the Crusades, focus was mostly on the places connected with the life of Jesus Christ rather than those of the prophets and other stories in the Old Testament. Roman Catholic and High Anglican doctrines have never, on the whole, emphasized the Old Testament as much as nineteenth-century Protestant Nonconformists. Nor have they been sympathetic to Zionism.

Most descriptions of the landscape of the Holy Land come from the Old Testament. For instance, Jerusalem, 'God's dwelling place' (Psalm 9) and 'God's headquarters on earth' (Psalm 102) is mentioned 656 times in the Old Testament, but only 139 times in the New. One reason for this is because the Old Testament is so much longer than the New Testament. Indeed, the New Testament has only 20 per cent of the number of words of the Old Testament. Another reason for the sparseness of descriptions in the New Testament is because it was between forty or seventy years after Jesus' death before his followers put pen to papyrus. By then they were far from where the events had taken place and, as said earlier, only three of the authors had been to Palestine. The books in the New Testament were written mostly in Rome and Syria. By the time it was written the inferno of war had destroyed the Jerusalem of Jesus with its thriving Jewish community and Herod's Temple with its High Priests. Archaeologists (and tour operators) often despair that the New Testament usually mentions only the name of a place, with few distinguishing features to identify it.[26]

Everyday practices entwine Jerusalem into Western life. The orientation of cathedrals, churches and synagogues is eastwards towards Jerusalem, and worshippers thus face the Holy City as they pray.[27] In the Christian faith, this means they are also orientated towards the place from where Jesus ascended into heaven and to where they believe he will one day return.[28] In Christian cemeteries the practice continues of burying the dead with their feet facing towards Jerusalem.[29] Lord Curzon summed this up when he described Jerusalem as the 'holiest space of ground on the face of the globe . . . to which all our faces are turned when we are finally laid in our graves in the churchyard'.

Many royal customs are also closely linked with the Old Testament, the Holy Land or Judaism. Since the time of Richard the Lionheart the children of the royal family have been christened with consecrated water brought in bottles from the River Jordan, near the place of Christ's immersion by John the Baptist. Since the sixth century words from the Old Testament have been used in the crowning ceremony of English kings and queens: 'Zadok the Priest and Nathan the prophet anointed Solomon king' (Kings 1:39).[30] Trumpets sound, then the monarch takes the oath with the right hand resting on a Bible. In England monarchs are anointed with oil to mark the beginning of their reign, as in the Old Testament – 'Then Zadok the priest took a horn of oil from the tabernacle and anointed Solomon. And they blew the horn, and all the people said, "Long live King Solomon!"' (Kings 1:39). Another tradition from the Old Testament relates to the two sceptres, as in Psalm 23. The longer rod is surmounted with a dove, the sign of equity and mercy.

The most unlikely of all the connections, though, is the fact that since the late thirteenth century all English monarchs have gone through the entire crowning ritual while literally sitting above a stone from Bethel, a village twelve miles from Jerusalem. This ancient stone weighing 336 lb and measuring 26 inches in length, 16 inches in width and 11 inches high, is a traditional backdrop to the coronation service. It is supposedly the very stone referred to in the Old Testament, used by Jacob, in about 1500 BCE as a pillow. He 'put under his head, and lay down in that place' (Genesis 28:11). 'He had a dream, and behold, a ladder was set on the earth with its top reaching to heaven; and behold, the angels of God were ascending and descending on it' (28:12). The stone had stayed in Jerusalem until the Babylonian siege around 586–583 BCE, when it was removed for safe keeping by the prophet Jeremiah. After a circuitous journey it ended up in Ireland for just under a thousand years. In the early sixth century it became a trophy of war and was moved to Scotland, where it was used in the coronation ceremonies of the Scots Dalriatic kings. Much to the wrath of the Scots, in 1296 this relic from the Holy Land, incorrectly known as the Stone of Scone – also known as Lia Fail, the Stone of Destiny, the Stone of Covenant, Jacob's Pillow, Jacob's Ladder, and the Saxum Fatale – was again a trophy of war. So meaningful was this stone to Edward I that he took it south to London where he had a new coronation chair built, which is still in use, with a special place for the stone under the seat, complete with spokes to protect it.

After the Stone was stolen by four Scottish Nationalists from Westminster

Abbey on Christmas Day 1950 and taken to Arbroath Abbey, it was located and quickly returned to London. Two years later, in June 1953, Queen Elizabeth II was the twenty-eighth English monarch to have the crown placed on her head while sitting over the stone. In 1996, the 700th anniversary of Edward's taking it from Scotland, the Scots requested its return. Since then it has been kept in Edinburgh Castle with a proviso from the Queen that it is returned for all coronations in Westminster Abbey. The connection of the holy stone to biblical history would be more apparent if it was known by the name of its provenance, Jerusalem, rather than the name Scone, the town where it had rested for just six centuries of its 3,500 year history. (Much the same applies to the so-called Elgin Marbles. It would be appropriate for these treasures to be called the Pantheon Marbles from the Acropolis, rather than by the name of the British ambassador who took them from Athens in 1801.)

The Old Testament was quickly disseminated all over Europe. As Greek translations had been in circulation well before the birth of Christ. In the third century BCE, King Ptolemy II (285–247 BCE) had ordered his librarian, Demetrius, to collect all the books of the world for his library in Alexandria. When Demetrius suggested a Greek translation of the Torah, seventy-two Jews, six from each tribe, travelled to Egypt. Their translation into hellenistic Greek, completed in seventy-two days,[31] was to become one of the foundations of Christianity.

Stories vary about how Christianity was brought to Britain. It most likely came with Roman merchants, traders and soldiers in about the third century. Many Anglo-Saxons took it up but lapsed back into pagan beliefs, it was centuries before the majority was converted.

By a strange twist of fate, within two centuries of the Romans suppressing the Jews in Palestine, Jewish history and its prophets became part of their religious beliefs, Romans began revering the holy places in the very city they had earlier destroyed. Through the medium of the Old Testament, they would be taking Jewish history and customs to the outer corners of their known world.

THREE

Queen Helena Goes to Jerusalem

But I have sent for him to answer this;
And for this cause awhile we must neglect
Our holy purpose to Jerusalem.

Henry IV, Part I; 100-102, William Shakespeare

Some historians say that after the death and Resurrection of Jesus, the most important person in the formation of the church was Paul, and that but for him it would not exist. Some go so far as to say that he coarsened the religion by making extensive use of a degenerate Judaism, of pagan religious practices and that he twisted the message of Jesus. Others argue that he laid the foundation of the Christian church. It is also disputed whether his conversion, or that of the Emperor Constantine,[1] who ruled his empire from Byzantium (Constantinople), had the most impact on the future of the church. Both converted after dramatic visions. Constantine had a vision of a flaming crucifix on the eve of a fierce battle. Recently it was claimed that this may have been the most implication-laden event in Western history.[2] Constantine's biographer, Eusebius (264–340), the 'Father of Church History' and bishop of Caesarea whose diocese included the city of Jerusalem, described the miracle:

> He said that about noon, when the day was already beginning to decline, he saw with his own eyes the trophy of a cross of light in the heavens, above the sun, and bearing the inscription, CONQUER BY THIS. At this sight he himself was struck with amazement, and his whole army also, which followed him on this expedition, and witnessed the miracle.[3]

No longer banned following the emperor's conversion, Christianity was now officially recognized throughout the vast Roman Empire. Eleven years after the Edict of Milan in 313, which formalized Christian civil rights, in 324, the year that Constantine moved his capital east to Byzantium, Christianity was made the State religion of the whole Roman Empire. With this recognition came a new dignity and new churches, but it was heavily encumbered with political and racial differences. Dissension, jealousy, intolerance, discrimination, maltreatment and bigotry between different patriarchs and bishops continued, as did bitter arguments about which writings and beliefs were divinely inspired, and which were of questionable origin. Later Islamic scholars would say that idolatry and polytheism seeped into Christianity at this time. 'The Christian community, while powerful enough to keep Constantine king, could not crush or eradicate idolatry,' wrote the twentieth-century Egyptian scholar Sayyid Qutb;[4] 'Christianity's principles became muddled and transmuted as a result of its struggles and conflicts, leading to the formation of a new synthetic religion, displaying conspicuously equal elements of both Christianity and paganism. . . . He [Constantine] deemed it in his interest and the interest of the two competing ideologies (idolatry and Christianity) to have unity and reconciliation . . .'.

Ideas and teachings about Jesus were as varied at this time as they were to become after the Reformation. The Cross, however, was accepted by all believers as the pre-eminent symbol of the Christian faith: the symbol of death, recalling the redemption of mankind through Jesus, it became the symbol for life. In the ancient world the Crucifixion, like the hangman's rope and the gallows in more recent times, was synonymous with shame and punishment. From the fourth century early Christians saw it differently and pointed out the universal presence of the Cross 'in Nature and in everyday life: the wings of a flying bird, the branches of trees, the projecting oars of galleys, the ship's mast and yard, the yoke of a plough, the handle of a spade, the nose and eyebrows of the human face. . . .'[5]

In 325 Constantine attempted to introduce uniformity and discipline into the scattered and diverse churches by setting up a council of Bishops of the Christian Church at Nicaea (the Turkish town of Iznik). Transport and accommodation were offered to all ecclesiastical leaders, from North Africa to Armenia, Persia, various parts of Asia, Syria, Palestine, Egypt, Greece and Thrace. However, few holy men came, other than those from Calabria, Carthage, Gaul, and Illyria. Eusebius spoke of around 250 bishops, but it was more likely to have been about 300: the figure of 2,000 in Arabic manuscripts probably included all the priests, deacons, and acolytes, and other men who already formed part of the Church hierarchy, who accompanied their bishops.

Clad in gold and covered with precious stones typical of Roman emperors before him, Constantine sat imperiously through the proceedings on a jewelled throne. Delegates brought together the different versions and translations of the twenty-seven books attributed to eight authors – Matthew, John, Paul, James, Peter, Jude, Mark and Luke – soon to be compiled into the most sacred first Christian book, the New Testament. Although it proved all but impossible to standardize the dates of Christmas Day and Easter, with the exception of two bishops, all agreed that the Nicene Creed proposed by Eusebius should replace the basic statement of Christian faith, the Apostles' Creed. In one form or another the Nicene Creed has come down today as 'I believe in one God the Father Almighty, maker of heaven and earth . . .'.

At the conference Bishop Macarius of Jerusalem met Constantine's mother, Helena (255–330) – Flavia Julia Helena Augusta, who had converted to Christianity before her son. Her zest epitomizes the energy common to many of the new followers of Jesus.

Speculation continues about whether Helena was the daughter of the king from Colchester of nursery rhyme fame – 'Old King Cole was a merry old soul, a merry old soul was he . . .' – or the daughter of an innkeeper in Bithynia (now in Turkey). Confusion may have arisen as she had lived in England during the years of her marriage to the Roman general Chlorus, who divorced her for a grander and younger woman. After the death of Chlorus in York, while leading the Romans against the Picts and the Scots, Constantine became emperor. His devotion to his mother was shown when, much to the jealousy of his wife, Fausta, coins were struck bearing his mother's profile.[6] Appalled by the bishop's story of the pitiful condition of the places connected with the life of Jesus in Jerusalem, she became an early pilgrim.

Undeterred by her age (she was at least seventy-two),[7] in either 326 or 327 Helena set off from Constantinople for Jerusalem, accompanied by courtiers. Nothing discouraged her, neither the precipitous terrain that had made King David's illustrious old city impenetrable to any but the most determined army, nor the sweeping changes and rebuilding that had taken place in the capital after devastation by two Roman armies during the three centuries since the death of Jesus, nor by the alterations caused by two major earthquakes.

Knowing that faith rather than fact would have to be used to locate the site of the Cross, Helena responded to this challenge by prayer which literally moved mountains. She directed that shovels, spades and picks be brought into action. The new Roman city of Aelia Capitolina had swallowed up Jerusalem's old streets, houses and walls, while other areas had been covered with rubble or new buildings. Using prayers, dreams, meticulous research and questioning to discover the folklore of what had happened 300 years earlier, Helena and the equally elderly Bishop Macarius supervised massive excavations. The task was daunting, comparable to that faced by an archaeologist in the year 1999 seeking the remnants of the life of a carpenter who had lived in London during the last days of Charles II in England.

Through prayer Helena finally located the site which was said to be the scene of the Crucifixion and Resurrection in the centre of the new town: a perpendicular rock face cut into the hillside with a low door, a vestibule and the inner chamber where she believed that the body of Jesus had lain. An old Jew named Judah told her that Hadrian had built a temple with a statue of Venus on Golgotha where the True Cross of Jesus was buried, intending to destroy all memory of it. Within weeks this pagan temple was pulled down and the ground under it excavated. The last days of Jesus on earth became real again – despite the city of Herod now being hardly recognizable. But such was Helena's passion in finding where the main events in Jesus' life had taken place that her conclusions were accepted and became part of history. The fourteen Stations of the Cross on the Via Dolorosa in Jerusalem were integrated into Roman Catholic ritual. Although these holy places were revered as such throughout the Christian world, centuries later Protestants would query them and find alternative locations.

Constantine rallied his workmen to ensure that the holy sites would be separated from the dirt and noise of daily traders. Magnificent churches, all rich in mosaics and gold, rose over places associated with the life and death of Jesus. Chief among these was the church of the Holy Sepulchre, built in 325–26 to a plan by the Syrian or Palestinian architect Zenobius, in the shape of a basilica – a central hall with double colonnades and an arched and domed recess at the end. The original design is now lost under a confusing accumulation of altars, chapels, and architectural styles, but originally a stately portico opened on to a courtyard on the site of the Sacred Cross and Crucifixion, the Holy Ground of Calvary and a series of open and closed spaces culminated in the Tomb of Christ which was enclosed by a rotunda with a wooden dome. Later this was covered and steps, steep and tall, took worshippers to the different levels. In order for the tomb to be evermore surrounded by the soft chant of praying voices, it was placed in the arched rotunda, in the centre of the church.

After its dedication in 335 the church of the Holy Sepulchre became the most sacrosanct place in the whole of Christendom. From that time onwards the veneration of the Cross intensified and the sanctification of the holy sites began. The church of the Nativity in Bethlehem, an octagonal structure with five naves and a star over the precious grotto on the site located by Helena as the exact place of Christ's birth, was also venerated. Another place of pilgrimage was the church of Eleona, built on the Mount of Olives where Jesus ascended to heaven. Churches and monasteries multiplied to such a degree in the Holy Land that hardly a town connected with the life of Jesus was left unadorned. Even the site of the miracle of the loaves and fishes was enhanced with a Byzantine mosaic. Pilgrims also began to visit Ein Karen on the River Jordan, birthplace of John the Baptist where he plunged into the waters and a church was built in his honour. Places revered in the Old Testament were soon marked by Christian churches – at Shiloh, at Gilgal near Jericho, at the Well of Jacob, at Shechem on Mount Gerizim and even in the Negev Desert. Church buildings were supplemented with monasteries and hospices to accommodate the increasing numbers of pilgrims.[8]

One bishop in Egypt[9] who lived much of his life in Palestine complained about these visitors who came from all corners of the world 'even from Persia and Britain'. Despairing at their numbers and dejected by many not being sufficiently pious, he discouraged prospective pilgrims by suggesting 'that it is as easy to find the way to heaven in Britain as in Jerusalem'.[10]

When the papal throne was transferred from Constantinople to Rome in 590, and Rome became the focus of the Christian religion, pilgrims continued to make their way along the old Roman roads, across Europe, the Balkans and Byzantium to the 'Holy Mountain' – Jerusalem – which God had called his 'eternal dwelling'.[11] Others sailed part of the way, some even went via Alexandria, others via Sicily.

The new religion caused people to travel in both directions. While pilgrims went south, missionaries went north, where soon the inhabitants exchanged the bloodthirsty gods of the Teutonic Valhalla for Christianity. Around the same time, forty monks led by the Italian churchman St Augustine[12] set forth to become missionaries among the heathen Picts and Scots. King Ethelbert, king of Kent, who was already married to a Christian from Paris, became a convert. Augustine became the first archbishop of Canterbury. Far away in Jerusalem, in May 614, the Persians invaded Jerusalem and set fire to the Holy Sepulchre. The roof and furnishings were smashed, but the basic structure remained intact. During the following century the building inspired by Queen Helena was carefully rebuilt and again stood in glory.

* * *

In the seventh century Jerusalem's status as the Holy City of David and Jesus was enhanced with the birth of the third monotheistic and Abrahamist religion, the faith of Islam founded by the prophet Mohammed. Islam quickly became the fastest-growing religion in the Middle East. Like Jesus few facts are known about Mohammed's youth. Born into the Hashemite clan of the Quraysh tribe in Mecca, the prosperous town situated on the trade route used by desert caravans taking goods north to the Christian Byzantine Empire, the prophet had married an older but rich merchant's widow, and led a conventional life. But when about forty years old, in a cave on the slopes of Mount Hira, a hill overlooking Mecca, he experienced uplifting visions and revelations. Voices told him he was the messenger of God, Allah, the creator of heaven and earth, and the words given to him by God through the messenger, the Angel Gabriel, became known as the Koran.

The doctrines of Islam continue some of the messages which were in the Old Testament, but fundamental differences separate it from either Judaism or Christianity. Mohammed believed that the same God had made revelations to earlier prophets, to Adam, Noah, Abraham, Isma'il, Moses and Jesus. When his teachings were scorned by merchants and his followers were persecuted in Mecca, Mohammed took flight to Medina in 622 and the new religion he founded flourished and escalated, as it has ever since. In Medina the Koran started a new phase which reflected the new reality of the Muslim state.

The word Islam means submission to God's will, and Islam attempts to place every dimension of human life under the explicit direction of God's will.[13] For Muslims 'There is no God but God!' They believe that Abraham, the father of Israel, was the first Muslim, and that Mohammed, not Jesus, was God's last prophet. It is a religion based on an insistence of total submission to God and to the dictates of the Prophet. It also shares many Judaic rituals and history, including the Psalms of David. God's revelations to Abraham and Joseph in the Old Testament are also embraced by Islam. Mohammed did not dismiss the New Testament, but declared that 'All earlier religions are paths to God.'

Mohammed is said to have come to Jerusalem in 628 and saw the site of the ancient Temple at a time when Mecca was hostile to him. He instructed his believers that, like the Jews and the Christians, when praying they must face towards the Temple at Jerusalem. This became the first Kibla (direction) for Muslims. Although it is often claimed that when the Jews refused to accept his doctrine, Mohammed said that Muslims must face Mecca, his birthplace, at prayer time instead of the Temple. But many Arabists dispute this, as the change of direction pre-dates this. As the new doctrine spread, and it did so at a rapid rate, it assumed a more Arab national character.

In Jerusalem, guided by the Archangel Gabriel, he is said to have ridden on his winged steed (Al Buraq) from the Temple Mount through the skies on his night journey to the highest heaven. (The Koran, or Qu'ran, Sura Al-Isra' 17:1) It was then that the five daily prayers became obligatory for all Muslims: faith, prayer, almsgiving, fasting and pilgrimage. From that moment onwards the Temple Mount, the Har Habayit in Hebrew and the Haram esh-Sharif, in Arabic, has become sacred to both Jews and Muslims, as is the area in front of it.

In 632, four years after his heavenly experience above the Temple, under Mohammed's chief disciple Caliph Omar, Muslim warriors on horseback conquered Jerusalem. In worn and torn robes, Omar humbly rode on a white camel into the centre of the Holy City. This time the population did not flee, since the tolerance of Islam was evident. Christians were able to run churches monasteries and hospices, but they could not ring bells. Islamic places of worship have no bells, altars, choirs or naves. Nothing broke the echoing chants of the muezzin who called Muslims to prayer five times a day. Jews, who had been forbidden to settle in Jerusalem under Roman and Byzantine rule now returned, to live in certain areas and build synagogues, schools and cemeteries. The three and a half centuries between the Arab invasion and the First Crusade were a period of fruitful spiritual and intellectual activity for Palestine Jews. They were forbidden, though, to visit the revered stone platform on which the great Jewish Temple had once stood and which Omar had ordered to be cleared of rubble and rubbish. A glorious edifice to Islam rose from the ruins. To mark the place of Mohammed's night journey to heaven, in 691 Umayyad Caliph Abd al-Malik built the Dome of the Rock with its golden dome, soon acknowledged as one of the architectural glories of the world. A shrine rather than a mosque, this expression of the ascendancy of Islam, became the third holiest place in Islam after the Ka'aba in Mecca and the Prophet's Mosque in Medina.

One of the many ornate inscriptions inside affirms that God is one and not three and that Jesus was an apostle of God. This is an example of how the standard Christian belief in one God to many Muslims appears to be belief in three Gods. In 1035, at the south end of the Temple Mount platform, a large mosque was built which came to be called al-Aqsa. Non-Muslims were forbidden to set foot on this area. Disputes over Jews visiting the Wailing Wall, their most sacred site, at the edge of the Haram became a bone of contention. As Mohammed's horse had been tethered to the Temple Wall, later to be known as the Western Wall or Wailing Wall, the area in front also became sacred for Muslims. Meanwhile, the primary Christian place of worship the church of the Holy Sepulchre had suffered from more disasters. In 746 an earthquake had caused structural damage to the dome. Just over sixty years later, in 810, another earthquake shook its very foundations, this time loosening some of the structural timbers.

The next calamity, though, came not from the heavens but from the Nile Valley. Al-Hakim, the fanatical and autocratic Fatimid caliph of Egypt from 996 (his cult spawned the Druze religion), set off on a mission to destroy churches. His act was rare. Muslims were not allowed to touch any Christian or Jewish place of worship. Under al-Hakim's instruction, masons stripped the courses of stones from the walls of the Holy Sepulchre until the floor was knee-deep in rubble. The Tomb of Christ was viciously destroyed; the millennium of his death in 1033 was celebrated amid ruins. Then a third earthquake, in 1034, destroyed much of what was left. But again the walls of the church rose up. In memory of his predecessor, the Byzantine Emperor, Constantine Monomachus rebuilt the church on the same site of the Tomb and the Crucifixion, copying the old model as much as possible. But reports that Oriental Christians were being persecuted by the Seljuk Turks began to circulate in Europe. At the Council of Clermont in France in 1095, Pope Urban II urged the need for a crusade to protect the holy places from the Infidels.

FOUR

The Crusades

May you deem it a beautiful thing to die for Christ in that city in which He died for us.

Pope Urban II, in his address of 1095 initiating the Crusades

The first Crusaders departed from various European cities in 1096, leaving behind them a blood-stained trail. In the name of God and under the banner of the Cross, on their way to the Holy Land Christian soldiers slaughtered thousands of Jews in Europe. This, however, was just a prelude to the carnage in Jerusalem itself in 1099. One chronicler estimated that over 10,000 Muslims were killed in the al-Aqsa Mosque, despite the fact they had surrendered. The shocking bloodshed brought fear and incomprehension throughout Syria and Palestine. Seven centuries later, retracing the sites of the slaughter during a visit to Jerusalem, William Makepeace Thackeray wrote, 'It was on Mount Zion that Godfrey and Tancred had their camp: when the Crusaders entered the mosque, they rode knee-deep in the blood of its defenders, and of the women and children who had fled thither for refuge: it was the victory of Joshua over again. Then, after three days of butchery, they purified the desecrated mosque and went to prayer. In the centre of this history of crime rises up the Greatest Murder of all. . . .'[1]

The Crusaders created two 'counties', Edessa and Tripoli, the Principality of Antioch, and in Palestine they set up the feudal Kingdom of Jerusalem under Godfrey of Bouillon, who became titular head – almost a king but not quite. But Godfrey died before the year was out and other prominent Crusaders consolidated their positions on the coast and formed the Crusader states – the Latin kingdoms of the East – giving themselves grand titles: Count of Edessa, Prince of Antioch and Count of Tripoli. Godfrey of Bouillon's brother, Baldwin, was elected the first king of the Kingdom of Jerusalem and was crowned on Christmas Day in the church of the Nativity at Bethlehem. Among the priorities of the Crusaders was rebuilding the church of the Holy

Sepulchre, and enlarging it to accommodate the increasing numbers of pilgrims arriving in the Holy City.

Each spring ships from Italian cities brought thousands of pilgrims for Easter, and the Latins took advantage of their presence to capture more towns and ports on the coast. In 1103 they took Acre, on the coast; in 1109 Tripoli; Beirut and Sidon fell to them in 1110 and Tyre in 1124.

The Crusaders were never able, however, to dominate the Levant beyond the line of the Lebanese mountains, and in 1187 the tables of conquest were turned. Saladin (Salah ad-Din), the mighty Sultan of Egypt and Syria, destroyed the Latin army in the Battle of the Horns of Hattin to the west of the Sea of Galilee. The fall of Jerusalem to the Arabs swiftly followed. Saladin's crossing of the River Jordan with an army of 20,000 foot soldiers and 12,000 cavalry, to retake the Holy City from the Christians, is seen as the first highlight of Arab victories in the Crusades. The giant Cross, the symbol of Christianity, that glittered high on the dome was quickly removed. In the words of Saladin's biographer,[2] 'A group of them scaled up to the top of the dome to remove the cross. When they reached the top all the people cried out with one voice.' Along with the Cross, the men dragged out four ivory chests of crosses, images, vases and other relics of 'Christian idolatry'.

Saladin purged the Holy City of Christians, and re-consecrated the great Mosque of Omar. A ship with black sails crossed the Mediterranean with the woeful news of the loss of Christian rule in Jerusalem. On learning of the disaster Frederick Babarossa, emperor of Germany, Richard the Lionheart of England and Philip Augustus of France responded by setting off on the Third Crusade. But this too was fraught with difficulty and mishap: Frederick drowned en route and the remaining two monarchs found on arrival they had a new and formidable opponent in the Arabian cavalry. Horsemanship in the Middle East was at its peak. Arab horses were much smaller, faster, more agile and manoeuvrable than the heavy northern horses, enabling their horsemen to use surprise tactics. One of these was to harry the flanks of the bulk of Crusader foot soldiers and pepper them with such a large number of arrows that they sometimes looked like hedgehogs or porcupines. Although slower and handicapped by having to carry men in bulky armour, the larger northern Crusader horses charged together and could mow down the enemy, rather like modern tanks. Richard failed to recapture Jerusalem. He stopped his advance in the surrounding hills overlooking the city. Whether this was because he anticipated defeat at the hands of Saladin or because he knew he did not have enough soldiers to hold the city will never be known, but after a siege lasting two years, Acre fell to Richard along with a narrow coastal area. Before he returned to England and France he arranged an armistice with Saladin that allowed Christian pilgrims to visit Jerusalem.

After Saladin died in the spring of 1192, competing Muslim factions began to shatter the fragile unity he had imposed on his dominions. This disunity allowed the Crusaders to take Beirut, Tiberias and Ascalon. Richard did not share in the victory, as he was far away in France trying to recapture lands and castles seized from him in his absence. He died in 1199, exactly a hundred years after the Crusaders had first taken Jerusalem. In 1219 the appearance of the city changed. The Ayyubid ruler of Damascus, El Malik El Muathim Isa, destroyed most of the old city walls (not rebuilt for three centuries). Ten years later Frederick II regained the Holy City in 1229, though this time the Crusaders held it for only thirteen years. Revered though it was, from the time of its final fall to the Muslims in 1244, Jerusalem played a static role as a pivotal place of worship – but little else. Far from the main caravan routes and lacking the vitality of an administrative or trade centre, this sacred city of faith, this city of dreams, was of neither political or economic importance. Even five years later when a new era in the East began as the mighty Mamelukes from Egypt, who had supplanted the Ayyubid family, fulfilled the aspiration of Cleopatra by capturing Palestine, the status of Jerusalem did not alter. And in 1291 the coastal strip also slipped out of Crusader control. First to fall was the Crusader castle at Acre, followed by the remaining Crusader towns of Beirut, Sidon and Tyre. Two centuries of crusading warfare were over. The next invader was Genghis Khan and his Mongols pressing in with his massive armies from the cold steppes of Asia.

Pilgrimages, smaller-scale crusades and trade continued, but, apart from the nearby island of Cyprus, Europeans ceased to control any large areas in the former Crusader kingdoms. Whether Francis of Assisi visited Jerusalem after his journey to Egypt is uncertain, but since the thirteenth century the voices of his monks, the Franciscans, with their rope belts knotted in imitation of their master, have filled the church of the Holy Sepulchre. These bearded brown-clad fathers have daily marched solemnly with candles in processions to the altar. Again the tolerance of Islam prevailed. Priests and monks from dozens of other religious orders were allowed by the Muslims to run Christian churches throughout the Holy Land.

This tolerance was not duplicated by Christians in Europe. Edward I, who lost all hope of overpowering Islam during his journey as a knight on the eighth and last Crusade, derived some satisfaction after his return to England in wreaking vengeance on the Jews. Roman Catholicism was by then the dominant religion on the continent. In the past seven hundred years, Europeans had turned their backs on paganism and regardless of their own language recited the same prayers in either Latin or Greek.[3] Pride in Christianity led to a hatred of anything that could not be assimilated. Gypsies and Jews were perceived as the main groups of infidels to have preserved their identities.

Before the Crusades the situation of the Jews had been tenuous, but tolerable. Now, in the midst of a sea of believers, clerics stirred the Christian masses into an anti-Jewish frenzy. Jews were offered the choice of Christianity or death. Everything continued to take Christianity away from its roots in the Jewish faith,[4] despite the inclusion of much that had originated with the Jews in Christian teaching.[5] Without the Jews there would be no Christian.

In 1306, sixteen years after Edward's drastic action against the Jews, France, which had a Jewish population of about 100,000, acted in a similar fashion. Any Jewish citizen who would not convert to the Roman Catholic faith was expelled. Henceforth, from time to time, persecution became a pattern in many countries in Europe, as did their exclusion from particular areas, jobs and universities. In some places they were forced to wear yellow stars: in others they bore the burden of the 'blood-libel', the belief that Jews sacrificed Christian children.

In contrast to the Jews in early Christian Europe who had mixed socially with their Christian neighbours,[6] medieval Jewry was now mostly confined to areas known as 'ghettos' (derived from a Venetian word meaning 'foundry') and frequently harassed. Here they kept alive their worship, their rituals, their ceremonies, their Hebrew language and their customs. Barriers were not put up just by gentiles. A strict Jew was forbidden to marry outside the faith, to eat at the same table as or go to the theatre with a non-Jew. Jewish agents collected the traditional equivalent of a half shekel from Jews abroad to send to the synagogue and the resilient small Jewish population in Jerusalem. After 300 French and English rabbis settled in Palestine in 1210, others followed, some just to die, others to live. Despite the dispersion, the spark of the Jewish connection with Jerusalem was always alive.

FIVE

The Wife of Bath Goes to Jerusalem

And thries hadde she been at jerusalem;
She hadde passed many a straunge strem;
At rome she hadde been, and at boloigne,
In galice at seint-jame, and at coloigne.
She koude muchel of wandrynge by the weye.
Gat-tothed was she, soothly for to seye.
Upon an amblere esily she sat,

General Prologue, Wife of Bath, 463–9, Geoffrey Chaucer

The inexhaustible Wife of Bath travelled to Jerusalem three times. In emphasizing her journey[1] in his classic description of English life, *The Canterbury Tales*, Geoffrey Chaucer showed just how popular Jerusalem then was as a destination. And by describing the Wife of Bath as a lusty, rather than a saintly type, he also illustrated that pilgrimages were not just for monks, abbots and the pious. Such journeys to the Eastern Mediterranean and other places associated with special saints were then on the increase. To earn merit for salvation pilgrims also travelled to Canterbury in Kent, the shrine at Walsingham in north Norfolk and Santiago de Compostella in north-west Spain. Many objects and relics, whether the bones of saints, alleged pieces of the cross, holy water from the River Jordan or statues, assumed deep spiritual meaning and were considered to bring blessings to anyone who touched them.

In the autumn of 1413, the last year of Henry IV's reign and less than twenty years after the Wife of Bath's last journey in 1387, Margery Kempe, the mother of fourteen children, set off for Jerusalem from King's Lynn, in Norfolk. From Yarmouth she travelled along the Rhine Valley to Venice where she took ship for Jaffa. Despite its being an 'as-told-to' autobiography, written down for her by male scribes, much has been made of the fact that her journals, faithfully transcribed into a book, are considered by some to be the earliest autobiography in English. Although known about, it was only discovered in the home of an old Catholic family in Norfolk around 1930.

Because she conveys a sense of the possibilities for women's piety in the later Middle Ages, the passage in which she bargains with her husband to have a celibate marriage and be free to go on pilgrimages is considered to be one of the most arresting discussions in medieval literature. But the victory of negotiating a breakthrough in marital arrangements does not overshadow her account of what a pilgrimage to Jerusalem then involved. She had almost nothing to say about geographical detail, but the book conveys her enthusiasm for Jerusalem:

> And so they went forth into the Holy Land till they might see Jerusalem. And when this creature saw Jerusalem, riding on an ass, she thanked God with all her heart, praying him for his mercy that like as he had brought her to see this earthly city Jerusalem, he would grant her grace to see the blissful city Jerusalem above, the city of heaven. . . . And so they helped her forth to Jerusalem. And when she came there, she said, 'Sirs, I pray you be not displeased though I weep sore in this holy place where our Lord Jesu Christ was quick and dead.'

A similar veneration of the Holy City is seen in the death of Henry IV who had been told that he 'should not die but in Jerusalem', and so when he was told that the Chapter House at Westminster Abbey was called the 'Jerusalem Chamber' he collapsed in a kind of fit when praying and died there 'according to the prophecy':

> It hath been prophesied to me, many years,
> I should not die but in Jerusalem.
> Which vainly I suppos'd the Holy Land.
> But bear me to that chamber; there I'll lie:
> In that Jerusalem shall Harry die.
>
> *Henry IV, Part II, iv 236–240, William Shakespeare*

Pilgrimages to the Holy Land were thought to bring spiritual reward and even salvation to the pilgrim, but for some were seen as a holidays or holy-days,[2] and had already become notorious as occasions for sexual promiscuity.[3] Just as with the tourism of later times, these journeys broke all sorts of inhibitions and barriers, especially of class. The journeys were not easy. Travellers endured fleas, mosquitoes, food poisoning and the other hazards of travel.

The numbers of ordinary Britons who risked seasickness and shipwreck to reach the Holy Land prompted William Wey, a Fellow of Eton, in the reign of Henry VI, to produce a travel guide stating the prices of inns in Venice, and what to see *en route*. On disembarkation in Palestine he advised his readers:

> When ye shall get your ass at Port Jaffa, be not too long behind your fellow, for an ye come betimes ye may choose the best mule or ass . . . and ye must give your ass man [for] courtesy a groat.[4]

Remote though it was, Jerusalem remained at the centre of world maps for centuries. Surrounded by unpromising country, this Oriental city was not on, or near, any trade routes or ports. Access was difficult. Wheeled transport was almost out of the question until the roads were repaired and rebuilt. The city was built on rock in the Judean hills, perched high above the desert, nearly 3,000 feet above sea level, with olives and fig trees growing among its stony valleys. During the winter, monks and pilgrims shivered in unheated churches. For those without horses or donkeys, the climb along the old mountainous road from the ports of Jaffa or Acre was arduous. Whether it was sheer relief that the journey was over, or an excess of religious fervour, medieval pilgrims would sometimes fall on their knees, tearing their clothes in an excess of ecstasy when they first caught sight of Jerusalem. Kites and falcons flew overhead and outside the walls, goats scrambled among the rocks. Here pilgrims found the plants of the Bible, the willow, oak, fig, date, olive, 'the lilies of the field', scarlet anemones, wild tulips, poppies and ranunculus. For some, just standing beside the walls where David, Solomon and Jesus had stood was the high point of their lives. Pilgrims returned from Jerusalem with their hearts filled with awe and wondrous tales of having followed in the footsteps of the most sacred man who had ever lived, of having seen the site of the Cross and of having kissed his empty Tomb.

As Jerusalem is not near any river or large water supply, it was frequently a thirsty city: in spite of its wells, hidden cisterns and the Roman aqueduct, water was usually in short supply. There was no agricultural hinterland so most food supplies arrived by camel, donkey or mule. As already noted, religion was Jerusalem's only real trade. The city was a mixture of magnificent churches, mosques and old dark stone houses, in narrow, clattering and often unswept streets. Its skyline was a silhouette of domes, minarets, spires, parapets and the huddled roofs of tile and corrugated iron.

From dawn to dusk the city rang with the sounds of the muezzins' calls to prayer from the minarets, Latin masses, dozens of languages and dialects. Religious orders from many different countries and denominations had turned Jerusalem into a cosmopolitan centre, with convents and hospices. With few exceptions, regardless of the era, until the twentieth century, it was usually run-down. Pilgrims were sold beads, crosses, effigies of the Virgin Mary, bottles of holy water from the Jordan, and pictures of saints painted on mother-of-pearl shells. In its roofed-in, at times fly-blown bazaars, men sat cross-legged beside piles of carpets, sandalwood, brass pots and old scent bottles, smoking their hookahs, waiting patiently for customers. Despite the noise and hubbub of the throngs, sometimes the only visitors to some shops were the sparrows hopping around looking for crumbs in the narrow shafts of light.

Each week three Sabbaths were celebrated. Friday was the holy day of the Muslims at the Mosque of Omar; from Friday sunset until three stars appeared in the Saturday-evening sky was the Jewish Sabbath at the Western Wailing Wall; Sunday was the Sabbath for the Christians at the church of the Holy Sepulchre. On Fridays monks shuffled along the Via Dolorosa paying tribute at the fourteen Stations of the Cross, winding their way between the overloaded donkeys and stick-wielding Arab boys, veiled women and men wearing either a turban or a fez. Century after century little changed. Jerusalem may have been 'holy', but bigotry, hatred and fanatical zeal formed hostile barriers between the different Christian religions and sects, giving rise to tension, unpleasantness and long-standing feuds.

The number of pilgrimages from England dwindled by the seventeenth century. Rome had taken over as the holy destination for Roman Catholics, while a journey to Mecca remained the cherished goal for Arabs. Pilgrimages were no longer valued by the Church: in England Protestants were exhorted to find salvation within themselves, not in places. The throngs of English pilgrims no longer made their way to the Holy Land but the printed word meant that it remained familiar. After a long struggle lasting nearly two centuries, newly translated and newly printed Bibles would bring visions of the Holy Land into millions of homes. At first, though, there was enormous hostility to translations. It was feared that personal judgment, based on the study of the Bible, would destroy the authority of the clergy. Who was qualified to translate the word of God? Apprehension was expressed that in the process of rendering the Bible, 'the jewel of the church', into another language, the nuances – the fine meanings of God's word – would be distorted or modified by the translator himself. Scriptures in English were equal to treacherous heresy. The long path ahead would be littered with burnt men, burnt books and burnt Bibles – and would lead to a renaissance of the Old Testament. Among other things it would also lead to querying many beliefs, such as Purgatory, introduced into the Roman Catholic Church in the late sixth century.

SIX

The Bible Begins to Speak with Many Tongues

Bibles laid open, millions of surprises.

'Sin', George Herbert

This epic endeavour began with the learned John Wycliffe from Yorkshire, the former master of Balliol College at Oxford, known as the 'morning star of the Reformation'. He bravely attacked the abuses of the Church, publicly queried the dogma of transubstantiation and produced religious tracts in English. In 1381 Wycliffe began the three-year task of translating the current Latin Vulgate version and produced the first complete version of the Bible in English. Although this was never printed and was later dismissed by scholars who sought a return to the roots of the texts, wishing to translate directly from Hebrew and biblical Greek, it was the first step to a complete and accessible Bible. It was not until 1455, in Germany, that Gutenberg's newly invented commercial printing press brought out the first printed Bibles, in any language.

Over half a century later, in 1517, two events occurred with far-reaching repercussions for the Jews. Firstly, in the summer the Turks, led by Sultan Selim the Grim, beat the Mamelukes, captured the Levant and began 400 years of Turkish rule. Jerusalem became but a part of the vast Ottoman Empire ruled from Constantinople. A prophecy in Isaiah (49: 7,16) was fulfilled: 'Foreigners will rebuild your walls and their kings will be your servants.' After an absence of 300 years, the walls around Jerusalem, dismantled and destroyed towards the end of the Crusader period, were rebuilt by Selim's son, Suleiman the Magnificent. He also resurfaced the exterior of the Dome of the Rock with blue-green tiles and, while building a series of fountains, improved and repaired the water system.

Secondly, in the late autumn of 1517 the religious upheaval which had been simmering in Europe for nearly a century exploded into an international débâcle. The division of Western Christendom into two camps, the Catholic and the Protestant, began after the Catholic monk Martin Luther hung his ninety-five theses on the church door in Wittenberg in Germany, and thus unleashed a force which would soon tear apart and break up the monopoly of the Roman Catholic religion in Europe. Large numbers of people now felt free to loosen the fetters that had constrained them from complaining against corrupt and exploitative priests, their demands and abuses. The idea that divine authority should be mediated only through priests and institutions was now challenged. Luther's idea of the supremacy of the written texts of the Bible struck a chord, especially with those who were sceptical about the clergy. Liberal though Luther's ideas were, he actually heightened anti-Jewish attitudes among Christians at a time when tens of thousands of stateless Jews, fleeing after the Spanish government issued an expulsion decree in 1492, were trying to settle in Germany, France and other European countries. Over 8,000 migrated to Palestine, more to other parts of the Ottoman Empire. For about a century the attitude of the Turks to the Jews was unexpectedly benign.[1] This was not the case in Germany. In his recent history of the Jews, Raymond Scheindlin states:

> Early in his campaign, Luther included in his critique of the church its persecution of the Jews, assuming that his attack on the popes and his appeal to the authority of the Bible would win Jews over to Christianity. When it did not, he turned on them as 'disgusting vermin,' urged Christians to treat them with enmity, and endorsed their expulsion from various German states.[2]

Just as Luther's preaching did not augur well for the Jews, it strengthened the stand against Protestantism in England. Here the church hierarchy saw anything to do with Luther and Protestantism as a threat, and for over fifteen years followers of the new faith were arrested and burnt at the stake. Nothing illustrates Henry VIII's dilemma about the Protestant religion more than the title of 'Defender of the Faith', bestowed on him by Pope Leo X in 1521 for his support in the battle against the new Protestant faith. In the very year that Luther was condemned as a heretic and excommunicated by a papal bull, Henry had written a tract, with help from Cardinal Fisher and Cardinal Wolsey, attacking Luther's views; and later Henry ignored the pope's repeal of his title.

In 1523 the Protestant William Tyndale escaped from England to the University of Wittenberg, and two years later, in Cologne, prepared the first copy of the New Testament for printing, which he had translated into English. At the last moment his place of refuge was discovered, but he managed to escape his would-be captors. Finally, in the town of Worms, on the Rhine, the first English translation of the Scriptures from the biblical Greek rolled off the presses. Smuggled copies were soon circulating in England.

By this time the Reformation had extended to Sweden and Denmark, and the breakaway sects were increasing. As Henry feared the spread of the Reformation and it reaching English shores, Cardinal Wolsey supervised a massive burning of 'Lutheran books', and Tyndale, who by now was experienced at camouflaging his movements, evaded arrest as he moved from place to place with his quill and Bible. Once the Reformation was established in Berne the hunt for Tyndale intensified. But in 1533 his translation of the first five books of the Old Testament were sent to England.

In England, from about 1534 onwards, when the Pope refused Henry permission to divorce Catherine of Aragon, his wife of nineteen years, all recourse to Rome was banned. Thomas Cranmer, the first Protestant archbishop of Canterbury, allowed Henry a divorce and conducted the marriage ceremony between Henry and the pregnant Anne Boleyn. This did not mean that England quickly changed from being a Catholic nation. Neither was there any sudden throwing out of the old dogmas and traditions, such as the belief in purgatory, the offering of prayers to saints, the use of devotional aids like rosaries, relics, incense beads and statues of the Virgin Mary. In ridding himself of the yoke of Roman Catholicism, Henry had given himself more power, and the dissolution of some 800 monasteries had enriched him with untold acres and wealth, but he had failed to bring in radical changes, and the words 'popery without the pope' echoed through the kingdom. The Church began to split into two camps, which would later be known, unofficially, as the High Anglicans or Anglo-Catholics, who retained much of the Catholic ceremonial and vestments, and the Low Church, which stressed simplicity in worship and reform.

Meanwhile, although Tyndale was arrested in Antwerp in 1535 by one of the king's agents, Myles Coverdale, who had earlier assisted him and worked on the as yet untranslated portions of the Old Testament, published the Coverdale Bible in Zurich. Much of this Bible, which was to be the basis of most future translations, had been translated by Tyndale, but, as an arch-heretic, he could not be acknowledged. The following year Tyndale was strangled and burned at the stake for heresy, but he died secure in the knowledge that people would now have personal access to both the Old and the New Testaments.

In 1539, in accordance with a proclamation by Henry that 'one book of the whole Bible . . . in English' was to be distributed to every church in the land and chained to the pulpit, Cranmer commissioned Coverdale to publish the 'Great Bible'. This, the first English Bible, was over fourteen inches in length. Seven editions were printed in the next three years. Acquaintance was not just restricted to the rich and the educated. By the decree of the king, every church was to provide a reader so that the illiterate could hear the word of God in their own tongue.

The Bible thus became the essence of the Protestant rebellion. Many people substituted 'the book' for the authority of the Church. Emphasis was now put on a simplified relationship to God, and scholars developed a profound interest in the Old Testament. Even though only a minority of people were literate, the Bible was read aloud daily in a wide cross-section of homes, churches and chapels. Many people felt that this put them in a direct relationship with God. Once new services were in English rather than Latin, and once the clergy widened the range of excerpts which were read, the Old Testament took on a new significance. This was not only because it forms the bulk of the Bible but because it was acknowledged as the Bible studied by Jesus, the book of his education, the book of his ministry, the book of his ancestry, which could be traced to the royal family of David, the book which had predicted his birth, the book he used to teach his disciples.[3] Many Christians now looked at Jesus in the light of his relation to Judaism and the Prophets.

When Henry VIII died in 1547 the impact of the Old Testament continued as reforms in favour of Protestantism were led for the next six years by the Bible-loving Cranmer. Henry left three children, two red-headed and one fair, Edward, Mary and Elizabeth who occupied the throne for fifty years. But none had children of their own, and so the crown passed to the lateral line three times, with no continuity between the reigns. With every new monarch the changes in religious practice were so spectacular that it would be another 150 years before the Protestant religion became firmly entrenched in England.

A mere ten years old when he succeeded his father in 1547, Edward VI, the son of Jane Seymour, showed his sympathy to the Protestant faith during his coronation when he requested a Bible to carry for the service. But when Edward's half-sister, Mary, the Roman Catholic daughter of Catherine of Aragon, succeeded him in 1553, she reversed her brother's policy, and executed and imprisoned reformers while reinstating Catholic bishops. Cranmer was just one of the 300 martyrs burned alive at the stake, and thousands of English Bibles were also consigned to the flames. After Mary's marriage to Philip II of Spain, which resulted in only phantom pregnancies, her persecution of Protestants earned her the name of 'Bloody Mary'. She and Mary of Guise, the Queen Regent in Scotland, were both damned by John Knox,[4] the Scottish Protestant reformer, who had taken refuge in Geneva with John Calvin, in his pamphlet *The First Blast of the Trumpet against the Monstrous Regiment of Women*.

When Mary died in 1558, Elizabeth, Henry's daughter by Anne Boleyn, succeeded to the throne. She showed her dislike of Roman Catholic pomp and ritual at her first State Opening of parliament by ordering the monks at Westminster to extinguish their ceremonial tapers: 'Away with those torches, we can see well enough'. Her half-sister's Catholic legislation was repealed, the Church of England was established as the State Church, Cranmer's [revised] Book of Common Prayer became the law of English liturgy, religious images in churches were to be destroyed by government order and punitive methods kept religious feuds in check.[5] The fine of one shilling imposed on any man or woman who failed to attend the parish church was obviously not always charged. Absenteeism was widespread and religious life in many parishes was at a low ebb. Many parsons, inclined towards self-indulgent lives, neglected the poorer members of their congregations. In 1581 parliament passed a law that conversion to Catholicism was punishable as high treason, and during the following two decades over one hundred priests and sixty laymen were executed. But a new social order based on the Bible was taking root, and by the end of Elizabeth's reign it would be the most popular book in the country.

Far from extinguishing their passion, the heavy hand of the state fuelled the resolve of Puritans. Among the first organized breakaway groups to emerge at this time and to sever links with the Established Church were the Congregationalists. In 1580, one of their leaders, Robert Browne, defined the principle of each congregation managing its own affairs, which led them also to be known as 'Independents'. Like the Baptists, their tenacity earned them a special place in the development of Puritanism. Wanting to purify (hence the term 'Puritan') the Church of its popish ways and return to early Christianity, they looked north of the border, where the church relied more on the Gospel and the Old Testament. To escape punishment, all members of the Low Church who became Puritans were forced to keep their beliefs secret.

In Scotland, however, it was different. Under the dynamic guidance of Knox, a distinct Protestant church had emerged. A year after Elizabeth's accession, Knox had returned to Scotland, pitted the sword in preparation for battle against the Catholic Church and inflamed the people. When civil war erupted Protestantism triumphed and the Church of Scotland became the State religion. Some Scottish divines spoke tenderly about Judaism as the 'elder' sister to the Church.

Knox presaged the emergence of a new era. To enable every Scot to read the Bible, schools were established, so that by the eighteenth century Scotland had one of the highest literacy rates in Europe. So distinct was the new Scottish church that when Mary Queen of Scots' son, James VI, came south to London as James I, after the death of Elizabeth in 1603,[6] English Puritans looked to him to make similar changes; but in vain.

In 1611, however, James authorized the King James Bible. In this new translation many facts differentiated it from earlier translations, which served to widen the gap between Roman Catholic and Protestant. Devout Protestants felt an intimacy with the history of the Jews and its biblical personalities were woven into Christian thought. Many people believed that the Bible was actually addressed to them, forgetting that it was about an Oriental race, at a stage of their culture dating back to the Bronze Age. This empathy would be more pronounced in the late eighteenth century with the Dissenters. As the Old Testament is so much longer than the New, people learned about Jewish lore, their wars, courage and death. It also helped the new readers in the sixteenth and seventeenth centuries, especially the English and Scots, identify with the pastoral life with its benevolence to strangers; pride of blood and family; migration and travel; long desert journeys; courage in battle and even input into the centrality of gardening to English culture with Isaiah's promise: 'thou shalt be like a watered garden.'

In earlier centuries the majority of Christians unable to read Latin or indeed their own language had relied solely on the clergy to translate and interpret the Bible. Now as the Bible became more widely distributed (by 1640 over a million copies had been printed in England alone) many people learned long passages by heart and felt that nothing stood between themselves and 'the book'. No one could add or subtract from the word of God. Most importantly, instead of just hearing extracts in sermons from the pulpit, which had been chosen and interpreted by priests, they could now read whatever *they* chose. The habit also began of daily Bible reading at home, starting with the words, 'In the beginning, when God created the universe . . .' in Genesis and finishing months later with the last verse in Revelations, in the New Testament, 'May the grace of the Lord Jesus be with everyone.' The Old Testament became a fund of powerful metaphors and images in conversation, with myriad words and polite culture saturated with biblical references.

No longer relying on orthodox interpretations from priests, people could now choose independently what they wanted to read or learn. But the Reformation was carefully policed and doctrine was still delivered from on high. Only those with university degrees – that is, clerics in orders – could teach and interpret the Scriptures at this time. The preface to the Authorized Version of the Bible sets out whose authority people were subject to in regard to its interpretation. Many preachers were imprisoned in cells with robbers and murderers, and even tortured, for preaching and teaching without a licence. So while people could decide for themselves, if their opinions did not coincide with official views, they had to keep those opinions to themselves if they did not want to get into trouble with authority. For the radical, breakaway Protestant sects such as the Congregationalists and Quakers, who emerged from the Puritan movements of the sixteenth century, individual conscience and the inner working of the holy spirit were of paramount importance. Definitions of heresy changed. The suppression of heresy, as well as the elimination of false teaching, became regular policy measures.

Not only did the new Bible have a deep effect on religion, it shaped the English language and literature. In his book, *In the Beginning*, Professor Alister McGrath says that the English Bible was 'the foundation of every aspect of English culture, linking monarch and church, time and eternity'. He adds that the influence extended to social, economic and political areas – and that it was also decisive in determining the British way of thinking about the Jews.[7]

An awareness and a close acquaintance developed with Jewish history. Characters such as Adam and Eve to Noah, Abraham, Moses, Samuel, David, Solomon and many more lived on in the imagination of Christians, and fuelled an interest in the Holy Land, its topography, people, and especially the four cities holy to Judaism, Jerusalem, Hebron, Safed and Tiberias. This familiarity was already well reinforced by art. Dozens of characters from the Hebrew Scriptures had been the subject of painters, sculptors, musicians and stained-glass artists.

As Barbara Tuchman shows in *The Bible and the Sword*, with the severance and separation with Rome, Protestants looked increasingly towards Jerusalem and the Holy Land, to the places where Christianity had begun, not where it had been interpreted. 'Wherever the Reformation took hold the Bible replaced the Pope as the final spiritual authority. The Palestinian origins of Christianity were stressed more and more in order to reduce the pretensions of Rome. Where the papal bull had ruled earlier, now the word of God as revealed in the Hebrew testaments to Abraham and Moses, to Isaiah, Elijah and Daniel, to Jesus and Paul governed instead. . . . After the publication of the King James version in 1611 . . . the Bible was as much England's own as Good Queen Bess or Queen Victoria.'[8]

* * *

Puritanism which became established in England with the newly translated Bible was impregnated with the ideas, language, arguments and history of the Old Testament. For Puritans, the Bible offered 'yet more light and truth', and so they discarded what they considered to be superstitious and corrupt observances and dogmas, and turned to 'the Book'. In 1618 the king horrified the increasing number of Puritans by announcing that people could dance, and take part in archery, leaping and vaulting on Sundays. Outlawed and dissatisfied, some Puritans fled to Holland. The Pilgrim Fathers who sailed to the 'New World' from Plymouth in the *Mayflower* in 1620 wanted to make a new holy land where they would be free from discrimination and other forms of persecution. One group was led by John Robinson, William Brewster and William Bradford; another by the Cambridge scholar and an ordained minister of the Church of England, John Smyth, the first English Baptist. Smyth's group became the earliest Baptists known by that name, but the first actual Baptist Church in America was set up in 1639 on Rhode Island by Roger Williams. Baptists, like other Puritans, sought the authority for their religion in the Bible, and strove to take religion back to its beginnings. In building 'the kingdom of Christ in America', they sought guidance in the Bible as interpreted by Puritan preachers.[9]

In the 103 years between Luther's hanging his notices on the church door and the sailing of the *Mayflower*, the Catholic Church had lost its monopoly in Europe. Jews had also lost their place as the most persecuted religious minority group in Europe, but they were still officially banned from living in

England. During these ten decades, despite the the renewed interest in the Hebrew Scriptures, no move was made to lift the ban. There were exceptions though. It appears that some Jewish physicians had been allowed to enter England to attend royal and aristocratic households;[10] that a man by the name of Mark Raphael crossed the channel to advise Henry VIII on his divorce; and that a German mining expert came to England to teach new mining methods. But these were rare cases.

The first call to restore the Jews to Palestine came in 1621, the year after the first Puritans set off for America. Sir Henry Finch, a Member of Parliament for Canterbury and legal adviser to King James I, published a small book entitled *The World's Great Restoration*, which urged that everything should be done to help the Jews return to the Promised Land: 'Out of all the places of thy dispersion, East, West, North and South, His purpose is to bring thee home again and to marry thee to Himself by faith for evermore.' Finch wrote at length and asked the English people and their government to support Jewish settlement in Palestine, rationalizing that it would fulfil biblical prophecy. Given that the whole of Syria had been conquered by the Turks nearly a century earlier his idea was theoretical. Finch was just one of a growing number of Christians who felt that the Bible promised the land of Israel to the Jews in perpetuity, and some restoration to them was needed if the Bible were to keep its promises. As Barbara Tuchmann points out, this was not for the Jews themselves, 'but for the sake of the promise made to them. . . . The return was viewed, of course, only in terms of a Jewish nation converted to Christianity, for this was to be the signal for the working out of the promise.'[11] James I, however, was offended by Finch's remarks that rulers should pay homage to a Jewish king, so Finch and his publisher were imprisoned until an apology was forthcoming. But his actions initiated Evangelical support for the Jewish people to return to Palestine, which was to increase over the next three centuries.

Religious tension between the Puritans and the Established Church became so extreme under King Charles I that it was a major contributory factor in the Civil War that broke out in 1642 between Royalist 'Cavaliers' and Parliamentarian 'Roundheads' (so named because of their short haircuts). The English Bible had helped to forge the religious fervour which was now manifested. With his battle cry, 'Lord God of Hosts!', Oliver Cromwell had victories celebrated with an emotive reading of the psalms; and he never lost a battle. After the execution of Charles I on 30 January 1649, the monarchy, the

House of Lords, the Anglican Church and the Great Seal of England were abolished, and Puritans, Baptists and Presbyterians could at last worship openly.

The Act of Oblivion, passed by parliament, released hundreds of Puritans from imprisonment. But, the issues that had dominated the earlier Protestant reformers still remained central to discussions and arguments: the role of the Bible, the nature of the sacraments and the authority within the Church. England was divided into ten large districts, over each of which Cromwell appointed a soldier with the title of major-general, to act as its governor. Acts were passed against swearing, duelling, horse-racing, cock-fighting and bear-baiting, and ways were introduced to enforce the keeping of the sabbath.

An interest in the Jews, especially among Puritans, was inspired by reading the Bible in its original tongue. John Milton, who wrote about the inaccessibility of paradise in *Paradise Lost* and who read and wrote Hebrew fluently, was made 'Secretary for Foreign Languages', and Cromwell suggested that Hebrew should be part of the curriculum in grammar schools. In his discourse on Oriental Tongues (1648) Christian Rane wrote that Hebrew 'makes us . . . to become Adam ourselves. Speaking Hebrew meant a person had more in common with the prophets and characters in the Bible. Risking the wrath of reactionaries, Cromwell later took steps to allow Jews to settle in England. Many would be converted, and he was attracted to their trading abilities, selling the generation of enormous wealth for England. Since there are references in the Book of Daniel and Deuteronomy to a prophecy that the Jews had to be scattered all over the earth before the Second Coming,[12] many people believed that the return of the Jews would hasten the arrival of the Messiah. Others thought that the 'end of days' was nigh. As Paul Johnson writes in *A History of the Jews*, 'The King's Puritan opponents, now effectively running the country, had always represented the philosemitic tradition there. The Bible was their guide to current events. They invoked the Prophet Amos to condemn Star Chamber. They adduced the case of Naboth's Vineyard as a prefiguration of Ship Money.'[13] Milton was not alone in linking the return of Jews to Christianity. In Book III of 'Paradise Regained' Satan argues with Jesus over David's throne:

> By him thou shalt regain, without him
> That which alone can truly re-instal thee
> In David's royal seat, his true successor.

SEVEN

In the Footsteps of the Old Testament

Whose distant footsteps echo
Through the corridors of Time.

'The Day is Done', Henry Longfellow

It is often said that Cromwell allowed the Jews to return to live in England. But it was not as straightforward as that. In the end all he felt he was able to do was to grant a number of dispensations to individual Jews. He[1] 'connived' at their settlement, but he did *not* authorize their resettlement. So mixed was the response among members of Cromwell's Council to the petition presented by the writer and publisher, Rabbi Manasseh ben Israel, when he arrived in London from Amsterdam in 1655, that the matter was referred to a special conference at Whitehall. Here, to everyone's surprise, twenty-five lawyers and the Chief Justice agreed that there had never been an official ban on Jews living in England; Edward I's expulsion in 1290 had been exercised purely by royal decree. This did not mean they could just arrive and settle in England. Strict terms of their readmission were vigorously debated, but no official decision, no conclusion, resulted. Despite this, Jews began to migrate.

In 1657 – less than two years after the conference at Whitehall – a house in Cree Church Lane was used as a synagogue, which curious Protestants, including Milton, visited. A cemetery was fenced off at Mile End and soon afterwards a Jew was admitted as a licensed broker at the Exchange without having to take the oath on the Church of England Bible. This foreshadowed the Court of the King's Bench allowing Jews to give evidence in a court of law by swearing on the Old Testament alone, rather than the complete Bible. Toleration of the Jews, whose population in Britain remained small, never exceeding 1 per cent, continued. (It is still the same today.)

Contrary to fears, the status of Jews in England became more secure with the Restoration of the Stuart monarchy in 1660 and the arrival of the popular and handsome Charles II – six feet two inches tall, with thick black hair – always to be remembered for his wit, mistresses and keen interest in science. Despite his intellect, the gap between his words, and his deeds was shown by his lack of piety, He pledged, but did not always grant, religious freedom. The Puritans, no longer the victors they had been under Cromwell's Commonwealth, were now the victims. For instance, the great Puritan John Bunyan, an inspired Congregationalist, was pilloried, persecuted and forbidden to worship. Freedom to worship God in his own way and freedom of speech were so important to Bunyan that he was prepared to be imprisoned for his beliefs. He was one of sixty Dissenters in Bedfordshire jail at the time. Charges against him read:

> That John Bunyan of the town or Bedford, laborer, . . . has . . . devilishly and perniciously abstained from coming to church to hear the Divine service, and is a common upholder of several unlawful meetings and Conventicles [meetings in secret places], to the great disturbance and destruction of the good subjects of this kingdom contrary to the laws of our Sovereign Lord the King. . . .[2]

While Charles's love life continued with a string of mistresses, in May 1662 the Act of Uniformity made the Church of England Prayer Book compulsory in church services throughout England, while the Corporation Act permitted only those who were communicant members of the Church of England and took the sacrament according to Anglican rites to hold public office. Despite his pro-Catholic manoeuvring, the Tory party supported Charles and the new Anglican and royalist strategy, but the Whigs disliked Charles's high Anglicanism and tried to limit his power. They also demanded toleration for Dissenters. During his reign and that of his brother James II, the Whigs set a precedent of association with the Dissenters that continued until the early twentieth century.

A protest by the Dissenting clergy against the demand for absolute loyalty to the king and the acceptance of the rule of the bishops and the payment of church tithes, led to an organized mass movement and the beginning of 'Non-conformity'. On St Bartholomew's Day, 24 August, the 'Great Ejection' took place across the country. Two thousand protesting clergy either resigned or were thrown out of their parishes. The main Nonconformist groups emerging were the Congregationalists and Presbyterians who joined the much older Baptists as the most popular Dissenting sects. All these denominations stressed personal worship, the importance of good deeds and salvation, the consequence of sin and repentance, and the truth which was found in the Bible, especially the Old Testament. Many continued – as is seen by surviving family Bibles – to read 'the book' in its original language, Hebrew. Soon, 'true believers' saw the evidence of the wrath of God. First was the Great Plague of 1665 that brought 100,000 deaths in London from bubonic plague. Then, before a year was up the Great Fire of London consumed St Paul's Cathedral, eighty-seven Anglican churches and 13,200 houses.

Parliament's extreme stand was opposed by Charles and in 1672 he issued an edict of toleration towards people of Dissenting faiths, 'a Declaration of Indulgence for Tender Consciences'. As a result of this proclamation Bunyan, having spent twelve years in Bedford jail, was freed. He was not rearrested when, in less than a year, under pressure from parliament and from Louis XIV, this declaration was annulled. But more restrictions were put through parliament to repress and restrict the growing number of Dissenters from holding influential positions. In 1673 the Test Act, which limited all public positions to members of the Church of England, was rushed through both houses. Two years later the king intensified his opposition to Dissenters by ordering bishops to take action against anyone failing to appear for Communion at their parish church. Thousands were arrested, including, for the second time, John Bunyan. Bunyan could not afford to pay even half the imposed £60 fine, and was sent to 'a dark, dreary, dungeon' for six months, where he wrote the first part of *The Pilgrim's Progress*.

Rather than being stifled by persecution many Nonconformists fled. In 1681 William Penn, an early Quaker, sailed for the New World and founded Pennsylvania in America as a Quaker refuge. At the same time, the Society of Friends, or Quakers, was formed by George Fox, from Leicestershire. His profound belief in the Bible led him to reject the need for creeds, paid ministers, the sacraments, formal services and oath-taking, putting the Quakers at the extreme left of Nonconformity. His followers also used 'thou' and 'thee' in everyday speech and wore plain clothes with no ornamentation.

When Charles II died, in February 1685, acknowledging Roman Catholicism on his deathbed, he left no legitimate children. His bevy of mistresses had sired several bastards, who became dukes, but no princes. The heir was Charles's brother James, a zealous Catholic convert. For two years the country was swept by anti-Catholic hysteria. But things boded ill for Protestants, Puritans and Jews alike. Honest and hard-working as he was, few English kings have been as unpopular as James. He was so morose that

Nell Gwynn called him 'Dismal Jimmy'. When his second wife, Mary of Modena, a Catholic, gave birth to a son, the succession by-passed his two Protestant daughters, Mary and Anne, a rumour that the baby had been smuggled into the queen's bed in a warming pan had such currency that it was parodied into a nursery rhyme:

Rock-a-bye baby, in the tree top.
When the wind blows, the cradle will rock.
When the bough breaks, the cradle will fall,
And down will come baby, cradle and all.

By 1688 the reign of James was over. At the invitation of both the Tories and the Whigs, an expedition led by William of Orange landed at Torbay, and the Glorious Revolution began. This *coup d'état* was a victory for representative government and freedom of religion. When William and his wife Mary, one of James II's two daughters, were crowned, a clause was inserted into the coronation oath, binding the king 'to the true Profession of the Gospell and the Protestant Reformed Religion established by Law'.[3] This commitment to maintain the Protestant faith has been recited at every coronation since. But members of the new breakaway religions still lacked equal rights. William's Toleration Act of 1689 permitted Nonconformists to worship publicly, though they remained second-class citizens and could not sit in parliament, hold public office or attend Oxford or Cambridge universities. Despite these limitations the Nonconformists had come a long way. As a mark of gratitude, a large group of Protestants in Northern Ireland later used William's title as part of their name – the Orange Order.

To facilitate his invasion of England, William had secured a loan from a Jewish financier, and whether it was because of this or for other reasons, throughout his fourteen-year reign he showed sympathy to the Jews. The Sephardic Bevis Marks Synagogue,[4] an architectural masterpiece designed by a Quaker and the third synagogue to be built in London since the thirteenth century, was completed. The future Queen Anne, another daughter of James II, is said to have presented one of the beams in its roof. As her husband, George, prince of Denmark, was the Admiral of the Fleet it was probably the mast from a man-of-war.[5]

Protestantism was firmly entrenched in Britain in the space of just one reign. To seal this, the Act of Settlement (1701) was introduced which ordered that no prince or princess married to a Roman Catholic could inherit the throne of England. William died in 1702 after his horse tripped on a molehill, fourteen years after he had landed at Torbay, and Anne became queen. She was not an attractive monarch. Alcoholism and excessive eating had made her fat, an attack of gout meant that she had to be carried to her own coronation. While religious toleration increased in her reign, Nonconformists still had to be discreet, as can be seen by looking at the life of the outspoken Nonconformist Daniel Defoe, author of *Robinson Crusoe* and *Moll Flanders*. The son of a butcher and pious Presbyterian, in 1702 Defoe was jailed and spent three days in a pillory as punishment for his satire *The Shortest Way with the Dissenters*. This lampooned the methods with which Church and State dealt with Nonconformists. But his was a rare example of persecution. Strong pockets of influential Dissenters in many towns set up their own schools, academies and chapels. In 1720 there were about 1,200 different congregations of which 350 were Baptists.[6]

Nothing illustrates the ambivalent attitude to those outside the Anglican Church, whether Nonconformist or Jew, more than the loud controversy over the 'Jew Bill' in England in 1753–4. The Jewish Naturalization Act put through parliament to improve the legal and social status of Jews and allow them to own land and to 'prefer bills in parliament without receiving the sacrament' was met with such agitation by noisy mobs and pamphleteers that it was repealed in less than a year. One legacy from this was the term 'the Jewish Question' which was first used at this time.

Towards the end of the eighteenth century a movement emerged within the Church of England itself. Whereas Congregationalists, Baptists, and Presbyterians were outside the Established Church, the Evangelical movement was a revival from inside. During its golden age, giants such as William Wilberforce and Lord Shaftesbury revitalized Christianity in England. Like Nonconformists before them, a large number of Evangelicals were effective in improving the morals, lives and miserable conditions for workers. Attempts were also made to establish free schools, reduce the number of drunks, gamblers and dissolute wife-beaters and, most of all, get people to attend chapel, kirk or church.

Anglican Evangelicals were one of the first religious groups to bring politics into the religious arena. The traditional Anglican clergy, distinguished for their politeness and good manners, had always considered it prudent to avoid political sermons. Not so the Evangelicals. Believing that improvement of the human condition was their moral duty, they began the impetus which resulted later in the great reforms in labour conditions. Wilberforce successfully campaigned to abolish slavery and among the many achievements of Lord Ashley, better known by his later hereditary title of Lord Shaftesbury, was improving the shocking and cruel conditions for women and children in mines and factories. Both also became members of the new missionary societies, including one which would change the history of Palestine.

Another controversial religious denomination that emerged at the end of the eighteenth century was the Unitarians. Unlike most Christians, who believe that God reveals himself in three persons, God the Father, God the Son (Jesus) and God the Holy Spirit (or Holy Ghost), the Unitarians rejected the idea of the Trinity, and gave a pre-eminent position to Jesus Christ as a religious teacher, while denying his deity. In a similar way they also dismissed the concept of hell. Their belief in one God gives them an affinity with the Jews, for whom, also, Jesus Christ is a religious teacher, not the son of God. Unitarians championed many causes, including religious freedom, not only for themselves, but for Roman Catholics, Jews and agnostics,[7] and also became active in politics, especially in local government. The determination of Florence Nightingale, a Unitarian, to improve the lot of injured soldiers and training within the nursing profession demonstrates their spirit. Another famous member was William Booth, the founder of the Salvation Army.

From the Evangelical Revival of the eighteenth century arose Methodism. In 1739, George Whitefield, newly ordained and banned from every pulpit in London because of his excessively Evangelical style, showed that the object of oratory is not always truth, but persuasion.

His fiery open-air preaching gave Nonconformity a new momentum. Within weeks he was preaching before audiences of 10,000, damning the clergy of the day as 'blind, unregenerate, carnal, lukewarm and unskilful guides'. Men and women received his sermons ecstatically as revelations of 'the word of God'.

Two months later the thunderous voice of the Revd John Wesley also rose over the heads of another huge open-air gathering in Bristol, and at a similar gathering in Hyde Park a large number of his 80,000 audience became 'brethren and sisters'. Loud 'Hallelujahs!' filled the air. Just before Christmas, at the end of the first year of preaching, the Methodist Society was formalized, with headquarters at Moorfields in London, and John's brother Charles published his first book of vigorous hymns, with favourites such as

'Hark! The herald angels sing'. Public response to Wesley or Whitefield, however, was not always positive. While addressing an audience of 10,000 at Moorfields, Whitefield was pelted with stones, rotten eggs and dead cats.[8] Wesley was often at loggerheads with the Church, but Methodism remained within the Church of England until 1795, four years after John Wesley's death, when it became a distinct body.

The celebrated Selina, Countess of Huntingdon, became one of the Methodists' most loyal and generous supporters, building a total of sixty-four chapels. But she was often at odds with Wesley, and ended up forming her own Connexion, quite distinct from his. The idea of extending her work outside the British Isles became a reality when her personal chaplain, Dr Haweis, became fascinated by the journals of Captain Cook's voyage to the South Seas, published between 1771 and 1782. Such was their impact that the London Missionary Society was formed and was soon thronged with willing candidates to take the Bible to India, Africa and other countries.

On 10 August 1796 the *Duff*, a ship of less than 300 tons, carrying thirty missionaries, a crew of twenty and suitcases full of Bibles, hoisted the mission flag, 'three white doves with olive branches on a purple field', and sailed for Tahiti to win over the lascivious heathens, the dancing girls who had seduced Captain Cook's sailors – and thus started the proselytizing movement which joined the Bible to the imperial flag. Many other well-endowed missionary societies followed. The London Society for the Conversion of Jews, as will be seen in the next chapter, had unexpected and far-reaching political repercussions.

At home, in England and Wales, the Evangelical spirit spread with a new passion, inculcating a belief in hard work, respectability and self-help, and the newly built Baptist and Methodist chapels in villages often drew larger crowds than the Church of England. Not to be outdone, though, between 1840 and 1876 some 7,000 Anglican churches were built. But the abuses often remained: parsons lived in spacious vicarages, mixed in the best county circles, cared about drinking good claret and old brandy, donned pink jackets to go hunting and employed curates to do their routine work.[9] In contrast, teetotal and upright Nonconformist and Evangelical converts purchased inns and imposed covenants on them stating 'no alcoholic beverages will be served'. Methodists in Cornwall renounced sugar in tea as a protest against the slave trade, and the habit lingered and spread. It was not long before the Methodists broke into competing sects such as the Primitive Methodists, with their rhetoric about Jehovah, damnation and the wrath of God, the Wesleyan Methodists, the Methodist New Connection, the United Free Methodist Churches and the Bible Christians. The Temperance Movement, campaigning against the evils of drink, was one of the few areas of common ground where all shades of Nonconformist denominations met.

The term Nonconformist was gradually applied to the growing congregations of Dissenters including the Baptists, Presbyterians, Congregationalists and Methodists, which claimed about a third of the adult population in England. By the nineteenth century there was no other Protestant nation that could match the British in knowledge of the Old Testament.[10] Soon sweeping changes were enacted that gave Nonconformists a political voice. First the Test and Corporation Acts were repealed in 1828, enabling Nonconformists to be elected to parliament, become councillors or hold public office. The Reform Act of 1832, the beginning of parliamentary reform, followed, dramatically enlarging the number of adult males in England who could vote. For the first time, Nonconformists, including three MPs from Manchester and Salford, areas with a large number of Jewish voters, were active in the political arena. Qualifications to vote differed in rural and urban areas. In town boroughs a uniform £10 household qualification became the basis of the vote, while in the counties it differed between leaseholders and tenants at will, from £10 to £50 per annum. Radical industrialists and the middle classes now influenced all levels of government, from town councils to the House of Commons and the link between middle-class political action and religion started to make a significant difference in politics. Most later jointed the Liberal Party which came into existence only in the summer of 1859 at a meeting at Willis's Rooms in St James' by a group of Radicals, Free Traders, Peelites, Gladstonian Liberals and Old Whigs, in order to combine to oust the government of Lord Derby. A large number of Radicals pushed for the disestablishment of the Church of England, for the redress of other Noncomformist grievances, for the widening of the franchise, for the limiting of the power of the House of Lord, Free Trade, and for limiting interference in foreign countries. The Conservative Party had been formed twenty-four years earlier, in 1835 with Sir Robert Peel's manifesto to the elctors of Tamworth (before the split in the Tory Party of 1846).

EIGHT

Lord Shaftesbury Campaigns for a Jewish Homeland

For his religion, it was fit
To match his learning and his wit;
'Twas Presbyterian true blue;
Fore he was of that stubborn crew
Of errant saints, whom all men grant
To be the true church militant;
Such as do build their faith upon
The holy text of pike and gun;
Decide all controversies by
Infallible artillery;
And prove their doctrine orthodox,
By apostolic blows and knocks;
Call fire, and sword, and desolation,
A godly, thorough Reformation,
Which always must be carried on,
And still doing, never done;
As if religion were intended
For nothing else but to be mended . . .

From the comic satire Hudibras, written to pour contempt on the Puritans,
Samuel Butler

In 1838 five Scottish clergymen, founders of a mission for 'the conversion of God's ancient people', arrived in Jerusalem eager to meet Jews and 'show them the way'. The leader, the Scottish Evangelical the Reverend Andrew A. Bonar (1810–92), was then just one of the many Nonconformist ministers working in missions formed in the early nineteenth century who believed that Christians had an obligation to these people to whom God had first revealed himself. Another missionary was William Wingate, the grandfather of Orde Wingate, the soldier who was later to become a hero of the Jews.[1] A minister with the Free Church of Scotland, he worked converting Jews to Christianity first in his native Glasgow, then Hungary and finally in the East End of London. The Revd Wingate, though, never became celebrated like Andrew Bonar whose work was making him nearly as famous as his brother, Horatio, the hymn-writer and author of such stirring lines as 'Father, beneath Thy sheltering wing . . .' and 'Here, O My Lord, I see Thee Face to Face . . .' Andrew Bonar's name was perpetuated indirectly because, twenty years later a boy would be named after him, who would be known all his adult life as Andrew Bonar Law. Paradoxically, his name, too, was to be associated with the Jews. Before becoming the first Conservative prime minister to be elected to office in the twentieth century, Andrew Bonar Law would be a member of the War Cabinet, the body which in 1917 would finally fulfil the aim of those passionate missionaries and allow the Jews to return to the Holy Land. As said earlier, this notion was not unlike that held by contemporary fundamentalist Christians. It was thought to fulfil biblical prophecy by bringing the Jews back to Palestine and, at the same time or soon afterwards, converting them to Christianity.

The first of the many steps which strengthened the British connection with the Holy Land over the next seventy-eight years and led towards implementing the 'Restoration of the Jews', took place in the year following Andrew Bonar's visit to the Holy Land.

Unlikely though it would appear, Henry John Temple, Viscount Palmerston,[2] Britain's brilliant Foreign Secretary, who had turned Britain into Turkey's strongest ally against France, supporting the Egyptian invasion of Syria, was responsible for the first moves which would culminate in Britain declaring a Jewish homeland within the British Empire. Palmerston, one of the most colourful of Queen Victoria's cabinet ministers, was usually drawn by cartoonists as a rather raffish and unconventional aristocratic character. Indiscreet amorous affairs earned him the nicknames of 'Lord Cupid' and 'Lord Pumice-stone', but did not detract from his becoming the most famous Foreign Secretary in the nineteenth century, a post he held intermittently between 1830 until 1855, when he became Britain's prime minister, a position he held, with the exception of one year, until his death ten years later.

In December 1839, Palmerston, at the age of fifty-five, married the 52-year-old widowed Lady Cowper, the mother-in-law of Lord Ashley. Palmerston scarcely had time for the wedding breakfast, so pressing were affairs in the

Middle East, with the occupation of part of Syria and Jerusalem by the Egyptians led by Mohammed Ali and his adopted son Ibrahim Pasha. Earlier, in 1831, they had begun his conquest of Syria, and within a year the late sultan had ceded victory to him. France, hoping to expand her base in the Levant and make herself the predominant Mediterranean power, was forming an alliance with him. Such an acute crisis had not arisen in the Middle East since Britain had helped Turkey to push Napoleon's army out of Egypt and Palestine between 1798 and 1801.

Palmerston signed an agreement in London with the Turks on 15 July 1840. Known as the 'Convention between the Four Powers and the Porte' [the name of the Sultan's government in Constantinople] it was also signed by Russia, Austria and Prussia.[3] The agreement was a threat to France, since if the French failed to withdraw their armies from supporting the Egyptian ruler, force would be used. Tension in Europe was high as the ship that took the message to Egypt waited for a reply before returning to England.

On the morning of 17 August 1840, while Britain was still waiting for the mail ship to come back from Alexandria with a 'yes' or a 'no' from Mohammed Ali, readers of *The Times* opened the newspaper at their breakfast tables to be faced with a long editorial telling them that 'the Jews, with all their faults must be regarded as among the first who essentially contributed to the civilization of the world, as the holders of a pure and simple faith . . .'. The article went on to explain the benefits of a Jewish homeland in Palestine, which would be good for both the Jews and the people of the British Isles:

> the minds of Jews have been earnestly directed towards Palestine, and that in anticipation of a reconstruction of the Jewish state many are prepared to avail themselves of the facilities which events may afford to return to the land of their fathers. It is not Jews only who anticipate this result; Christians are becoming equally impressed with the conviction, are endeavouring to create facilities and to remove obstructions, and are intently watching those coming events whose shadows are believed to be now passing over the political horizon. A noble lord who has given his attention to this matter is circulating queries, which will be found in a subsequent column, with a view to ascertain the real feelings and expectations of the Jews: and 'the belief of an approaching restoration of the Jewish policy, and that no lasting solution of the eastern crisis can be expected till this takes place, a community of English gentlemen have lately memorialized all the Protestant

monarchs of Europe on the subject. The scriptural grounds on which this belief rests do not belong to our province, and we notice the proposed restoration of the Jews solely as what may be deemed a new element of the Eastern question. Until this element shall assume some more definite form than has yet been given to it, it can be scarcely considered ripe for public discussion, nor can any satisfactory judgment be formed whether its introduction will tend still further to complicate the question, or to facilitate its adjustment. The Jews, although bereft of their temple, their city, and their country, have never ceased to be a people. In the East, they are found scattered, wandering, oppressed, despising, and despised, cultivating a peculiar literature, divided into hostile sects, cherishing hopes ever disappointed and never abandoned. In Europe, an Asiatic people, they partake largely of European civilization; but amidst the diversities of language, of custom, of occupation, and of opinion, they seem with invincible tenacity. . . . It is for the Christian philanthropists and enlightened statesmen of Europe to consider whether this remarkable people does not present materials which, when collected and brought into fusion under national institutions might not be advantageously employed for the interests of civilization in the East. . . . All who have paid any attention to modern Judaism know that, especially in recent years, the minds of Jews have been eagerly directed towards Palestine; and that, in anticipation . . . of the Jewish state, many are prepared to avail themselves of the facilities which events may afford, to return to the land of their fathers. . . .

Despite the optimism of this article, and Turkey's reliance on Britain, Palmerston failed in his efforts to persuade the sultan that an increase in the number of Jews settled in Palestine would be to his advantage. But British diplomats in Constantinople and Jerusalem did succeed in increasing Jewish immigration. Indeed, the good relationship between the British Consul in Jerusalem and Turkish officialdom[4] also helped lay the foundations for subsequent farming schemes and settlements.

There was an enormous contrast between the dandy-like Palmerston and his new step-son-in-law, the dour and almost saintly Lord Ashley. He and his father-in-law became firm friends, however, and were two of the best-known names in government during the reign of Queen Victoria. Both were involved in the idea of the British government creating a Jewish homeland. Despite belonging to the Low Church, Ashley was a traditional Tory Member of

Parliament, gifted, with a compassion rare in his age. A deeply pious Christian and one of the most active politicians in the Evangelical movement as well as promoting factory reforms,[5] he helped push through anti-slavery legislation, temperance movements, orphanages and schooling. Other reforms initiated by him included legislation to provide care for the insane, ten-hour days for factory workers, and the banning of young boys as chimney sweeps. His inspiration was from the Old Testament. He believed the literal truth of every word of the Bible.[6]

His passionate faith in the Jewish Scriptures came not from his father, the sixth Earl of Shaftesbury, or his mother, but from his mother's maid who became his nanny, Maria Millis, an Evangelical Christian. His biographers stress that she was the source of practically all the love he experienced as a child.

The inspiration to make Palestine a home for the Jewish people was part of his upbringing, his firm belief in the divine predictions in the Bible, and belief in the 'restoration' of the Jewish people to the Holy Land as a fulfilment of prophecy. Just like the many Puritans in Cromwell's time, Ashley was then one of the many Protestants who believed that the Second Coming[7] required the conversion of the Jews, and their restoration to Palestine. Conducting his own life according to a literal acceptance of the Bible, he styled the Jews 'God's ancient people' and like other keen Bible scholars, he had learned Hebrew at Oxford so that he could study the original texts of the Old Testament. Touchingly, he wore a gold ring inscribed with the words 'Pray for the peace of Jerusalem; they shall prosper that love thee.'

Ancient prophecies such as Isaiah's prediction that the Gentiles would bring the Jewish people back to their land could be fulfilled by allowing the Jewish population in Palestine to expand, and Ashley saw the so-called 'Eastern Question' as an ideal opportunity to further the return of the Jews to the Holy Land. In one of his diary entries he says that, '. . . Palmerston has already been chosen by God to be an instrument of good to His ancient people'.[8] Concluding on an optimistic note he added, 'After dinner left alone with him. Proposed my scheme, which seemed to strike his fancy; he asked some questions, and readily promised to consider it.'

At the Public Record Office[9] in Kew there is a letter from Palmerston to Lord Ponsonby, the idle but brilliant British ambassador to Constantinople. This is probably the first written request from Britain to form a Jewish homeland in Palestine:[10]

> There exists at the present time, among the Jews dispersed over Europe, a strong notion that the time is approaching when their nation is to return to Palestine. . . . It would be of manifest importance to the Sultan to encourage the Jews to return . . . their thoughts have been bent more intently than before upon the means of realizing that wish. It is well known that the Jews of Europe possess great wealth; . . . any country in which a considerable number of them might choose to settle would derive great benefit from the riches which they would bring into it.[11]

Ashley noted in his diary of 24 August that his stepfather-in-law had written to Ponsonby to direct him to open intercourse with Reshid Pasha, respecting protection and encouragement of the Jews. Five days later he wrote:

> The newspapers teem with documents about the Jews. Many assail and many defend them. The Times . . . has stirred up an immense variety of projects and opinions . . . time when the affair of the Jews shall be . . . fully before the world! . . . What a stir of every passion . . . in men's hearts.[12]

Pursuing his cause with energy and commitment, Ashley was aware that it would not be supported by commercially minded Britain unless it furthered the interests of the empire. The previous year he had reviewed Lord Lindsay's *Letters from Egypt, Edom and the Holy Land* in the *Quarterly Review*, and pointed out the advantages of Palestine as a British sphere of influence; it could become a place where cotton, silk, madder and olives could be grown and exported to England.

His support of the powerful Evangelical movement within the Church of England was shown in many ways, some controversial. His encouragement of preachers to hold religious services in large theatres and music halls instead of churches caused such an outcry that he was forced to defend his actions in the House of Lords. Horrified critics said that Christianity would be compromised if it were associated with such scenes of frivolous entertainment.

Among Ashley's diary entries of the many conversations he had when dining with Palmerston show that whenever he could he seized the chance to urge the prime minister to persuade the Turkish government to allow Jews to settle in Palestine. One such entry reads, 'The ancient city of the people of God is about to resume a place among the nations, and England is the first of Gentile kingdoms that ceases "to tread her down".'

* * *

After the Crusades England's direct links with the Holy Land had been few. Politically, Britain and Prussia were jealous of the growing influence of France and Russia, both of whom had a network of churches, monasteries and hostels there. So the idea of setting up a competing Protestant church by the British and Germans seemed a logical move. At a London Jews Society meeting in May 1838 there was much excitement when members heard of a development in Jerusalem. When told that a lay pastor there was looking after a small Protestant congregation, consisting of a few converted Jews and visitors, the bishop of London donated £10 to start a fund to build an Anglican church in the centre of Jerusalem with a bishop to look after the needs of 'Protestant Christians'.

Enthusiasm for the scheme meant that the king of Prussia gave £15,000, a sum which would be matched by funds raised by the London Society for Promoting Christianity Amongst the Jews (the LJS), known as the London Jews Society the earliest and most popular of the Jewish missionary societies. Although it was decided that a bishop would be appointed alternately by Britain and Prussia,[13] the first one was to be English. As it ensured the influence of European Protestantism in the area, the archbishop of York and the bishop of London had approved of the plan for a bishop of Jerusalem, and for a Jewish convert to fill the post. This was also supported by the Lutheran Church[14] (the religion of Queen Victoria's mother and future husband). The decision, though, was controversial. Among the many reasons given for John Henry Newman, one of the leaders of the Oxford Movement, leaving the Anglican Church and becoming a Roman Catholic was the creation of a Protestant bishop in Jerusalem. This blending of the Anglican religion with the Lutheran progressed despite enormous hostility – even though each Lutheran would be ordained into Anglican orders before consecration and subscribe to the thirty-nine articles and if an Anglican he was to agree to the Confession of Augsburg.[15] Michael Solomon Alexander, a converted rabbi, who was professor of Hebrew at King's College, London, was chosen and prepared for the role.

The next move was political: a British Consulate was set up in Jerusalem. The consul, W.T. Young, was told to cover an area similar in size to the ancient limits of the Holy Land. Palmerston, at the suggestion of Ashley, also issued instructions to other British Consuls in the East to 'give protection' to the Jews in Palestine and other Turkish dominions. Young reported the results of a census, which revealed that 9,690 Jews were sufficiently poor, oppressed and stateless to be eligible for British help. Young, though, according to the British Consul-general at Alexandria, was spreading his wings too far. The Foreign Office in London received a strong complaint from him. Young 'was 'granting British protection in an indiscriminate manner to all Jews'.

The British Consul then had a unique role. This was the first time that the Jews in the Holy Land had had a voice. Cocooned in their religious rituals, they had lived for centuries in the narrow streets of the Orthodox Quarter of old Jerusalem, or the smaller centres at Safed, Tiberias and Hebron. These indigenous Jews, known as the old Yishuv (a Hebrew word meaning 'having dwelled'), claimed descent from Jews who lived in biblical times and had survived there for thousands of years. As said earlier, for the first hundred years after the conquest by Selim in 1517 the attitude of the Turks to the Jews was benign. In the seventeenth century, though, things changed. Howard Sacher says that the 'Turks proceeded to make life increasingly difficult for Christians and Jews alike.' This stance continued so that after the city of Safed was shattered by an earthquake in 1837 'no more than 6,000 Jews altogether lingered on in the four holy cities [Jerualem, Safed, Hebron and Tiberias]. Taxed and tyrannized as they were to within an inch of their lives, they regarded their ordeal essentially as a testament of repentance.'[16]

Over the years the numbers of resident Jews had been supplemented by migrants, many pious European Jews who had migrated in their old age so they might die on holy soil. Some found jobs as tinkers, shoemakers and spice merchants but for the majority, intensive biblical study and prayer dominated their days. Just as Jerusalem's Christian nuns and priests relied on foreign alms, many Jews eked out an existence living on remittances. There was always the fear that a war might cut off this finance. The dead hand of the *Challukah* – money from collections abroad from co-religionists – lay on more than half this population. Little could any of them have realized that far away in London an English peer was using political sway to improve their future in Palestine.

In September 1839 Ashley gave yet another document to Palmerston for the 'recall of the Jews to their ancient land'. The time was near for their restoration to the soil of Palestine; the governing power should solemnly engage 'to establish the principles and practices of European civilization'. Between 1839 and 1841 not only was the 'chapel' attached to the stately British Vice-Consulate near the Jaffa Gate in Jerusalem, but Palmerston raised the question of Jewish immigration with the authorities in Constantinople. The proposal was no idle dream. This was the height of the crisis in which Britain was checking not just French but Russian expansion in the Middle East. Turkey needed Britain's support.

'The Consul's Chapel', later called Christ Church, was a ploy for getting around Turkish restrictions on building more churches in the Holy City. Paid for by the LJS it was the first Protestant Church in Jerusalem. Palmerston made no objection to a church being attached to the new British Consulate, even one that was a blend of Anglican and Judaic practices. Placed on the communion table was the traditional seven-branched candlestick, the menorah, services were read (as they still are) in Hebrew, and the first bishop was a Jewish convert. The new church was a constant reminder of the aims of Christian Zionism: to turn Jews towards Christianity and restore them to the Holy Land. Devotional books were also in Hebrew – the LJS had paid to have the New Testament translated into Hebrew in 1817 and into Yiddish four years later. The liturgy of the Church of England, however, was not published in Hebrew until 1837. The mission was also practical with a medical mission and later a hospital.

Even though it was attached to the British Consulate and officially part of it, the money for the Chapel, came from the LJS. Founded in 1809, this society had immense social prestige and political patronage. William Wilberforce, the leading Evangelical who led two great crusades to abolish the slave trade and later to free the slaves, was one of its early active members. Queen Victoria's father, the Duke of Kent, was president for eleven years, and Ashley was president for over thirty. Its motto, from Romans 1:16, 'to the Jew First', referred back to the early days of Christianity, and to the Apostles' statement that the Jews were to be converted before those of other faiths, as 'the world should be evangelized through the Jews'.

The beliefs of Shaftesbury and his fellow millennialists were then widespread. In 1844, on a visit to Jerusalem, Thackeray was impressed by the unpaid American Consul-General of Syria and Jerusalem, who believed that the Second Coming was nigh and that the Jews were all about to return to Jerusalem. Thackeray commented that 'he expects to see the Millennium in three years, and has accepted the office of consul at Jerusalem, so as to be on the spot in readiness.' As well as providing a lively description of the rival Christian churches in Jerusalem – and making clear his contempt for the tatty squalor and the bogus claims of the Christian relics merchants – he wrote a report on the straggling congregation at Christ Church:

> The English mission has been very unsuccessful with these religionists. I don't believe the Episcopal apparatus – the chaplains, and the colleges, and the beadles – have succeeded in converting a dozen of them; and a sort of martyrdom is in store for the luckless Hebrews at Jerusalem who shall secede from their faith. Their old community spurns them with horror; and I heard of the case of one unfortunate man, whose wife, in spite of her husband's change of creed, being resolved, like a true woman, to cleave to him, was spirited away from him in his absence; was kept in privacy in the city, in spite of all exertions of the mission, of the consul and the bishop, and the chaplains and the beadles; was passed away from Jerusalem to Beirut, and thence to Constantinople; and from Constantinople was whisked off into the Russian territories, where she still pines after her husband. May that unhappy convert find consolation away from her. I could not help thinking, as my informant, an excellent and accomplished gentleman of the mission, told me the story, that the Jews had done only what the Christians do under the same circumstances. The woman was the daughter of a most learned Rabbi, as I gathered. Suppose the daughter of the Rabbi of Exeter, or Canterbury, were to marry a man who turned Jew, would not her Right Reverend Father be justified in taking her out of the power of a person likely to hurl her soul to perdition? These poor converts should surely be sent away to England out of the way of persecution. We could not but feel a pity for them, as they sat there on their benches in the church conspicuous; and thought of the scorn and contumely which attended them without, as they passed, in their European dresses and shaven beards, among their grisly, scowling, long-robed countrymen.[17]

As Marvell had observed earlier, 'Till the conversion of the Jews . . .' most Jews silently and politely resisted attempts to be converted. Conversion was much more successful in England, where some Jewish families were motivated to break their connections with the synagogue so as to become accepted and move more easily in mainstream society.[18] This often stemmed from a desire to conform rather than from an intrinsic belief in Christianity.

Young was replaced by the equally religious James Finn, who served for seventeen years as British Consul in Jerusalem, from 1846 to 1863. He also carried on the tradition of pressurizing the local pasha to enforce Jewish rights, and to deal with any case of persecution. As the European presence in Palestine grew, so did investments and the number of pilgrims, missionaries and tourists. In the first half of the century these included Gustave Flaubert and Benjamin Disraeli. The description of Jerusalem in Disraeli's novel *Tancred*, in 1847 shows how he fell under the city's mystical aura sixteen years earlier:

> . . . we saw the Holy City. I will describe it to you from the Mount of Olives. This is a high hill, still partially covered with the tree which gives it its name. Jerusalem is situated upon an opposite height which descends as a steep ravine. . . . As the town is built upon a hill you can from the opposite height discern the roof of almost every house. In the front is the magnificent mosque built upon the site of the Temple. A variety of domes and towers rise in all directions. The houses are of bright stone. I was thunderstruck. I saw before me apparently a gorgeous city. Nothing can be conceived more wild and terrible and barren than the surrounding scenery, dark, strong, and severe; but the ground is thrown about in such picturesque undulation. . . . Except Athens I never saw anything more essentially striking, no city except that whose sight was so pre-eminently impressive.
>
> . . . This week has been the most delightful of all our travels. We dined every day on the roof of a house by moonlight; visited the Holy Sepulchre of course, though avoided the other *coglionerie*.

* * *

Ashley stood at the crossroads between Christianity, the Jews and the furtherance of their cause in the Holy Land. Equally active was the Jewish philanthropist Sir Moses Montefiore, a prosperous London Jewish stockbroker. Montefiore who earlier used his influence to combat anti-Jewish disturbance and is remembered for his intervention in Damascus, where he managed to get the Turkish authorities to release some Jews who had been unjustly accused of ritual murder. In 1840 he gave Jerusalem its first printing press, which, as the city was expanding at an unprecedented rate, was urgently needed.

The erection of the Protestant church had goaded the Italian and French Roman Catholics, the Greek Orthodox and others to extend their activities. Competition between rival Christian religions and national interests intensified. All used various ploys to get around restrictions on building new ecclesiastical and national edifices. The Russian Orthodox Church and the German Lutherans were especially determined not to be outdone.

In one decade the British Consulate went from being the sole Western consulate in Jerusalem to being just one of six. Prussia established a consulate in 1842; France and Sardinia in 1843; the United States in 1844; and Austria in 1849. Russia continued to maintain a consulate in Jaffa.[19] But it was only the British Consul who had instructions to look after all Jews, no matter what their nationality. This role was on a par with that of the French, who traditionally looked after Roman Catholics in the Holy Land, and the Russians who did the same for members of the Greek and Russian Orthodox Churches.

Foreign government agencies of other European countries soon found, however, that they had to deal with problems concerning the Palestinian interests of their Jewish nationals. The Holy Land was becoming a focal point for the Christian world. By the mid-nineteenth century American and British missionary institutions, schools, colleges and hospices were expanding rapidly, but France still led in the numbers of missionaries and educational establishments. Exports of oranges, liquorice, sesame seed, almonds, rugs, hides, olive oil, soap and opium also increased. And another sphere of foreign influence had opened up: biblical archaeology. Edward Robinson, a Connecticut Yankee, on foot and horseback, began the first archaeological survey of the Holy Land to seek out the exact locations of places mentioned in the Old Testament and the roots of Christianity.[20] This matching of ancient texts and artefacts with assumed biblical sites attracted scholars and archaeologists from all over the world. Ashley, like many Christians, closely followed this unearthing of the remnants from the days of the Scriptures which 'proved the truth of the Bible'. Not to be forgotten also were the artists like David Roberts and William Holman Hunt who travelled to the Middle East and helped bring images in the Bible alive.

Meanwhile, because occasional fights took place between the different Christian denominations, Muslim policemen were posted inside and outside the main churches to keep peace between the Catholics and the Greek Orthodox Christians. Finn said that the weapons used in 'such warfare were indeed carnal, even bodily fists, besides crucifixes and huge wax tapers taken from the very altars . . .'.[21]

One of the differences between Greek Orthodox and the Roman Catholics was over the bread used in Communion. The Catholics believed in the use of unleavened bread as used by the Jews at the Passover. The Greeks passionately believed in using leavened bread to signify that Christ had risen.

This bitter rivalry and animosity of the competing groups of 'warring monks' at the church of Holy Sepulchre was described by a visiting member of the clergy, W.H. Bartlett, who said that they regarded 'one another with deadly hatred, exhausting every artifice of petty intrigue to supplant each other in the possession of these gainful shrines, and often coming to blows in the very holiest places'.[22] During one fray in the Grotto of Bethlehem the blessed Silver Star denoting the spot where Jesus was born was wrenched from its foundations and disappeared.[23] The repercussions of this theft soon echoed across Europe: the Crimean War was about to begin.

NINE

From Jerusalem to the Crimean War

'Forward, the Light Brigade!'
Was there a man dismay'd?
Not tho' the soldier knew
Some one had blunder'd:
Their's not to make reply,
Their's not to reason why,
Their's but to do and die:
Into the valley of Death
Rode the six hundred.

'The Charge of the Light Brigade Balaclava', Alfred Lord Tennyson

Jerusalem's importance and fascination to the Christian world was the initial cause of the Crimean War of 1854. This was Britain's first major conflict after Waterloo and the only major conflict involving the main European world powers in the ninety-nine years between Waterloo and the First World War. The opening dispute was over the apparently minor matter of a key. Centuries of acrimony and competition over the right to hold the custody of the churches in the Holy Land spread into a spiralling quarrel between the French emperor, the Russian tsar and the Turkish sultan. Karl Marx, then working as a journalist, was cynical about the causes although he never visited the Middle East. In the *New York Herald Tribune* of April 1854, he analysed the situation:

> Imagine all these conflicting peoples beleaguering the Holy Sepulchre, the battle conducted by the monks, and the ostensible object of their rivalry being a star from the grotto of Bethlehem, a tapestry, a key of a sanctuary, an altar, a shrine, a chair, a cushion – any ridiculous precedence! . . . these sacred rows merely conceal a profane battle.[1]

Accusations and quarrels escalated. Should the Protector of the Christian holy places of Christendom in Jerusalem and Bethlehem be the Roman Catholic or the Greek Orthodox Church? The Roman Catholic countries had ties with the Holy Land, especially in northern Syria, stretching back before the Crusades to Charlemagne who had secured the right of protecting the holy places from the Caliph Haroun-al-Raschid. In modern times it had continued with Francis I who had negotiated the first capitulations with the Turks on the model later adopted by other western powers. As the traditional guardian of all Catholics in the Levant, France had grown into the leading foreign power in the area. The numbers of Roman Catholics in either Jerusalem or the whole of the Ottoman Empire, though, was small in comparison to the Orthodox churches. The number of Orthodox pilgrims, especially from Russia, had increased so much that by the 1840s they outnumbered Catholic pilgrims by 500 to 1. Regardless of the changing figures, the French, according to Thackeray, never missed an opportunity to stress their historical status. All French visitors to Jerusalem, all resident priests and guide books, he said, spoke of their role in the following terms: 'La France, Monsieur, de tous les temps a protégé les Chrétiens d'Orient . . .'.[2] But they did now have a real grievance. Orthodox monks were progressively excluding Catholic monks from entry to some of the holiest shrines.

Intransigent in their stand, the Russians put up a strong counter attack. The majority of the Christian churches in the Ottoman Empire had more connections with Russia than with France. Both the numbers of resident Roman Catholics and the numbers of Latin pilgrims to the Holy Land paled beside either members of the Orthodox churches or Orthodox pilgrims. The ten to thirteen million Orthodox Christians in the Ottoman Empire were augmented each year by thousands of Orthodox pilgrims from Russia who streamed into Jerusalem, bringing money and support for both the churches and the patriarchs. In his capacity as *de facto* head of the Orthodox Church in Russia, the tsar resented any threat to the rights of any Orthodox Church wherever it was, especially by France.[3] The appointment of the Patriarch of the Orthodox Church in Constantinople, who was regarded as the leader of the entire Orthodox Church. had to be confirmed by the sultan.

In 1852 Napoleon III wanted confirmation of his role as the patron and defender of Roman Catholics in the Holy Land, and rushed an envoy to Sultan Abdul Medjid in Constantinople. Tsar Nicholas I also sent a series of demands, including the right to protect all Orthodox Christians throughout the Ottoman

Empire, a prerogative held for centuries by the Greek Orthodox Church. Both sides in the contest had powerful support.[4] The tsar, under the pretext of religious concerns,[5] began moving troops to the Turkish Romanian provinces and called on his people to wage a holy war in defence of their co-religionists in Turkey.[6] Russian-Turkish hostilities began in October 1853.[7] And so the dispute over the church of the Holy Sepulchre ended up on the cliffs above Balaclava and Sebastopol, hundreds of miles away from Jerusalem. Britain, concerned about trade on the overland route to India and alarmed at the expansionist policies of the 'Russian bear', sent gunboats to the Dardanelles. In this holy war Protestant Britain was fighting on the side of Muslim Turkey against Christian Russia. But Russophobia swept across Britain.

This bitter war, remembered for the gallant yet suicidal Charge of the Light Brigade, was also a landmark in communications, the first war in history which could be followed daily in Britain. Each day the legendary war correspondent, William Russell, sent reports to *The Times* by the newly invented telegraph. His graphic tales of the army's mismanagement brought the government crashing down and Palmerston in as prime minister.

If Russell was the hero of the war, the heroine was Florence Nightingale. After volunteering for duty she took thirty-eight nurses with her to Scutari in 1854 and introduced compassion, discipline, sanitation and efficiency into the care of the wounded. Organizing the barracks hospital she struggled to save young men from the most formidable enemy of the war, cholera, and managed to reduce the hospital mortality rate. But in two years 21,000 British soldiers died – more by disease than enemy fire. The collective disasters led to major reforms in the British army to end outmoded military traditions, such as the selling of commissions. The Crimean War was a watershed in many ways. Not only was it the first to use railways, iron-clad steamships, mines and the telegraph and photography, but it eventually led to far-reaching changes such as the emancipation of the serfs in Russia. These are well known. The war, though, is seldom remembered for provoking diplomatic exchanges that led to the lifting of restrictions on Jews and Christians owning land in Palestine.

As British gunboats steamed to the Crimea in May 1854, an extraordinary request was made by the Foreign Secretary, the Earl of Clarendon, in a letter to Constantinople. He suggested that '. . . the sultan should be moved to issue a *firman* granting the Jewish people power to hold land in Syria or any part of the Turkish dominions.'[8] The Porte in Constantinople, though, remained unwilling to grant concessions that might result in a Jewish national movement within its territory. Thus no such order was issued. But in the following year, before the war had finished, and while Turkey was still relying on Britain, Montefiore obtained permission to buy land near Jerusalem and Jaffa. Previously the small amount of acreage which the Jews had been able to use had been acquired by using legal fiction. During 1854 the first Ottoman loan was floated in London. But later, at the height of the Crimean War, due to pressure from the foreign bond market, the Porte had to declare itself bankrupt. At the end of the war, while restructuring the massive debts, the British government again took the opportunity of insisting on reforms.

Once peace terms were agreed in Paris in 1856, the Allies managed to contain Russia for another fourteen years. The Black Sea was now neutral and the Danube again became an open waterway. In Jerusalem, though, the fight over the custodianship of the holy places, which had started the war, remained unresolved and the *status quo* unchanged. But within a decade the appearance of city was dramatically changed due to postwar reforms resulting in a building boom which followed.

Montefiore's purchase had marked a new era of building and expansion. The 1867/8 Land Law which permitted foreigners to purchase land, enacted by the Porte, meant that soon suburbs encircled the old City of Jerusalem. In 1869 a Jew called Joel Moshe Salomon and six of his friends also purchased land outside the city walls, which was named Nachalot Shiv'ah.[9] The effect of opening up Jerusalem can be seen by comparing the Jerusalem with the city described by Karl Marx fourteen years earlier. By 1868 there were, according to the *Jerusalem Almanac*, twenty-one synagogues, twenty-one convents and eleven mosques. 'The sedentary population of Jerusalem numbers about 15,500 souls, of whom 4,000 are Mussulmans and 8,000 Jews.'[10]

Russia reinforced her position in the old argument about precedence by spending huge sums on ecclesiastical buildings. Having acquired a large area to the north-west of the city, they named it the Russian Compound, and built massive construction outside the walls of the old City. A Muscovite church with glittering onion-shaped domes changed the skyline. Rocks were blasted, land was levelled and soon four hospices to accommodate the annual influx of Russian pilgrims were completed. Prussia, too, made her mark. Not only was a Lutheran church built in Jerusalem and Teutonic Knights Templar colonies re-established, archaeologists started searching, among other things, for the lost tomb of the German Crusader, King Frederick Barbarossa. Crates of newly unearthed antiquities found their way to Berlin.

Hotels were also built for package tours to the Holy Land, initiated by Thomas Cook, who set up an office in the old city. Tours became immensely popular after the new road inland from Jaffa was built in 1867. A steady stream of travellers included eccentric romantics, intrepid explorers, diplomatic consuls, risk-taking businessmen, religious pilgrims, missionaries and members of various benevolent societies. The American impresario P.T. Barnum dispatched an expedition to collect biblical antiquities for public display. This was followed by hundreds of books on the Holy Land including Mark Twain's, *Innocents Abroad*, which sold 67,000 copies in just one year. Even Twain, while seeing Jerusalem as a neglected city, found himself so overwhelmed that he wrote 'that I am actually in the illustrious old city where Solomon dwelt, where Abraham held converse with the Deity, and where walls still stand that witnessed the spectacle of the Crucifixion'.

As Jews could now become landowners, farmers and settlers, they were no longer limited to towns. This heralded the beginning of large-scale migration from Russia and the first *Aliyah*. Each wave of immigration was called an '*Aliyah*', meaning the 'ascension' or 'going up' of the Jews, as individuals or groups, from exile or diaspora to live in Eretz Yisrael, the Land of Israel. Thirty to forty thousand immigrants settled in a series of farms between 1882 and 1903. At first these newcomers were called the 'New Yishuv', but soon became known as the 'Yishuv'. In just over two decades twenty-eight well-organized agricultural settlements were set up, supporting about 5,000 people, including workers and their families.

The continuing importance of Britain to Turkey was evident in 1862 during the visit of the Prince of Wales, the future King Edward VII. Although non-Muslims were not permitted to enter the Dome on the Rock or the al-Aqsa Mosque, an exception was made for the prince by the Ottoman Sultan. This cooperation between Britain and Turkey manifested itself in many ways: the British government later sent naval officers to help modernize the Turkish navy; commercial enterprises were encouraged. The French countered this by sending army experts to Constantinople.

Just how varied the interest in the Holy Land was at that time can be seen by the wide range of people, including distinguished academics and clergymen, who helped set up the London-based Palestine Exploration Fund in 1865 to advance archaeological diggings and biblical research. The Queen was patron and Ashley was president and its prestigious members included the Dean of Westminster Abbey, Arthur P. Stanley, and Sir George Grove, who founded the Royal College of Music and the dictionary that bears his name. At the opening ceremony Finn urged the large audience not to 'delay to send out the best agents . . . to search the length and breadth of Palestine, to survey the land, and if possible to go over every corner of it, drain it, measure it, and, if you will, prepare it for the return of its ancient possessors, for I believe that the time cannot be far off before that great event will come to pass . . .'.[11]

Soon two major projects were under way. Jerusalem was the scene of the first. In 1867 a team began work under the direction of Charles Warren, and for three years excavated tunnels and subterranean chambers in the vicinity of the Temple Mount. The second project, the six-year Survey of Western Palestine, soon followed. Claude Conder, Horatio H. (later Lord) Kitchener and a team of eighteen Royal Engineers were sent to Palestine in 1872 to make an exact ordnance survey of the country. Their diligence revealed the full extent of Britain's interest in Palestine as a strategic base. Every rock, every curve of each river was recorded. Among Kitchener's recommendations was the appointment of a British Consul at the port of Haifa, a place he said would be an excellent railhead to the 'shortest way to India'. In 1875 the survey was interrupted when both Kitchener and Conder were badly injured by Arabs. As Conder was slow in recovering, Kitchener took over command.

Kitchener's religious mapmaking for the Palestine Exploration Fund was briefly taken over by General Gordon. This Evangelical Christian had served at Sebastopol in the Crimean War, crushed the Taiping rebellion in China in 1864 and later worked for Ismail Pasha, the Khedive of Egypt, opening up vast regions of the equatorial Nile. After becoming Governor of the Sudan in 1877 he had tried to bring in a measure to put a stop to the practice of black inhabitants being sold into slavery to serve Islamic families in Arabia. In Palestine, Gordon, who looked on the Bible as a reliable source of history, derived immense pleasure from finishing the cartography in 1882 and 1883. Lytton Strachey described him as 'a solitary English gentleman . . . wandering, with a thick book under his arm, in the neighbourhood of Jerusalem. . . . His . . . sunburnt brickred complexion . . .', but results from his visit resonated through the Christian world. He, like other Protestants before him, challenged the authenticity of St Helena's alleged site of the Crucifixion as the correct place of Jesus' Crucifixion. A stony outcrop on the side of the hill below Damascus Wall, was, he was convinced, the true site. Part of his evidence was the hill's similarity to a human skull with two caves resembling eye-sockets. The New Testament says that Christ suffered outside the city gate, at 'the place of the skull' ('Golgotha' in Aramaic, 'Calvary' from the Latin). Gordon's theory was supported by a Jewish first-century tomb which was probably used for Christian worship near the supposed Crucifixion site which had been unearthed earlier. For years the *Palestine Exploration Fund Quarterly Statement* had been dominated by discussion about the authenticity of the sites and was stimulated by Gordon's article in 1885. Many visitors today feel that his competing site, now referred to as the Garden Tomb or General Gordon's Garden, outside the Damascus Gate, is more genuine than the dark urban interior of the church of the Holy Sepulchre.

These are just some of the events surrounding the official Jewish return. During the near two centuries that elapsed between the first well known manifestations of Christian speculative thought about the Jewish return from the time of Oliver Cromwell to the Crimean War, there was a long line of non-Jewish theologians, poets, writers and statesmen who reinforced Jewish desires. Even Jean Jacques Rousseau in *Emile* (1762) had his say. Among his revolutionary ideas on education, the simple life, the familial bond, domestic happiness and pleasures he wrote: 'I do not think I have ever heard the arguments of the Jews as to why they should not have a free state, schools and universities, where they can speak and argue without danger. Then alone can we know what they have to say.'

TEN

Gladstone, Lloyd George and the 'Eastern Question'

She stands, a thousand-wintered tree,
By countless morns impearled;
Her broad roots coil beneath the sea,
Her branches sweep the world;
Her seed, by careless winds conveyed,
Clothe the remotest strand
With forests from her scatterings made,
New nations fostered in her shade,
And linking land with land.

'England and Her Colonies', Sir William Watson[1]

A high-profile Nonconformist whose childhood had been steeped in the Old Testament became the next Member of Parliament to identify strongly with the idea of the Jews returning to the Holy Land and making a homeland for them. Joseph Chamberlain, the famous monocled, orchid-wearing ex-mayor of Birmingham, was one of the most dazzling political figures in London in the 1880s. A reformer, he had been drawn into politics by his wish to improve conditions for the working man. Something of a demagogue when mayor of Birmingham from 1873 to 1875, he had won accolades for transforming the city into a model of municipal development. While president of the Board of Trade in Gladstone's second ministry, he had excited and angered both rich and poor with his 'unauthorized programme', smallholdings of 'three acres and a cow' for each agricultural labourer. After his bid for compulsory purchase of land for artisans' dwellings and compulsory free education, his ideas caught the public imagination. He had become Birmingham's most popular citizen and was affectionately dubbed 'our Joe' and 'a bonny fighter', while his opponents called him a 'red revolutionary'.

Coming from a prosperous Dissenting family in Birmingham, Chamberlain belonged to the Nonconformist tradition that stretched back to the Puritanism of Bunyan and Milton. He was also one of the first Nonconformists to hold high government office in Britain who in the next fifty years would steer events towards what became the future state of Israel. Chamberlain's endeavours to find a homeland for the Jews helps to confirm the opinion of Nahum Sokolow, who was later president of the World Zionist Organization,[2] 'that religion, and especially the Bible, was one of the most potent agencies in the formation of political and moral theories in England', adding that, 'the history of the Zionist idea was interwoven with that of religious opinions'.

Chamberlain's family were Unitarians, imbued with the Protestant romance with Zion, so succinctly described by Ian Buruma in *Voltaire's Coconuts*, 'They read the Old Testament, adopted Hebrew names, looked for Lost Tribes, prayed for Christ's Second Coming and petitioned [in 1649] for the return to England of the people of Israel.' Entering local politics in his youth when working at the West Midlands' biggest screw manufacturer, Nettlefolds (later expanded into GKN), which was owned by a relative, Chamberlain delighted in lecturing audiences of hard-nosed Birmingham businessmen on their 'false economy'. The 'true economy', he said, lay in spending and investing in the homes, streets and schools of the working class. This would enhance the productivity of workers, beautify and civilize the towns and build up their prosperity. When he first entered politics he was known as 'Radical Joe', but by the end of the century, he had been transformed into a 67-year-old aggressive imperialist with a keen interest in the Boer War of 1899, in which Britain suffered initial reverses.

In 1903 Chamberlain, then colonial secretary in Balfour's Conservative government, held in-depth discussions with the 42-year-old Theodor Herzl,[3] who had started the Zionist movement. Out of the estimated 9½ million Jews in the world at the time, 7½ million lived in Europe, the majority in Russia, where life was often harsh and degrading. Chamberlain now set out to support the nascent Zionist movement by offering them some of the vast territories at his disposal as chief minister of the largest empire in the world. But where?

Herzl, a frustrated playwright and actor, but successful journalist and theatre critic for the prestigious liberal Viennese newspaper *Neue Freie Presse*, had aspirations to being on the stage. In Vienna he had absorbed the manners of the sophisticated Austrian capital, where among his contemporaries were the two pioneers of psychoanalysis, Sigmund Freud and Alfred Adler, as well as the composers Anton Bruckner, Johannes Brahms and Gustav Mahler, the music director of the Imperial Opera. In 1895 Herzl had formed the World Zionist Organization in Vienna, calling for an individual land and state for Jews, '*die letzte Anstrengung der Juden*'. With energy and imagination he pulled the ambitions of the scattered Jews into a worldwide political movement aiming to create a nation where Jewish people could legally immigrate *en masse*, without having to creep in by the back door[4] past Turkish officials. His 100-page pamphlet *Der Judenstaat* (The State of Jews) published in 1896 went into reprint after reprint. Before taking on the cause of Zionism, Herzl was one of the new 'non-Jewish Jews'. His father, a businessman, had displayed an almost casual attitude to Judaism, and his great-uncles, like the parents of Karl Marx and Felix Mendelssohn, had converted to Christianity. Herzl, too, was indifferent to some of the traditions in Judaism (his son was not circumcized, for example). But when in Paris covering the Dreyfus Trial, Herzl was appalled at the hatred against Jews. After the first Zionist Conference in Basle in 1897, the World Zionist Organization quickly grew into a network of offices and annual conferences in different European capitals.

* * *

With the British occupation of 1882, Egypt became a part of the British Empire but never officially a colony, since it still belonged to the Ottoman Empire. The British agent and consul general, Lord Cromer, backed by British troops, was the real power in the country, while the puppet khedival government provided a façade of authority. In 1869 the Suez Canal had been opened, shortening the journey from Britain to India and Australia by several weeks. Most of the shares were owned either by the French or the high-flying khedive, Ismail Pasha, the viceroy of the sultan of the Ottoman Empire; but spectacular extravagance forced him to sell his share. In 1875, with a loan of £4 million from Lionel de Rothschild's[5] bank, Disraeli purchased this holding. (A decade later Lionel's son, Nathaniel, became the first Jewish peer in England.)[6] Britain's unofficial occupation of Egypt increased as Egypt's debt increased. Britain was not alone in usurping Ottoman territory in North Africa. France then took Tunisia, Algeria and Morocco, followed later by

Italy's taking of Libya. To ensure she kept her dominant role in the 'scramble for Africa', Britain began to look at other corners of Africa.

In 1902 Chamberlain suggested that the Jews should make a homeland on the delta and river area in the Sinai Desert around El Arish (near today's Egyptian/Israeli border), on the threshold of Palestine and the Mediterranean. Bordering the only river between Israel's southern limits and the Nile delta, this foothold could be a stepping stone to Palestine. Knowing his Old Testament well, Chamberlain was pleased to offer a place with biblical associations – it is only about 120 miles north of Mount Sinai, where Moses had received the Ten Commandments. This could also have helped the British safeguard the canal and have further extended British influence in the Middle East. While the Zionists discussed the Egyptian proposal, a firm 'No,' came from Lord Cromer in Cairo although various groups later tried to revive the idea.

After touring Africa to look at ways to consolidate Britain's colonies and maximize their strength, Chamberlain offered the Zionist Committee 6,000 square miles in the Guas Ngishu plateau in the East African Protectorate as a homeland. Wanting to help the Jews and perhaps also to conciliate the Zionists because of valuable Jewish investments in the empire, especially in the Rand mines, on 24 April 1903 Chamberlain suggested to Herzl, 'On my travels I have seen a land for you – Uganda. It is hot on the coast, but in the interior the climate is excellent for Europeans.'[7] He found the present wuite population 'sparse' and recommended considerable immigration.

This was the first time that a government had entered into negotiations with representatives of the Jewish people, and it set a precedent for the British in finding a secure place for the Jews under the British flag. But it also had a significance that is usually overlooked. It started David Lloyd George, then a forty-year-old backbencher, on the quest of finding a homeland for the Jews, which would culminate fourteen years later with Palestine. Between July 1903 and 1905 he acted in a private capacity as a solicitor for the Zionists in this proposal. His relationship was very much on professional lines and had nothing to do with the fact that his maternal grandmother, who died when Lloyd George was five in 1868, was called Rebecca Samuel. (Many Welsh families, unable to use their Welsh surnames, adopted names from the Old Testament.) The Lloyds themselves trace their ancestry back into the mists of Celtic history on the Lleyn peninsula. As noted earlier, Lloyd George enthusiastically drew up the first documents submitted to the British government for a Jewish homeland. At this time he still relied on income from his legal firm to support his wife and four children. Members of Parliament were not paid salaries until 1908. After his younger brother, William, joined the practice he had set up with Arthur Rhys Roberts, a solicitor from South Wales,[8] he was able to use a large percentage from it as the base on which to build his political career.[9]

After long negotiations with Chamberlain, the offer was officially made by Sir Clement Hill, of the Foreign Office, to Herzl's London representative, Leopold J. Greenberg. Later the editor of the *Jewish Chronicle*, Greenberg, was acting as an intermediary between Herzl and Chamberlain. Like Chamberlain, he came from Birmingham, and knew him from old, had lengthy discussions in the spring and summer of 1903. Greenberg first tried to employ the services of a lawyer from the British East Africa Company, but when this proved impossible he wrote:

> Lloyd George as you know is [a] Member of Parliament. He therefore knows the ropes of these things and can be made useful to us. Besides which he is a great authority on Uganda, etc. which means much. The next cause of delay was the desire of Mr. George to quietly ascertain beforehand what the British government were likely to assent to, so that the form in which it is sent in may be acceptable.

In a footnote to his book *The Balfour Declaration*, Stein added that 'this was Lloyd George's first contact with the Zionist Movement', giving his source of the above letter from Greenberg to Herzl as 4 July 1903, adding that it had been published by Oskar K. Rabinowicz. The scheme introduced Balfour, as well as Lloyd George, to the idea as it was floated in 1903, coinciding with Balfour's term as prime minister between 1902–6. An adjoining footnote by Stein says, 'The project would clearly have required the approval of the Prime Minister, Balfour, and was in fact actively supported by him.' Balfour's endorsement is confirmed in his Introduction to Nahum Sokolow's weighty tome, *History of Zionism*, published in 1919: '. . . in the early years of this century . . . I did my best to support a scheme devised by Mr. Chamberlain.'

Lloyd George's long proposal (Appendix 5) was attached to a letter dated 13 July to Chamberlain and submitted to the Foreign Office where it was examined by a government legal expert, C.J.B. Hurst, who wrote lengthy notes in the margins. The proposal then went to the Marquis of Lansdowne, the Foreign Secretary.

On 14 August Clement Hill sent the following letter to Greenberg, ready for him to read out aloud at the Sixth Zionist Congress:

> His Majesty's Government must always take in any well-considered scheme for the amelioration of the position of the Jewish Race. . . .
>
> If a site can be found which the Trust and His Majesty's Commissioner consider suitable and which commends itself to His Majesty's Government, Lord Lansdowne will be prepared to entertain favourably proposals for the establishment of a Jewish colony or settlement, on conditions which will enable the members to observe their National customs. For this purpose he would be prepared to discuss (if a suitable site had been found and subject to the views of the advisers of the Secretary of State in East Africa) the details of a scheme comprising as its main features; the grant of a considerable area of land, the appointment of a Jewish Official as chief of the local administration, and permission to the Colony to have a free hand in regard to municipal legislation and as to the management of religious and purely domestic matters, such local autonomy being conditional upon the right of . . .

When the Ugandan offer was debated at the congress in Basle, Switzerland, in August 1903, the majority of reactions were hostile, and the Zionist movement nearly split up. Herzl, though, persisted in promoting it as as a temporary refuge, a 'night shelter' for Jews in Russia in immediate danger. By a vote of 295 to 178 it was decided to send an investigatory commission to Africa. Such a colony would not, according to Herzl, affect the ultimate aim of a Jewish settlement in Palestine. But he failed to convince many in the audience, including one woman who ran on to the platform and tore down the large map of East Africa hanging at the back. She, like the majority of Zionists, felt that nothing should deflect them from the return to Palestine. Two years later, at the Seventh Zionist Congress, a unanimous resolution rejected the East African offer and called for increased colonization in Palestine. Historically rooted Jewry revolted against a 'New Palestine' and caused confusion among Zionist supporters. Even though the East Africa scheme came to nothing it was to bear fruit later with the Balfour Declaration.

* * *

Among the immigrants who came to England in 1904 was Weizmann, who had a doctorate in chemistry from the German University of Fribourg. When Herzl died of a heart attack in the same year at the age of forty-four, his confidant David Wolffsohn, who took his place, was a lacklustre president. In 1911 Professor Otto Warburg of Berlin took over and vigorously improved the settlements in Palestine. Weizmann[10] then had no position in the organization but this did not stop him promoting Zionism in England. In 1906 he married a Russian doctor, Vera Chatzman, who had received her medical training in Geneva, and soon afterwards they were both nationalized as British subjects. Unlike her husband she was inclined to be snobbish, and was said to have the aloof air of a French-speaking Russian aristocrat.

In the year of his marriage Weizmann met Balfour and converted him to the cause of Zionism at a meeting at Manchester's Victoria University where Weizmann was a lecturer in chemistry. Balfour recalled the failure of the Uganda project and asked Weizmann both why it had been rejected and why the Jewish people were so determined to have Palestine. Weizmann replied that the British had London but the Jews did not have Jerusalem, adding that it had belonged to them 'when London was a swamp'. Balfour told his niece and biographer Blanche Dugdale, 'It was from that talk with Weizmann that I saw that the Jewish form of patriotism was unique.'[11] In her insights into her uncle she said she remembered that in her childhood she imbibed 'from him the idea that Christian religion and civilization owes to Judaism an immeasurable debt, shamefully ill repaid'.[12]

But at that stage in Palestine there seemed little hope of a Jewish homeland. A letter dated 7 March 1911 from the British ambassador in Constantinople[13] to the British Foreign Secretary, Sir Edward Grey, shows the anti-Zionist bias of the new government of the 'Young Turks'. In contrast to the previous British ambassadors in the nineteenth century who stood up for the Jews in Palestine, Lowther identified with the Turks. After the unsuccessful counter-revolution in April 1909, official opposition to Jews within the Ottoman Empire was becoming both prejudiced and entrenched:

> In 1909 the masses of the Turkish and other populations here began to notice the extent to which the influence of Jews and Salonica Crypto Jews were monopolizing finance, commerce and the machinery of State, while during the last year the conviction has been growing that this influence is being used to further the objects of Sionism [*sic*]. . . .[14]

The following letter, sent on 17 March 1913, paints a vivid picture of opposition to an increased Jewish presence in Palestine:

> Jews are free to travel, reside and hold property etc. in other parts of the Ottoman Empire and it was only when the Zionist movement appeared from the language of its expounders to aim at the establishment of a Jewish polity in Palestine that the Turkish Government initiated the restrictive measures which it is now sought to be removed . . . [as referred to in Dr Max Nordau's letter in *The Times* of 30 December 1912].
>
> Besides the political reasons which have led the Ottoman Government to oppose Zionism in the form of 'unrestricted immigration of non-Ottoman Jews into Palestine', it also felt it necessary to take this course owing to the Opposition of the local Muslim Arabs who on economic grounds objected to the large influx of foreign Jews backed up by subsidies from wealthy Jewish Associations, thus rendering it impossible for the native Arab to compete with the newcomers. Further the Ottoman Government is particularly sensitive to all matters connected with Jerusalem which also contains the Holy Sepulchre and other places to which Christians, and particularly those of the Oriental branch, attach such importance, especially in view of the causes which contributed to the Crimean War. It was consequently alarmed at Zionist projects as set forth by Dr Herzl in his book on the subject styled 'The Jewish State'.
>
> . . . it might be difficult to support projects of the kind without perhaps giving umbrage to the Arabs, and in view of our position in Egypt, H.M.'s Diplomatic Agent and Consul in Cairo [Lord Kitchener] to whom I am forwarding copy of this dispatch, would doubtless be better able to judge of the attitude which His Majesty's Consular offices in Syria and Palestine should adopt in this matter. . . .

Looking at the problems in Palestine for Jews, it is little wonder that the majority leaving Europe migrated to other countries. Those who came to Palestine were a small fraction of the estimated 2.75 million who poured out of Russia and Eastern Europe between 1882 and 1914. Most went to the United States of America, to Britain, to Argentina and to Australia. A surge of Jewish refugees from Russia followed the assassination of Alexander II in 1881. During terrifying pogroms Jews and their property were mercilessly attacked and conditions for Jews, particularly in the towns and villages of southern Russia, deteriorated, with thousands of Jews rendered homeless and penniless. Much courage was needed then to migrate to Palestine. Fifty years earlier, Lord Byron, who died while fighting for Greek liberation, wrote:

> The wild-dove hath her nest, the fox his cave, mankind their country – Israel but the grave.

ELEVEN

With a Spade, a Rifle and Hope

The Turkish Government does nothing but collect taxes for itself in as a loose a manner as formerly; – it returns no protection, and allows of no improvement . . .

James Finn in a letter to Earl of Clarendon, Jerusalem, 1 January 1857

Despite a severe economic crisis in Palestine during and after the Turkish–Russian war, twenty-six families of Orthodox Jews from Jerusalem purchased a tract of land in the Sharon Valley, six miles from Jaffa, built mud huts as homes and called the farm Petach Tikvah, Gate of Hope. This, the first Jewish agricultural settlement in Palestine, initially failed. Although it was later revived with financial support from Baron Edmond de Rothschild, crop failure, malaria and hunger led the original pioneers to return to Jerusalem, A letter in the Foreign Office file from the British Consul in Jerusalem, N.T. Moore, dated 30 July 1879, describes the general depressed situation at the time:

At no former period of my sixteen years' residence in Palestine has the condition of the country been so deplorable as at present. Various causes contribute to this depression. The drain of nearly all the able-bodied men for the late war, scanty harvests, insufficient rain, high prices, and the ruinous loss inflicted on hundreds by the stoppage of the payment of the interest on Turkish Government securities . . . wide-spread destitution and industrial and commercial stagnation. Wheat and grain are at double their normal prices; this year's crops are again meager; of the 12,000 conscripts . . . probably not more than a quarter have returned. . . . The corruption and endless abuses in every branch of Turkish administration are too well known. . . .[1]

The consul then went on to despair about the shortage of trees which were 'cut down and sold for fire-wood, the peasants next took to digging up the roots which now constitute the common fuel of every house and establishment in the town . . .'. The deforestation, he added, was worsened by 'flocks and herds which roam over every hill and valley and crop up every green shoot that shows itself above the ground . . .'. In an effort to create shade and stop soil erosion settlers brought new trees and plants which would grow rapidly and endure heat and low temperatures. Among these were the eucalyptus and paperbark from Australia and the Sabra cactus (*Opuntia ficus-indica*), that strange prickly pear cactus from the deserts of North America, with their flat pads looking like large leaves which were grown into protective hedges. These foreign plants would all root and seed their way over the hills and valleys, changing the appearance of the biblical landscape forever.

Buying and selling land in Palestine was complicated – and expensive – as each sale required ratification by the local pasha. Sometimes negotiations were drawn out because of disputes about ownership or inheritance. There had been no land registry law until 1858.[2] Prices were often inflated, and the ground usually poor. Much land appeared to be a waterless wilderness of tumultuous hills broken by rocky valleys with stones ranging in size from pebbles to boulders a couple of feet high. The built-up terraces of biblical times were now a bygone system of agriculture. As well as denuding the country of trees, for over a thousand years the Arabs had used so much animal dung for fuel that the soil was deprived of its usual nutriments, and the nomadic Bedouin had allowed too many sheep to graze on the sparse grass.

Jews, however, were not the only new settlers. The arrival of large numbers coincided with a general opening up of the country, to tourists, to trades and to new ideas. As Palestine was believed by many to be God's chosen place, an American settlement of 167 immigrants was formed on the outskirts of Jaffa in 1866. Consisting mostly of farmers, carpenters, blacksmiths and tradesmen who belonged to the newly established 'Church of the Messiah', they came to await the Second Coming. A letter from the acting American Vice-Consul in 1866 to the British Consul in Jerusalem explained that they wanted to 'live and die in the Holy land, as they beleive [*sic*] that before long, great changes will take place i.e. as I hear from them, the gathering together of the Jews from all parts to this country and the advent of Christ.'[3] The inability of the colony to tackle the local bureaucracy meant that it lacked a licence and their applications to purchase land were never approved. The colony's failure was compounded by unusual farming conditions, a cholera epidemic which killed many of the children, and the alcoholism of its leader; which led to a complete collapse of the colony within eighteen months and the dispersal of the inhabitants. A letter from the British Consul dated 2 July 1868 summed up some of the difficulties: 'The failure of the American settlement at Jaffa, indeed, is but a repetition of the fate of previous similar experiments made under better auspices. In present circumstances, both as regards the country itself and the still unsettled question of land tenure by foreign subjects in Turkey . . . there seems little hope of success attending these enterprises.'[4] But as the first group of Americans left, a larger group of pious families from Swabia, predominantly from the north-eastern outskirts of Stuttgart, in the south-west of Germany, emigrated, due to their religious difference of opinion or interpretation of the scriptures with the Evangelical-Lutheran Church. Like so many Nonconformists, it was the Bible, not the teachings of a state church, that they revered. Calling themselves the German Temple Society, and members of the Templars, they settled in Haifa – named after the Arabian fishing village. Khaifa, (now the city centre of today's Haifa) then took over the land of the failed American colony, calling it Jaffa-Walhala. In the following seven decades they established altogether seven settlements and next to the Jews were the most dominant non-Arab settlers. Apart from the two mentioned above these settlements were at: Sarona, founded in 1871; Jerusalem, which unlike the others was an urban colony, set up in 1873, near the subsequent railway station; Neuhardthof was founded in 1892; Wilhelma in 1902; and finally at Bethlehem in 1906.

The dismal collapse of the first American colony was soon balanced by the enormous success and prestige of the German settlers and by the second wave of American colonists. In 1881 Horatio Spafford, a Chicago lawyer and church leader, his wife Anna and a group of fifty Americans took over a pasha's old palace and a farm in east Jerusalem. Life was often a struggle, but the institutions they established, including a school and a hospital, became social centres of significance. Their generous hospitality became so renowned that it eventually developed into a boarding house (now the ever-popular American Colony Hotel). Another settler around this time, who was a positive force in the first stages of Jewish colonization, was Laurence Oliphant, friend of the Prince of Wales and journalist, traveller and Christian Zionist extraordinary who had earlier sent requests to the sultan about the possibility of large-scale Jewish migration to Palestine.[5] With his wife Alice, Oliphant set up a settlement on the coast at Haifa, south of Acre.

Jewish migration to Palestine progressed fitfully. Baron de Rothschild financially supported various schemes, purchased 125,000 acres for the community and saved the early settlements from collapse, especially the new large-scale farming enterprises, in which people struggled – 'dunam after dunam,[6] goat after goat' – withstanding the malarial mosquitoes, their own lack of capital and the resentment of the locals who were displaced by their presence. The repercussions from land sales, whether wasteland in areas which were vastly underpopulated, or land which had been used by tenants, were far-reaching. Fellahin (peasants, or husbandmen) were pushed from their traditional sources of livelihood, as were those who for centuries had subsisted on a share-crop basis by contracts with large landowning families, also known as the 'effendis'.[7] Most of the land farmed by Jews was purchased from Arabs, often rich absentee landlords – only a small acreage was from peasants, usually when bankrupt or suffering from crippling tax arrears. Some Arab cultivators refused to move from land which they saw as their own. The new land registration law of 1858 had meant that landlords could override communal rights of tenure. Ownership was often disputed, especially as members of the Arab upper classes had registered large areas of land which the fellahin also said was their own, but being illiterate had not registered. Sometimes it was only discovered that they had ceased to be the legal owners when the land was sold to Jewish settlers by an absentee landlord.

Much land had been tenanted or used by nomadic Bedouin, who had roamed with their precious sheep, goats, horses and camels for centuries, making it difficult for them to respect the new ownership. Springs, rivulets and even wells had generally been regarded as communal property. If it had been the Bedouins' custom to use a certain spring or well at a certain time of the year they wanted to continue to do so. It usually rains only during the winter, that is, between November and March, when the west wind blows in from the Mediterranean. For nearly eight months the land is dry and parched. In September and October, the tail end of the dry season, large areas do not even boast a blade of grass and a well can be a matter of life and death.

The heaviest rain is near the coast, where it falls in torrents, and decreases as the winds lessen, further east. In some areas, such a small amount of rain falls that viable agriculture had been nearly impossible. Now with irrigation and what was dismissed as 'a few bags of phosphate and lime', orange and olive groves sprang up, together with fig trees in former desolate fields around the Sea of Galilee and Jaffa. The Arabs saw the arid and stony ground bloom as it responded to an injection of capital, modern techniques, diligence and skill. The new settlers persevered. They carried stones from the fields, built irrigation ditches and terraces and planted more and more trees – some just for pleasure and shade. A few industries were established. In Jaffa, for instance, one immigrant started a short-lived metal factory employing 150 people, making parts for farming tools and carriage wheels. Huge areas, long abandoned, were now productive. The Jaffa orange, with its thick skin which made it more suitable for the long journey to export markets, contributed to the increase of trade. Prosperity driven by foreigners appeared as a threat to the Arabs who at different times urged the government in Constantinople to prohibit Jewish immigration and land purchase.

* * *

In the early nineteenth century there were no publicized cases of politically inspired attacks by Arabs on Jews, but even so farms and settlements, no matter if they were owned by Arabs, Turks or Jews, were guarded against marauders. High fences and armed guards were needed to safeguard residents, workers and landowners, and also their groves of citrus fruit, olives and other crops. 'Adroit thieves' was a term used sometimes by travellers to describe the Bedouin. Travelling across the deserts in Arab countries could also be hazardous, even for Arabists like Sir Richard Burton. Both Disraeli and Thackeray on their visists to Palestine wrote about having to travel in parties 'well mounted and well armed'. The values of the Bedouin were different and perplexing. On the one hand they had a deep feeling for human fellowship and hospitality, and respected individual courage and personal bravery, but on the other they looked upon stealing from some of the people they considered rich – including the Jews – as fair game and called such defenceless people *Awlad al-mitah* ('Children of death', the Arabic term for orphans). Letters in the British Consulate files during the nineteenth century despair at the enforcement of law and order. Incessant tribal warfare, which undermined security, had become worse during the Crimean War, as Turkey had withdrawn most of its troops from Palestine. It was the same after the Russian–Turkish war of 1878, with armed skirmishes leading to chaos in many places.[8] In Britain once again Russophobia swept across the country. Large crowds gathered in Trafalgar Square waving the Ottoman crescent and star flag while singing:

We don't want to fight,
But by jingo if we do . . .
The Russians shall not have Constantinople!

In Palestine an anti-Jewish policy was re-emerging. In 1883 more constraints were introduced, requiring visitors to depart within three months. But in 1888 the Ottoman government had allowed foreign (non-Ottoman) Jews to settle in Palestine provided they did so singly and not *en masse*. Then in 1891 prohibition against the immigration of Russian Jews was renewed and more strictly enforced. A year later, Jews were forbidden to buy land, with the exception of those who were Ottoman subjects and those who did not belong to the category *en masse*.

Arguments put forward by the British Consulate in Jerusalem led to some laws being rescinded. But during all the years of these bans, thousands of Jews entered the country, aided by the inevitable *baksheesh*, and as it was delicately explained in a Zionist report, 'it was always possible to get round the individual official with a little artifice'.[9] Despite a series of edicts limiting land purchases enormous progress had been made. By 1900 the Jews in Eretz Israel numbered 50,000.

In 1906, the government changed in Constantinople. A group of army officers, known as the 'Young Turks' or the CUP, the Committee of Union and Progress, mutinied and embarked on taking over the government. Two years later elections were held in which they won all but one of the seats in the Chamber of Deputies. Eventually, in the spring of 1909, a coup was staged by a triumvirate led by Enver Pasha. Sultan Abdul Hamid II was deposed and his half-brother Mehmet Resat assumed the throne in his place, albeit with reduced powers. This nationalistic movement made Turkish the medium for all schools throughout the empire, yet at the same time took heed of Arab complaints and fears about Jewish expansion. The new Turkish government restricted immigration and suspended all land transfers to Jews in both the Jerusalem district and the province of Beirut.

But as before, immigrants still managed to filter into Palestine. During the Second *Aliyah*, which had begun in 1905 and finished in 1914, about 40,000 Jewish immigrants settled. During its second year (1906), among the single immigrants to arrive in Jaffa was twenty-year-old David Gruen, soon to change his name to David Ben-Gurion, from the small town of Plonsk, in Poland. Like his father, an unlicensed lawyer who was active in

Chovavai Tzion, an early movement which sought to make Palestine a homeland for the oppressed Jews of Eastern Europe, Ben-Gurion abandoned his law studies at Warsaw University and became a zealous Zionist. He and other teenagers in Plonsk founded a Zionist youth society, called after Ezra, the ancient priest and scribe. Members took a solemn oath that they would never speak any language but Hebrew to each other and that they would labour for 'the dissemination of Hebrew culture among the working youth'.[10] Like others, they started updating Hebrew from being just a biblical language into one that could be used as everyday speech. The Jews not only lacked a motherland, they also lacked a mother tongue.[11] So much progress was being made with bringing this new Jewish language into use that Yiddish now had a competitor. In America, in the New York Public Library on Fifth Avenue, the scholar Eliezer Ben-Yehuda started the long task of adapting biblical Hebrew into a usable language and produced a sixteen-volume dictionary.

On arrival in Israel Ben-Gurion found that life was tough, conditions harsh, the climate hot and muggy and mosquitoes sometimes rampant. Much of the land was hard, work was scarce, and he frequently suffered hunger and relapses of malaria. But for four years he worked on and off as a labourer on various Jewish settlements of orange groves and vineyards, from Petach Tikvah to Sejera. In 1910 Ben-Gurion moved to Jerusalem where he and Yitzhak Ben-Zvi, the intellectual from Poltava in the Ukraine who became his lifelong friend and later a president of Israel, were part of the editorial staff of the new party paper, *Ahdut*. The following year they were elected as delegates to the 11th Zionist congress in Vienna. Both were active in Poale Zion, the socialist international trade union, and managed to entrench the branch in Palestine. Ben-Gurion went to Constantinople to study law so that he would be able to defend and further the cause of Zionism.

Deeply influenced by socialism and the theories of Leo Tolstoy, John Ruskin and William Morris, who believed there was virtue in working manually and in intellectuals becoming 'hewers of wood', Ben-Zvi said that there was 'no redemption for our nation in our homeland unless each of us labours with his hands . . .'.[12] This idealism was a common link between many of the new settlers.

Along with Rachel Yanait, whom he later married, and Eliyahu Golomb, who would later command the Haganah, Ben-Zvi was one of the founders in 1908/1909 of the first secret defence force, Hashomer, the Watchmen. The name was taken from Isaiah XXI (11,12):

> He calleth to me out of Seir, Watchman, what of the night? Watchman, what of the night? The watchman said, The morning cometh, and also the night: if ye will inquire, inquire ye: return, come.

No public security existed then in Palestine. Physical valour and self-defence were the only ways of surviving and gaining the respect of the Bedouin. Photographs show members looking like a cross between American cowboys and Arab sheikhs, with flowing headdresses, riding boots and bandoliers of bullets. But it was not just a matter of fighting. Some studied Arabic and learnt about Bedouin law and Arab customs. Many were respected by the Arabs, and, according to Koestler, 'Many of them had become blood-brothers of influential tribal elders, and were called in to arbitrate in disputes or settle blood-feuds.' In his *History of Jewish Self-Defence in Palestine* Golomb described how security was integrated into everyday living:

> In those days there were no buses. Even a mule was an exceptional luxury. The settlement was often completely isolated and special steps had to be taken to ensure the food supply. The settlers had to ford ditches and flooded wadis after the heavy rains, and pass alone through Arab villages bringing food from the nearest town. . . .
>
> The Arabs of the neighbourhood of a new Jewish village, having sold to the settlers the land on which the village was erected, afterwards tried by constant raids to make life impossible for them; and by chasing them away, to regain possession of their land – in addition to the houses erected on it. In Petach Tikvah, there was an additional source of trouble. Two tribes wished to sell part of their land to the Jews, and when the settlers purchased from one tribe only, the other began to attack the settlement. Since they knew that the Jews observed Saturday as the day of rest, they staged all their attacks on the Shabbath. Stamper (one of the early 'Watchmen') a scrupulously observant Jew, had often to summon the settlers to their posts straight from the Synagogue, to defend the settlement with cudgels and knives.

There were always fewer than one hundred members of the Hashomer – certainly not enough members to protect all the settlements, which by now numbered over thirty, with about 10,000 workers. The startling appearance of these settlements was described by T.E. Lawrence as he travelled through

Palestine working as an archaeologist in Syria, and collecting material on Crusader castles. In a letter to his mother in August 1909 he described how Renaissance painters were correct to place Jesus and his disciples feasting in a pillared hall, 'or sunning themselves on marble staircases: everywhere one finds remains of splendid Roman roads and houses and public buildings, and Galilee was the most Romanized province of Palestine . . .'. He went on to say that the Romans did not come across '. . . dirty, dilapidated Bedouin tents . . . Palestine was a decent country then, and could so easily be made so again. The sooner the Jews farm it all the better; their colonies are bright spots in a desert.'[13]

Like earlier Jewish settlers they poured on bags of nitrogen, lime and phosphate and the desert bloomed into vineyards, wheat fields, orange groves and new crops and seeds from experimental research stations, staffed with scientists. In 1906 the agronomist Aaron Aaronsohn discovered specimens of wild wheat (*Triticum dicoccoides*) at the foot of Mount Hermon, near Rosh Pinah. World wheat crops had deteriorated through centuries of intensive inbreeding, but by crossing wheat hybrids with Aaronsohn's wild wheat species, crops were transformed, making them less prone to disease and more inclined to produce higher yields.

* * *

In 1909, twelve Zionist settlers stood on the sands a few miles north of the ancient port of Jaffa, drew the outlines of a city in the sand dunes and named it Tel Aviv, meaning 'Hill of Spring', a name used in Herzl's book in which he set out his blueprint for a Jewish state. This completely new town, which grew up between newly planted trees, would soon become a brash boom city, a contrast to Jerusalem. Despite their disproportionately small numbers in the rest of Palestine, the Jews were a majority in Jerusalem. One of the reasons for this was because the city, although religiously significant for the Muslims, had never been an important political and administrative centre in the Ottoman Empire.

* * *

For thirty years, from 1876 to 1909, Sultan Abdul Hamid II – Abdul 'the Damned' – played the European powers against one another. His successor, Mehmet V Resat, indulged in similar games. So did the leader of the

'Young Turks', Enver Pasha, who became the Minister of War and the head of the triumvirate which ruled Turkey since 1908. More incursions were made into the Ottoman Empire in 1912–13 in the First and Second Balkan Wars, when Bulgaria, allied with Serbia and Greece, declared war on Turkey. Peace was only made in October 1913. Diminished though the Ottoman Empire now was, it still stretched in an arc from Turkey around the eastern Mediterranean to Syria, Palestine, Sinai and Egypt, and it contained the three Holy Cities of Islam, Mecca, Medina and Jerusalem. The biggest threat to Turkey was the Entente Cordiale, formed in 1904 between Britain and France, which expanded into the Triple Entente to include Turkey's old enemy, Russia. According to these agreements, each of these countries was to provide mutual aid in the event of aggression.

TWELVE

From Peace to War, November 1914 – March 1915

A place of dream, the Holy Land
Hangs midway between earth and heaven
'The Holy Land', Harriett Prescott Spafford

Kaiser Wilhelm II of Germany declared war on France on 3 August 1914. At midnight on 4 August 1914, on behalf of Britain and her empire, King George V declared war on Germany. Two million German soldiers started heading for Belgium and Holland *en route* for Paris. All over Germany, soldiers in field-grey uniforms and spiked helmets raised the spirits of every German as they marched and boarded troop trains bound for the frontier. Flag-waving crowds thronged streets and railway stations cheering the soldiers and blowing kisses, pressing on them gifts of flowers and cigarettes. Calling the 1839 Treaty of London, which guaranteed Belgian neutrality, 'a scrap of paper', the German army believed it could take Paris in a 'swift knock-out blow'. To avoid the French frontier fortresses on the French–German borders, soldiers marched over the flat plains of Belgium and Holland, on the new arc-shaped route to the French capital.

A seemingly endless stream of soldiers tramped or rode through Belgium's meadows and picturesque woods of high summer. Peaceful farmland was disturbed. Poppies, buttercups, cornflowers and hedge mustard on the road verges were crushed by the weight of jackboots, the first of many. Waving fields of wheat and corn waited, never to be harvested; unploughed fields waited, never to be sown. It was a glorious August. Men sang '*Die Wacht am Rhein*' ('The Watch on the Rhine') or the song which was then Germany's national anthem '*Heil dir im Siegerkranz*' ('Hail to You in the Victor's Laurels') sung to the tune of England's 'God Save the King'.

Next came the requisitioning of animals and the felling of trees. Artillery fire from both sides turned land that was once bountiful countryside into a lunar landscape. Within two weeks seven German armies were being hurled into France and Flanders. No other European army could match either the size or strength of the German forces, said to comprise 10 million men. Steam locomotives, pulling cars packed with troops, guns, food, medical supplies, blankets, artillery ammunition, hand grenades and bullets headed west. The Kaiser believed it would take a mere six weeks to conquer Paris. He put his faith in the Schlieffen Plan, as devised in 1895 by Count Alfred von Schlieffen, whose dying words in 1913 had been, 'Only make the right wing strong'. Despite Schlieffen's admonition, nervous German commanders actually weakened the right wing in favour of the 'hinge' of their great turning movement. German and French armies fought a colossal 'Battle of the Frontiers' but on the right the weakened German advance petered out.

Britain and France urgently wanted Germany to become engaged against Russia in the east, for only then would she be forced to divert troops from France. Crammed trains pulled tens of thousands of shamefully ill-equipped Russians towards the forests of East Prussia. As predicted, the Kaiser quickly relocated two army corps from the Western Front to stop the Russians penetrating into the heartland of Germany. When they met the Germans in battle at Tannenberg on 29 August 1914, the Russians were virtually annihilated.

In Britain new recruits, who had been enrolled in response to posters with slogans such as 'King and Country' and 'Come on Boys, Follow the Flag', suffered because of deficiencies in rifles, uniforms, boots, horses, metal horseshoes, and specialist personnel such as blacksmiths and farriers. As Lloyd George, who was then Britain's Minister of Munitions, wrote in his *War Memoirs*, 'Army authorities had neither barracks in which to house these men, uniforms in which to clothe them, nor weapons with which to drill and train them.' Volunteers, often trained in civilian clothes or bits of old uniforms, improvised with broomsticks instead of rifles. Some huts lacked roofs, windowpanes or beds. Improvised latrines were sometimes just poles over communal pits.

Twenty days after Britain's entry into the war, the troops of the British Expeditionary Force, the BEF, were outflanked and forced to pull back from the Belgian town of Mons. In the following week, in a series of bloody and costly battles, the British and French troops halted the German advance on Paris. A million men were in combat for five days. In one phase, fighting raged over a front of 140 miles. One Prussian wrote, 'Our men are done up. They stagger forward, their faces coated with dust, their uniforms in rags. They look like living scarecrows.'

This, the decisive Battle of the Marne, in which Parisian taxis famously drove troops to the front, saved the French capital. German forces retreated to the River Aisne. The Russians insisted that it was they who saved the city because their troops had kept the Germans and Austrians engaged on the Eastern Front, thus diffusing the German onslaught. Indeed, the Allies now owed a moral debt to the Russians.

Germany's 'race to the sea' to take the Channel ports of Boulogne and Calais was frustrated in November 1914. The men started to dig in. With optimism the Kaiser continued to tell his troops they would be 'home before the leaves fall'. But the autumn leaves began to fall and the rains came, and soon the battlefields turned into a wilderness of mud, trenches, grim places filled with water, where hundreds of thousands of soldiers existed like troglodytes. By November 1914 both sides were bogged down on the Western Front in a stalemate that nobody had expected. This deadlock had to be broken. Politicians cast about for a diversionary theatre of war to break the impasse in France. Turkey was still neutral, but not for long.

* * *

In his palace near the Golden Horn on the Bosphorus, the fury of Sultan Mehmet V Resat against his old friends the British and the French knew no bounds. The day before announcing war on Germany the British had confiscated Turkey's nearly completed dreadnought battleships, the *Sultan Osman I* at Armstrong's shipyard on the River Tyne and the *Reshadieh* at Vickers' shipyard. On the advice of the new First Lord of the Admiralty, Winston Churchill, they were impounded. As they had been paid for by coins dropped into collection boxes in villages in Turkey, Britain's action embittered the whole Turkish nation. But Britain's guarantee to Turkey of the absolute integrity of her dominions if she remained neutral was repeated by the Ambassador in Constantinople. The seventy-two British naval advisers and staff under Rear-Admiral Arthur Limpus, who were working in Constantinople to modernize the Turkish navy, remained, carrying on their duties as usual. Limpus did not leave the city until 17 September 1914, when he travelled to Malta, while most of the British naval personnel did not depart until November. Until then, Vickers Ltd., the British armaments firm, supplied Turkey with munitions alongside her competitor, Armstrong, Whitworth & Company Ltd. operating a thirty-year lease under the name Société Impériale

Ottomane Co-interéssée des Docks, Arsenaux et Constructions Navales, of the dockyards and arsenal of the Golden Horn. This was owned jointly by the Turkish government and the two British armament companies. Sir Basil Zaharoff, the Turkish-born international financier and arms dealer, known as 'the merchant of Death' or the 'mystery man of Europe', worked closely with both the Turkish and British governments. Vincent Caillard spent many years in Constantinople as president of the council of administration of the Ottoman Public Debt before returning to Britain to become financial director of Vickers. Wyndham Deedes was another Briton taking a leading role in Turkey; he trained the gendarmerie and was known as 'Deedes Boy'.

Three months passed before Turkey entered the war at the beginning of November. When she did so Prime Minister Asquith, at the Lord Mayor's Banquet, made it clear that Britain had finally abandoned her traditional Eastern policy. With unusual vehemence he said that it had been the 'Ottoman government who had rung the death-knell . . .'.[1] But the 'Eastern Question', which had dogged British politicians, especially Palmerston and Gladstone, and the rest of Europe in the nineteenth century, was not to be concluded as easily as that. The problem was still there as, indeed, it still is. All that happened was that everyone changed sides and the old policy was now reversed. Britain started planning the future of the Arab territories in British hands. In his memoirs, Herbert Samuel, then President of the Local Government Board, said that in a discussion the day following the Lord Mayor's Banquet, Lloyd George had told him that he was 'very keen to see a Jewish State established in Palestine'.[2] A few days later Samuel pointed out to Grey that 'the jealousies of the great European Powers would make it difficult to allot [Palestine] to any one of them'. He provocatively added that 'perhaps the opportunity might arise for the fulfilment of the ancient aspiration of the Jewish people, and the restoration there of a Jewish State'.

This was the first time that Lloyd George had publicly aired his enthusiasm for a Jewish homeland since being a member of the cabinet. Samuel and Balfour must have known that he had earlier acted privately as solicitor to the Zionists, but whether other colleagues knew, is not recorded. The Register of Members' Interests in Britain was only introduced in 1974. Then, and only then, were members prohibited from engaging in any advocacy on behalf of clients or former clients. Among Lloyd George's other clients was the Shell Oil Company, which had led him into close contact with several Jewish financiers including members of the Rothschild and Marcus Samuel families (but a different family from that of Herbert Samuel, who was to play such a decisive role in the Jewish homeland).

A further suggestion for the projected homeland was that 'British influence ought to play a considerable part in the formation of such a State', since the 'geographical situation of Palestine, and especially its proximity to Egypt, would render its goodwill a matter of importance to the British Empire'.[3] When composing a memorandum to the cabinet, Samuel consulted Lloyd George. He must have been well aware that Lloyd George was not only sympathetic to the idea but had been the author of the 1903 Draft Agreement, which could now act as a precedent.

Meanwhile, some politicians presented a strong case for an invasion of Turkey. This, it was argued, would prop up the hard-pressed Russians by delivering a shattering blow to Germany's power and prestige. Most of all it would get the men out of the trenches, back into open warfare.

* * *

Towards the middle of November 1914 the sultan threw into the war what had once been the strongest arm of Islam, declaring a holy war, a jihad against the infidel, he exhorted Muslims to unite.[4] This was reinforced by five fatwas (religious rulings) by Sheikh al-Islam, the highest Muslim authority in Constantinople. Germany, too, backed the scheme to inflame the whole Muslim world against Christians, to destroy the influence of the Allies everywhere. Meticulous in his prayers – and almost equally devoted to brandy and liqueur[5] – the sovereign of the Ottoman Empire hoped to incite the whole Muslim world to rise up against his new enemy and her Allies. In Turkey religion and state were as yet not separated, so the sultan was also the caliph of Islam and keeper of the insignia of the caliphate, including the Prophet's mantle, and was the guardian of the two holy places, Mecca and Medina in the Hejaz. The ramshackle Ottoman Empire still extended from the Black Sea to southern Arabia, and was maintained by huge numbers of Turks garrisoned in Palestine, Syria and the Hejaz. With its holy cities of Mecca and Medina, the Hejaz was the southernmost part of the Ottoman Empire, and under the control of Sherif Hussein, who was answerable to the sultan. It was provisioned by the recently constructed German-built Pilgrim's Railway running from Damascus. Every ship using Britain's Suez Canal had to sail past the coast of the Hejaz and Jidda, the port of Mecca, which annually received a huge influx of pilgrims, mainly from Africa, India and the Dutch East Indies.

Unlike jihads issued in previous centuries, this was supported also by the government of a Christian country, Lutheran Germany. According to Liman von Sanders, the German general stationed in Constantinople, being allied with Christian states and German and Austrian officers serving in the Turkish army gave the holy war an air of unreality.[6] Germany planned to use the jihad as an extra weapon and started having the words translated and printed into incendiary pamphlets, which were then distributed and which would spark off unrest and rebellion among Muslims and reach all countries with large Muslim populations, including India, China, Persia, Syria, Palestine, Egypt, Algeria, Libya and Morocco.

These calls to holy war, recited in every mosque and printed in every newspaper throughout the Ottoman Empire, were greeted by cheering crowds, bands, drums and speeches in Constantinople. The cheers echoed and resonated from Jerusalem and Tel Aviv, to Baghdad to Cairo – anywhere where there were Muslims. A consular agent at Safed reported an increase in disturbances around Galilee against Jewish settlers, fomented by the Bedouin tribesmen excited by the prospect of war – and the sultan's jihad. On the whole, however, there were few mass risings. But in the inhospitable terrain of the Yemen the Islamic extremists entered the Aden protectorate and installed themselves both in the highlands and near the port, the vital coaling station for British ships entering and leaving the Suez Canal. If they got to the coast it would threaten the British Red Sea route and the Germans could launch their U-boats. The British responded with a blockade of the Red Sea, leaving the Turks nothing but the overland route and the famous Hejaz or Pilgrim railway to send critical military supplies and reinforcements to their garrisons at Mecca and Medina. Soon, though, the British would be sabotaging this route as well.

Turkey hid her preparations to invade both the Caucasus and the Egyptian front. Signs of extensive military operations were few. Simultaneously with the declaration of the jihad, all able-bodied men between the ages of eighteen and forty-five were forced to enlist in the Ottoman Army ready to take their part in the multi-fronted war against the British in Egypt, and stopping the Russians fulfilling their desire to dominate the Balkans as an outlet to the Mediterranean.

Unlike German soldiers they did not march in formation – the roads in the Ottoman Empire had always been rough, and in mountainous regions there were seldom even paths or tracks between villages. Miscellaneous Ottoman conscripts passing through the streets were described by the ambassador in Constantinople, Henry Morgenthau. 'A motley aggregation of Turks, Circassians, Greeks, Kurds, Armenians, and Jews, showing signs of having been summarily taken from their farms and shops. . . .'[7]

The fact that America hesitated for two and a half years before entering the war meant that they could maintain embassies and consulates in countries which were Britain's enemies, such as Germany, Austria and Turkey. 'Arabs, bootless and shoeless, dressed in their most gaily coloured garments, with long linen bags (containing the required five days' rations) thrown over their shoulders, shambling in their gait and bewildered in their manner, touched shoulders with equally dispirited Bedouins, evidently suddenly snatched from the desert.'

* * *

Turkey had been slow to enter the war for many reasons. News of the assassination of Archduke Ferdinand, heir-apparent to the Austrian throne, in Sarajevo, three months earlier, on 28 June 1914, had appeared to be yet another incident in the centuries-old dramas of the Balkans. Disraeli's 1878 Treaty of Berlin, which had taken much of the Balkans out of the Ottoman Empire, had not brought peace. Most in the government in Constantinople had no desire to enter another war that could well exhaust the Ottoman army, already drained by their war against Italy in 1911, which had been followed by the two disastrous wars in the Balkans.

Most arguments were in favour of Turkey staying neutral. If Turkey joined Germany, and Germany lost, the country would lose everything, including the Holy Land, Mesopotamia and the Hejaz.

From the moment Britain entered the war, naval blockades, the threat of torpedo attacks and mines had deterred shipping in the Mediterranean, putting an abrupt end to most trade. Administrators, both civil and military, in Jerusalem and Jaffa, suspicious of secret conspiracies and spying, naturally imposed an embargo on Jews sending or receiving goods or letters. In Jerusalem, where the majority of people relied on food and money coming from elsewhere, many inhabitants would soon collapse from starvation, malnutrition or disease. Despite imaginative assistance and handouts by the Christian churches and groups such as the American colony, many of the poor of Jerusalem were soon forced to subsist on bark, roots, watermelons and sesame seeds. The traditional *chalukkah*, the dole and food supplies donated by pious Jews in Europe and America, seldom got through. Limited food and medicine, though, came from the United States as Morgenthau, who happened to be a non-Zionist Jew and diplomat of a neutral nation arranged limited assistance.

The Reverend Otis Glazebrook, the American consul in Jerusalem, in a cable back to America, said, 'Military authorities seizing supplies of foreigners. Protests unavailing. Violation of domicile continues. Sixteen thousand troops concentrated at Nablus without visible support. Reign of military terrorism. Great distress prevails. American Jewish Community beseeches financial aid and food from America. Will you transmit appeal? Urgent.'[8]

Djemal Pasha, the Minister of the Navy and one of the three most powerful men in the Turkish Empire, went to Damascus to take command of the Fourth Army and become governor and military commander of Greater Syria, which then included Palestine. His hanging of offenders in public during his four years as governor of Jerusalem and Damascus caused him to be referred to as 'the Bloodthirsty'. But his ruthlessness against all suspects, especially foreign-born Jews, who might leak information to their relations in enemy countries, was one reason why British Intelligence in the Middle East during the war was so inadequate. As Allied consuls had been expelled, foreign Jews became subject to Turkish law. Alexander Aaronsohn, brother of the agronomist, said, 'Upon the Arabs [war] acted as an intoxicant. Every bootblack or batman felt that he was the equal of the accursed Frank [European invaders], who now had no consul to protect them; and abuses, began immediately.' Anyone found with any sort of Zionist document, or any members of the Hashomer, the group who had earlier set themselves up as settlement guards, was threatened with death. There were fears of a bloodbath similar to that which was soon to be carried out against the Armenian Christians.

Despite his order to confiscate all arms, Djemal's policy is unclear at this time – who was tortured, who was hanged, will never be known. But he certainly detained 500 Russian immigrant Jews before their deportation to Egypt. Other Jews were sent to internment camps north of Jaffa, awaiting expulsion,[9] others still were sent to work in labour gangs. All enemy aliens had to become Ottoman subjects or leave the country. The small number who retained British certificates of protection, a policy of Palmerston's which had lasted until 1890, made preparations to depart for Egypt, but others faced repatriation to Russia, a prospect few could contemplate.[10]

Without even a day's warning or time to pack their belongings, on Tuesday 15 December 1914 gun-carrying police rounded up Jewish residents in Jaffa, ordering them to go immediately to the port. As there was no harbour in the shallow port of Jaffa, Jews rushed to procure places in rowing boats to take them out to the American cruiser *Tennessee* which was about to depart from Jaffa for Alexandria with refugees. Even when the sea was rough – and it often is between the winter and spring months of November and May and both anchorage and boarding can be unsafe – they were rowed out to the swaying vessel. German-born Arthur Ruppin, who stayed on in Palestine because he carried a German passport, wrote in his diary, 'We are now losing within a few days more people than we gained during years of immigration . . .', and then described the scene at the harbour, 'I had to watch whole families with their hurriedly collected belongings – old people, mothers and babies – being driven on to the boat in infinite disorder.'

Despite increased detention and expulsion, Ben-Gurion saw no alternative to joining the Ottoman army. When his application was refused, he and Ben-Zvi managed to start recruitment for a Jewish militia to help Turkey defend Palestine against Britain, France and Russia and set up what they called the Yishuv Ottomanization Committee. Joining the Ottoman forces would not only help defend Palestine, their actions would also add to the Jews' claim to being permanently settled there. And, most importantly, it meant they would be fighting against the Russians, not with them, as would be the case if they left Palestine and enlisted in the British army. Most Jews, who had experienced the whiplash of the tsarist regime, did not want to fight on the same side as Tsarist Russia, which had treated the Jews so abominably, and they looked on the idea of fighting with the British as becoming Russian patriots, a condition they could not then countenance. Among Jewish recruits from Palestine in the Turkish army was Moshe Shertok (later Sharett), destined to be the first foreign minister and the second prime minister of Israel. Another was Dov Hos, who was later deputy mayor of Tel Aviv, and who eventually ended up in the British army.

The Turkish authorities knew that Ben-Gurion and his followers were Zionists and socialists, and suspected them of being a fifth column of the British, but it seems did not find their secret stores of guns and bullets from the Hashomer cache. Djemal saw them as the dangerous nucleus of a Jewish army. After the militia was broken up, Ben-Gurion was manacled and imprisoned awaiting either a labour gang or deportation. In his *Memoirs* he recounted how in the courtyard of the prison in Jerusalem he met one of his old Arab friends, Ihie Effendi, from his two years as a law student in Constantinople. When the Arab asked, 'What are you doing here?' Ben-Gurion replied, 'I'm being expelled from the country.' This was followed by a remark that was Ben-Gurion's first indication of the new Arab nationalism, 'As a friend of yours, I'm very sorry to hear it. As an Arab, I am pleased about it.'

Ben-Gurion's expulsion order was stamped in bright red letters, 'Expelled for ever from the limits of the Turkish Empire'. He and Ben-Zvi, 'the twins', were soon on board a filthy refugee ship, crowded and insanitary, zigzagging its way around the coast, taking them to the chief port of Egypt, Alexandria.

As they sailed across the Eastern Mediterranean, another expedition was also heading for Egypt. Djemal was assembling his massive army to cross the Sinai Peninsula to the Egyptian border, ready to wreck British shipping by cutting off the Suez Canal. Ben-Gurion could not have anticipated that this invasion would cause the British government to change its attitude to Palestine. It emphasized the ease with which troops coming from Palestine could sabotage the Suez Canal. The need to extend the buffer zone around Egypt would be more apparent than ever before.

THIRTEEN

In the Realm of the Pharaohs

Therefore shall the strength of Pharaoh be your shame,
And the trust in the shadow of Egypt your confusion.

Isaiah 30:3

Alexandria appeared flat and low in an early-morning haze; smoke drifted through the late January sunshine. Passengers stood around on the wharves in awkward, perplexed groups, enjoying the fresh air after four days below deck. They had just walked down the gangplanks from the *Tennessee*, the American ship that in December 1914 and January 1915 was providing a free shuttle service for refugees from Jaffa and Jerusalem. English officers with breezy, cheerful voices seemed to be all over the place. The Jews were safe in port, but where were they to go? Stories of overcrowding and problems at the refugee camps, now with 9,000[1] men, women and children, made them hope and pray that another destination would be suggested.

Egypt, which Napoleon had called the crossroads of the world, the meeting point of the three continents of Europe, Asia and Africa, was now on its way to becoming a vast British military camp in the Middle East, a springboard from which to attack Turkey, Palestine, Syria and Mesopotamia. Anxious to keep the Suez Canal, the lifeline to Britain's colonies and dominions, open, the place was filling up with British, Australian and Indian soldiers. Within a few weeks of Turkey's declaration of war, British officials in Cairo had deposed the pro-Turkish sultan of Egypt in a bloodless coup, and replaced him with the pro-British Sultan Ahmed Fuad (the grandfather of King Farouk).

Alexandria was bristling with activity and bustle, especially the harbour, crowded with thickets of masts and funnels. The war had been going on for only five months and was still centred on the Western Front, but already Cairo, Alexandria and Port Said were at bursting point. Some of the more resolute refugees, like Ben-Gurion and Ben-Zvi, who had been interrogated by the British as suspect aliens on arrival at the end of March, were making plans to continue their journey and find a passage to New York. Neutral America still showed no indication of entering the war. Most of the refugees, however, had little choice but to stay in Egypt and await their fate. Like their biblical ancestors, their presence in the land of the Nile was in no sense their own choice.

The British provided the refugees with barracks, money and a special department for refugees' affairs. Help also came from the large groups of Jews in the south-west of the city, descendants of those who had lived there since Cleopatra had paid dearly for dallying with Julius Caesar and Mark Antony. The first refugees had been temporarily herded into the Hotel Metropole, 'a stuffy unattractive building which sounded finer than it really was'. Four hundred went to live in a converted cinema, which was donated by a local Jewish businessman. With the help of soldiers from the Australian Expeditionary Force, which had recently arrived in Egypt, 1,200 were moved into the military barracks, under the charge of the kindly Mr Hornblower in the suburb of Gabbari surrounded by sand, huts, tents and soldiers with fixed bayonets. Temperatures in Egypt during the winter of 1914/15 were lower than usual, and even soldiers complained of ice-cold nights and having to sleep on groundsheets in the open until tents arrived from England. It was worse for the refugees. But soon temporary sheds and kitchens were put up to take the overflow.

Between 10,000 and 12,000 of the 18,000 deportees and refugees from Palestine and Syria ended up in Alexandria. Loneliness, lack of cash, squalor, overcrowding, flies and a feeling of desperation gave rise to both a lingering odour and endless internal tensions. Disputes were varied. Ashkenazis and Sephardis would not eat from the same soup-kitchens; language, too, became a source of domestic conflict. In the refugee camp a small group of former students from the Gymnasium in Tel Aviv remained mute if addressed in anything but Hebrew. They considered European languages to be the languages of exile.

The barracks were a far cry from Shepheard's Hotel, the giddy centre of social life 130 miles away in Cairo. With its palm trees and aspidistras, men in linen suits and women in crêpe de Chine dresses, thick damask tablecloths set with the heavy silver-plated cutlery, Shepheard's was the most famous attraction in Egypt after the Pyramids. Not far behind were the tennis courts and wicker chairs on the lawns of the smarter clubs such as the Turf Club and the Khedivial Sporting Club (Ghezira).

While such places represented another world, and most refugees would have welcomed any alternative to the dreary and crowded life in the camp, only a small number considered volunteering to serve in the British army. There were several reasons for this. First, because of the requirement for the oath of allegiance, only British nationals could then serve as soldiers in the British army. Secondly, as we have seen, Russia was hated by a large number of Jews who had suffered from their merciless pogroms and persecution. While the majority in the camps were pro-English, most, but not all, were unequivocal in their reluctance to fight on the same side as Russia. So the Jewish refugees were divided as to whether to back Britain and her ally Russia, or Germany – until the war the Zionists had their head office in Berlin.

The lack of intelligence about Turkish troop movements was hampering the Allies, and contributed to the resounding defeat of the Russians by Turkish troops at the foot of the Lesser Caucasus, at the end of December. Worse was to come. The British did not realize that 25,000 Turkish troops were being assembled to cross the burning sands of the Sinai Peninsula to attack the Suez Canal under the command of Djemal Pasha. Extraordinary though it was, this man, who was Minister of the Marine and whose real place was surely in the navy, was leading a campaign across a near waterless desert.

At the end of January, Djemal was only a few hundred miles away from Alexandria. In just two weeks, in seven night marches, his army of 22,000 Anatolian Turks, Armenians, Kurds and Arabs with 11,000 camels crossed the 150 miles of desert. Speed was imperative, as the Turks and the Germans hoped that the Egyptians would still be fired up by the pamphlets containing the words of the jihad from Constantinople. Egypt seemed ripe for a popular uprising. The British occupation of Egypt was so unpopular that Djemal was in no doubt that the Egyptians would assist their fellow-Muslims and rise against the Infidel. Djemal wrote in his memoirs, 'In any other than the rainy season it would be impossible to attempt to cross this waste with an expeditionary force. . . . Even a force of only 10,000 men could not be brought through. As the rainy season in this desert comprises the months of December and January only, it was necessary to conclude the operation in those two months or postpone it to the same season in the next year.'

As they marched, dragging guns, boats and pontoons towards the Suez Canal so they could cut it off from the rest of Egypt, rain set it. Before he had left Constantinople Djemal had made a public declaration, 'I shall not return to Constantinople until I have conquered Egypt!' On hearing that Djemal had been hailed the 'Saviour of Egypt', Morgenthau was provoked to liken his stance to that of Mark Antony: 'Like his Roman predecessor, his private life was profligate; like Antony, he was an insatiate gambler, spending much of his leisure over the card table at the Cercle d'Orient. Another trait which he had in common with the great Roman orator was his enormous vanity.'

On 3 February the Turkish flotilla was launched on the Suez Canal, only to be repulsed by British and colonial troops. By evening the Turks retreated, leaving 700 prisoners and having suffered 2,000 casualties. Djemal had failed. Both the Germans and the Turks had overrated the Muslim faith as a force for unity, as the Egyptians had remained indifferent to their co-religionists. But flawed as this attack had been, it forced the British to maintain large forces in Egypt which might otherwise have been used to advantage against the Turks in other parts of the Middle East or against the Germans in Europe.

Soon, however, the British would support an Arab revolt in the Hejaz which would take the Holy City of Mecca out of the Turkish Empire.

* * *

Jews and Arabs had never fought against each other in battle until Gallipoli, in May 1915, when a large number of Arab officers were sent there as part of Djemal's way of quashing the growth of the Arab nationalist movement. At Gallipoli, Jew also fought Jew. Exactly how many Jews were in the Ottoman army is not known, but there were half a million Jewish soldiers serving in the German and aligned armies. In Germany itself, at least 100,000 Jews, including 4,000 officers, were enlisted.[2] Alongside them were 300,000 Jewish soldiers in the Austro-Hungarian forces, including 25,000 officers. None of them, though, commanded a specifically Jewish regiment. The Turkish army, which comprised around 2,700,000 men, included about 20,000 Jews spread among various regiments. France had about 55,000 Jewish soldiers, of whom 9,500 were killed in action. A far larger number of Jews fought against the Allies than were in the British or French armies. Counting *all* Jewish soldiers in the regiments of the British Empire, they only numbered an estimated 50,000, of which 2,300 were from Australia and of whom 8,600 were killed in action.[3] Many distinguished themselves in battle and five were awarded the Victoria Cross.

In January 1915 the British War Council agreed 'to bombard part of the Gallipoli Peninsula with Constantinople as its objective'. Not only did Britain send the largest fleet of warships ever assembled, the fleet itself was led by the *Queen Elizabeth*, then the largest battleship in the world. On 19 February the fleet set off to take the legendary peninsula. But defeat followed. Most of the damage to the British ships was caused by brilliant new technology, underwater mines, explosive charges fitted with detonators to make them blow up when hit beneath the waterline. After eight hours the British ships returned. The mightiest sea power the world had ever known had been held in check by a much smaller nation, because of new technology. Two further attempts met with equal failure.

The War Cabinet in London decided to send a combined naval and armed force of 75,000 troops, including 16,000 Australian and New Zealand troops. These men would storm over the peninsula, capture the fortified mountain slopes and overwhelm the Turks and, with reinforcements, continue to Constantinople. Owing to the steep terrain at Gallipoli there was no role for mounted troops there, at least not in the early stages. One thing that would be needed, though, would be mules, both for transport and for an ambulance service.

Two Russian Zionists, Captain Joseph Trumpeldor and Vladimir (Ze'ev) Jabotinsky met for the first time in 1915 in Alexandria, and were soon working together to raise a Jewish battalion to fight the Turks. Jabotinsky, then an energetic 36-year-old journalist and writer and one of the most colourful characters in modern Jewry, was on an assignment for his Moscow newspaper. He had translated Dante's *Inferno* into Hebrew in his spare time, and a couple of his essays had won praise from Tolstoy. Short in stature, excitable, earnest and a non-stop talker, in conversation he could switch quickly between English, Russian, German, French and Hebrew. Born in Odessa, and known for his charm, he had earlier combined work and study in Switzerland and Italy while earning his living by writing articles for Russian newspapers. As well as being talented he had been an active member of the Odessa self-defence force and a keen Zionist. When he visited the refugee camp in December he was pleased to find 'a lively Zionist atmosphere'.

For the reasons stated above the efforts of Jabotinsky and Trumpeldor to form a Jewish battalion were not getting very far. To get around the problem of swearing an oath of allegiance to the king, Sir John Maxwell, the British commander in Egypt, designated the 'Zion Mule Corps', as a support, not a fighting, unit. Their job would be to bring water and ammunition to the front, with the help of mules, and take the injured to base. Despite the ill-feeling towards Russia, 650 men enlisted. Their commander, Lieutenant-Colonel John 'Pat' Patterson, a regular army officer in the Royal Engineers who had fought in the Boer War fifteen years earlier, made sure they were armed; they were issued with some of the 2,500 rifles captured from the Turks during their Suez débâcle. He also persuaded the military authorities to provide his men with kosher food and unleavened bread for their Passover celebration during their training in Egypt.

Patterson, a wiry, moustached Irishman in solar topee and jodhpurs, had reinvented himself, from a private in the Dragoons to gentleman adventurer on the fringes of colonial society. The author of a book based on his adventures in Uganda and Kenya, *The Man-eaters of Tsavo*, his name was esteemed among big-game hunters in Europe and America. He was once at the centre of a scandalous love affair immortalized in Ernest Hemingway's short story made into a Hollywood movie of the same name, *The Macomber Affair* (1947), with Gregory Peck playing Patterson. In yet another safari melodrama, *The Ghost and the Darkness* (1996), he was portrayed by Michael Douglas.

Responses to the formation of the new corps were mixed. Jabotinsky, disgusted at the Jewish unit being downgraded into 'a donkey battalion', left for England. He said that both its name and its role were demeaning and asked, 'Will Jews enter Zion on mules?' For the corps itself, army life and mule-training proved more than challenging. One member, M.A. Teram, later wrote:

> Sleeping on the ground proved rather a trial, while shaving, a novelty to the majority, was enforced, with the result that the first-aid tent had lines of men lining up outside with bleeding chins, waiting to have their cuts attended. What mules! Originated from the interior of Africa, they were wild, and had never had a saddle on their backs. For a few days the men who had never handled a saddle and the mules who had never seen one hated each other with fiendish intensity. Many a bruise, a broken leg or arm was reported. In three weeks they were informed to pack up for the Front – for Gallipoli. Our regiment which was composed of 600 men were shipped aboard two boats at Alexandria. At Limnos our ship ran aground and . . . pulled on a rope as thick as a tree trunk, trying to bring the relief ship close to the stranded vessel. And then commenced the transfer of mules and stores through the long weary night – all for the rebuilding of a Jewish State in Palestine.[4]

Trumpeldor, quiet and dignified, joined Patterson as deputy commanding officer of the mule corps. Described as 'a romantic figure', he was tall, handsome and fine-featured, with the bearing of a gentleman officer. Coming from the northern Caucasus, Trumpeldor, a vegetarian and socialist, had been strongly influenced in his youth by the model of collective communal life at a nearby farming commune set up by followers of Tolstoy. After losing his left arm almost to the shoulder when fighting during the seven-month siege of Port Arthur in the 1904 Russo-Japanese war, he had gone back to the front, winning four Crosses of St George and becoming one of the tsar's first Jewish officers. He had taught himself to dress, shave, eat, shoot a gun, and ride, with one arm but, unable to continue practising as a dentist, he studied law before joining the new wave of young idealistic socialists coming to start a new life in Palestine in the agricultural commune of Degania (cornflower).

From first to last the Gallipoli campaign was hindered by mismanagement and weak command. This was demonstrated even while the ships were loading. With 80,000 Allied troops gathering in Alexandria waiting to board the fleet, dozens of agents in Cairo and Athens were able to convey the news of the preparations to the Turks, who, under the command of the German Liman von Sanders and Mustafa Kemal, started safeguarding the fifty-two miles of headland at Gallipoli against attack.

The Zion Mule Corps, comprising 600 muleteers and their mules, was divided into four groups, each with a Jewish and a British officer. Loading animals on to ships was not easy at the best of times, but with men who had only trained for three weeks, getting them into pulleys and hoisting them up to the decks of the *Hymettus* and *Anglo-Egyptian* without breaking their legs was more than difficult. When the invasion took place on 25 April 1915, the Germans and Turks had had plenty of warning and, as unsettled weather had delayed the invasion, time to prepare their defences. Half the mule corps disembarked with the 29th Division at Cape helles with Patterson and Trumpeldor, and the other half at Ariburnu – the 'Cape of Bees', named after the wild bumble bee colonies in the cliff face, which became known as Anzac Cove, the acronym for the Australian & New Zealand Army Corps who were based there.

For some undisclosed reason, the 300 muleteers at Anzac were sent back to Egypt after two weeks. The other 300 continued to serve, despite the difficult conditions, with distinction. Deadlocked at three beachheads, each hemmed in by apparently impregnable positions on higher ground, the British invasion was a complete disaster, despite about 480,000 Allied troops taking part in the campaign.

As spring progressed the weather became oppressively hot and diarrhoea and dysentery were rife. As the bodies of the dead rotted huge flies known as bluebottles filled the air and crept over the food, bringing with them more dysentery and enteritis. At the end of November it rained ceaslessly for twelve hours. Trenches became canals, dugouts became cisterns, and raging torrents ran through gullies. Then the wind changed to the north as the frost set in. At midnight snow began to fall, and at daybreak the whole peninsula was white. Water supplies were still desperately inadequate as the regular supply from the boats could not be landed.

With British casualties of over 200,000, including 43,000 dead and 90,000 evacuated sick, the Gallipoli campaign has been rated as one of the greatest disasters in British military history. In contrast to the campaign itself, the departure of the troops in December and January was a triumph, without losses. After the evacuation Liman von Sanders described in *Five Years in Turkey*[5] 'wagon and automobile parts, mountains of arms, ammunition and entrenching tools' left behind. The saddest thing he found were the rows of dead horses 'shot or poisoned' but quite a number of horses and donkeys were still wandering around, and were turned over to the Turkish artillery.' Once back in Egypt the Zion Mule Corps was disbanded. But their excellent performance augured well for the future of the formation of another all-Jewish unit within the British army.

The catastrophic failure of the Gallipoli campaign was a victory for the 'Westerners' who argued that it was better to concentrate as much force as possible in France and Belgium. As the whole operation had been strongly promoted by Churchill, its failure counted against him, and for a while, hindered his progress in the government. His theory that the campaign would take Turkish pressure off the Russians, and would also create a diversion from the deadlocked Western Front and counter Turkey's threat to the Suez Canal, had been wrong on every count. Until there was a change of government in Britain it would now be more difficult to put forward a case for an invasion of Palestine.

Despite the disaster, in Alexandria 120 men of the Zion Mule Corps volunteered for enlistment in the British army. On their trip back to England their ship was one of the casualties of war, and was hit either by a submarine or mine. Clutching on to the wreckage, all 120 men managed to get ashore, and, in a roundabout way, arrived in England after many adventures. Already

Jabotinsky, Trumpeldor and Patterson had arrived in London and all three were exerting pressure on the authorities for a separate battalion of Jews to be formed. But requests for these men to become a separate troop in the 20th London Regiment were refused.

* * *

Jabotinsky was then staying in rooms at 3 Justice Walk, off Old Church Street, Chelsea, which Weizmann had rented as a small house was within walking distance of both the Lister Institute on the Thames and the Smith Street Synagogue. Trumpeldor was living nearby at 29 Shawfield Street, off the King's Road. Throughout the bitter winter of 1916/17, Jabotinsky had continued his effort to raise a combat unit of Jews to fight in Palestine. He walked from Chelsea to government offices in Whitehall, knocked on doors and handed in his beautifully printed visiting card.[6] Born politician that he was, Jabotinsky would not have succeeded without the support and connections of Weizmann, who wrote in his memoirs, 'It is almost impossible to describe the difficulties and disappointments which Jabotinsky had to face. I know of few people who could have stood up to them, but his pertinacity, which flowed from his devotion, was simply fabulous. He was discouraged and derided on every hand. . . . The Zionist Executive was of course against him; the non-Zionist Jews looked on him as a sort of portent.'

Trumpeldor and Jabotinsky, with help from Amery, then presented a petition to Lloyd George, requesting the formation of a Jewish Legion. As an earnest of his unwavering belief in the need to weld Jews together into a cohesive fighting unit, Jabotinsky then signed up as an ordinary soldier with the 20th London Regiment. Jewish people, he argued, needed to acquire military discipline and prove themselves in the eyes of the world by taking part in winning the land they wanted to inhabit.

FOURTEEN

A New Empire from Cairo to the Persian Gulf

Ye daughters of Israel, weep over Saul,
Who clothed you in scarlet with other delights,
Who put on ornaments of gold upon your apparel.
How are the mighty fallen in the midst of battle!

1 Samuel 1:24–25

On 6 December 1916, the day Lloyd George was made prime minister, the rains came in Mesopotamia. And came in torrents. Earth was turned into mud; the loamy soil became a slimy surface, the Tigris was clogged up with yellow sand and so heavy was the rain that it swept away bridges. At night men, wet and cold, did not have enough shelter. It seemed as if once more a British invasion was to be hampered by the weather; but somehow the aircraft managed to bomb enemy trenches. Major General Stanley Maude, with his 150,000 troops, had started a second invasion towards Baghdad a few months earlier. Lurching with their heavy loads, horses, mules and camels squelched their way through mud, and the soldiers were never sure if their rifles would fire, or jam. This campaign, which had begun modestly in Basra in 1914, had been fraught with high casualties, death, disease and few successes, but the territory was needed by Britain because of the oil in the Persian Gulf area and for its strategic position as the Arab world's frontier with Persia, Afghanistan and India. Before the war the Anglo-Persian Oil Company had built an oil refinery in Southern Iran which supplied most of the petroleum needed by the British armed forces during the First World War. As the oil was transported to the British Protectorate of Kuwait in the Persian Gulf, it was imperative to keep control of the area. Eleven months earlier, in January, February and March, during abortive attempts to relieve the garrison at Kut, the number of those killed, wounded or starving had been worryingly high. Even dogs, cats and horses had been eaten. When the death toll had reached 38,000, the garrison had hoisted a white flag. The 13,000 survivors marched off into captivity in Turkey. Half died on the march or during imprisonment.

The war was going badly for the Allies. On 15 December when Haig was briefly back in London, he and Robertson saw Lloyd George in Downing Street. Haig wrote in his diary: 'He pointed out the need for an early success and was anxious to make an attack on El Arish and so towards Jerusalem . . .'. Spiralling death rates had forced the British government to introduce conscription. Not even at the height of the Napoleonic Wars had this extreme measure come into force. Under the Military Service Act of 1916 any able-bodied British male unmarried national aged between eighteen and forty-one (soon to be extended to fifty-one and married men) was forced to sign on and take the oath of allegiance to the king. Jews born in Britain were considered British subjects, even if their parents had not been naturalized, but as most were foreign-born the majority could not take the oath. At least 10,000 Jews, of whom 1,140 were officers, had volunteered before conscription. Confusion over status was seen in an article in the *Jewish Chronicle* in November 1915. It gave examples of recruiting officers saying 'Lord Kitchener does not want any more Jews in the Army' and 'We are not enlisting Jews'.[1] But accusations that Jews, especially in the East End, were not joining up continued. Weizmann pleaded with local Jews to support the Allies. But he was met with a disheartening response.

* * *

On Sunday 11 March 1917, in soaring temperatures and in the midst of an almost blinding dust storm, Baghdad fell. Within hours a captain of the East Kent Regiment hoisted the Union Jack on the Citadel. As the remainder of the 100,000 British troops advanced, the sun caught the gold-covered minarets and domes of the great mosques. Later, in the heart of the city, the British gunboat flotilla anchored in the river opposite the mansion of the former governor, now the British residency. By the end of the campaign 52,000 men would be dead, including the Commander-in-Chief Maude, and more than twice that number wounded, among them Clement Attlee, who was evacuated to Bombay via Basra. The situation in Iraq remained dire for both the conquered and the conquerors. Hunger, disease and death were rampant.

Soon 3,000 British administrators would start arriving. Baghdad was the third of the legendary cities of the Ottoman Empire to be captured in the past year. The first had been the Turkish garrison in Medina and a month later, Mecca. These had fallen during the Arab Revolt initiated by Sherif Hussein, descendant of the prophet Mohammed, guardian of the holy places in Mecca and Medina and as such an influential figure in the Muslim world. The actual field operations of the revolt in mid-1916 were led by Hussein's sons, Feisal and Abdullah, assisted by British liaison officers, including T.E. Lawrence who would immortalize the revolt in *Seven Pillars of Wisdom*. The next city which the Allies planned to take would be Gaza. And then, Jerusalem.

Baghdad partly vindicated Lloyd George's policy of swinging away from the Western Front; but it was obvious that the destinies of the world still hinged on the coming campaigns on the Western Front.

The War Cabinet in London had a new problem. It had hoped that Russian troops would force Mosul from the north. But three days before the fall of Baghdad, on 8 March 1917, the Russian Revolution had broken out in Petrograd. Tsar Nicolas abdicated a week later, ending the 300-year-old rule of the Romanov dynasty. The withdrawal of Russia's army would be a catastrophe for the Allies – worse would be Russia making its own peace with the Germans. One belief current at the time was that support for Zionism would detach Russian Jews from the Bolshevik party, which would help keep the Revolution moderate and also ensure that Russia remain an ally of France and Britain.[2] But the moderate provisional government was soon to be overturned by the Bolsheviks with their cry for 'Peace and Land', which appealed to soldiers and peasants. As they were led by Vladimir Ilich Lenin (whose brother had been executed by Nicolas's father), who was said to be half-Jewish, and Leon Trotsky, who was also Jewish, along with some other revolutionaries responsible for organizing the November Revolution, their actions fuelled anti-Jewish feelings.

* * *

Then Turkey turned the tables on Britain. Their first major victory against the Turks in Mesopotamia was still being celebrated when the British lost the battle of Gaza of 26 March 1917. The city was encircled by British forces, who entered overnight, but by the next morning were forced to retreat. At least 1,500 British dead were buried by the Turks, who also took a large number of prisoners and captured twelve machine-guns and twenty of the latest automatic rifles. In all the British dead were at least 4,000. But as General Murray's report to the War Cabinet was optimistic he was ordered to attack again. It was imperative that he break through into Palestine.

Palestine and Egypt have always shared an extensive frontier on the Sinai Desert. Britain like every earlier ruler of Egypt, from the pharaohs and Cleopatra to the Mameluks,[3] cherished the ambition of having a foothold in Palestine. The Mameluks and Fatimids had actually achieved this in the last thousand years. Whoever controls Palestine can prevent hostile penetration into Egypt. Since 1869 the Suez Canal became a priority for Britain. Britain also needed a deep port in the eastern Mediterranean, such as Haifa on the Palestine coast, as a destination for an overland pipe from the Persian Gulf through which oil could flow and be shipped out.

General Smuts reinforced Lloyd George's policy by saying that the initiative should be seized from the flagging hands of the French on the Western Front and that the British should invade Palestine. The second Battle of Gaza in April was another disaster, with British losses totalling 6,444 men. Since Lloyd George had taken over as prime minister the British army had been beaten by the Turks in two battles at Gaza/Beersheba, even though in the second confrontation the British army had resorted to a careful use of gas. Insidious fumes of toxic gases had been part of warfare in Europe since 1915, but chemical warfare had not been introduced into the Middle East until then. This time, though, it failed.

Turkish defences were so formidable that eighteen months had passed since Murray's army had advanced from the Suez Canal slowly across the desert of the Sinai Peninsula. 'Wriggling across the desert like giant pythons', were the words used by military historian B.H. Liddell Hart. Mark Sykes in Cairo telegraphed London that if the British army in Egypt was not reinforced, it would be necessary 'to drop all Zionist projects . . . Zionists in London and USA should be warned of this . . .'.

The War Office responded by sacking Murray. There were plans for an even larger invasion into Palestine and Syria. As Lloyd George's first nominee as commander of this operation, Smuts, decided to stay in England, where he could help set up the League of Nations, General Sir Edmund Allenby, a cavalry officer, was recalled from France and appointed to lead the Egyptian Expeditionary Forces.

When Allenby visited Downing Street *en route* to the new front in the Middle East in the late spring of 1917, Lloyd George asked him to speed up the taking of Jerusalem, giving him less than six months to get through the Gaza/Beersheba gateway and over the steep barren hills of Judah to the Holy City. The capture of Jerusalem was seen as desirable and 'as a Christmas present for the British nation'. It was felt that a victory and a diversion were required for the public to offset the news of the horrific death toll in Europe. No other destination on earth could have had such a spiritual or sentimental appeal. As Muslims had been in control of the Holy City for over twelve centuries, the idea of its conquest stirred the imagination of Christians throughout the world.

Lloyd George also instructed Allenby to read *Historical Geography of the Holy Land* by Sir George Adam Smith, former professor of Old Testament Subjects at the United Free Church College, in Glasgow.[4] The book covered over 150 biblical sites and the routes of all the invading armies of the past. Lloyd George added jokingly that it probably contained more of practical value than could be found in War Office surveys. This popular book, summarizing the work of the energetic surveyors of the Palestine Exploration Fund, was with Allenby, along with his Bible, when he departed from Charing Cross on 21 June. The Bible, which he read daily, was so important to him that when he was ennobled he became Lord Allenby of Megiddo, the Old Testament battlefield which he was to turn into a twentieth-century theatre of war.

To oblige the War Cabinet, Allenby planned a rapid breakthrough at Gaza. He received extra aeroplanes, battalions and battleships, and also 10,000 cans of asphyxiating gas to knock out the Turks. At fifty-seven, with his clipped moustache and his immaculate uniform with its gold braid and tabs, he was set in his ways and castigated anyone who split infinitives (even in a telegram) or looked untidy. In his younger days his appearance had earned him the nickname of 'apple pie', but on the Western Front his explosive temper was so notorious that he was referred to as 'the Bull', and he was said to make grown men shake. Brigadier-General Archibald Wavell, who served under him, wrote, '. . . in spite of his volcanic outbursts of temper, his attitude to men was at bottom kindly and tolerant'.

FIFTEEN

The Jewish Legion

But I say unto you, swear not at all, either by heaven, for it is God's throne; nor by the earth, for it is his footstool, neither by Jerusalem; for it is the city of the great King.

Matthew 5:34–35

On 7 July 1917, in broad daylight, a fleet of twenty-two Gotha aircraft flew from Germany across the sea and dropped bombs on the East End of London. Buildings crashed to the ground, huge fires ignited and 195 civilians were killed or wounded. British anti-aircraft guns had failed to hit even one plane. All twenty-two planes flew safely back to Germany. This had been the largest raid on London to date, and a tremendous outcry followed. What was Lloyd George's War Cabinet doing? Amid the uproar a small paragraph appeared in *The Times* on 28 July, stating that the War Office's arrangements were nearing completion for a Jewish infantry regiment which would wear a representation of King David's shield as a regimental badge. A month later, on 23 August, a notice appeared in the *London Gazette* inviting Jews to join the newly formed special Jewish regiment. Jabotinsky's persistence had paid off. These announcements coincided with plans for an even larger invasion into Palestine and Syria. Only a month had passed since Allenby had arrived at the British camp east of Gaza to reorganize the battalions and prepare to break through into the Holy Land.

Some Jews joined up to fight for 'King and Country', others to strengthen the cause of Zionism. Tremendous adjustments had been made to bring this unit into being, but the intensifying struggle against Germany allowed for changes that would have been unthinkable in peacetime. Not since the Catholic Relief Bill of 1829, which had taken away the legal impediments stopping Roman Catholics taking a commission in the army, had so many obstacles been removed so quickly. But this was war.

To have a separate named unit fighting with the Allies was the first practical step for the Jews in making 'the Return to Zion' a reality in the new post-Ottoman era. The War Office hoped the unit would attract Russian Jews living in Britain who fell outside the conscription net. But why, it was asked, should Hebrew- and Yiddish-speaking troops be destined for Palestine in special units, with kosher food, and yet be an integral part of the British army? There were no Methodist, Presbyterian or Catholic regiments. But there were units of men with specific interests or backgrounds, such as the recently formed Artists' Rifles or the Pals' Brigades composed of soldiers from different towns or men of common interests. The Gurkhas from Nepal, also, had always been a welcome adjunct of the British army.[1]

The setting up of the Jewish Legion was the culmination of the persistent efforts of Jabotinsky and Trumpeldor. Jabotinsky might have been short of supporters, but among them were the energetic Amery and Ormsby-Gore, both of whom had earlier worked in the Arab Bureau in Egypt. Both also were Members of Parliament, assistant secretaries to the War Cabinet and had the full authority of junior ministers. Amery once explained that minor though his title was, it allowed him to sit in the House of Commons without having to answer questions there.

Distinguished by his brilliance (and by being even shorter in height than the prime minister), Amery, then forty-five, became champion in Whitehall of both the Jewish Homeland and the Jewish Legion. He frequently spent time at St James's Park, in the high-ceilinged rooms of the Athenaeum Club in Pall Mall, a club which attracted intellectuals. Genealogists have recently revealed that Amery was himself half-Jewish. His mother, Elisabeth Leitner, a Budapest Jewess, had converted to Christianity. With financial help from her brother she had put her son through Harrow, where he won a scholarship to Balliol and became a Fellow of All Souls, Oxford. Whether he acted as the non-stop negotiator for Zionist causes because of his ancestry, or because of his Protestant upbringing, will never be known. What is more certain is that without Amery's backing and his contacts with the War Secretariat, it is unlikely that the Jewish Legion would ever have been formed.

Amery persisted throughout 1916. In 1917 he laid Jabotinsky's petition before the War Cabinet. He was given much support and encouragement by Patterson, who stayed at the Cavalry Club in Piccadilly when in London and was keen to head another Jewish unit. He had become a passionate Zionist since his command of the Zion Mule Corps in Gallipoli. An outsider who had risen from private to officer, he did not fit in with the usual British officer set, but had found a niche for himself with the Jews. Many Jews believed that the land would be restored to them by prayer and waiting. The presentation of the petition coincided with more talks on the Jewish homeland and also with amendments in the recruitment of foreigners into the British army. An agreement with the other Allied governments now allowed each country to enlist the resident nationals of another. Russian Jews could now sign on more easily. The downfall of the tsar had lifted another barrier, and diluted much Jewish bitterness against Russia.

* * *

Jabotinsky persisted in his proposal that the Jewish Legion should only fight against the Turks in Palestine. Opposition came from all quarters. The fact that the Jews had a non-combatant image was used against them, as was the fact that they were generally regarded as an unknown quantity as fighters. The Earl of Derby, then the Minister of War and a born negotiator, decided personally to sort out the problem. Bluff, blunt and boisterous, this friend of King George V had more of the air of a down-to-earth farmer than a peer of the realm. With his huge girth and loud laughter, Derby was one of the last of the great English magnates to enjoy political power gained from the ownership of land. Derby's solution to Jabotinsky's suggestion was to deprive the Jewish Legion of the name 'Jewish', and treat it as any other British regiment to be sent wherever required. But this was not an acceptable solution, and Wickham Steed, then a journalist for *The Times* and soon to be its editor, saved the day with an editorial in which he ridiculed the War Office for concerning itself with a handful of plutocrats, stressing that the unit's Jewish character must be safeguarded and it should be sent only to Palestine. Derby again changed his mind. The regiment would be purely Jewish after all and it would be sent only to Palestine. But the use of the Hebrew name and badge would be delayed. This unique unit was listed on the rolls as the 38th Battalion of the Royal Fusiliers, the City of London Regiment, but the press always referred to it as either 'the Jewish Regiment' or 'the Jewish Legion' or 'the Judeans'.

Tradition and precedent were to be broken, but compromises abounded. Regimental distinctions would only be granted once the regiment had proved its capabilities, once it had been blooded in battle. The soldiers could wear the six-pointed Star of David, the *Magen David*, on their sleeves; the words on the signboard outside the London recruiting office were in Hebrew; a Jewish chaplain was enlisted, the Revd Leiber Falk (who named his son Balfour), as were kosher cooks to prepare special food; instructions were to be given in English and in Hebrew – not the frequently used Yiddish; Saturday would be a day of rest; and so far as military exigencies permitted, other religious festivals, like Passover and Yom Kipper, could be celebrated.

One reason for the hostility felt towards the Jewish Legion was that its formation was the first practical outcome of the Lloyd George coalition's known commitment towards the Jewish homeland. While the Legion was a reality, the undertaking made by the British government to set up a Jewish homeland could only be notional until the Turks were driven out of Palestine. A few battles would have to be fought before any part of the Holy Land could become part of the British Empire. Only then could it be coloured pink on the atlases of the world, like India and Australia.

The announcement of the formation of the 38th Battalion added another dimension to the Jewish-Zionist debate. Jews were seen as nationalists without a country; most were foreigners; many could not speak English. How could an army unit comprise people who had no national territory of their own? Complications also arose, as the word 'Jew' referred to a religion and could also be the name of a race. The journalist and historian Lucien Wolf, an anti-Zionist who believed that the Jewish population should go no further than enjoying equal political rights with the other inhabitants of Palestine, protested that it was dangerous for the Jewish people if it was accepted that the Jews were a separate nationality or race. Such a definition would give European countries cause to expel Jews, rather than consider them citizens of the country they lived in. But the perception of Jews as a separate nationality was the very point that Weizmann, who had been elected as president of the British Zionist Federation in February, used to strengthen the case for Zionism.[2] The *Daily News* printed an article on 17 September 1917 by the Right Hon. G.W.E. Russell, who quoted Wolf, 'The Jews are neither a nation within a nation, nor cosmopolitan'. He added that they were 'an integral part of the nations among whom they live, claiming the same duties. . . . They need no special standard, no differentiating motto. They are soldiers of the country to which they belong.'

Questions were asked as to why support should be given to the World Zionist Organization, which had been mostly active in mainland Europe. During the war its headquarters had been moved from Germany to Copenhagen, not to London.

Some of the strongest opposition to the Jewish Legion came from the Jews themselves who pointed out that Jews in such a unit might end up fighting fellow Jews conscripted into enemy armies. Just how improbable it was that the British should have created a unit of Jews can be seen by looking at the armies of other countries. No counterpart to the British Jewish unit then existed in the French, Russian, Austro-Hungarian or German armies. So when Britain created a Jewish Legion before announcing its commitment to a Jewish homeland, the news was a shock. Arguments against it ranged from soldiering being incompatible with Judaism to Zionism being too closely identified with Britain. Most young, able-bodied Jews in Palestine had either been exiled by the Turks, sent into labour gangs or conscripted into the Turkish army so life could well become perilous for the Jewish women, children and old men in Palestine. If a Jewish Legion were formed within the framework of the British army, would the Jews of other countries suffer reprisals? The divergence between Zionist and non-Zionist Jews of the time was constantly aired in newspaper articles and letters.

One argument in favour of the Jewish Legion was that it would attract Jews, especially American and Russian Jews, to the Allied cause – and, perhaps, 'Jewish banking money'. Further concessions widened the recruitment net. Jewish soldiers serving in any British regiment could request a transfer. The process, though, was slow. Among those who applied and failed was the poet Isaac Rosenberg, then serving with the Royal Lancasters on the Western Front. It took four months for Russian-born Lieutenant Eliezer Margolin, who had served at Gallipoli and on the French Front, to be moved across. He underwent such a lengthy process of formally resigning before he could enlist with the Royal Fusiliers that it is unlikely that he would have managed to make the arrangements if he had not been in England recovering from an injury sustained in France. He had spent five years as a child with his parents in Palestine before migrating to Australia, and was keen to go.

The majority of Jews in the different Allied national armies did not try to become part of the legion. Most of the 5,000 Jews who enrolled were new recruits who enlisted after the regulation forbidding non-British nationals to enlist was relaxed. Only half were British-born or naturalized British citizens, the remainder being Russian Jews, including East End tailors, or Jews from Allied and neutral nations, from the Argentine and Poland to the United States and Romania. That fourteen languages were spoken in the legion is indicative of this varied background.

The role of the Jewish Legion in the Middle East, would always be overshadowed by Lawrence and his colourful band of Arab Irregulars led by Feisal and Nuri Bey. Like the Legion, this Arab army was active then in Palestine and Syria only because it suited British policy, and it, too, was working towards the same aim as other men in the Jewish Legion, to gain territory once the Turks were beaten. At this stage Arabs and Jews fighting side by side for the same goals did not appear to be incompatible.

SIXTEEN

The Fateful Embrace in the 'Garden Suburb': the Balfour Declaration

Do good in thy good pleasure unto Zion: build thou the walls of Jerusalem.

Psalm 51:18

On 2 November 1917 a group of politicians sitting either in 10 Downing Street or its walled garden, looking across Horse Guards' Parade from the garden hut that would be remembered as the 'Garden Suburb', were about to make a grandiose gesture towards the Jews. Nearly 1,800 years may have passed since the carnage wrought by Titus, but the historic connection of the Jewish people with this city from which they were banished was, it was hoped, to be restored. Eight members of the War Cabinet, together with Balfour, Amery, Sykes and Ormsby-Gore, finalized the blueprint for Jewish nationhood. Time was short. In a few days, with luck, Allenby's army would break through the Gaza/Palestine gateway and finish 400 years of Turkish rule. And the War Cabinet was about to add a third declaration to its two earlier agreements over territory in the Middle East.

First, there was the series of letters written in late 1915 and early 1916, known as the Hussein–MacMahon correspondence; and secondly, the Sykes–Picot Agreement between the French and the British made secretly in 1916. Letters between Sir Henry MacMahon on behalf of Britain and Sherif Hussein of Mecca on behalf of the Arabs, during the period 1915–16, laid down the terms of what the British would cede to the Arabs in return for Hussein initiating an Arab rebellion against the Turks in return for national independence after the war. As neither the precise borders of the future Arab state were agreed upon and as Palestine was not named in any of the letters, its status has been a source of dispute ever since. This correspondence remained secret until towards the end of the war, as did the Sykes–Picot Agreement. This agreement was also ambiguous over borders and the future administration of Palestine. Attached to the agreement was a map which marked in red zones of British influence and in blue zones of French influence. But because of Palestine's importance to three religions it had been marked as a brown zone, with this explanation: 'Palestine, with the holy places, is separated from Turkish territory and subjected to a special regime to be determined by agreement between Russia, France and Great Britain.'

The War Cabinet now needed a clear way to keep the French from disputing British control over Palestine. There was discussion as to whether Russia's withdrawal was enough to invalidate either the clause or the agreement: the regime change in Russia after the March Revolution nullified all Russia's contracts with the Allies. Would Georges Picot, who was then in Egypt, claim either a share in the administration or compete for control of it for France? French colonial pretensions dated back to the time of Napoleon. In the nineteenth century, France had set up a network of businesses and excellent schools in the Levant. In the Sykes–Picot agreement, France was to exercise direct control over the greater part of the Galilee area, while Britain would control the small territory around the Haifa-Akko bay. The remaining areas of Palestine, excluding Beersheba and the Negev Desert, were to be under joint administration. But the British did not want the French either on the threshold of Egypt or on the outskirts of the canal. One of the advantages of creating a Jewish national home in Palestine was that it gave a valid reason for blocking the French from taking the territory and stopping them relying solely on the earlier agreement.

Discussions about the possibility of a Jewish homeland in Palestine continued. Like many resolutions during the First World War, the policy of forming a settler-colony of Jewish people in Palestine was not debated in either the House of Commons or the House of Lords. The decision was made behind the closed doors of the War Cabinet (not to be confused with the War Secretariat, the Imperial War Cabinet or the cabinet itself), which had its first meeting on 9 December 1916, after Lloyd George succeeded Herbert Asquith as prime minister. Full details of conversations were not contained in the minutes of these meetings, nor were the conclusions.

Apart from ordering the invasion into Palestine in December 1916, Lloyd George's fascination was shown in his secret negotiations for peace with Turkey. Within months of becoming prime minister he entered into a dialogue with Basil Zaharoff, the international arms dealer whom he later knighted, to negotiate a separate peace with the sultan on condition that Britain was awarded Palestine and Mesopotamia. Lloyd George asked Zaharoff to attempt to negotiate a peace with Enver Pasha. He wanted Arabia to be independent, Armenia and Syria to have autonomy within the Ottoman Empire but for Mesopotamia and Palestine to become British protectorates with a relationship similar to that of Egypt to the Ottoman and British Empires before the war. France, Russia and Italy were not mentioned at all.[1] The meeting came to nothing, but Lloyd George's terms once again show his priorities to secure, at least, the area around Britain's oil supply. 'Motorization of the army' was the new slogan, but much oil was being used by the navy and the new Air Force. Without oil a great power is not a 'great power'.

In one of the papers in the bulky file F6/16 on the matter it is indicated that 'the Chairman' was a cover for Lloyd George himself. Under the headline 'Summary of Chairman's Personal Views', six lines spelt out a route to peace: 'To give as his personal opinion that Allies do not desire destruction of independent Ottoman State nor surrender of Constantinople but freedom of Straits to be secured. Arabia to be independent. Mesopotamia and Palestine to be Protectorates on analogy of Egypt before the War. Autonomy for Armenia and Syria. Capitulations to remain abolished and generous treatment to Turkey as regards finance. (handed to me by Mr Bonar Law)'. It was signed with initials VC – Vincent Caillard, a director of Vickers.

Another statement, dated 9 January 1918, marked 'Handed to me by Mr J.T. Davies, the PM.'s Private Secretary at 10 Downing Street, at 3.30 p.m. 9 Jan. 1918 . . . These reached Mr Z. before he started' mentions the sums of five million pounds sterling and two million pounds being paid to Turkey in return for the opening of the Dardanelles and the withdrawal of Turkish troops north of the railway line from Haifa to Deraa.

* * *

In London in the summer of 1917 the Garden Suburb group was enlarged to seven with two newcomers, Smuts and Edward Carson. This barrister, leader of the Ulster Unionists, MP for Dublin University and Attorney-General, was famed for his defence of the Marquess of Queensberry, the father of Oscar Wilde's lover, Lord Alfred Douglas, in Wilde's unsuccessful action for criminal libel. Carson had asked Wilde, 'Did you ever kiss him?' Wilde replied, 'Oh, dear no. He was a peculiarly plain boy . . .'. Wilde was subsequently prosecuted and imprisoned for homosexuality. As Wilde's biographer has written, 'What made Carson finished Wilde.'[2] Although christened into the

Church of Ireland Carson was a direct descendant of one of Oliver Cromwell's top generals and was so inclined to Ulster Protestantism (that is, Presbyterianism) that he was called the 'King of Ulster'.

Smuts's inclusion in the War Cabinet was fortuitous for Zionist policy. Born in 1870 in the Cape Colony, he had fought against the British in the Boer War and gone on to hold several cabinet offices in South Africa. Weizmann persuaded Smuts that it would be an historic justice to restore the People of the Book to the Land of the Bible, and the two men became lifelong friends.[3] An ardent Zionist sympathizer, Smuts felt an affinity with the ancient Hebrews, and put forward arguments in favour of the Jewish homeland and an invasion of Palestine. His outlook, common among many Dutch Reformed Protestants in South Africa, is seen in the speech 'I need not remind you that the white people of South Africa, and especially the older Dutch population, has been brought up almost entirely on Jewish tradition. The Old Testament, the most wonderful literature ever thought out by the brain of man, the Old Testament has been the very matrix of Dutch culture here . . . the day will come when the words of the prophets will become true, and Israel will return to its own land.'[4]

In early 1918 Austen Chamberlain, half-brother of Neville and son of Joseph, and raised as a Unitarian like his father, was added to the War Cabinet, along with Sir Eric Geddes, the First Lord of the Admiralty, who had been born in India, and was a Scottish Presbyterian. Minister for Transport Geddes was praised by Haig in a letter to his wife: 'Such a good fellow and has been the greatest help to the army in the matter of railways, roads, docks, etc.'.

When Arthur Henderson, who had taken over the leadership of the Labour Party during the war due to Ramsay MacDonald's pacificism, went to Russia to investigate the new Bolshevik government in Moscow in July 1917, his place in the War Cabinet was taken by George Barnes, another Labour man of Scottish ancestry and a Congregationalist. His memoirs *From Workshop to War Cabinet*[5] demonstrate his wit, especially when describing Lloyd George:

> . . . [he] like Father O'Flynn, has 'a wonderful way wid him.' In a physical sense he has not been endowed with any adventitious aid to power, for he is not a commanding figure, being under medium height and having a rolling gait as of a man top heavy. His power is in his daring assurance. He would descend on occasion upon the cabinet as from Olympian heights to deliver himself of a message as from the Gods and, hey presto, we would find ourselves borne along on the torrent of his words.

Lloyd George wanted to include his good friend Churchill either in his cabinet or appoint him as a minister, but, as he wrote in his *War Memoirs*, 'Unfortunately, the Tory Ministers, with the exception of Mr Balfour and Carson, were unanimous in their resolve that he should not be a member of the Ministry, and most of them made it a condition precedent to their entry into the Government that he should be excluded.' He went on to describe Bonar Law's 'profound distrust of him'. When, on 17 July, Churchill was given Lloyd George's old job as Minister of Munitions, Lloyd George wrote that 'Tory antipathy was so great that for a short while the very existence of the government was in jeopardy.' From then onwards, Churchill, an early supporter of the Zionist cause, joined in some of the Garden Suburb meetings.

* * *

Weizmann, meanwhile, called by Smuts the 'New Moses,'[6] was ceaselessly promoting the cause of the Zionists (Balfour and his under-secretary also his cousin), the tall, stooped, hawked-nosed Robert Cecil (later Lord Cecil of Chelwood), gave support for the idea of a Jewish homeland. But all this talk would come to nothing without a massive military invasion to push the Turks out of Palestine. The British needed to follow the paths of the Pharaohs and Mameluks before them, and move troops up from Egypt to Jerusalem. If Britain were to become the conquering nation its hand would be strengthened at the negotiating table against French claims. By defeating Turkey, Palestine, Mesopotamia and, perhaps, Syria would be brought under British control. Lloyd George told Lord Bertie, '. . . that the French will have to accept our protectorate; we shall be there by conquest and shall remain . . .'.[7]

Imperially minded Britons knew that since Napoleon's massive fleet had landed in Alexandria in 1798 the French had wanted to hold the Holy Land. French missionaries were active throughout Syria and Palestine, and their schools had transformed thousands of intelligent but illiterate Arabs into well-informed intellectuals, writers and poets. A Jewish homeland would provide a rational reason to block the French from taking too much territory in the Levant, and Jews would create a reliable and strong client population. Their presence would guarantee Britain a hold on this strategic area. If the Allies won the war, France would take the place of Germany and would be the most powerful nation on the continent. France's power would need to be checked. Britain did not want France also to be the dominant power in the Middle East.

At the end of 1917 the war was still going badly for the Allies in France. No one could forecast who would ultimately win. Mutinies were threatening the fighting spirit of the French army, and the German and Austrian forces were about to break through the Italian lines. When the United States declared war on Germany (but not on Turkey) Balfour led a 25-man delegation to Washington, asking for food, ships and money. The serious danger of Britain's financial collapse at the end of 1916 was saved by the United States's offer of massive loans. A request was also made to America for the speedy dispatch of troops to the Western Front. Balfour then went north to Canada, where conscription was being introduced. By the time he returned to England on 9 June he had been away for two months. During his absence, discussions had continued within the War Cabinet about the Jewish homeland, and a Jewish Legion. More thrust and vigour had also been put into the invasion of Palestine.

* * *

The millet system had provided a reasonably satisfactory *modus vivendi* between Muslim and Jew within the Ottoman Empire. In common with other foreigners living in the empire, Jews had special rights and privileges, including exemption from some taxes, called capitulations.[8] As Ottoman Jews had not been a source of trouble to the government, no national movement had developed against them, such as those against the Christians and the Armenians.[9] Nor had anti-Semitic violence taken place in Arab lands against Jews. Voltaire and Edward Gibbon had admired the tolerance of the Ottoman Empire to religious minorities. So, when the idea of increasing the number of Jews was discussed in London, it did not seem an unreasonable idea, especially as it was assumed that the move would also bring three commodities: money, expertise and energy. Lloyd George's former secretary, Dr Thomas Jones, explained, 'Palestine needed ports, electricity, and the Jews of America were rich and would subsidise such developments.'[10] Another point in favour of the Jews was their track record of transforming barren land. The new homeland, instead of being a country of Arab emigration, would become one of Arab immigration. Ormsby-Gore maintained that Jewish agronomists would make the desert bloom. The quality of life for the Arabs, too, it was thought, would be improved.

Since the wave of new settlers in the Holy Land after 1880 there had been many incidents, mostly over land tenure by displaced former tenant farmers or by landless Bedouin. Fences did not frighten the wild Bedouin tribes, compelled by drought, locusts and poverty to lead a nomadic existence. Their time-honoured grazing rights for their sheep and goats was often a matter of survival – as were old wells where they could dip their buckets. The creep of civilization has led to similar displacements throughout the world.

For decades the conflict between the Arabs and Jews has been so bloody that people wonder how the British ever agreed to increasing the Jewish population in Palestine. But the incessant Israeli–Arab struggle is not an extension of an old blood feud;[11] such a feud never existed. The Arabs and Jews living in Palestine *before* the First World War were not at each others' throats. Large numbers of Jews were well established in other parts of the Ottoman Empire. Muslims and Jews had lived in the Holy Land together for well over a thousand years, since 636 CE when Mohammad's successor, the Caliph Omar, captured it from the Byzantines. The only interruption had been the Crusaders. Always at the mercy of the Arabs there had been problems and antipathy, but no riots interfering with the slow pace of life. Indeed, the absence of conflict or persecution in the Holy Land had attracted Jews from Russia to seek refuge there. Despite tensions Muslims considered Jews as a 'People of the Book', respecting their religion while sharing their prophets and their God. Resentment and objections began only towards the end of the nineteenth century, when immigration numbers increased. Sustained organized hostility did not begin until *after* the First World War.

* * *

Apart from the revolt in the Hejaz, a well-organized independence movement in Egypt, and the Syrian movements around Beirut and Damascus, Arab nationalism, centred on the area later known as Palestine, was still in its infancy and lacked solidarity. The area was then known by its Arab-Muslim name of *al-Ard al-Muqadass* (the Holy Land) or *Surya al-Janubiyya* (Southern Syria) and had not been a separate political entity for 2,000 years. Nationalism was centred further north around Beirut and Damascus, which were open to American and French influences. Despite pleas for clemency from Feisal, Djemal had hanged at least twenty-one Arab nationalists, mostly intellectuals and musicians, in the city squares of Damascus and Beirut in August 1915 and May 1916. By this extreme action, and by sending Arab army officers suspected of being associated with secret societies, to distant fronts, such as Gallipoli, Djemal put a stop to any uprisings. One of the first of these Arab secret societies was Al Jamiyyah al Arabiyah al Fatat (the Young Arab Society, known as Al Fatat, not to be confused with Al Fatah, or Fatah, of the Palestine Liberation Organisation). Another was al-'Ahd ('the covenant between members and Allah in the service of the Fatherland'), a society of officers with a special sign language. Passionate and dedicated, they were all ready to take up arms to defend their own land and pay for its freedom with their lives. Many, including Nuri al-Sa'id, went on to become ministers in the future governments of Syria, Iraq, Transjordan and Lebanon. Membership, though, before and during the war was limited due to the fear of Turkish reprisals.

The nationalist rebels in Syria executed by the Turks during the war were mostly former pupils of one of the ninety-five American schools in Syria. American Protestant missionaries had established schools in Beirut in the 1820s, and all instruction was in Arabic, not English. One of their first tasks had been to translate the Bible into Arabic and print it on the first modern printing press in the Levant. At these schools, on the eve of the war, 5,300 students[12] were learning a new pride in their culture and history. The Syrian Protestant College, which had opened in 1886 in Damascus, was a throbbing intellectual centre, the very heart of the Arab Renaissance. The majority of Arabs then wanted reforms and independence within the Ottoman Empire, not autonomy. Nor were they seeking European 'liberators'. This was seen in 1916 when Australian prisoners-of-war from the Sinai, roped together, were paraded through the streets of large towns during their journey to the prison camp of Afion-Kara-Hissar in Turkey. Far from being welcomed, local men threw small stones at them and women hissed.[13] Paul Johnson sums up the effect of the Turks smashing the Syrian nationalist movements in *A History of the Jews*.[14] 'If the Arabs as a whole had been properly organized diplomatically during the war – if the Palestine Arabs had been organized at all – there is not the slightest doubt that the [Balfour] Declaration would never have been issued. Even twelve months later it would not have been possible. As it was, Weizmann pulled the Zionists through a brief window of opportunity, fated never to open again.' For by the time the war was finished and the peace treaties settled, the problems inherent in creating Jewish territorial rights in a country where Arabs had lived for more that 1,200 years were well manifested.

SEVENTEEN

Judah's Broken Shell

O weep for those that slept by Babel's stream,
Whose shrines are desolate, whose land a dream;
Weep for the harp of Judah's broken shell;
Mourn – where their God hath dwelt the godless dwell.

And where shall Israel lay her bleeding feet?
And where shall Zion's songs again seem sweet?
And Judah's melody once again rejoice
The hearts that leap'd before its heavenly voice?

Tribes of the wandering foot and weary breast,
How shall ye flee away and be at rest!
The wild dove hath her rest, the fox his cave,
Mankind their country – Israel but the grave.

'O! Weep for Those That Slept by Babel's Stream', Hebrew Melodies, Lord Byron

King Solomon's port on the Red Sea coast, Aqaba, was captured from the Turks on 6 July 1917 by Arab Irregulars led by Lawrence, and quickly became a vast tented base camp for Arab Irregulars. After the disastrous two failures at Gaza, this success gave the enigmatic scholar-hero Lawrence immense, and well-deserved, prestige. With charm, and his almost insane risk-taking and imaginative tactics, Lawrence had gained the confidence of the Arabs, who called him *el Aurans, Laurens Bey* or the *Emir Dynamite*. The sultan's jihad to incite the Arabs to revolt against the Allies, especially the British in Egypt, had failed. In contrast the methods used by the British to stir the Arabs to revolt against the Turks were proving more successful. Lawrence's star had risen quickly in the year since he had gone to Mecca after the British government had started backing the Arab Revolt against the Turks in the Hejaz. Extensive aid to 'nourish' the revolt had come in the form of massive quantities of guns, bullets, gold and camels, together with bilingual English army advisers. While leading the Arab Irregulars with Feisal, from the Hejaz to Palestine and Syria, Lawrence showed himself to be a guerrilla leader of genius, combining raids on railway lines with stirring up revolt among the Arabs. Feisal, who often wore belts of jewelled pistols and daggers and had been raised in almost suffocating luxury, felt himself equipped to take on the role of a king in the territories they were soon to capture. He was attended by five young black Abyssinian slaves, a legacy of the trade which General Gordon had tried to stamp out.

Lawrence's victory in Aqaba coincided with the arrival of Allenby. During this time, Allenby met Lawrence in Cairo, where they co-ordinated plans for British and Arab advances across the River Jordan. Lawrence had been in Arabia for four months, and in the last month alone he had clocked up 1,400 miles on the back of a camel. Fed up with vermin, he 'wanted a bath, and something with ice in it to drink: to change these clothes, all sticking to my saddle sores in filthiness: to eat something more tractable than green date and camel sinew'. Lawrence's unemotional feelings about eating his own camels was revealed in the piece which he wrote in the *Army Quarterly* in 1920:

> and there was never a fear of starvation, for each of us was riding on two hundred pounds of potential meat, and when food lacked we would stop and eat the weakest of our camels. Exhausted camel is poor food, but cheaper killing than a fat one, and we had to remember that our future efficiency depended on the number of good camels at our disposal. They lived on grazing as we marched (we never gave them grain or fodder), and after their six weeks on the road they would be worn thin, and have to be sent to pasture for some months' rest, while we called out another tribe in replacement, or found fresh riding-beasts.

The meeting in Cairo between Lawrence and Allenby was a success, despite Lawrence writing, 'He was hardly prepared for anything so odd as myself – a little bare-footed, silk-shirted man offering to hobble the enemy by his preaching if given stores and arms, and a fund of two hundred thousand sovereigns to convince and control his converts . . .'.

Allenby was then planning the third British attack against the Turkish fortified defence system of Gaza. Extra troops had arrived from the Salonika Front and Aden because if this failed the invasion of Palestine would not be possible. In October telegrams from London instructed Allenby to quicken his pace. As the autumn leaves began to fall in Europe and the winter rains were again about to turn the battlefields of candle-lit trenches into wildernesses of mud, Lloyd George wanted a victory to counter the appalling losses in Haig's battle of Passchendaele. In just days the Holy City would fall. The occupation of the Jaffa-Jerusalem line was an immediate objective. So eleven months before the war ended, on 2 November 1917, the invasion began which would lead to Britain usurping the Ottoman Empire as the most powerful country in the Middle East. It was also the first time Englishmen had invaded the Holy Land since the Crusaders had lost their territories there in 1291.

A section of the British middle and upper classes had a tendency to be pro-Arab and entertained a fascination for Oriental cultures and the half-known world of 'minaret and muezzin . . . camel and veil and palm'.[1] They clung to images of deserts stretching into pink horizons, tents, caravans of loaded camels, sheikhs, palm-trees, domes and the ceaseless round of *louche* pleasure in the seraglio, and collected paintings of harem interiors often with images by French and British artists featuring either a woman with partly bared breasts or an English gentleman lounging on a divan, turban on his head, smoking a hookah. Despite critics declaring much to be 'wholly invented phantasmagoria,' books about the East had been popular from the mid-eighteenth century including Voltaire's *Candide*, whose heroes had found peace near Constantinople; the Arabian novel *Vathek* by William Beckford with its strong tendency towards the esoteric; and Goethe's poems, such as 'Mahomets Gesang'. In 1799 the term 'Orientalist' was first used in England and 'orientaliste' in France.

Not only did the British have a reputation for being pro-Arab, over 100 million Muslims lived in British colonies within the British Empire, from Borneo to Africa. George V was the Supreme Governor of the Church of England, but not even the sultan-caliph of Turkey could boast so many Muslim subjects. Increased sensitivity to the needs of the Muslims had been shown since the Indian Mutiny in 1857, when Muslims and Hindus had revolted on hearing that cartridges were greased with the fat of pigs (anathema to Muslims) and cows (sacred to Hindus). But it would have been almost impossible for the British then to have consulted local Arabs as Palestine was still enemy territory.

* * *

The Turkish line on the Gaza Front was formidable and commanded by one of the most respected generals of the war, General Erich von Falkenhayn, the former chief of the German General Staff and later the conqueror of Romania.[2] In Palestine the Turks, in anticipation of the British advance, were getting tough on the remaining Jews. Among the houses which were commandeered were the two stone houses and the adjoining kitchens in the Degania Kibbutz as lodgings for German pilots. Some of the members, including the parents of young Moshe Dayan, moved into the loft of the cowshed, while others camped in the partitioned sections of the empty granary. The months of November and December 1917 were so cold and wet that the future hero of the Israeli army caught pneumonia and nearly died.

While the men of the Garden Suburb sat at No. 10 Downing Street Allenby's massive army of over 100,000 men, 50,000 horses and squadrons of aircraft was breaking through the Beersheba/Gaza fortifications. As well as ammunition they had a new weapon, asphyxiating gas. This was first time in history that it had been used effectively outside Europe. Allenby unleashed the contents of 10,000 shells to float across the formidable trench system and barriers at the third battle of Gaza on 1–2 November 1917. Murray had attempted to use it in the second battle of Gaza six months earlier but it had been ineffective.

After taking Gaza, Allenby broke through the Turkish lines and on 4 November started up the coast to Jaffa. By chance this was the 9th of Ab [in the Jewish calendar, also known as Tish'ah B'av], the anniversary of the destruction of Jerusalem by Titus. But Allenby could not pursue the Turks quickly in one continuous advance to Jerusalem as the Turks kept up an intense rearguard action with machine-guns. The desperate lack of water held back the exhausted horses.

* * *

On the same day as Allenby unleashed his artillery barrage on Turkish positions at Gaza, Balfour, issued the declaration that bears his name. Talks with leading Jews, such as Weizmann, and Lord Rothschild, the head of the dazzling Jewish banking family and unofficial leader of the Jewish community in Britain, had continued during the summer. This undertaking to create a 'national home for the Jews' is one of the most controversial outcomes of the First World War and considered by some to be the founding charter of the state of Israel.

Yet again more reasons for retaining Palestine as an Anglo-Jewish colony were aired. It would strengthen the strategic position of Egypt and create a buffer zone for the Suez Canal, a 'land bridge' linking India and Egypt, bringing together the British imperial territory in Africa and Asia and forming an endless chain of imperial possessions from the Atlantic to the Pacific oceans. Yet again, another motive was that Palestine could be used as a route for troop movements from the Mediterranean to the Persian Gulf and India.

But arguments against making such a colony continued. Would such a settlement be either ethical or strategic? Was forging a colony of a Jewish migrant population in a land which was more than 90 per cent Arab contentious? Would it adversely affect the standing of Jews in Britain and throughout the world? In May 1917 a letter had appeared in *The Times* which warned of a future calamity if such a homeland went ahead. This had the effect of not only producing a counter-letter but also of stirring more members of the Jewish community to rally around the Zionists.

Vocal opposition to the Jewish homeland came from a small number of Jews who regarded Zionism with grave misgivings. Edwin Samuel Montagu, the Secretary of State for India and member of the cabinet (not the War Cabinet) stood up at one meeting and said that he was a 'Jewish Englishman'; then turned to Lloyd George, saying, 'All my life I have been trying to get out of the ghetto. You want to force me back there!' Zionism, he said, was 'a mischievous political creed'. His argument reflected the attitude of David Alexander, president of the Board of British Jews, and Anglophiles such as Claude Montefiore, president of the Anglo-Jewish Association.

If the Jewish people had a homeland, according to Montagu, European countries would have an excuse to deport Jews by saying, 'Go back to your *own* country.' Smug anti-Zionists, comfortably integrated into English life with a niche in English society, overlooked the fact that they were a minority. They were, they said, just as much citizens of Britain as any Christian, forgetting that the Aliens Bill of 1905 had restricted Jewish immigration. Recent news of pogroms in Russia was a reminder that most Jews were usually outside society, segregated into ghettoes and frequently persecuted. Anti-Zionists looked on the idea of a separate homeland as a form of segregation. They did not want Weizmann, however Anglophile his tastes, telling them to settle in the Judean desert, or to till the orange groves of Jaffa. There certainly was opposition outside the War Cabinet, but Curzon was the only actual member to oppose the Jewish homeland. On 26 October 1917 he wrote about the half a million Syrian Arabs:

> a mixed community with Arab, Hebrew, Canaanite, Greek, Egyptian, and possibly Crusaders' blood. They own the soil, which belongs either to individual landowners or to village communities. They profess the Mohammedan faith. They will not be content either to be expropriated for Jewish immigrants, or to act merely as hewers of wood and drawers of water to the latter.[3]

He then added:

> Now what is the capacity as regards the population of Palestine within any reasonable period of time? . . . What is to become of the people of this country, assuming the Turk to be expelled, and the inhabitants not to have been exterminated by the war? There are over a half a million of these.

Apart from Curzon and Montagu, few men in the inner government anticipated the drawn-out Arab-Israeli turmoil that lay ahead. But even a glance at the correspondence in the Foreign Office files for the few years before the outbreak of the First World War – letters from Lowther to Grey – would have revealed the tensions likely to be ignited by such a sudden move. Why Grey, the former Foreign Secretary, nor Lowther were not called in is not known.

On 3 September the War Cabinet had been close to issuing a statement of intent, but wrangling over the wording brought delay. Sykes composed a version which visualized a 'Jewish National Home with liberty of immigration to Jews . . . and the Hebrew language to be officially recognized.' This, though, like other versions, was pushed aside. The cabinet was so divided about the wording of what Koestler described as a 'promise by one nation to a second of the country of a third',[4] that Amery was asked to redraft the note to meet the objections of both the pro-Jewish and pro-Arab camps. Amery noted in his diary,[5] 'I had drafted the finally agreed text about 6 October for a cabinet at Milner's request.' In the entry for 31 October, he wrote, 'After lunch Weizmann and Aronson came in, the cabinet having at last agreed to issue the declaration on Zionism, and fell on my neck with gratitude for my efforts on their behalf.' Amery's draft, based on two other versions by cabinet members, was approved:

> I have much pleasure in conveying to you, on behalf of His Majesty's Government, the following declaration of sympathy with Jewish Zionist aspirations which has been submitted to me and approved by the cabinet.
>
> His Majesty's Government view with favour the establishment in Palestine of a National Home for the Jewish People, and will use their best endeavours to facilitate the achievement of this object, it being clearly understood that nothing shall be done which may prejudice the civil and religious rights of existing non-Jewish communities in Palestine, or the rights and political status enjoyed by the Jews in any other country.
>
> I should be grateful if you would bring this declaration to the knowledge of the Zionist Federation.

Full of ambiguities, it was very different from the draft of July; it was now a dual obligation to both the Jews and the Arabs. 'The national home' was now 'a national home'. The phrase 'regards as essential for the realization of this principle the grant of internal autonomy to the Jewish nationality in Palestine' was changed to 'nothing being done which may prejudice the civil and religious rights of existing non-Jewish communities in Palestine . . .'.

Lloyd George wrote in his *War Memoirs* that issuing the declaration at that time was part of his propagandist strategy, and added that, 'Propaganda on both sides probably played a greater part in the last war than in any other.' Although the declaration, in the form of a letter, was sent to Lord Rothschild on 2 November, it was not printed in a newspaper until it appeared in *The Times* a week later, on Friday 9 November.

As well as the tactical advantages to Britain, there was a strong belief that the idea of a homeland would win over to Britain influential Jews in Germany, Russia and the United States. This was considered an especially potent factor in public opinion in the United States, where there were at least three million Jews, many of whom, it was commonly thought, wielded enormous influence in financial and political circles. The United States was fast becoming home to the largest, richest and probably the most secure Jewish community since Abraham left Ur of the Chaldees,[6] controlling banks and financial institutions. Lord Robert Cecil, the Foreign Office under-secretary, summed this up when he said, 'I do not think it is easy to exaggerate the international power of the Jews.' Winning worldwide Jewish support, especially in the United States, was certainly high on the list of suggested motives behind the Balfour Declaration. The German government, extraordinary as it may now seem, were reluctant to lose their position as the main bastion of Zionism. Adolf Hitler's Nazism would not be born for another twenty years. Germany tried to maintain itself as the seat of the Central Office of the Zionist Organization, which had developed in the Austro-Hungarian Empire and Germany, not in England. Most of the members, at this stage, were in fact drawn from Russia's six million Jews.

* * *

In his scholarly analysis of the peace settlements after the First World War in *A Peace to End All Peace*, David Fromkin emphasized the influence of the Bible on policy formation and implementation. 'Biblical prophecy was the first and most enduring of the many motives that led Britons to want to restore the Jews to Zion.' In spite of the British tendency to glamorize Arab countries, Nonconformist ideas appeared to be a more persuasive force in shaping the attitudes of the politicians towards British sponsorship of Zionist aspirations. Generation after generation had heard the Bible read in church each Sunday, and many had a copy at home, which was studied daily. In many cases, the Bible was the only book, certainly the principal book. Its cadences, its music, its phraseology, sank into men's minds. In remote villages it was the chapel, the church and the kirk that gave people their first music, their first literature and first ideals and philosophy, their first lessons in reading, their first moral code, their first sense of belonging.

In the nineteenth and early twentieth centuries, as trade and factories multiplied, many working-class Nonconformists rose to join the middle classes and tended to join the Liberals, who advocated civil and religious improvements. G.M. Trevelyan in his *English Social History* said that 'the leading Conservatives in each town and village were usually the keenest churchmen; while most active opponents were Whig and Liberal, Dissenters or anticlericals. The lower-middle and working classes attended the same chapels and took part in the same religious activities. Politics in the nineteenth century were as much a matter of denomination as of class.' The left wing of the Liberal Party was mostly composed of working-class radicals and men who had surmounted earlier poverty, men who would later be attracted to the Labour Party, which was formed in 1906.[7] D.W. Bebbington in *The Nonconformist Conscience*[8] said that Nonconformists of all shades were drawn to the Liberals in the hope that they would abolish their practical grievances, 'The politics of Nonconformity were overwhelmingly Liberal up to the First World War and beyond . . .'. He added that it was attractive because the Liberals had 'inherited the Whig advocacy of the principles of civil and religious liberty. Only from the Liberals could Nonconformists expect redress for their disabilities'.

Thus many of the new champions of industry had risen from Nonconformist backgrounds, The separation between the humbler section of society and those who could imperiously call themselves 'gentlemen' or were 'gentlemen born' was marked by differences between Church and Chapel. Unlike many English aristocrats who were reared on the classics and could speak with warmth of the Peloponnesian War and quote Thucydides, for Nonconformists their main point of reference was the Bible. Apart from learning lines from the classics, among the social hurdles to be crossed before the newly enriched could be seen at glittering social gatherings in the drawing-rooms and clubs of the upper classes, was religion. Nonconformist denominations continued to be socially tainted because of their immense appeal to 'the lower orders'. The Church of England, one of the pillars of the gentry and aristocracy, could be used as a rung on the ladder to acceptability.

Another rung could be climbed by joining the Conservative Party. In 1848 the Chartist theologian Jacob Cadley described the Church of England as 'the Tory Party at prayer'. This was echoed thirty years later by Matthew Arnold, who accused the Church of being 'devoted above all to the landed gentry and to the propertied and satisfied classes generally'. The landowner, stockbroker and banker still stood for Church and Tory, Mr Disraeli and the promise of heaven; mason, miner, wheelwright and blacksmith now stood for Chapel and Liberal, Mr Gladstone and salvation from hell-fire.

Gladstone's family is an example of the successful use of religion on the crowded nineteenth-century road of upward mobility. This Grand Old Man of British politics was once described as, 'Ah, Oxford on the surface, but Liverpool below'.[9] He had been a Conservative for the first half of his political life and then a Liberal, and was prime minister four times between 1868 and 1894 before leaving office half-blind and half-deaf aged eighty-five. The grandson of a Presbyterian corn merchant in Leith who had left school at thirteen, his father had gone south, rising quickly from grain dealer to making a fortune from sugar plantations in the West Indies with slave labour. Eton, that citadel of upper-class education, then, it appears, seldom put up barriers to any *parvenu* from the merchant classes. In his biography of Gladstone,[10] Roy Jenkins quotes a contemporary comment made in 1811 that there were 'enough Liverpool Etonians to fill a coach'. While such a *parvenu* could not become a gentleman by stiffly aping his 'betters', his children could acquire what Thackeray called the 'diabolical invention of gentility' at such schools and meet influential friends, as was the case with the sons of Nonconformist families such as the Gladstones, Chamberlains and Baldwins. Baldwin admitted that the classification of English schools was on the lines of 'social rather than educational distinction: a youth's school badge has been his social label'.[11]

Raised as a God-fearing Presbyterian, Gladstone senior moved across to the Church of England and built and endowed two churches in Liverpool (the 'livings' of the Church were then chiefly the property of the aristocracy) before sending three of his sons to Eton. Mrs Gladstone had also converted to become a member the Established Church, choosing Low Church Evangelicalism. While retaining his mother's love of the Bible and adopting the reforming zeal of the Nonconformists, Gladstone became a High Anglican who went to church every day. Evenings were sometimes spent trawling the dimly lit streets of London's West End 'rescuing' prostitutes. On Judgement Day, he believed, he would have to defend all his thoughts and actions before God, so he felt he had to act accordingly.[12] His book *The Impregnable Rock of Holy Scripture*,[13] published during his last term at 10 Downing Street, was described as a 'Defence of Biblical infallibility by Evangelical British Prime Minister'. One of his phrases is still quoted: 'I have known ninety-five of the world's great men in my time, and of these, eighty-seven were followers of the Bible. The Bible is stamped with a Speciality of Origin, and an immeasurable distance separates it from all competitors.'

* * *

The treacherous hills around Jerusalem were a formidable barrier. Like previous warriors before him, Allenby soon discovered that Jerusalem was no easy city to conquer. Since the Crusaders had left in 1291, no European troops had invaded. Even Napoleon, with his newly founded Camel Corps, in which each camel carried two French soldiers in sky-blue uniforms with white turbans, had not risked detouring from the coastal route when bringing his forces up from Egypt to storm the ancient ports of Jaffa and Acre.

Forming a depot at Jaffa, Allenby then wheeled his troops into the Judean-Samarian hills on 18 November. The rainy season had started early. Dust and dirt had become slippery mud as the loamy soil mixed with water. Loaded camels and horses lost their footing, and those at the gallop slipped and fell. As the terrain and the dreadful weather restricted the use of both horses and vehicles, infantry dominated the taking of Jerusalem. There were no head-on battles, just continual guerrilla warfare. Boulders and scrub gave excellent cover to the Turks. At times it seemed that, like Richard the Lionheart, Allenby's forces would never get to the Holy City. Men shivered in the cold and wet. Over 18,000 Allied casualties occurred while turning the Turks out of the defensive positions on those perilous mountain roads. As the men marched, fire came at them from the Nebi Samwil Mosque, the burial place of the Prophet Samuel, on a high ridge before the last hills and valleys into Jerusalem. Richard the Lionheart had been forced to turn back here. It is said that he had hidden his face with his shield on the heights in order that he would not see the city he would never conquer.[14]

This battle was about to fulfil a long-held wish by a line of British Evangelicals and Nonconformists that stretched back to the Puritans and to the time when the *Mayflower* set sail for the New World.[15] It would also allow the descendants of the Jews in the Diaspora to return to the Holy Land. Restoring an ancient and persecuted people to their lost country was an inspiring vision for those who had been immersed in the Bible from childhood. To increase the number of Jewish people in Palestine would also fulfil prophecies, such as Isaiah's prediction that the Gentiles would bring the Jewish people back to their land (Isaiah: 49).

Ronald Storrs, the son of an Anglican vicar in London, who became the first governor of Jerusalem during the initial nine years of rule, who had briefly been part of the War Cabinet Secretariat, wrote of how the religious element was mixed with other motives: 'Behind the adoption of so novel a thesis [the Balfour Declaration] by the most level-headed cabinet in the world on the recommendation of a Russian Jew [Weizmann], there were alleged to lurk other considerations than mere eagerness for the fulfilment of *Old Testament* prophecy. British espousal of the Hope of Israel would, it was hinted, serve triply our interests . . .'.[16]

EIGHTEEN

Sunrise in Jerusalem

In the gold of morning we march; our swaying shadows are long; We are risen from sleep to the grey-green world and our limbs move free. Day is delight and adventure, and all save speech is a song; Our thoughts are travelling birds going southward across the sea.

'Shadows', Palestine 1918, Siegfried Sassoon

The sun rises over Jerusalem from behind the Mount of Olives, and when it rose on Sunday 9 December 1917 a new era was about to begin. Jerusalem was back in Christian hands. The final offensive by the British army had begun with an artillery barrage after midnight the day before. But during most of the crossing over the rocky hills guns had been able to give little support in the advance which had relied on rifle and machine-gun fire, followed by the bayonet.[1]

By nightfall the advance army was at Bethlehem. Unknown to the British the administration was preparing to evacuate. At about 2 o'clock the next morning weary Turks began to file out of the old city through the Jaffa Gate, with everything from electric generators to food, paintings, furniture and portable treasures. Once defeat had appeared inevitable, the Turkish governor, anxious not to harm the holy places, whether Muslim, Jewish or Christian had retreated with his staff north-east to Damascus. The city of Jerusalem must fall without a shot being fired. A suitable document and the keys to Jerusalem were given to the mayor, Hussein Effendi al-Husseini, and the chief of Jerusalem Police, Haj Abd al-Kadir al-Alami. Monks, rabbis, imams and others joined the little procession as they went to find some British officers so that a formal surrender could be enacted. On the way they visited a hospital run by Bertha Spafford Vester, the daughter of the founder of the American Colony. Someone quickly pulled a sheet from one of the beds and tied it to a broomstick to make a flag of truce.

Two British soldiers near the Arab village of Lifta, among the north-west hills of Jerusalem, had gone ahead to search for a few eggs for breakfast.

Other versions of the story – and there are at least seven – say they were looking for a well so they could fill buckets. When they confronted a group of men wearing tarbooshs on their heads and carrying their limp white flag, the cooks felt inadequate to receive the honour and rushed off to find two outpost sergeants. An excited message was sent to high command. Soon Brigadier-General C.F. Watson, of the 180th Brigade, 60th Division, arrived and received the keys of the city. But they were then returned to the mayor because another, more senior, general, the divisional commander, Major-General J.S.M. Shea, wanted to accept them in a more dignified manner. And so started the saga of three decades of colonial settlement in Palestine.

A news blackout on the fall of Jerusalem was imposed for a day. Knowing that the capture of the city would stir the imagination of the whole world, Lloyd George wanted to announce it personally to the House of Commons. It was also an opportunity for favourable publicity about the eastern campaigns. Applauded as a 'Christmas present to the British nation', the news hit the front pages of most newspapers in Europe. To celebrate 'the liberation', Westminster Abbey's bells rang out in triumph, the first time they had rung in three years. This was followed by the ringing of thousands of other church bells in Britain and across Europe. But little did the Europeans who rejoiced know of the full horror of the deaths and injuries incurred during the assault over the hills. In Jerusalem, too, the church bells rang, as people were overwhelmed with joy at the re-establishment of Christian rule after an interval of 730 years. For the first time in four centuries Muslim police were no longer guarding the church of the Holy Sepulchre.

The men in the War Cabinet may have been a thousand miles away, but they were following every move, even the protocol of which flags could be displayed. Because of the unique character of the city and the difficult political and diplomatic questions, instructions were telegraphed that no flags should fly. The flaunting of national symbols, especially those of the French and the British, let alone the Arabs, could easily have provoked more tensions, so in the end it was decided that just a small token Union Jack was to fly from the bonnet of Allenby's car.

On Tuesday 11 December – by chance, the day of the Jewish feast of Hanukah – Allenby made his official entry into the Holy City.

The great Jaffa Gate in the old City wall was opened for the momentous occasion. Security was made easier as most of the population already lived outside the formidable ochre-coloured walls of squared stones. These walls, the glittering dome of the mosque of al-Aqsa, and a sheaf of minarets, dominated the city, even though the Jaffa Road, running through suburbs containing consulates, the American Colony, hospitals, shops and a few hotels, was already thought of as the main street. It is not known who realized that the man about to declare the independence of Jerusalem was a direct descendant of Oliver Cromwell, but there is a certain irony that just 261 years after Cromwell had allowed the Jews back into England, his descendant, Edmund Henry Hynman Allenby, on behalf of the British nation, was doing the same for them in Palestine. According to Allenby's biographer, Brian Gardner,[2] 'In the eighteenth century some powerful blood was injected into the family when a direct descendant of Oliver Cromwell . . . married Hynman Allenby . . .'. The location chosen by Allenby for the historic announcement was close to the entrance of the Jaffa Gate, beside the Tower of David and opposite Christ Church, the place which represents the beginnings of British Protestant interests in Palestine – another connection which would have pleased the Evangelicals. According to the census taken in 1912, the Jewish population of Jerusalem had risen to 45,000, while the Arab population had remained at 25,000. Both had now dropped by over half, if not more – and more in other areas.

Directions were given for Allenby to dismount his horse before arriving at the Jaffa Gate and humbly walk through on foot, past the guard of honour of soldiers from England, Scotland, Wales, Ireland, Australia and New Zealand. The War Cabinet wanted a simple, un-militaristic entrance, completely different from the Kaiser's theatrical parade nineteen years earlier when, with much pomp, he had ridden through the Jaffa Gate on a horse. Now the British officers, wearing their uniforms of jodhpurs and tunic jackets, their highly polished riding boots glittering in the morning sunshine, took their places on a temporary wooden dais beside the entrance to the Tower of David. If only Shaftesbury, who had done so much for the restorationist movement and who had predicted the arrival of the modern day Cyrus, had been there. On 24 July 1840 he had written, '. . . prospects of the Jewish people. Everything seems ripe for their return to Palestine. . . . Could the five Powers of the West be induced to guarantee the security of life and possessions of the Hebrew race. . . .'[3]

Beside Allenby stood Picot, who now called himself the French High Commissioner for Palestine and Syria, and twenty officers including Lawrence who had come to report on the failure of the Arab Irregulars in blowing up a railway bridge in the Yarmuk Valley. In *Seven Pillars of Wisdom*, aware of the privilege in being there, he wrote that the ceremony was 'the supreme moment of the war'. Not even Sir Reginald Wingate, the former governor-general of the Sudan, who was then high commissioner of Egypt, was allowed to be present at this exclusive ceremony. British aircraft flew overhead as the proclamation was recited loudly in English, French, Arabic, Hebrew, Greek, Russian and Italian:

> . . . since your City is regarded with affection by the adherents of three of the great religions of mankind, and its soil has been consecrated by the prayers and pilgrimages of multitudes of devout people of these three religions for many centuries, therefore do I make known to you that every sacred building, monument, holy spot, shrine, traditional site, endowment, pious bequest, or customary place of prayer, of whatsoever form of the three religions, will be maintained and protected according to the existing customs and beliefs of those to whose faiths they are sacred.

In her memoir *Our Jerusalem* Bertha Spafford Vester described watching the ceremony from the balcony of the Grand New Hotel, '. . . witnessing one of the great events of history . . . the whole Christian world outside of Germany and Austria was jubilant. People in the streets were crying at their deliverance. I saw a Jew embrace a Greek priest, and his tall clerical hat. . . . Truly we could sing with the Psalmist, "Then were our mouths filled with laughter and our tongue with smiling. . . . The Lord hath done great things for us, therefore we are glad."'

Peaceful though Allenby's taking of the city was, he had to cope with two threats to British occupation. First, counter-attack by the Turkish army, which was only three or four miles down the Jericho road to the east, and some six or eight miles to the north, was imminent. He was anxious to step up the capture of Jericho and then Transjordan. Secondly, France's shared claim to the Holy Land was asserted at the picnic lunch which followed. Picot, who had rejoined the advance a few days before the fall of Jerusalem, reminded Allenby of the earlier Sykes–Picot agreement which he had personally composed with Sykes. In *Seven Pillars* Lawrence described how 'salad, chicken mayonnaise and *foie gras* sandwiches hung in our wet mouths unmunched, while we turned to Allenby and gaped. Even he seemed for a moment at a loss. . . . But his face grew red: he swallowed, his chin coming forward (in the way we loved), whilst he said, grimly, "In the military zone the only authority is that of the Commander-in-Chief – myself."' He knew that Lloyd George was vehement in wanting only British control, not shared control. He added that War Cabinet instructions were that Jerusalem 'should be kept under martial law so as to avoid Franco–Italian complications' and that a military administration would be set up pending the Peace Conference. The fall of Jerusalem meant yet another new phase in tension between Britain and France over the division of the Middle East.

* * *

In Palestine during the early days of the British administration one of the men who ensured the viability of the homeland was Wyndham Deedes, an Evangelist who later became a famous social worker among the poor in the East End of London. His knowledge of Turkish civil administration, coupled with his ability to speak Turkish fluently, meant that he was one of the soldiers then entering the Old City of Jerusalem who would stay on long term in the administration.

As Chief Secretary and the second most senior person in the administration, Deedes, who was 'essentially Christian religious, rather than political',[4] felt a tremendous responsibility to safeguard the lives of the people whom victory had placed under British control. His benevolence was such that another member of the staff called him 'a modern saint'. The military administration in Palestine was mostly pro-Arab, but this was not the case with Deedes. His three years of office as Chief Secretary of Palestine were to be the most decisive in the early period of the homeland. A deeply religious man, he once told a colleague that he wanted to do everything he could to hasten the Second Coming.

Small, pale and painfully thin, for years Deedes thought nothing of working a fifteen-hour day, leaving scant time for meals, money or conventional pleasure. His career had been far from conventional. As a passionate member of the Low Church, he had scant time for ceremony but cared deeply for individuals, whoever they were. Like Evangelicals before him, he brought his faith in active Christianity to bear on whatever he did. The fact that he was half-Jewish appeared to have little bearing on his attitude. His father was from an old landed family in Kent, but his mother, the daughter of a Jewish doctor whose wife had been converted to Christianity, had become a devoted member of the Church of England. After taking a commission in the King's Royal Rifle Corps he had served in the Boer War. (When asked about the horrors of this war he had replied, 'Well, anything was better than Eton.')[5] In 1910 he was 'lent' by the British to the sultan of the Ottoman Empire to help reform the Turkish gendarmerie, where he quickly learnt to speak Turkish and Arabic. At the outbreak of the First World War he returned to England, then went to Gallipoli and Cairo as an intelligence officer.

Deedes' profound belief in the Jewish people and in the Bible helped him through the problems of setting up the administration. Streets were strewn with all kinds of litter, both animal and human. Wherever he went there were ragged starving children moaning and whining, veiled women so thin that their bones almost pierced their skin, beggars offering a perpetual chorus of prayers. The Turks had taken food stores with them, which combined with the effects of the disastrous harvest in 1915 caused by a locust plague, followed by another poor harvest, had diminished supplies. To make matters worse Jerusalem itself was starving. Fuel was scarce if not unobtainable. There was no electricity and nights were dark and cold. Deedes' first job was to help organize blankets and food. Supplying Jerusalem, and safeguarding existing supplies lest even more people in the city starved to death, were formidable tasks. Another duty was the burying of the military and civilian dead. Epidemics of typhus and cholera were a continual threat. As donkeys and mules managed to keep their balance on the slippery ground more easily than horses, they ceaselessly plied backwards and forwards across that 50-mile tract from Jerusalem to Jaffa, laden with thousands of tons of food, clothing, bullets – and once a typewriter for a new office.

The whole machinery of everyday life had broken down. There was no postal service in operation, no police, no organized transport, no machinery for the collection of taxes, national or local. Banks had ceased to function, shops were empty, peasants had stopped bringing their goods to market, there was no buying or selling, and schools were closed.[6] In a letter to his mother Deedes told of the failure of 'currency, taxation of all sorts, trade, commerce, municipal affairs, relief, justice . . .'. Water, too, even in the rainy season, was a serious problem, the troops alone accounting for large quantities, and as Storrs pointed out, 'the sudden demand for bath water contravening all tradition'. The nearest rivers or lakes were well over 2,000 feet below the level of Jerusalem. Even in the time of Jesus, the local springs and Roman aqueducts had been woefully inadequate.

The threat of being cut off from supplies meant that the corridor to the coast was heavily guarded. Allenby and most of the officers were preoccupied with pushing the Turks, who were regrouping and rearming, out of the surrounding area. While the Turks still held all of Palestine and Syria north of Jerusalem and all territories east of the Jordan Valley, the British were now dug in on a crooked line from west to east across Palestine, from a point ten miles north of Jaffa eastwards over the coastal plain, the hills of Judea to a few miles north of Jerusalem and then across the Jordan Valley.

* * *

After centuries of poor Ottoman administration and a large number of absentee estate-owners, much of the countryside had become derelict. The Promised Land was now far from being 'the land of milk and honey' of the Bible. Centuries of neglect had been exacerbated by the Turks, who during the war had seized the crops and left practically no seed to be cultivated. On top of this, oak, eucalyptus trees, vineyards and olive groves had been cut down within a 10-mile radius of the railway to counter the fuel shortage. When locomotive coal for the steam trains was unavailable the Turks used felled trees and dried camel dung as fuel. Storrs was appalled at finding an area recently denuded of 10,000 olive trees. Some villagers also had the habit of cutting down trees in an act of revenge, as a traditional way to inflict injury on an enemy. Trade, too, was at a standstill. So little olive oil was being processed that not much soap was being manufactured. The acute shortage of oil was also because there were few experienced men to harvest the trees as the Arab labourers had been conscripted into the Turkish army.

While Storrs and Deedes set to work in the administration in Jerusalem, Allenby initiated the breakthrough, which would take the British to the other side of the Jordan. Rain continued to turn plains into seas of mud and water. A raging storm on Christmas Eve and Christmas Day 1917 washed away parts of the railway and hundreds of camels in the transport columns lay down in the water and died. Neither food for the troops nor forage for the animals could be procured. Four days after Christmas the Turks made an abortive attempt to retake the city, but they, too, were hampered by the rain and mud. Blue skies did not return until early in January.

* * *

At Crown Hill Barracks, near Plymouth in Devon, 800 new Jewish soldiers were training hard for the further battles in Palestine. Anxious to join Allenby's troops before the remainder of Palestine was conquered, the Jewish Legion worked ceaselessly. Days were filled with endless drills, saluting, signalling, shooting at imitation targets, bayonet fighting and fatigue duties – a familiar routine for all British infantry units. Heavily laden with backpacks, wooden rifles and bandoliers of bullets, the new soldiers learned to march 110 paces to the minute. Atypical of these often idealistic but untried warriors was the sculptor Jacob Epstein. His influential friends had tried to have him assigned as an official war artist but Haig had personally vetoed the move. During one march, unable to take another step, Epstein collapsed in a stony field and by the time the Jewish Legion were boarding their ship, he was in a military convalescent hospital suffering from a nervous breakdown. His welcome discharge from the army did not come until 25 July 1918.

Despite the lack of any military background most men, according to the Jewish Regiment Committee, 'unlikely material though they may have been', were 'singularly free from crime; drunkenness is unknown . . . they have gained many prizes for boxing, musketry, etc. and have at all times displayed a high intelligence which has greatly impressed the non-Jewish officers. It is a matter of curious interest that our boys beat all other troops in Palestine in boxing'. The 'Wet Canteen' selling beer was closed down because of lack of customers, and not because they were taking a cue from George V's pledge of total abstention for the duration of the war. Jabotinsky said that they were 'the one white battalion which had no drunkards in its ranks'. But they did enjoy books and music. A travelling library was assembled and the Band Committee supplied trumpets, drums and fifes and they learnt marches including 'The Boys of the Old Brigade', 'Light Cavalry', 'The Dear Homeland', 'Down South' and 'Gipsy Love'. Little could any of them have visualized the conflicts that lay ahead. The Jewish Legion would be seen as a physical representation of the Balfour Declaration and the Zionist movement which so many of the British officials in Palestine opposed.

NINETEEN

'If I forget thee, O Jerusalem!'

By the rivers of Babylon, there we sat down, yea, we wept,
When we remembered Zion . . .
How shall we sing the Lord's song in a strange land?
If I forget thee, O Jerusalem, let my right hand forget her cunning.
If I do not remember thee, let my tongue cleave to the roof of my mouth;
If I prefer not Jerusalem above my chief joy.

Psalm 137

The last year of the war brought marked vicissitudes for the Turks. Despite the loss of Baghdad and Jerusalem they were buoyed up by the collapse of Russia. In March 1918 Lenin and Trotsky pulled Russia out of the war with their famous Treaty of Brest-Litovsk, according to which Germany gained huge areas of western Russia, including virtually the whole of the Ukraine, Russia's bread basket. Alarm was felt in the West not only because of Germany's territorial acquisitions but because the Kaiser was bringing his troops from the Russian to the Western Front. On 21 March the long-expected German offensive in France opened. As late as Easter 1918 the Germans thought they would win the war.

The outlook was dismal. Reinforcements from the Turkish armies in Asia Minor moved south to Palestine ready to put up a good fight against the British. The German 'sink at sight' U-boat campaign against merchant cargo ships supplying British ports was crippling industry. But on the plus side, Austria-Hungary and Bulgaria were weakening and Americans were enlisting in the United States Army, which had entered the war the previous year.

Allenby, though, was about to lose some of his best troops. The British army needed fresh reserves of tough, experienced soldiers. Sunburnt men from the Egyptian and Palestine fronts were soon embarking for France, about to exchange their mobile life in the desert for the trenches in Europe, 'the mincing machine' of the Western Front. As these soldiers departed for France the Zionist Commission arrived. Ormsby-Gore, who was at that time assistant secretary to the War Cabinet and had keenly supported the Balfour Declaration in the previous year, was now the official liaison officer of the newly created Zionist Commission. This body, of course, was considered the nucleus of the government of the Jewish homeland. Weizmann, who was given credit for the Balfour Declaration, was unofficially spokesman and leader of the delegation which included among its members James de Rothschild, Lieutenant Edwin Samuel, Israel Sieff, a director of Marks & Spencer, Leon Simon, who was later knighted, Joseph Cowen, Commendatore Levi Bianchini from Italy, Professor Sylvain Levi from France, and Dr David Eder, a psychiatrist. One of Dr Eder's patients, D.H. Lawrence, was so distraught not to be able to consult Eder in England that he threatened to follow him to Jerusalem. Jimmy Rothschild combined this job with that of his role as a senior officer in the second Jewish battalion, the 39th. His father, Baron de Rothschild, had financed, to an unprecedented extent, farming settlements in Palestine. In his book *Waddesdon Manor*, Michael Hall says that 'Weizmann found James, for all his occasional patrician *hauteur*, far more approachable than his autocratic and by now elderly father, and a close friendship grew up between them.' Jimmy, an expert on Shakespeare, a man of the turf who collected expensive horses, fine paintings, motorcars and mansions, was always remembered for carrying a small steel cylinder containing a collapsible chess-set.

Dame Miriam Rothschild remembers her third cousin Harry Dalmeny (later the Earl of Rosebery), who was ADC and later assistant military secretary to Allenby, telling her that his job overlapped that of censor and he had noticed that 'Weizmann was a little put out because Dalmeny's cousin Jimmy got all the attention'. Dalmeny's mother was a member of the Rothschild family and was another stepping stone between the Jewish Legion and the General Staff. Balfour's cousin, Lord Eustace Percy, was also on the staff.

The Zionist Commission started planning medical services, schools and a variety of social services within the Jewish community; it would be almost a state within a state. Naturally, the British military administration accepted another layer of authority with scepticism and irritation. Life was not easy in the Holy City. Flora Solomon, the Jewish wife of a British army officer, described Weizmann's reaction to Jerusalem on arrival, 'The scientist in him gazed upon the multitude of religious sects, sniffed the crumbling slums within its walls, noted the absence of sewerage and typewriters, then decided to transform this place by building a university. But soon the soporific took command, and seven years would elapse before the first lecture-hall was ready.'[1]

* * *

Already the Turks had managed to retake Erzurum in eastern Turkey which Russia had occupied in 1916. They continued to dig themselves in, barely more than ten miles north of Jaffa and Jerusalem. Rolls of barbed wire were still tangled through formidable cactus and prickly pear hedges. Even when everything seemed quiet, apart from for the occasional desultory exchange of tank and artillery fire, the silence was deceptive. The obstinate Anatolian peasant turned Turkish infantryman, 'Johnny Turk', 'Jacko', 'Joe Burke' or 'Adbullah' was still a stubborn fighter. Near the front men reported an almost continuous barrage of shells and bullets.

In Jerusalem itself much time was spent enlisting the help of relief organizations, both Christian and Jewish, for the refugees, the homeless and the sick. Something had to be done to get more cereals, grains and medical supplies up the hills. Life would improve once the 300 miles of standard-gauge track and pipeline bringing supplies from Egypt was completed. The section between Kantara and Gaza was now being extended up towards Lydda, the town where St George had slain the dragon. Progress was slow. The forced labour gangs from the 120,000 conscripted Egyptian fellahin toiled from dawn to dusk, but it grew only ten miles a week. Guns, water and food came, but now there were vast armies and prisoners of war to feed as well. Little could come from Europe.

The grievances of the disparate Arab tribes, plus deputations from the religious groups including Muslims, Druzes, Maronites, Armenians, Copts and Assyrians, were time-consuming. Quarrels between them were interminable. But they were not the only hostile groups. There were also the bishops, archbishops, archimandrites, rabbis, monks and imams. Another problem was the divided proprietorship of the church of the Holy Sepulchre between the Roman Catholics, the Greek Orthodox and the Copts. Each complained at any infringement of their rights, whether it be to change the position of a lamp, a picture, to mop the floor or carry out repairs. The Russian Emperor had given an annual stipend towards the maintenance of the Holy Sepulchre, but now, with the new revolutionary government, no money was coming.

At this time a new and bitter hostility was added to the religious divisions within the city. The Orthodox Jews, who had existed in Jerusalem for thousands of years with few interruptions, believed that divine, not mortal or political, intervention,[2] would bring the return of the Jews to Jerusalem. The arrival of the Zionists was viewed by them with alarm and suspicion. Arguments about who would have the majority in the newly formed City Council of Jerusalem Jews, a body to ensure that Zionist views would be audible, resulted in the Orthodox Ashkenazi Community Council. Storrs described some of them as 'fur-hatted, ringleted Rabbis . . . the only tongue they all understood was an ultra-German Yiddish, though individuals spoke Arabic and French . . .'. Tensions in other matters between the Orthodox and Zionist Jews continued unabated. The Jews divided themselves into three groups, the Sephardi, the Ashkenazi and the different strains of extreme Orthodoxy who looked upon the others as heretical.[3] Edward Keith-Roach, a member of the British Administration in Palestine for over thirty years, described some of the divisions: 'The Christians were particularly venomous in their hatred of members of other Christian churches. Even among the Latins or Roman Catholics there were many internal clashes, especially between the Patriarch and the *custos* the head of the Franciscans, who was in charge of Latin interests in the holy places.'[4]

As the area that the British already called Palestine on documents was being governed as Occupied Enemy Territories Administration, the new administrators – led by other members of Intelligence apart from Deedes – were forced to retain the laws and structure of the old Ottoman government and change them as little as possible. International law dictated that no alterations could be made until after the territory was awarded to a conqueror as part of a peace treaty. But there was no question of pausing to consolidate the British position in Jerusalem. The War Cabinet decided that a concerted push towards Damascus had a good chance of a quick victory.

Smuts and Amery travelled from England and went first to Egypt and then to Palestine where they spent most of February getting reports to take back to the War cabinet. In their absence the feud between the 'Westerners' and the 'Easterners' exploded, with the generals complaining that not enough troops had been sent back to Europe from the Middle East. Sixty thousand exchanged a mobile life in the desert for a harrowing existence in the trenches. Even so Allenby's army still comprised 69,000 men including 6,000 French troops, 540 guns, 62,000 horses, 44,000 mules, 36,000 camels and 12,000 donkeys. There were also huge numbers of reserves, soon to be supplemented by the Jewish Legion, small though their numbers still were.

Wavell, in his biography of Allenby, described how Allenby consulted the Bible daily, and how when they were mapping out some strategy Allenby once gazed intently at the hills, saying suddenly, 'Look at the big rock in front of us! That must be just about the place where Jonathan and his armour-bearer climbed up and attacked the Philistine garrison.' A graphic description of Jonathan's feat as told in Samuel followed. A few hours later when they moved on to another position, Allenby gave the officers around him a detailed description of one of Joshua's battles that had taken place there.

* * *

In England on 20 January 1918 the Jewish Legion was ordered to mobilize. In London they had the rare privilege of sleeping one night in the Tower of London before marching through the streets of the City. Describing their reception during the march, Jabotinsky wrote of '. . . tens of thousands of Jews in the streets, at the windows and on the roofs. Blue-white flags were over every shop door; women crying with joy, old Jews with fluttering beards murmuring, *Shehecheyanu*; and the boys, those "tailors", shoulder to shoulder, their bayonets dead level, each step like a single clap of thunder, clean, proud, drunk with the national anthem, with the noise of the crowds, and with the sense of a holy mission, unexampled since the day when Bar-Kochba, in Betar, not knowing whether there would ever be others to follow and take up the struggle, threw himself upon his sword.' The climax of this march was the taking of the salute by the Lord Mayor, with a few generals from the War Office in attendance, a moment captured on film for a British Pathé newsreel. Lloyd George is alleged to have said at the time, 'The Jews might be able to render us more assistance than the Arabs' in the Palestine campaign.

On the day of the London march Jabotinsky was made commander of a platoon of around sixty men and a lieutenant. His promotion, as he explained, was not achieved without surmounting more hurdles: '. . . according to the British constitution no foreigner may be an officer in the army. Patterson used to say, laughingly, "There are only two exceptions, the Kaiser and you – and he's out."' Three days later, on 5 February, the men of the Jewish Legion reached Southampton and set off for Egypt via Cherbourg. It took ten days for the 800 men under the command of Patterson to cross France to Marseilles, Genoa and Taranto, where they took ship to Alexandria, arriving on 1 March.

As soon as the 38th battalion had left Britain, a second Jewish unit, the 39th Royal Fusiliers, was being formed under the command of Margolin, comprising mostly the Jewish volunteers from America plus *émigrés* from Russia. Soon this would be augmented with recruiting in Salonika and Buenos Aires – and news was received that the 40th battalion was being formed in America.

* * *

Having arrived in New York in 1915, Ben-Gurion and Ben-Zvi founded the *He-Chalutz* (Pioneer) movement of America to promote the idea of young Jews settling in Palestine after the war. They travelled to over thirty cities, and disappointing though the response was, they set up a network which they were able to use in their recruitment drive for the Jewish Legion following the arrival of a cable on 21 February from the War Office in London saying, 'You can give undertaking that Jewish battalions will be drafted to Jewish units in Palestine, if medically fit and when trained.' Ben-Gurion and Ben-Zvi also campaigned among the rank and file of Poale Zion. Attitudes changed after the official American propaganda campaign got under way. Singers, musicians and actors like Charlie Chaplin and Irving Berlin made Americans more enthusiastic about their participation, a difficult task as America had remained neutral for the first twenty months of the war. Wilson had been returned as president in 1916, for his second term, with the campaign slogan, 'He kept us out of the war'. So his announcement of participation in April 1917 had come as a shock, especially as conscription was also being introduced. Jews, mostly immigrants with only their first naturalization papers, who were not subject to the newly imposed draft, could now join the Jewish Legion.

The imminent departure of the Jewish Legion to Palestine via England cut short Ben-Gurion's first semblance of home life since he had migrated to Palestine nearly a decade earlier. Parting from his new wife, a Russian-born nurse, Pauline Munweis, who was now awaiting the birth of their first child, was difficult. On the evening of Sunday 5 May a farewell banquet was held in Clinton Hall 'for the Legionnaire comrades . . .'. Three weeks later, Ben-Gurion swore allegiance to the British Crown, received his soldier's pay and then, with 300 other volunteers, assembled on East Broadway. As they marched loud cheers came from people who had come to watch their historic departure.

Their route took them along 42nd Street to the Jewish Legion Committee office on 22nd Street. Eventually they arrived at a pier at Newark and began their circuitous journey to Palestine via Canada, England and Egypt. First they embarked on a boat that took them to Fall River, Massachusetts. From there a train took them via Boston to Fort Edward, Canada, where they arrived on 1 June. At every station crowds of Jews greeted them, showering them with gifts of cigarettes, chocolates, socks and soap. After three weeks training the new soldiers were on a ship to England, where like the men of the Jewish Legion before them, they trained in Devonshire.

* * *

Meanwhile, in Cairo the High Commissioner took the salutes of the 38th Fusiliers when they marched before the gate of the Residency, and listened to their band playing *Hatikvah* – the national hymn of the Zionist movement – set to a Moldavian-Romanian folksong. This welcome did not prepare the soldiers for the cynicism directed at them by some of the British officials. On returning from headquarters at Beer Jacob, Patterson noted bitterly, 'From the moment of disembarkation it was made plain by the army staff that our arrival was deeply resented. The anti-Jewish Chief of Staff, General Louis Jean Bols, did his best to destroy us, but failed miserably.' Allenby, who had inherited from Kitchener an antagonism to 'fancy regiments', also often showed a coldness towards the Jewish Legion, but he got on extremely well with Weizmann and other Zionists in the Commission. Patterson described his first brush with hostility after their arrival:

> I had an interview with the Commander-in-Chief, who told me quite frankly that he was not in sympathy with the War Office in sending this Jewish Battalion to Palestine, and he did not want any further addition such as I suggested to his Forces. . . . This policy of General Allenby and his Chief of Staff came as a shock to me, for I knew that it was the settled intention of His Majesty's Government to support these Jewish Battalions, and the Jewish claim to Palestine . . . I found, to my amazement, that the policy adopted by the Staff towards this Jewish Battalion, and the Jewish problem generally, ran counter to the policy of the Home Government. Alas! It seemed that another Pharaoh had arisen who knew not Joseph; and once again we would be expected to make bricks without straw. . . .

> Instead of this new unit being helped and encouraged, we were on the contrary, throughout our service in the E.E.F. made to feel that we were merely Ishmaelites, with every hand uplifted against us.[5]

Patterson continued to note how they 'were pushed around from brigade to brigade, and from division to division . . .'. But as momentum was kept up, a recruiting office was set up in Egypt; a Jewish ward at a hospital in Cairo was staffed by nurses sent out by the Jewish Welfare Fund, a recruiting squad was sent north to Palestine. Within fourteen days of opening a recruiting office, 370 Jewish recruits left Tel Aviv for Ludd *en route* to the new training centre of the Royal Fusiliers in Egypt. One report stated that, 'There is an undoubted and sincere wish to "do their bit" (an expression they have already learnt) as a token of gratitude to England for their liberation, and a wish to range themselves side by side with those who are fighting for the preservation of freedom . . .'.[6] Those enlisted in Jaffa, despite the terrible food shortages in Jerusalem, were 'first class'. Medical examiners found the majority 'as good as the finest men recruited in England in the early days of the war'.

James ('Jimmy') de Rothschild, with the help of Margolin, also enlisted more Palestinian Jews. These were organized as the 40th Battalion of the Royal Fusiliers and sent to Egypt for training. Just before Passover the numbers enlisted in this battalion were 2,000. Jabotinsky later gave the exact figures: 'Only one and a half battalions, with a nominal numerical strength of 1,500, actually took part in the campaign. The rest were still in training in Egypt. But by the beginning of 1919 we had more than 5,000 men in our three battalions. . . .' His breakdown was: '34 per cent from the United States, 30 per cent from Palestine, 28 per cent from England, 6 per cent from Canada, 1 per cent Turkish war prisoners, 1 per cent from Argentina.'

* * *

On 5 June, after twelve weeks of being toughened up by strenuous drill, the men of the Jewish Legion were jammed into low-sided open railway trucks. Fifteen hours after they had left Kantara near the Suez Canal, well before dawn, the train stopped and the 881 men and 33 officers, covered with sand and soot, were ordered to fall in and stand to attention. Patterson, dressed in full uniform, told them that they were at last fulfilling the ancient Jewish wish of returning to Eretz Israel (the name given to the area of Judea, Galilee,

Perea and Negev in the Old Testament). Trumpets sounded, and the Revd Leiber Falk, with Bible in hand, recited a simple prayer in Hebrew. Patterson found a biblical analogy in the sparks and flames from the train engine – the children of Israel had been led by a pillar of fire in the same desert. Deeply moved, the men climbed back into the trucks. Before dusk they arrived at the railhead at Ludd to see the Palestinian hills in all their beauty and glory. There was no appropriate place to pitch tents so they were marched through the night to bivouac in the British camp at Surafend. The next day, Allenby inspected them and plans were made to move them to the front. British positions had scarcely advanced since the capture of Jerusalem. Nor had they become any quieter.

Local Jews from nearby settlements in Richon le Zion and Mount Carmel came to welcome the Jewish Legion, bringing clusters of grapes, wine, olives, a variety of other edible produce and home-made blue and white flags and banners. They also showed the men how to shake ripe figs from the trees before the birds ate them. As in all Muslim countries, alcohol was banned. Under the Arabs the land of the old vineyards of the Bible had fallen into disuse – until wine-makers from France arrived with Baron de Rothschild.

After Jabotinsky, Patterson and the first group of Jewish soldiers had gone to Palestine, a second Jewish battalion, the 39th Royal Fusiliers, was formed in Britain. This comprised Jewish volunteers who had arrived with Ben-Gurion and Ben-Zvi from the United States and Canada, plus *émigrés* from Russia, under the command of Margolin. Once they set up camp in Egypt, the battalion expanded with more Palestinian Jewish volunteers.

Soon, ninety-two Jews who had been in the Ottoman army and taken as prisoners-of-war by the British, were sent up from prison camps in Egypt. These local recruits had the advantage of having a thorough knowledge of the country and speaking Arabic, which helped them to take many prisoners. Some newcomers, like Elimelekh Zelkovich ('Avner'), a former officer with the Turks, became a pioneer military strategist and instructor.

A few days after being inspected by Allenby, the Jewish Legion was moved to the front on the silvery chalk hills of Samaria, halfway between Jerusalem and Shechem (Nablus). Beyond the villages of El Bira and Ein Sinia a road took them to a narrow valley known by the Arabs at Wadi-Ed-Jib. Here, near two deserted Arab villages, Abouein to the left and Jiljiliah to the right, was their first front. Jabotinsky described their position as 'a long chain of hills, about 2,500 feet high, running from west to east. North of the hills is a deep valley, and on the other side of this valley a second parallel chain of hills even higher than the first.' The legion was based on the first. Two miles away the Turks patrolled the second, with their camp 200 feet below the summit on the far side of their hill.

Occupying hilltops facing No Man's Land, the legion spread out over a four-mile front. Much patrolling was done under cover of darkness. At night, each man, silencing his heavy military boots by wrapping them in thick rags, would set off with a compass, rifle and a sealed envelope containing a map and the route that had to be taken. On night patrols across No Man's Land, groups of from eight to twelve men would infiltrate the Turkish lines. As they did this without warning, they often overwhelmed enemy positions. Sometimes they climbed up the enemy's hill to within 200 feet of an observation post. When the Turkish soldiers saw them, they responded with their rousing war cry, 'Allah! Allah! Allah!' Rounds of gunfire would follow. On other occasions the Jewish soldiers who spoke Arabic or Turkish would call out, 'Come to us – we'll give you food!' and sometimes persuade a few Turkish soldiers to change sides. Within a week a rumour in the Turkish ranks hinted that there were friends among the Jews who spoke Turkish and who offered better things. Sometimes six or more prisoners would return with the patrol.

In mid-July the men were introduced to gas exercises. Jabotinsky described how they had to 'adjust heavy anti-gas contrivances to our stomachs and to wear them all day, and every morning we rehearsed the adjustment of gas masks. We were told that this had to be done because of the receipt of information that the Turks had begun gas exercises.' He did not know that the British had introduced chemical warfare to the Middle East in the last two battles at Gaza.

The going was hard; the broken ground in the foothills favoured the enemy. Every step forward when climbing the hills released an avalanche of stones. Much of the earth was so stony that the delicate cushion-like feet of the camels tore and bled. Lack of water, too, caused problems. Day and night, men, camels and horses came under intermittent rifle and machine-gun fire at short range. Routine intensified: marching, digging, wiring, standing to arms before dawn. The Jewish Legion, now a perfectly co-ordinated military unit, could advance with precision. Two weeks of rest, following the month in the mild climate of the Shechem front, was cut short. The 38th Battalion received an order to proceed eastwards via Jerusalem to the Jordan Valley – where the Turks still held both banks of the river.

An anniversary, not celebrated, occurred on 4 August 1918, the day the First World War entered its fifth, and what was hoped, its final year. The effective strength of the battalion was now thirty-one officers and 765 men. After bivouacking at Ramallah they camped outside Jerusalem. Some of the men visited the Wailing Wall and saw the barren crest of Mount Scopus, near the new military cemetery. Weizmann had recently laid the foundation stones here for a university. There were twelve in number – twelve to symbolize the twelve tribes. One was laid by the Mufti of Jerusalem, who represented the Muslims. The men of the Jewish Legion had been forbidden to attend the ceremony, but Weizmann had laid a stone 'in the name of the Hebrew army'.

Respite in Jerusalem was brief. Taking the road through the valleys leading to Jericho the Jewish Legion headed towards Talaat el Dumm, one long descent from 6,000 feet. Finally, they came on to a plain near the Tomb of Abraham, and then proceeded north to Jericho. Their new home, near the Wadi Mellaha by the Jordan, appeared to lack the slightest trace of vegetation, not even a thorn or thistle. Near here the River Jordan flows down the deepest gash in the face of the earth, until it vanishes into the Dead Sea, at 1,290 feet below sea level. The serpent is almost the first creature mentioned by name in the Old Testament – and in Palestine there are eighty different species of reptiles, including lizards, geckoes and thirty-five species of snake. Here the soldiers saw many examples of these cold-blooded creatures.

The Jewish Legion was placed in a pivotal position. Now integrated into 'Chaytor's Force' under the command of the quiet and retiring New Zealand general of that name, the legion joined the extreme far right of Allenby's army. Beside them were two battalions of West Indians, a Scottish field artillery battery, an Indian mountain battery and the Anzac Mounted Division.

Dispersed over a line of nine to ten miles on seven small mountain forts, forming a chain from north to south, the position of the Jewish Legion was both dangerous and weak. They had no artillery support – not one cannon between them. In contrast, the Turks on the other side of the valley had seventy cannon, including one terrifying piece of German machinery, nicknamed 'Jericho Jane'. The men also had the ignominy of being fired on by a British cannon, which had been seized from the British in March when Allenby had first attacked the Turks north of the Dead Sea.

Occupying the Jordan Valley, one of the hottest places on earth, was precarious, but a necessary preliminary to taking Amman (ancient 'Philadelphia', with its Roman theatre). As well as depriving the Turks of supplies by boat on the Dead Sea from the grain-bearing districts near Kerak, the presence of the army also cut off their line of retreat. The Turks held the northern section of the wadi, and its right and left flanks.

The Jews toiled and sweltered until the Turks, the malaria-carrying mosquitoes (*Anopheles bifurcatus*), dysentery or other poisonous bites claimed them as victims. The slightest breath of wind raised a cloud of dust. Sand jammed weapons and after firing fifteen or twenty shots the rifles were often too hot to hold. Men developed a squint against the fine flying sand and the ever-glaring sun. In mid-August temperatures soared to between 110 and 126°F, leaving many men, because of dehydration, on the verge of unconsciousness. Added to this, the fine dust was suffocating and caused coughing. A rumour persisted that 'no European man had ever spent a summer' there. There was no shade, just the odd shadow of the sand dunes, a rare cluster of date palms, the battered pup tents and thatched huts. Food – in fact everything – was full of grit, sand, insects and more insects, lice, fleas and loathsome sandflies. Men sometimes woke to find scorpions, not to mention spiders, under their groundsheets. Among the snakes sighted were fat and terrifying horned adders. Like the other troops the men were 'conditioned' to the thirst. Habitual thirst, it was said, hardened men. But all it did was make them excessively dehydrated and lead to incipient kidney stones and other problems.

The men found the water salty and bitter to the tongue. It blistered the lips if drunk. Near their camp was a narrow stream of salty water, no more than a yard wide but a paradise for malarial mosquitoes. Water carts were supplemented by large, oblong copper boxes, usually carried on camels or carts. The water of the River Jordan, so sweet and swift running, was under constant fire and observation from Turkish posts. Above their camp, on either side of the narrow valley, were whitish-grey hills hiding strange, twisted, mutilated rocks – part of the wilderness in which Jesus Christ was alleged to have spent his 'forty days and forty nights' wrestling with the devil.

In the Jordan Valley elaborate charades were staged to make it appear that the British forces there were still present in significant numbers. Every effort was made to indicate that the 'Big Push' would be coming from the Jordan, not from the flat area near the coast where the majority of Allenby's troops were well hidden in groves of citrus and olive trees north of Jaffa and around Ludd. One of the ways devised to create the illusion of massive troop movements was to undertake constant patrols. Other ingenious devices were the creation of dummy tents; the provision of large amounts of forage for horses, the lighting of unnecessary smoky fires and sending huge dust clouds into the air by towing bushes behind mule-drawn sleighs. Perhaps the most extreme of all the charades were the staged marches. The West Indian and Jewish battalions marched down the valley in the scorching sunlight one way, then were returned to base at night in lorries with muffled engines, ready to repeat the same exhausting and debilitating march the following day. To ensure that these ruses could deceive any German planes in the area, pilots flew low to test sorties.

Further false impressions were given with fictitious wireless messages from the old Desert Mounted Corps headquarters near Jericho, while a wireless receiving station had been set up earlier on the Great Pyramid itself to intercept enemy messages. False rumours in the bazaars quickly suggested that the grand Hotel Fast in the old city would be Allenby's advance headquarters for the coming offensive. All the rooms were booked and notices were pinned to hotel bedroom doors with the letters 'GHQ'. As early as May the manager, Caesar, the famous head waiter from the Continental Hotel in Cairo, received notice that all his accommodation would soon be required. When two sentry boxes were placed at the entrance more whispers went from the bazaars to Turco-German Intelligence.

While plans for the coming invasion into Syria were being finalized, the same cynicism that had greeted the Jewish Legion on arrival was again evident. Only sheer necessity prompted their inclusion in the advance. It was unfairly said that the majority were East End tailors, stunted, ill-nourished and ghetto-bred, who had hitherto led sedentary lives, and who would not, it was feared, perform well under intense fire. Patterson himself wrote, 'A little tailor, snatched from . . . Petticoat Lane, who had never in all his life wielded anything more dangerous than a needle . . . adept in the use of a rifle and bayonet. . . .' As a result of this cynicism, only about half this regiment were destined to fight alongside the 38th Royal Fusiliers.

In August the Jewish volunteers from the United States and Canada, forming the third Jewish regiment, the 40th Royal Fusiliers, commanded by Lieutenant-Colonel Samuel, arrived in Egypt. Ben-Gurion was made a full corporal, Ben-Zvi a lance-corporal, and they sewed their stripes on their uniforms with much pride. Jewish volunteers and former prisoners of war who had come over from Palestine, included Eliyahu Golomb, Dov Hoz, Berl Katznelson, and several former members of the Hashomer. But by the time they were transferred from Egypt to Palestine, it was too late to see action. Instead of taking part in open battles they were doing nonsensical drills, exhausting themselves in 'make-work' projects, and becoming more frustrated by the hour.

Above: Empress Helena, mother of Constantine, travelled to Jerusalem to sanctify the Holy Places. *(Photo © Gary Davies, Magnetic Island)*

Left: The church of the Holy Sepulchre, originally built by Constantine on the site of the Crucifixion after Helena's pilgrimage to Jerusalem. *(Author's Collection)*

Known for his devout Christian beliefs and philanthropic work, Anthony Ashley Cooper, 7th Earl of Shaftesbury, was also one of the first British politicians to campaign for the return of the Jews to the Holy Land. The winged silver figure of Eros in Piccadilly Circus was built as a memorial to his generosity. *(© The Illustrated London News Picture Library)*

During Churchill's twenty years as a Liberal or Coalition Liberal Member of Parliament (1904–24 he often worked closely with David Lloyd George. Although a firm friend, Lloyd George was unabl to include Churchill (whose reputation had suffered as a result of the Gallipoli campaign) in hi War Cabinet but by July 1917 he felt strong enough to make him Minister of Munitions. *(© Th Illustrated London News Picture Library)*

ght: Approaching
usalem. For mile
er mile British
ldiers went up the
t, steep Roman road,
rough the Judean
lls, with gorges and
uffs on either side.
re, at last, they ride
the road below the
lls of Jerusalem.
) *Frank Hurley
llection, State Library
New South Wales)*

Left: The Battle for Jerusalem, November/December 1917. Infantry dominated the taking of Jerusalem. There were no head-on battles, just continual guerrilla warfare. *(© Frank Hurley Collection, State Library of New South Wales)*

1915 the Zion Mule Corps, comprising 600 muleteers and their mules, was sent to Gallipoli, ving the way two years later for the formation of the Jewish Legion. This watercolour of the llipoli Peninsula was painted by Frances Cadogan, whose future son-in-law, Major Sir Anthony lmer, led the 'Sea Lion' expedition from Haifa with twenty-three members of the Haganah. *(By d permission of the artist's granddaughter, Lady Christopher Thynne, the former Antonia Palmer)*

Portrait of C.R. Ashbee by Frank Lloyd Wright. One of the key figures in the British Arts and Crafts movement, after the British invasion, between 1918 and 1922 Ashbee worked on the restoration of Jerusalem. *(© By kind permission of Felicity Ashbee)*

The entry of General Allenby into Jerusalem 11 December 1917. There was a new blackout for a day as Lloyd George wanted to personally announce this 'Christmas present to the British nation' to the House of Commons. *(© The Rothschild Archive)*

Reading the Proclamation from the steps at the base of the Tower of David, which had stood when Christ was in Jerusalem. Although the British occupied Jerusalem in December 1917, the Turks were still close by ready to retake the city. *(© The Rothschild Archive)*

nes de Rothschild and the Zionist Commission arriving in Palestine. William Ormsby-Gore was ison officer of the commission, while members included James de Rothschild, Lieutenant Edwin muel, Israel Sieff, a director of Marks & Spencer, Leon Simon, who was later knighted, Joseph hen, Commendatore Levi Bianchini from Italy, Professor Sylvain Levi from France, and David Eder, a psychiatrist. *(© Waddesdon, The Rothschild Collection (Rothschild Family Trust))*

Chaim Weizmann (centre) and members of the Zionist Commission, 3 April 1918 at Rishon -Zion, the winery which had been founded in 1882, and where David Ben-Gurion had worked iefly in 1907 treading grapes. *(© The Rothschild Archive)*

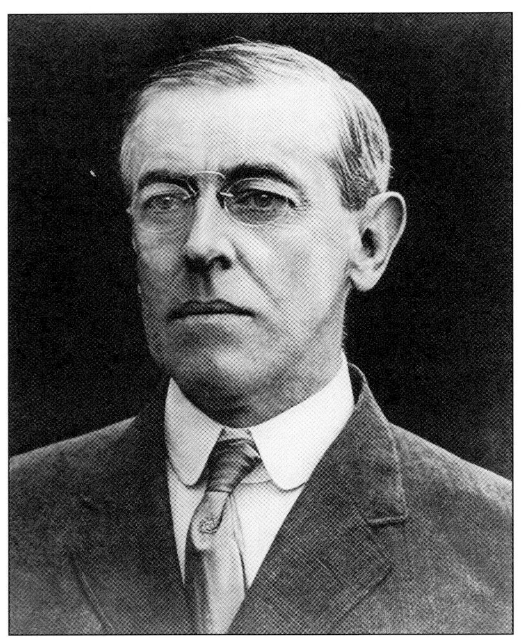

President Woodrow Wilson. The year 1917 was a turning point in the First World War, with the outbreak of the Russian Revolution in March and the United States' entry into the war in April. Britain would not have been able to establish a homeland for the Jews in Palestine after the First World War without the support of Woodrow Wilson. *(© The Illustrated London News Picture Library)*

An 'Arabian Nights' touch was added to the Peace Conference in Paris 1919 by delegates in turbans and fezes, the most outstanding of whom was Prince Feisal (centre), who pushed himself forward as the future king of Syria. Behind are General Nuri Es-Sa'id, who in 1921 became the first prime minister of Iraq, T.E. Lawrence ('Lawrence of Arabia') and Captain Pisani of the French Mission. The Allies recognized Feisal as leader of the Arab Delegation but not as ruler of Syria. *(© Hulton Getty Archive)*

Canadian-born Scottish statesman Bonar Law in conversation with Lloyd George at Cannes a few weeks before the Chanak crisis, which led to the collapse of Lloyd George's coalition in 1922. Lloyd George's stand in September and October of 1922 against Turkey led to the collapse of the Coalition government and the appointment of Bonar-Law as prime minister, the first Conservative to hold that office since 1905. *(© Hulton Getty Archive)*

President Kemal Ataturk of Turkey. Mustafa Kemal won fame as a commander in Gallipoli, but the tables were turned when he was defeated by Allenby's forces on the road to Damascus in 1918. Dissatisfied by the occupation of Constantinople by the Allies in 1919, he led an independence movement against the Allies, which he won in 1922. *(© Hulton Getty Archive)*

Orde Wingate, one of the most charismatic generals in the Second World War, first came to fame during his two and a half years in Palestin (from September 1936 to May 1939), with his night patrols, 'moving ambushes' against Arabs threatening the oil pipeline to Haifa. Ben-Gurion said that 'Wingate's doctrines were taken over b the Israel Defense Force'.
(© Special Forces Club, London)

May 1948: the signing of the Proclamation of the state of Israel by David Ben-Gurion, a survivor the Jewish Legion and both Israel's first prime minister and first minister of defense. Today t Israeli Defense Force is regarded as one of the most formidable armies in the world. But this cou hardly have been predicted by anyone who saw its unlikely and humble beginnings. The Isra army can trace its history back to the First World War and the 38th Battalion in the Royal Fusilie London Regiment, known as the Jewish Legion. (© The Illustrated London News *Picture Library)*

TWENTY

'The Turks Must Go!'

Th' inhabitants of old Jerusalem
Were Jebusites: the town so call'd from them;
And theirs the native right –
But when the chosen people grew more strong,
The rightful cause at length became the wrong:
And every loss the men of Jebus bore,
They still were thought God's enemies the more.
Thus, worn and weaken'd, well or ill content,
Submit they must to David's government.

'Absalom and Achitophel', John Dryden

'The Psalms of David and a cloud of unseen witnesses seemed to inspire our work. "Build ye the walls of Jerusalem." We put back the fallen stones, the finials, the pinnacles, and the battlements, and we restored and freed from numberless encroachments the mediaeval Ramparts, so that it was possible to "Walk about Zion and go round about her: and tell the towers thereof: mark well her bulwarks, set up her house". . . We repaired, cleaned, and cleared many hundred tons of modern Turkish barrack rubble, the Citadel, generally known as the Tower of David, which crowns the lower courses of the Hippicus and Phasael towers recorded by Josephus . . . a building contractor had stolen some twenty tons of Roman stonework which he carried off by night on the backs of donkeys . . .'.[1] So wrote Storrs as he described the challenge of restoring and safeguarding Jerusalem's ancient heritage. A born showman and intellectual, fluent in French, Arabic and Italian, during his ten years first as Military Governor, and then as Governor of Jerusalem, Storrs showed enormous imagination in his task and revelled in being in the East.

At his side was a champion of the Arts and Crafts Movement in England, 58-year-old Charles Robert Ashbee, silversmith, architect, designer and town planner. This well-known disciple of William Morris had set up the first Arts and Crafts village in Chipping Camden, Gloucestershire, which became home to the Guild of Handicrafts, with 150 East End craftsmen. After a decade, cheap mass-produced imitations of their work had led to its demise, and when war broke out Ashbee had gone to Cairo to teach English at the Sultania Training College. Storrs, who had heard him lecture while at Charterhouse, invited him to come to Jerusalem to make two reports, one on the buildings, and another on workshops, schools and crafts. Ashbee was given the title 'Civic Adviser' and was soon climbing over the walls of the old City – which he restored and on top of which he created a rampart walk – inspecting a Zionist knitting factory, riding out to the villages to engage masons, or diplomatically drinking bitter coffee with the Grand Mufti. In an article in *The Times* of February 1919, under the heading 'Reconstruction in Jerusalem', he wrote of the contrast 'between the Jerusalem of man's imagination . . . and the actual Jerusalem left us by the Turk . . . a picturesque but filthy medieval town . . .'. It would be another year before Ashbee's wife, Janet, and four daughters, who became pupils at the American Colony School, arrived to join the growing British community.

The guns could still be heard, but parts of the old *suqs* were transformed, with women and men weaving on looms set up by the American Red Cross. In other old buildings a revamped kiln was used to revive the art of making brilliantly coloured medieval tiles. Nearby at pottery wheels, men and women made vases, bowls, ewers, goblets, beakers and plates; centres were set up where women embroidered and made lace. In Hebron glass-blowers turned sand into colourful glass for Government House on the hill. Over King Solomon's stables in the Temple area attempts were made to imitate the furnaces and kilns in which the tiles had originally been fired for the Great Mosque. Nor was education forgotten. A building in the Municipal Gardens was turned into a Reading Room stocked with newspapers and periodicals in English, French, Italian, Arabic, Greek and Armenian, with frequently updated war bulletins.

The new administration looked on their inheritance with respect and awe. Ashbee was aided by two more architects and engineers from England and on 18 April 1918, four months after the invasion, orders were issued forbidding the use of stucco, concrete and corrugated iron within the ancient city. It was made a crime to demolish, erect, alter or repair the structure of any building in or near Jerusalem without the written permission of Ronald Storrs himself. Another order prohibited advertisements. Although Storrs referred to the clusters of convents and monasteries built near the northern and western walls as 'colossal and hideous', as they had thrown the ancient walls out of scale with the rest of the city, in the end he had no choice but to acquire one as an office and headquarters, as nothing else suitable was available.

Storrs soon discovered 'the power of the name of Jerusalem'. The ease with which he raised money abroad for conservation projects in the ancient city, which now included the restoration of the al-Aqsa Mosque, amazed him. Through his Pro-Jerusalem Society, the School of Music and the Chamber of Commerce he and Ashbee managed to lay the foundation of many trends.

The 'power of the name Jerusalem' was also seen in the extraordinary success of a film made by Lowell Thomas, a Princeton-educated American journalist who had been sent to Europe to write propaganda news stories for America, and who arrived on the Western Front in 1918. He was left with a dilemma: if he filmed the truth about the terrible conditions of life in the trenches, it would put Americans off the war. An alternative was suggested by John Buchan, author of *Greenmantle*, and director of the newly formed Department of Information in London. Soon, with cameraman Henry Chase, Thomas was on his way to Jerusalem, where he stayed at the American Colony with Bertha Spafford Vester. Thomas made two films, the first on Allenby and the second on Lawrence. It was Thomas who dubbed Lawrence 'Lawrence of Arabia' and portrayed him as an idealistic British officer who usually wore full Arab dress and who helped Feisal fight for Arab freedom in the Holy Land against Turkish oppressors. A penchant for dressing up in Eastern costume had, until just before then, been the rage among sections of the intelligentsia – as personified by the languid portraits of Lady Hester Stanhope in extravagant versions of Arab attire. Even the ever-correct Lord Kitchener, during his four years mapping the Holy Land, had been photographed posturing in Arab dress.

* * *

Allenby's plan was to break through enemy lines, hitting the Turks from behind. This was the strategy he had used in the assault on Jerusalem – concealing intentions and then surprising his opponents by acting out a charade of secrecy and deception. For months he devised all kinds of ruses to hoodwink the Turks into believing the push would be along or east of the Jordan Valley, whereas the strength of troops and ammunition was being concentrated in the coastal area.

The Allies were divided into three columns, one to rush along the coastal route and the other two through the desert and mountains. Lawrence, with the Arab army and Feisal, would go to Deraa and proceed on the final leg with the British army. As always in this hilly country, the operation had to be carried out before the start of the rainy season at the end of October.

The British army advanced with special military units of both Arabs and Jews on their flanks. One of the roles of the Jewish Legion, in their series of fierce actions in September 1918, was to clear the way to Amman for Lawrence and his Arabs. The Arab army was a separate and independent entity controlled by the family of Sherif Hussein. They co-ordinated their advance with Allenby but were not under his direct command. In contrast, the Jewish Legion was an integral part of the British army and the men had to salute and conform to British army regulations. Both armies were to become disillusioned by the perfidy of British politicians, and some of the former members of each were to find themselves the main pawns in the tangled affairs from which many of today's problems in the Middle East stem. Both also contained men who were to go on to find fame, and who were to receive the Distinguished Service Order for bravery in operations against the Turks, during Allenby's taking of Damascus.

* * *

The 2,000 men of the Jewish Legion were anxious that the American volunteers, including Ben-Gurion, now in Egypt, should come to help them hold the extreme right flank west of Jericho. But the authorities refused to listen. 'We had the most exposed piece of front to guard which it is possible to conceive,' wrote the Legion's commander, Patterson, 'and we were so badly supported by guns, etc., that, had the Turks made a determined attack in force, we would probably have been annihilated. It was an extraordinarily risky position in which to place a raw battalion.'[2]

* * *

On 19 September each of the Allies in the advance had rations for two days plus an emergency quota of basics and biscuits. Allenby had asked a senior administrative officer about the prospect of receiving supplies. On hearing an abrupt 'Extremely rocky, sir,' he had grunted, 'Well, you must do your best!'

and gave instructions to push the troops forward on short rations – they needed to get to Amman and Damascus before the winter rains came. Feeding and watering the 80,000 troops, including 57,000 infantry and 12,000 cavalry, in the advance was fraught with problems.

On the other side of Palestine, near the coast, the main British force commenced their intensive bombardment near Jaffa, ready to sweep around the rear of the Turkish flank to block their line of retreat. Holding the 7th Army with a strong frontal attack, the British cavalry burst through the right of the Turkish line, and then started advancing north. As soon as news of this arrived in the Jordan Valley Turkish fire increased.

At 6 p.m. the Jewish Legion and the rest of Chaytor's forces stepped into action. The enemy dropped shells. The barrage commenced. Two hours before midnight one of the Jewish patrols drew heavy rifle and machine-gun fire. Patterson wrote in the Regimental Diary, 'Enemy appears to be nervy.' The quietness was deceptive. Men in patrols sent out the next day to check if enemy trenches north of the Wadi Mellaha were being evacuated, were blasted with rifles and machine-guns. Four men went missing.

El Salt (the ancient Ramath Gilead) was the destination of the Jewish Legion. It had to be secured before Amman and Damascus could be taken. The 38th battalion, together with Margolin's two companies, was to form 'Patterson's Column'. Their first job was to capture each side of a ford on the River Jordan in a dauntingly broad section. With hidden currents and whirlpools beneath its murky surface, it flows so fast and is so deep that with the exception of one place, the Umm Esh Shert ford, crossing was near impossible. Centuries of tracks leading here had worn into a natural road through an area known as 'the ditch', about a mile wide, a couple of hundred feet deep and thickly covered with shrub and bush. This hollow was mirrored on the opposite side of the river. Orders were to clear the ford and then to advance to the town of El Salt in the Hills of Moab.

Collecting the various Jewish units across the 10-mile front took the entire night. At the same time patrols were sent out to No Man's Land to see if the Turks were still in their forts. Only two were occupied. With no artillery the Jewish Battalion emptied their machine-guns on them. The response was quick. Gunfire again echoed through the valley. Abruptly, though, at 3 a.m. there was silence. This turned out to be misleading. The patrols brought back grim news. The deepest part of the valley was jammed with troops on both sides of the river.

Patterson's men waited. Their order to clear the way for three brigades of horsemen to cross the Jordan was proving nearly impossible. Nothing could be done until 'the ditch' was emptied. With hushed movements, the Jews moved in a long line at its edge. Huge boulders and rocks obstructed their view. The Turks were out of sight below, but kept watching in anticipation. Another day passed. And yet another night. Tension mounted. Everyone felt relief when at dawn on 22 September one of the companies at the north end of the line sent down a unit. They were to drive away the Turks from the edge of the wood lying under their sector of the ridge. Leading them was Lieutenant Cross, accompanied by Captain Julian from Ireland, who wanted to inspect the conditions for his camels and mules. But Cross was ambushed by Turks with machine-guns and taken prisoner. Julian was shot, falling on the stony ground, unable to move. Risking being shot himself, a soldier dragged him to the side, out of the line of fire.

Grudgingly, Patterson had to admit defeat. The attempt to take 'the ditch' had again failed. But taking the ford was imperative. The next night they would try again with different tactics. Chaytor's Australian cavalry were impatient to break across to the eastern side of the Jordan where they had a rendezvous planned with Lawrence, Feisal, the Arab regular army and the ragtag band of Arab Irregulars to join up and take Amman and Damascus.

On 23 September Jabotinsky and a small group of men again advanced in the dark to clear the ford. As malaria had robbed Jabotinsky's company of almost a hundred men and all but three officers, he was forced to compromise. To make up for the deficiency, he kept one Lewis gun and gave the remaining seven to the two officers, Barnes and Abrahams, who hid behind a cluster of boulders.

At midnight, Jabotinsky left the ridge. Dragging the Lewis gun, he led the company assured of continued cover from his guns behind the boulders. He then went into the open hoping that reports that there were no Turks lurking behind the scrubby bushes were true. A hundred paces from the hills he halted again and sent out scouts to reconnoitre. Jabotinsky got the Lewis gun set up in an elevated position covering the east and west banks of the river. The night was not very dark so camouflage was difficult. Leaving Sergeant Moskow with twenty men, he went forward with the rest to search the nearby bush, made up of shrubby, thorny vegetation, low and densely packed. Two men, a Londoner and one soldier from the Zion Mule Corps, marched ahead; twenty paces behind them, the party followed in a long, widely spread line, extending from the banks to the rocks which are the boundary of the Jordan 'ditch' on the west. They heard shots only once. Jabotinsky signalled to the men above behind the boulders. They opened fire with the Lewis guns. For five minutes the enemy replied. With bayonets fixed the men of the Jewish Legion waded knee and waist high through mud and water. This time they managed to push their foes completely out of an area on the right bank of the river for a distance of about a mile. Jabotinsky showed such courage that he was decorated for bravery. The chances were that the reply had come from the rearguard of the retreating Turks.

Before sunrise, Jabotinsky saw the scouts from another company of the Jewish Legion, who were scrutinizing the upper portion of 'the ditch'. He indicated that the ford was clear. The colonel telephoned to General Chaytor's staff. Jisr ed Damieh was captured and the advance across Umm Esh Shert had cleared the west bank. At last the horses could now gallop through. Lying on its side in the stream was the mighty cannon – 'Jericho Jane' – pushed into the river, never to be used again.

Just after daybreak the battalion withdrew from the outpost line and proceeded to concentrate on the Aujah bridgehead. Simultaneously, with swords outstretched, the Australian horsemen galloped up the riverbanks, relentlessly pursuing the retreating Turks. The Turks panicked. Everywhere there were dead animals. For some unexplained reason the Turkish soldiers shot their own draught horses and mules. Then they burned the dry grass in their retreat, and the heavy black smoke in the windless heat was so thick that men lost sight of each other. Into the flames of grass the Turks dropped untouched packages of ammunition. Other pouches were left in a trail strewn over the hills, exploding when the flames roaring through the dried-out vegetation engulfed them. This smoke combined with the dry dust churned up by so many marching men, reduced visibility and made breathing difficult. Jabotinsky wrote that, 'Patterson, who still remembered the Boer War in the hot African sun . . . had never endured more painful progress.'

Margolin's American infantry marched behind the cavalry, but keeping up with the thundering horses was impossible. Soon they were miles, then days, behind. After crossing the Jordan at the Gorania bridge, a few miles south of Umm Esh Shert, towards El Salt, they were joined by Jabotinsky and his company. This was close to where Joshua and his men had crossed the Jordan before heading over the Moab Hills. Men, too hoarse to yell, lost sight of each other. Sometimes they tripped over dead bodies – horses or men. But on they marched further and further away from the river to the foot of the Hills of Moab.

The climb was merciless. The gradient of the hill was one in about twenty. All water bottles were by now empty. Jabotinsky, describing the climb, said, 'And the men and the NCOs had to carry, in addition to their rifles and ammunition, bulky kit-bags as large as a four-year-old child, packed chockful with shirts, socks, shoes and everything else kindly provided by His Majesty, including razors and tins of polish for polishing buttons. . . . The officers, who had only kitbags to carry, helped as much as they could . . .'.[3]

Dust hung low without a breath of wind to disturb it. Instead of air, the men breathed dust, grimacing as they swallowed it, gasping like fish on dry land. Man after man fell out of the line. It was just as bad on the hills because the smoke rose up from the valley. Whenever someone collapsed to the ground, a soldier nearby would drag him up. On they went. They now understood why the retreating Turks had abandoned so much gear. Jabotinsky, finding a Bedouin with an ass, took the animal – reluctantly giving a receipt – and loaded it with the packs of some of the weaker men. Half a day's march from El Salt, Jabotinsky and his men were ordered back to the Jordan Valley to take charge of 900 Turkish and 200 German and Austrian prisoners. At about five o'clock the men rushed down the rocks into the valley to bathe in a stream and to drink their fill of fresh, cold water from the Me Nemerim.

By 4.30 in the afternoon of 23 September, El Salt was encircled and captured. Margolin, later made military governor, and his men, exhausted by marching and fighting in the heat, stayed to secure the town. In a typed letter to the former president of the United States, Theodore 'Teddy' Roosevelt, dated 20 October 1918, Patterson described the activities of the Jewish Legion:

> I was at this time commanding a Force officially known as 'Patterson's Column' composed of the 38th & 39th Bns R.f. We pursued the Turks to El Salt and personally I went to Amman where I saw the surrender of the Turkish Army on the East side of the Jordan. Amman is the ancient Ammon mentioned in 2nd Samuel chap. II. . . . The Turkish Army being now 'knocked out' there was nothing more for my Column to do, so we recrossed the Jordan and camped at Jericho and finally re-entered Jerusalem in Triumph, bringing with us about 4,000 prisoners.

> The 38th and 39th are now encamped some 9 miles from Jaffa resting after our arduous fights and marches. How arduous these were will be gathered from the fact that I have at this moment many Officers and men of the 38th Bn. In Hospital, mostly fever cases from the Jordan Valley. . . . Is it not a strange thing the whole movement which led to the freeing of Palestine was actually pivoted on Israel (i.e. the Jewish Bns) holding the enemy on the Jordan?[4]

A week later, on 1 October, Damascus fell. Beirut followed on 7 October and finally Aleppo on the 26th. The toll of British casualties since the campaign had started at the end of 1916 was 12,640 lives left behind in graves on the Sinai coast, outside Gaza and Beersheba, in Jerusalem on Mount Scopus, in Ramle and Haifa.

Chaytor praised the Legion in dispatches. He also personally told the men: 'By forcing the Jordan fords you helped in no small measure to win the great victory gained at Damascus.' He pointed out that they alone had managed to carry the line from the Aujah bridgehead across the Mellahah and Abu Tellul defences. Members of the Legion were scathing that Allenby did not mention their role when he thanked the various sections of his army. But in his report he had written, 'On the night of 23rd September the Jewish battalions captured the Jordan ford at Umm Esh Shert.' Many of the soldiers saw this omission as yet another example of Pro-Arab and anti-Zionist attitudes in the military administration.

Guns were not silenced until the armistice between Turkey and the Allies, the Mudros Treaty, was signed on 30 October 1918 on board a British battleship. The realization that the war had been lost at such cost did not seem at first to demoralize the Turkish army. There were no mass desertions. At that stage Germany had still not considered an armistice, even though political unrest in Germany was rampant. The German army was running out of replacement recruits and their effective divisions were poorly equipped. It was not until President Wilson's Fourteen Points were put forward as a basis for peace terms that the Germans agreed to consider an armistice. The actual signing took place after the German Republic was proclaimed at 11 a.m. on Monday 11 November 1918 – the 1,568th day of the war.

On the day the war ended Lloyd George had invited Weizmann to 10 Downing Street for lunch. Weizmann related in his memoirs, 'I found the Prime Minister reading the Psalms; he was moved to the depths of his soul and was, indeed, near to tears. The first thing he said to me was: "We have just sent off seven trains full of bread and other essential food, to be distributed by Plumer in Cologne." . . . At three o'clock he had to be at a Thanksgiving service in the Abbey, and at a quarter to the hour I watched him emerge from the door at Number Ten, to be overwhelmed immediately by a cheering crowd and borne, shoulder-high, from my view.' But the blockade against Germany was enforced until the disarmament terms of the Armistice were carried out and the peace formalized.

TWENTY-ONE

After the Armistice with Turkey

O Jerusalem, Jerusalem, thou that killest the prophets, and stonest them which are sent unto thee, how often would I have gathered thy children together, even as a hen gathereth her chickens under her wings, and ye would not!

Matthew 23:37

The Armistice with Turkey left Allenby master of all Palestine and Syria. It had taken eleven months from the time he had broken through at Gaza when he drove the Turks out of Palestine and Syria. The horrors of the last four years of war were over, but now the problems that had been encountered on arrival in Jerusalem were repeated. Palestine became Occupied Enemy Territory, OET under the British, while the French had the coastal portion of Syria from Alexandretta to Acre, including Beirut and the Lebanon, OET North. The area from Aleppo to Damascus to the east of the French zone was OET East, under Arab administration led by Feisal. All were under the authority of Allenby who was now based in Cairo, where he would soon take over from Reginald Wingate as high commissioner of Egypt.

The Zionist Commission attempted to act as a buffer, a liaison body between the Jews and the military administration. Problems arose in all directions. Orthodox Jews continued to disagree with the Zionists; the Arabs were getting ready to show ways of expressing their alarm at the proposed increased Jewish presence; there was discontent among some of the soldiers in the Jewish Legion.

Ben-Gurion, Ben-Zvi and the rest of the 40th Battalion continued to feel resentful at their slow transfer to Palestine. Living in tents at Tel al-Kabir, they had spent four months on dreary duties such as guarding prisoners and lines of communication. But on 4 December 1918 Ben-Gurion, almost four years to the day since he had been pushed out of Jaffa, was back in Palestine. His battalion had been transferred to Surafend, a base dominated by units of Australian and New Zealand soldiers, because so many men in the

38th Battalion were ill with malaria that replacements were needed. Pleased though they were to be in Palestine they were soon fed up with the incessant drill, physical exercises, route marches and squad drills. Like soldiers everywhere, they wanted to go home. One day Ben-Gurion decided to walk five miles to Jaffa to see a political colleague about forming what would later be the Histadrut, the General Federation of Labour for Jewish Workers. He knew that the guiding principles for the election of a National Assembly, a body that would decide on matters of the community and liaise with the British, were in the process of being drawn up; he wanted to ensure that all workers, whether they lived in towns or were agricultural labourers, had a voice.

Ben-Gurion ended up staying the night in Jaffa. And the next. Back at the camp Ben-Zvi knew that if his absence was prolonged, he would be severely disciplined. Five days passed before he returned to Surafend. Margolin, his company commander, refused all excuses. Punishment included demotion from corporal to private, being moved to another company, less pay to send to Paula in America and being parted from his friends. The only possible way to continue his political activities was to appeal to the Zionist Commission – Weizmann was twelve years older than Ben-Gurion, and from a similar background in Russia, by now he sometimes assumed an aloof attitude. Ben-Gurion's biographer, Shabtai Teveth,[1] wrote that Weizmann was 'Blind to the potential of the workers' movement and to its strength, he did not think that unification of the workers' parties was a cause worthy of intervention with the military high command to obtain long leaves for Ben-Gurion . . . Eder and Weizmann considered Ben-Gurion a "political agitator" unworthy of their notice.' This, the first time their paths crossed, set a pattern. Over the next thirty years both Ben-Gurion and Weizmann would devote their lives to the same aim but using entirely different means and methods. They often clashed.

Ben-Gurion requested a discharge. But each month his demobilization papers failed to come through. Another summer passed, and another winter. Troops in Europe and the Middle East waited impatiently to board battered railway carriages, trucks and ships to take them home. Across Europe troops demonstrated, demanded action and in late January 1919 5,000 British troops at Calais mutinied. All over Europe, all over the Middle East, hundreds of thousands of soldiers, impatient at the slow demobilization, wanted to get back to civilian life. But not all troops could be demobbed. Thousands were stationed from Berlin to Jerusalem, from Baghdad to Damascus, to maintain and to enforce order. In Germany soldiers ensured that the November Armistice was honoured; in Ireland they were needed to deter more revolt; in Mesopotamia, rebellion was out of hand; on the Afghan and north-western frontier of India fighting had again broken out; and in Russia civil war was tearing the country apart. In February 1920, the men were shovelling snow after a blizzard that had brought waist-deep snowdrifts. Some men applied to settle, and during leave visited farms and kibbutzim where they made niches for themselves, keeping belongings there in anticipation of their release. When, at one stage in 1919, most British units had been demobbed or moved back to England or to Egypt, where rebellions had broken out, the soldiers in the Jewish Legion represented a quarter of all the British infantry regiments still stationed in Palestine.

In December 1919 the first battalion was described as the 38th Battalion Royal Fusiliers (1st Judeans). But over a year had passed from the time when they had proved themselves in combat, until they were given this Jewish name. The badge chosen, the seven-branched golden candlestick, the menorah, with the Hebrew word for 'forward', *Kadimah*, inscribed on it, had symbolized the Jewish people through the ages. The 40th Battalion also had a name change, to the '40(S) PALESTINIAN Battalion Royal Fusiliers'.

Unlike Ben-Gurion and many others, though, there were men like Jabotinsky who did not want to be discharged. They struggled to stay an entity as a permanent militia under arms so they could defend and guard the Jewish settlements. Arab violence was increasing and it became clear that some sort of Jewish guard was required.

But the British military were nervous of having an armed Jewish force. There was a distinct need for powerful control at the top, and they were determined to fill this role themselves. A Jewish unit whose role was to face Arabs would, they believed, cause further conflict.

Signs of rebellion in the Jewish Legion were also showing. So restless and impatient were some of the Americans in the 38th and 39th battalions to receive their discharge papers that a small mutiny blew up. Two courts martial and stiff sentences of penal servitude caused much bitterness. Finally, three years after the last battles against the Turks in the First World War had been won, the Jewish battalions were finally disbanded.

A core of men still wanted to remain in the Jewish Legion in Palestine, but many, dejected by what they regarded as mistreatment at the hands of the military administration, started clamouring to go home. Many later went to the United States, Australia and elsewhere, but over 400 of the soldiers stayed on, usually working on smallholdings and farms. Ben-Gurion, like the majority of the men in the 40th battalion, received his discharge in April 1920. In the same month Bols wrote to London urging that the newly arrived Zionist Commission should be abolished.[2]

When Jabotinsky made a farewell address to the departing soldiers he reassured them that the fruits of their efforts would form the future state of Israel:

> . . . Far away, in your home, you will one day read glorious news, of a free Jewish life in a free Jewish country – of factories and universities, of farms and theatres, perhaps of MP's and Ministers. Then you will lose yourself in thought, and the paper will slip from your fingers; and there will come to your mind a picture of the Jordan Valley, of the desert by Raffa, of the hills of Ephraim. . . . Then you shall stand up, walk to the mirror, and look yourself proudly in the face. Jump to attention and salute yourself – for 'tis you who have made it.

* * *

The status of the Jews in Palestine was uncertain until the Balfour Declaration was passed at the Peace Conference in Paris. The carving up of the Ottoman Empire's territories was yet to be finalised, but in Jerusalem the British continued as if Palestine was already part of the British Empire. Everywhere there was resentment about the welter of British pledges and counter-pledges made during the war to the French, to the Jews and to the Arabs. Palestine had become the 'twice Promised Land' in that the Sykes–Picot agreement, made in 1916, contradicted the earlier 1915 Hussein–MacMahon correspondence containing pledges to the Arabs. The Arabs have pointed out ever since that the Balfour Declaration had made Palestine the 'thrice Promised Land'; but the War Cabinet insisted that it had been excluded from any undertakings made to Hussein.

Confusion was also caused as the War Cabinet had never defined the exact meaning of either 'home' and 'homeland'. Delivered with so much enthusiasm and, as far as the Jews were concerned, with so little precision, it gave the officers reasons to support the Arabs, who outnumbered the Jews by nine to one as it stated 'that nothing shall be done which may prejudice the civil and religious rights of the existing non-Jewish communities in Palestine'. It was plain to anyone that because of their superior numbers, any agitation on the part of the Arabs would be far worse than any similar action by the Jews.

The first Chief Administrator in Palestine, General Sir Arthur Money, rejected charges about the existence of anti-Semitism in the army, but privately complained about 'Balfour, Lloyd George and their long-nosed friends'. In *Cross Roads to Israel*[3] Christopher Sykes said that the temporary military administration which was the first to rule Palestine after the Turkish defeat, became notorious for anti-Zionist bias: 'In a short time . . . the army was against Zionism and against the whole conception of maintaining a garrison in Palestine as part of Zionist policy.' Sykes went on to quote the moderate Zionist Horace Samuel, who accused the military administration of making 'every Arab realize that it was absolutely an open question whether a Zionist or an Arab policy was to be eventually adopted, to allow the impression to be broadcast that the administration favoured an Arab policy and that the policy of HMG could be deflected by the requisite amount of vim and determination.'

Some officers thought that strife and instability would persuade those in London to drop the scheme. There was, though, no chance of that happening while Lloyd George was in power. Indeed, for the rest of their lives the majority of men in the War Cabinet, especially Lloyd George, Milner, Bonar Law and Smuts, as well as Balfour, remained faithful to the Balfour Declaration and went out of their way to further its aims.

* * *

In Syria the French and the Arabs were both pushing their claims with passion. Wavell[4] described how the French, furious at what they saw as British encouragement of the Arabs in Damascus 'complained that British officers were openly supporting the Arab claim to control the whole of Syria, and they accused Allenby himself of partiality'. The French claim to Syria, acknowledged in the Sykes–Picot agreement, was now ignored by the British. Allenby himself wrote at the time, 'All nations and would-be nations and all shades of religions and politics are up against each other and trying to get me to commit myself on their side.'

In the middle of 1918, before the invasion of Damascus, in anticipation of future negotiations Allenby had suggested to Weizmann that he made a journey to visit Feisal in Aqaba, where Feisal expressed the necessity for cooperation between Jews and Arabs. In early 1919, Feisal, Lawrence and Weizmann were all in Paris for the peace conference, where one of the unanswered questions would be, why did Feisal not produce the correspondence between his father, Sherif Hussein and MacMahon to further the Arab cause? And why was Ibn Sa'ud, of the Nejd, who headed the Wahhabi movement, not present? During the war the British had given support to Hussein and a subsidy to Ibn Saud in return for his neutrality and cessation of hostilities against the Hejaz. Contrasting Feisal's warm relationship with Britain, some observers already saw a gradual worsening of relations between Hussein and Britain and predicted that Ibn Sa'ud, the fighting prince of the Nejd, supported by a strict Muslim sect, the Wahhabi, was ready to move against Hussein and to occupy the Hejaz and take over the administration of the holy places. The idea of his renaming the area Saudi Arabia was not on the agenda of the peace conference, but would, in the not too distant future, become a reality. On 3 January 1919, Feisal signed an agreement recognizing the Zionists' right to be in Palestine. In return Feisal expected Zionist support to be shown in Paris for his claim to Syria. The Paris meeting had been preceded by a convivial dinner hosted by Lord Rothschild at the Ritz in London, where Weizmann, Milner, Feisal and Lawrence were among the guests. Feisal accepted all the European dishes but refused pork and alcohol.

TWENTY-TWO

The Peace Conference

I am black, but comely, O ye daughters of Jerusalem, as the tents of Kedar, as the curtains of Solomon.

Song of Solomon 1:5

The Paris Peace Conference opened with much pomp on 12 January 1919 on the Quai d'Orsay. Paris was crowded with politicians, royalty, lawyers and military leaders of both nations and aspiring new nations. Crammed with advisers, 500 journalists and all manner of hangers-on, the conference was dominated by Wilson, Lloyd George and Georges 'Tiger' Clemenceau. Uninvited and absent were Russia, Turkey and Egypt – Russia had become the scourge of Europe, synonymous with Bolsheviks, the Reds, the communists and Lenin, and one of the aims of the Peace Conference was to stifle Bolshevism by surrounding it with a circle of strong states. Just as 1848 is known as the year of revolutions in Europe, 1919 could be called the year of nationalism. Europe boasted twenty states and nations at the outbreak of war. Five years later it comprised thirty-one. But in contrast to Europe, the Arab minorities who had lived under the yoke of the Ottoman Empire would be slow in gaining their independence.

The First World War had been the gravedigger of empires, kings and emperors. Instead, many other countries, like Poland, Czechoslovakia and Hungary, that had earlier been part of the greater empires, were now independent. As the gilded thrones of Kaiser Wilhelm II, the tsar of Russia and the emperor of Austria joined the rusting debris of tanks, guns and mines, new boundaries divided up their old territories. The throne of the sultan of Turkey would also soon be added to the rubble of the battles, for the war would act as a catalyst for his abdication.

As the delegates ponderously planned the future of the world, none realized that it would take eight long months or that the carve-up of the Middle East would remain partly undecided. The future Jewish homeland was again at a decisive juncture, and again by chance a Nonconformist politician helped advance the aims of the Jewish people. Despite opposition from his advisers Wilson was about to ensure that the Balfour Declaration was implemented. He had given his tacit agreement to its wording while it was being drafted in London in 1917, but in Paris opportunities abounded which could allow him to change course. Some supporters of the Jewish homeland were anxious that giving the Jews special status and rights in Palestine could conflict with his 'Fourteen Points'. Wilson had put himself up as the champion of small nationalities wanting self-determination. To his famous Fourteen Points he had added his 'Four Principles', which elaborated the theme of 'No annexations, no contributions, no punitive damages', and in addition were the 'Five Particulars' which emphasized the prohibition of secret treaties.[1] Wilson referred so often to his Fourteen Points that the Prime Minister of Australia, Billy Hughes, complained that 'Wilson and his fourteen points bore me! Even God Almighty has only ten!'

Lawrence made sure that the Arabs were given the correct diplomatic courtesies, had access to telegraphic facilities and took part in meetings with Clemenceau, Lloyd George, and other leaders, all the time putting forward the case for Hashemite rule in Syria and Iraq. In March 1919 the Zionist case was put forward. Weizmann spoke, then Feisal, with Lawrence as his interpreter, agreed to these proposals.[2] As the best known of the four sons of Sherif Hussein of Mecca, Feisal was determined to be king of Syria (as it turned out he became king of Iraq). His remarks about encouraging Jewish immigrants to settle in Palestine in the interest of both communities were sprinkled with phrases about the reputation of the Jews for expertise, brilliance and money. This plea was to strengthen his own plea for ruling Syria. Ironically, the Palestinians gave Feisal their support. They did not want their territory to be truncated, but to stay, as it had been for 2,000 years, as part of Syria. In Paris the two Arab delegates from Palestine were overshadowed by Feisal and Lawrence and they had no impact. However, in Palestine itself protest against a Jewish homeland was gathering. The first Palestinian National Congress of the Muslim-Christian association convened during the month the conference opened. Before the Balfour Declaration, the Arab nationalist organizations around Jerusalem had had no sharp edge and no mass following. It was the threat of increased Jewish presence that gave them impetus.

The apprehension of Curzon, who, in Balfour's absence, was acting as Foreign Secretary in London, was expressed in a letter written on 16 January which reported the view of Allenby and other officers in Jerusalem: 'a Jewish *government* in any form would mean an Arab uprising, and the nine-tenths of the population who are not Jews would make short work of the Hebrews.' Curzon, whose concerns may have sprung from seeing the problems between Muslims and Hindus during his five years as Viceroy of India, cautioned those in Paris that 'the pretensions of Weizmann and Company are extravagant and ought to be checked'.[3]

Lloyd George and Balfour continued to believe that the Arabs would back their idea of the Jewish homeland as they were standing up against the French taking over Syria. Indeed, Lawrence drafted a letter which was published in the *New York Times* on 5 March 1919, in which Feisal said that there was room in Syria for a Jewish home and that he hoped the Jews and Arabs would work together to reform the Near East.

Christopher Sykes, who had access to his father's papers, wrote in *Cross Roads to Israel*, 'Ridiculous as it seems to-day, many British political and military thinkers at the time . . . considered that an increase of French authority in Syria, especially in the form of a Protectorate or a similar system, would gravely imperil our communications with India, and in all seriousness many policy planners put forward the proposition that Britain should supply advisors to governments and obtain maximum concessions; should, in effect if not in name, establish British protectorates over the whole Arabic-speaking world, as a safeguard against the rapacity of France!'[4] Feisal was attempting to pursue a middle of the road policy regarding the French. Within weeks Allenby was called to Paris. He, like most of the British, seemed determined to exclude France from all effective influence in the Middle East and put Britain into the leading position in the Arab states. But after being in Paris for barely a day and a half he received an urgent summons to return to Egypt, where rebellion had broken out.

* * *

Anti-Zionist memoranda were pouring in from all over the world. Curzon sent a letter from London querying the term 'national home', adding that it might mean two quite different things to Balfour and to Weizmann. 'He [Weizmann] contemplates a Jewish state, a Jewish nation, a subordinate population of Arabs and others ruled by Jews, the Jews in possession of the fat of the land and directing administration.' At the Peace Conference Lloyd George caused confusion by referring to an area with a quote from the Old Testament, 'from Dan to Beersheba'. Beersheba, in the south, was well known, but nobody was too sure where Dan was situated. After consulting reference books, it was found to be in the extreme north, near the Golan Heights.

The fight to get the Jewish homeland proposals passed was not going smoothly. Would Wilson, a Bible-loving college professor of Scottish and Irish descent, consider Jerusalem to be Christendom's biblical patrimony? Barnes gave a vivid description of this cold, imperious president:

> Wilson was a somewhat remote and solitary figure in Paris. He was accommodated in a palace in the city, to which there was access only through a barrier of French and American soldiers and detectives, and he was seldom seen away from it except when driving out, or at plenary sessions, or visiting the United States staff headquarters. . . . Probably his aloofness, while it created a bad impression, was due only to intense preoccupation. . . . President Wilson came to Europe occupying a unique position of moral ascendancy in the world and he returned to America broken in health and reputation.[5]

On 3 March 1919 Wilson said, 'I am persuaded that the Allied nations, with the fullest concurrence of our own Government and people, are agreed that in Palestine shall be laid the foundations of a Jewish Commonwealth.' This vision was echoed later in the year by Smuts; when talking of an increasing stream of Jewish immigration into Palestine, he said, 'in generations to come, [there will be] a great Jewish state rising there once more'.[6]

Nothing deterred Wilson, not even scepticism about Zionism with his forceful Secretary of State, Robert Lansing, who advised him 'to go very slowly' when formulating support for Zionism. On Wilson's insistence the King-Crane Commission was dispatched to the Middle East to discover the wishes of the people. Wilson ignored, though, the subsequent report, possibly because was because one of the members of the commission, Charles Crane, a wealthy American, did not hide his sympathies for the Arabs. After listing Arab grievances the report concluded that the Zionists should forget about Palestine.

Theories as to why Wilson gave an affirmative answer were many. One claimed that he wanted to attract votes from Jews at the coming election. Another was that he wished to retain the support of leading Zionists, especially the Supreme Court Judge Louis Brandeis, the leader of the Zionist

Organization of America, the Harvard lawyer Felix Frankfurter and others. In the middle of the conference Brandeis went to Palestine and returned with a favourable report.

But Wilson's attitude was also likely to have been the result of his Presbyterian childhood in the manse. The president's appreciation of the Jewish heritage can be seen in this quotation by Cecil Roth in *The Jewish Contribution to Civilisation*,[7] in which he expands the point that the Jewish people are largely a product of the Bible:

> In Woodrow Wilson's expressive words, 'if we could but have the eyes to see the subtle elements of thought which constitute the gross substance of our present habit, both as regards the sphere of private life, and as regards the action of the state, we should easily discover how very much besides religion we owe to the Jew.'

There was no back-stepping about Palestine. At the end of the conference it was clear that while decisions had been made, nothing on the Middle East had been concluded. Finality would have to wait until April, in San Remo in Italy. The Treaty of Versailles pertained only to Germany. Separate treaties were made for each of the nations who, with Germany, had been part of the central powers. Meanwhile, in his absence Feisal temporarily installed his younger brother, nineteen-year-old Zaid, as regent in Damascus with ex-army officers as government officials. These khaki-clad officers were described by Gertrude Bell when she visited Damascus around that time. On entering the king's house she found it full of Arab officers[8] and a throng of black Abyssinian eunuch slaves who had been imported from Mecca. Wilson returned home to Washington after the Peace Conference only to suffer a debilitating stroke. His second wife, Edith Bolling Galt, a widow whom he had married when he himself had become a widower in 1915, virtually governed in his place.

TWENTY-THREE

Arab Riots Begin

Where peace
And rest can never dwell, hope never comes
That comes to all.

'Paradise Lost', John Milton

The year 1920 was the turning point for Palestine's two neighbours, Syria and Mesopotamia. Feisal was unilaterally made king of Greater Syria, including what later became Palestine and Jordan, on 8 March. The Syrian National Congress, which 'elected' him, comprised mostly his own staff officers. But it was a hollow coronation. No European country recognized Feisal in his new role. Within a week of the coronation all attempts at a peaceful solution had irretrievably broken down; within five weeks the former deputy commander of the Zion Mule Corps would be dead and the founder of the Jewish Legion imprisoned. Serious Syrian Arab rioting began in Damascus, when rioters hurled themselves at the French for refusing to accept Feisal's new status. Clubs and knives were augmented with hoards of ammunition and weapons plundered from Turkish stores and dugouts. It is often said that the 'rioting crossed the border into Palestine'. But this arbitrary border did not exist then either physically or in the minds of the inhabitants – only on the maps of the politicians.

A month after Feisal's coronation, all hopes for his reign collapsed. The rioting crept south and the Jews found that they had the Arabs at their throats.

Bedouin tribes attacked Jewish settlements in Upper Galilee, in the area near the new border between the French in Syria and the British in Palestine. They began to roam[1] around this area in large bands, mounted or on foot, raiding even Arab villages for loot. Once these bands of Bedouin were joined by Arab nationalists from the villages, the raid became politically oriented. Bearing knives and sticks they entered Zionist settlements, and at Tel Hai, then a village of no more than five or six wooden buildings surrounded by desert, on 1 March 1920, and killed eight Jews, including Trumpeldor, who was shot in the stomach. His death became a story of exemplary heroism.[2] (A museum was built on the the much-visited reconstructed site.)

The British administration neither gave the Jews adequate security, nor allowed them to organize their own defence. When the Jewish Legion was disbanded, some of the members who stayed on in Palestine went further than, as Weizmann put it, 'a psalm on their lips, and a spade in their hands'. As well as having one hand on the plough, it was equally necessary, they decided, to have the other on a sword; and so they went ahead to form the nucleus of a 'grassroots' secret army. Realizing that they would survive in Palestine only if they had armed protection, they retreated underground to train and arm themselves in order to defend Hebrew settlements against Arab attacks. It would be another year before it was given a name, Irgun HaHaganah HaIvri BeEretz Israel (the Jewish Defence Organization in Palestine) or Haganah, one of the most successful clandestine armies in history. Like all underground armies, the Haganah's continued existence depended on its remaining secret, so early records are scarce and figures and dates differ. Dov Hos, became one of its most active leaders. As the Zionist Organization refused to countenance any illegal military force, the Haganah was run by the same men as those who started the Histadrut (the General Federation of Jewish Labour).

Training was held at night. Shortages of weapons plagued its operations from start to finish. Often, as quickly as guns and ammunition were smuggled in they were confiscated. Today the Haganah museum in Tel Aviv shows how arms were hidden inside farm machinery, and how hand grenades and Sten guns were made in clandestine kibbutz workshops. One home-made grenade had the letters USA stamped on it[3] to mislead the authorities so they would not suspect locals of making it.

Not only did the Haganah have to guard their land, the process of Jews buying it was also proving difficult. First, vendors often found it complicated to prove title to land, especially that which had been held in common under Ottoman rule. Secondly, the British Transfer of Land Ordinance, introduced in 1920, included clauses to safeguard Arab tenure of land but sales frequently involved the British police expelling peasant farmers while the vendor enjoyed the financial rewards. Hugh Foot recounted the bitterness aroused when land changed hands, giving an example at Wadi Hawarith, 'It was a large stretch of land inhabited by Arabs in tents and shacks. Eventually, after long court cases, it was decided that they must be evicted. I had the dreadful job of going in with police, knocking down their tents and small structures and turning them off.'[4]

Golomb, a young intellectual socialist, who was already well known for his roles in both the Hashomer and recruitment for the Jewish Legion in Palestine, now shaped the clandestine force in which all able-bodied Jews could serve. Within a year it was joined by the Hashomer. Whereas the Hashomer had been an elite force, the new guard was to be a democratic militia. Soliders enlisted into the Haganah took an oath of allegiance on a Bible in the home of Golomb.

As with the earlier Hashomer, it was often the case that when the Jewish pioneers convinced their Arab neighbours that they were self-reliant and could put up a fight for their rights, attacks ceased. At this stage the actions of the Haganah were to defend, not to attack. Self-defence impressed the Arabs. It is unlikely that the early Jewish settlements would have survived if soldiers, either in an official or unofficial capacity, had not been guarding them.

These riots were followed by the first violent anti-Jewish street riots in Palestine. On 4 April 1920, crowds were massing on the Jerusalem-based pilgrimage to Nebi Musa, the place which Palestinian Muslims believe is the burial place of Allah's prophet, Moses, a forefather claimed by both Jews and Muslims. Each year, people from outlying regions marched to Jerusalem to pray first at the al-Aqsa Mosque, and then continued down to Jericho to Nebi Musa. On this occasion, a large crowd from Hebron suddenly paused. One of Jerusalem's leading Muslims, Haj Amin el Husseini, addressed them from a balcony about the scandal of the French attitude towards the newly crowned King Feisal. Other Arabs joined in the angry speech from nearby balconies. The police made what turned out to be a terrible mistake: to hurry up the now delayed crowd so they would get to the mosque quickly, they changed the route of the march, so that the pilgrims, instead of going around the outside of the city wall to the Damascus Gate, went through the Jaffa Gate. Shorter though this route was, it cut through the Jewish quarter. Stones began to fly and soon stores were being looted and Jewish passers-by attacked. Mattresses, chairs, tables and people were thrown out of the houses. Shots were fired.

With fellow-members of the newly formed Haganah, Jabotinsky, already distressed by the death of his friend Trumpeldor, rushed to the site of the uproar echoing from the old city. Soon afterwards British troops blocked the gates, allowing no one to enter or leave. There were no British constables on duty in the old city, nothing but a small Arab police detachment under a young British lieutenant. Four days of rioting and bloodshed followed. Eventually the police and troops succeeded in pushing the rioters into the mosque. The toll of what was to be later known as the 'Bloody Passover' riots, as they coincided with the Jewish Passover, was six Jews killed, 211 wounded and two women raped. Haganah retaliation left four Arab dead and twenty-one wounded.

Jabotinsky was stripped of his commission and decoration and, like the nineteen members of the Haganah who were also arrested, sentenced to fifteen years' imprisonment. Public outrage echoed in England and was so loud that a government court of enquiry was held in Jerusalem. While the Jews said that the British military had encouraged the rioters, the military officials blamed the Jews. The fact that the riots had spread from Damascus was overshadowed by complaints by the Arabs that too many Jews were about to take refuge in Palestine due to the recent pogroms in the Ukraine, which had already caused the deaths of 60,000 Jews.

Richard Meinertzhagen (the name is not Jewish but from Bremen in Germany), who like Clayton, Deedes and Lawrence was from Military Intelligence in Cairo, accused the military administration of a pro-Arab bias. He claimed that Colonel Waters-Taylor had encouraged the instigators of the riots, including Haj Amin el Husseini, in order 'to show the unpopularity of Zionism'. He followed this up with a letter to the Foreign Office saying that Allenby was unsympathetic to furthering the Balfour Declaration. Allenby, who was still High Commissioner of Egypt, sacked him. Within a month London sent orders for the military administration in Jerusalem to be replaced with civil servants. Meanwhile, Jabotinsky, in prison, started translating Sherlock Holmes into Hebrew, then turned to the Omar Khayyam. He finally settled down to *La Divina Commedia*, on contract for a Jewish publishing house in America.

Reports of the riots were sent to Lloyd George and other members of the government before the beginning of the conference at the seaside Italian resort city of San Remo in April 1920, where representatives from Britain, France, Italy, Japan, Greece, and Belgium were assembling. Far from dissuading Lloyd George to cancel plans for the Jewish homeland, it made him hasten arrangements to replace the military with a civil administration and he invited Herbert Samuel, who was at the conference, to be the first High Commissioner. Once the concept of the homeland was formally accepted and signed by the principal Allied powers, Britain applied to the League of Nations for a mandate, while the French applied for one for Syria and Lebanon. This new term was invented by Smuts to replace the words 'colony' or 'protectorate' and fit in with the new colonial outlook of administering a country only for as long as it took to stand on its own feet. The conference also decided that Kurdistan should be autonomous, that Armenia should be independent and that there should be a Greek presence in western Turkey. When the Jews heard that the Balfour Declaration had been accepted, there was dancing in the streets and toasts were drunk in wine from the vineyards in Palestine. They were especially pleased to hear of Articles Four and Six. While number four specified that the mandatory power had to recognize a Jewish Agency which would represent the Jewish people as they worked to establish their national home, number six permitted Jewish immigration.

The delegates had hardly left the conference before the French, realizing that Feisal was but a puppet of the British, intensified their military force to throw him out of Syria. He was therefore forced to leave Damascus at the end of July 1920, and depart for London. Hostility to French rule was so intense that 90,000 French troops, mostly North African Arabs and black Senegalese, were stationed from Damascus to the borders. But riots continued. Feisal's brother Abdullah was meanwhile heading towards Syria with about 200 Bedouin and thirty officers to stir up trouble in southern Syria. Across Syria's newly imposed borders once again there was rioting. Violence flared up in Jerusalem on 2 November, the third anniversary of the Balfour Declaration. But it was far worse in Mesopotamia, where local resentment against British rule resulted in fierce insurrections. Despite the presence of 65,000 troops, bombing raids carried out by Royal Air Force planes and the British rushing in more battalions from India, anarchy ruled for three months.

* * *

By 1920 many wives had joined their husbands in Palestine for a 'tour of duty' and a social life, atypical of British colonial regimes of the day, developed. Unlike India and certain places in Africa there were no exclusive clubs serving large gins, with snooker or billiard tables. There was, though, a little tennis, a small group of regulars playing bridge in the evenings over whiskies and sodas, 'a little jackal chasing' with the Ramle Vale Hunt and riding in the Ludd Hunt point-to-point. A few packs of foxhounds had been sent from England and the head of the new gendarmerie set up the Lydda

Hunt. A few thoroughbreds had also arrived but race meetings were rudimentary in their displays and always had an amateur country carnival air about them. There were a few dances held in rooms decorated with a sprig or two of myrtle or orange blossom, but even so everything seemed different from the usual colonial set-up.

Some conflicts arose between the Jews and the British administration purely because British officials were often more able to understand the Arab peasant, who had little to say, than the sharp, argumentative Jewish intellectuals from the cities of Europe. As one officer put it, 'The Arabs have the lazy charm and humour of the Irish and even more natural dignity despite their squalor. One can't help liking them. . . . I am afraid that our policy in Palestine is more than a little tempered by our personal preference for them, rather than rational impartial treatment between them and the Yids.' In contrast, the Jews were vocal, often raising problems and apt to point out any flaws in the administration – and many spoke neither French nor English.

Koestler summed up the attitude in his semi-autobiographical novel *Thieves in the Night*, 'The trouble of course was that they were white – white natives, who has ever heard of such a thing? And on top of it they were all university professors or whatnots. Thought they were cleverer than oneself, and yet couldn't even offer one a decent cup of tea at their parties, or carry on a really nice conversation. Had to show off all the time with their bookishness and the languages they knew and what clever-clever fellows they were. . . .' He went on to add:

> But at least with those Arabs one knew where one stood; they were natives and knew their place. Their notables were polite and dignified, the mob picturesque and obsequious. If occasionally they did some rioting or shooting that was only natural for what could one expect from them. Look how they lie about on their backs and stomachs, ignoring one, instead of jumping to attention when a Major and the ADC's wife inspects them. Good heavens, if they dared to behave like this in Roonah! . . . [Poonah, India]

In the Jerusalem of the 1920s a Muslim woman who discarded her veil and appeared bare-faced and bare-kneed would have been quietly 'put away'. The Arabs did not approve of the ultra-modern habits of the Jewish residents in Palestine, and especially disliked the way some girls came into town dressed in tight-fitting shorts and aertex shirts or heavily made up in sleeveless and low-cut dresses. But despite the constraints, Jews and Arabs did mix, especially at work, in government offices and in factories. They were often seen eating and joking at the same tables in canteens such as at Ruppin's Palestinian Electricity Company, or the Salt Company or Novomeysky's Potash Company at the Dead Sea – establishments which made a point of using mixed labour. Ben-Gurion never lacked confidence that Jews and Arabs might one day reach direct agreement. Many Jewish leaders, such as Judah Magnes, who later became president of the Hebrew University, were fluent in Arabic. But Keith-Roach, the long-serving British administrator, said in his memoirs[5] that 'I never met a Jew in an Arab house, nor an Arab in a Jewish one.' He then mentioned the point, usually ignored, that Arabs complained about Jewish expansion, while they 'continued to sell their land to Jews'.

* * *

From a guard of honour to ceremonial artillery salutes, everything was mustered so that colonial pomp could dignify the arrival at Jaffa on 30 June 1920 of Sir Herbert Samuel as High Commissioner in Palestine, for a five-year appointment. Just as Samuel had earlier been the first professing Jew to sit in a British cabinet, as Home Secretary under Asquith, now he was the first Jew to govern the Holy Land since Pompey captured the Temple in 63 BCE. Many Jews hoped that he might one day follow Disraeli and become prime minister.

Clothed in tropical whites, with a plumed and cocked hat, he climbed into an armoured car, then a special train took him up the Judean Hills to Jerusalem. Samuel's first act was to grant an amnesty to all political prisoners, including Jabotinsky. One unpopular move was his appointment of Haj Amin el Husseini, who was suspected of inciting the Arabs to rebellion, as the Muslim Mufti ('expounder of the law') of Jerusalem. The leading religious and political personality in the city, he was violently anti-French, and, like many Palestinian Arabs, he called himself a Syrian. For two generations his family had held the office of Mufti, but now his position as president of the newly created Supreme Muslim Council also gave him importance throughout the Arab world. There were also those Arabs who supported the ethnic type of Arab nationalism that favoured a united or federated Arab state.

Samuel turned the leaky official residence, the Augusta Victoria Hospice on Mount Scopus, into a viceroy's mansion in miniature.[6] Ashbee and his team of local masons, plasterers, blacksmiths, weavers, cabinetmakers, potters and glassblowers, made the house an Oriental Arts and Crafts palace. Flora Solomon wrote, 'Up on the hill, as we referred to the High Commissioner's residence, Beatrice Samuel transformed a portion of the premises into a replica of her environment in Porchester Terrace. She queened it over the officials' wives, insisting we call her Auntie Bea. At her side a real niece was in constant attendance . . . Helen . . . She and I shared a certain fame in being the only two women in Palestine with our own motor-cars.'[7]

* * *

Balfour continued his role of promoting the Jewish cause. In July 1920, when addressing a mostly Jewish audience at the Albert Hall in London, he said that Britain had 'freed them, the Arab race, from the tyranny of their brutal conqueror', the Turk. The Arabs, he hoped, would not grudge 'that small niche, for it is not more geographically . . . being given to the people who for all these hundreds of years have been separated from it'. Determined to obtain a solid foundation for the Zionists, Balfour never missed an opportunity to further the aims of the declaration that bore his name. He told Lord Hardinge:

> Our Jewish friends, who are not always easy to deal with, sometimes get dreadfully perturbed over the matters of comparatively small moment. But the question of frontiers is really vital, because it affects the economic possibilities of developing Palestine; and on these economic possibilities the success or failure of Zionism. The experiment, in any case, a bold and rather hazardous one, though, in my opinion, is well worth attempting. But it must be given a fair chance.

Soon afterwards, at a meeting in Carlton Gardens, Churchill, Balfour and Lloyd George told Weizmann 'that by the Declaration they had always meant an eventual Jewish state'.[8]

TWENTY-FOUR

Riots and a Royal Visit

And we are here as on a darkling plain
Swept with confused alarms of struggle and flight,
Where ignorant armies clash by night.

'Dover Beach', Matthew Arnold

By February 1921 the crisis became so acute that the control of Palestine, Iraq and Arabia was transferred from Curzon at the Foreign Office to Churchill at the Colonial Office. One of Churchill's main jobs was to cut administrative expenditure, which in 1920 alone had cost the British taxpayer thirty-seven million pounds.

According to Robert Graves in *Lawrence and the Arabs*, Churchill immediately offered Lawrence the post of adviser 'with the promise of a fair deal if he would help to put things straight in the East'. Now Britain's gifts to the Hashemite family of Mecca were to be extended to include even crowns, thrones and further generous allowances from Whitehall. Churchill was told by Lawrence that Feisal had agreed 'to abandon all claims of his father to Palestine in return for the throne of Iraq for himself, and the throne of Transjordan for his brother Abdullah,' adding that 'they tend towards cheapness and speed of settlement'.[1] This was contrary to what had earlier been decided by Britain, and ignored the character and individuality of the geographic regions in this land between the Tigris and the Euphrates. When the divisions had originally been discussed by the British, Mesopotamia was going to be divided into two separate kingdoms, Iraq itself (lower Mesopotamia) with Abdullah as its ruler, and Jesireh (upper Mesopotamia) with Jesireh's younger brother Zaid at its head. But now a consolation prize was needed for Feisal for losing Syria, and if Baghdad, Basra and Mosul were joined together, the area would be bigger than Syria.

A month later Churchill and Lawrence were on their way to Cairo. Once and for all a conference of Middle Eastern experts, including Gertrude Bell, the brilliant archaeologist and Arabist, who was Oriental Secretary in the new administration in Baghdad, would decide the boundaries and rulers of the new British territories in the area. The result was that Mesopotamia, instead of becoming two kingdoms, was unexpectedly expanded into just one large area. Palestine, on the other hand, which had been under one administration since capture, was divided into two smaller areas. Britain held the mandate for both the eastern and western banks of the River Jordan, and at the suggestion of Lawrence, Churchill offered Abdullah the post of emir of the eastern side of the Jordan, which would be known as Transjordan (Jordan), with Amman as its capital. So instead of being installed in Baghdad with a kingdom to rule, Abdullah was given an emirate (princedom) of eastern Palestine. This meant that the Jewish homeland would be reduced in size to just 10,000 square miles and be limited to the western side of the Jordan. Thus 77 per cent of what had been designated as Jewish homeland went to Abdullah, leaving just 23 per cent as Palestine. The idea of a new state ruled by a son of Sherif Hussein of Mecca had not occurred to Churchill before Lawrence had suggested it.

Prudence dictated that the announcement about the new king of the future state of Iraq be deferred until Feisal had left London, so he was hastened to Mecca, the holiest site in Islam, from where he would travel to Baghdad. This was a carefully calculated move to demonstrate the strength of his claims to the throne as a descendant of the Prophet Mohammed. With much pomp, Feisal soon arrived in Iraq, a country in which he had never before set foot. In *Sultans in Splendour* Philip Mansel says that Feisal 'described himself with resignation, as "an instrument of British policy".'

Certainly Feisal had no knowledge of the local tribes and spoke a different dialect of Arabic from any in the area. As a Sunni Muslim he was also in a religious minority. Between 1921 and 1936 the country was divided by a ratio of five to seven between the Sunnis and the Shiites – at one stage 71 per cent of cabinet posts were held by Sunnis. Feisal was given a coronation and a palace; his son was awarded a place at Harrow; and the number of British officials increased in Baghdad. As Iraq had no historical traditions as a state, few of the Kurds, the Turkomans or the Arabs in the newly proclaimed country thought of themselves as Iraqis. There was no distinct culture as groups and races lacking any sense of unity had been scrambled together. Nomads and shepherds were just two of the loud and discontented voices. The Kurdish cities were the loudest. Hopes, which had been raised in the 1920 Treaty of Sèvres for an autonomous Kurdistan state, were now overruled.

On 23 March Churchill and Lawrence caught the train with its hard wooden seats held up by chains, which went along Allenby's old supply track via Gaza and up to Jerusalem. This was Churchill's first trip to the Holy Land. He was not a religious man, but thirty-four years earlier, during his first term at Harrow, one of his essays had been set in the time of John the Baptist, when the land 'lay at the feet of the Roman, who was then at the apex of his glory'.[2] Earlier at preparatory school in Brighton he had written to his parents to say he had won two prizes, one for English and one for Scripture.

They had only been one day in the Holy City when riots broke out in Haifa, in which two Arabs were killed. Members of the administrative staff at Government House were impressed by Churchill's relaxed attitude. 'He did a lot of work in bed and I had several interviews with the future Prime Minister in his pyjamas, while Mrs Churchill walked about the room in a homely way', wrote Keith-Roach, adding that Lawrence 'enjoyed king-making and glided in and out of our offices like an elf'.

Churchill received a dignified request from the Arabs to abolish the Jewish homeland and to set up a national government 'elected by the Palestinian people'. But he was not persuaded. He also explained to Abdullah that the Jews would be allowed to enter Palestine and that Abdullah would have to pledge not to undertake any anti-French or anti-Zionist activity. In exchange for his undertaking Britain paid him generous aid, including a large sum annually to maintain a police force and army.

During his week in Jerusalem, Churchill visited the usual holy sites and the military cemetery on Mount Scopus to see the 2,000 graves of the British soldiers lost just a few years earlier in the taking of Jerusalem. Nearby, on the site of the Hebrew University, he planted a palm tree and made a speech saying, 'The hope of your race for so many centuries will be gradually realised here, not only for your own good but for the good of all the world.'

Churchill estimated that 90 per cent of the British army in Palestine were opposed to the Balfour Declaration. General W.N. Congreve, commander of the British armies in Egypt and Palestine, like many officers, made no effort to hide his prejudice. Later in the year, in October 1921, he sent a circular to troops saying that 'Arabs . . . were the victims of an unjust policy forced upon them by the British government . . .'. John Shuckburgh, an administrative officer, when passing the circular to Churchill, remarked, 'It is unfortunately the case that the army in Palestine is largely anti-Zionist and will probably remain so whatever may be said to it.'

Racial problems intensified. To calm the atmosphere following more Arab riots in May 1921, Samuel set up the Haycraft Commission of Inquiry. The Commission reported that the outbreak of Arab violence was provoked by anxiety in the face of British pro-Zionist commitments: 'Arab disappointment in the non-fulfilment of promises of independence and to their fear of economic and political subjugation to the Zionists.' The Arabs quoted a line from MacMahon's letter, 'Great Britain is prepared to recognise and support the independence of the Arabs'.

* * *

On 1 May 1921, International Workers' Day parades were taking place all around the world to show the solidarity between the many labour and socialist organizations. But in a rally at Tel Aviv scuffles broke out between Jewish communists and Labour Zionists, and the British army fired into the air. The gunshots were misunderstood by the Arabs in nearby Jaffa. Thinking that the gunfire was the beginning of a Jewish attack on them, the Arabs started to riot. Jaffa was still the principal port of disembarkation for immigrants, so tension between Arabs and Jews was already high. Settlements were attacked and once again the Jewish quarters in the old City were under fire. This time the riots took on a political and religious dimension with slogans like '*Itbabu al yahud!*' ('Slaughter the Jews') and '*Falastin bladna wa al yahu clabna!*' ('Palestine is our land and the Jews our dogs'). Terrorism spread towards various Jewish settlements, including Hadera, Rehovot and Petah Tikvah. At Petah Tikvah, the first of all the Jewish settlements, Abraham Shapira, a pioneer of the Hashomer defence, managed to keep the Arabs at bay.

Although the Zionist Executive in Jerusalem had persuaded the British authorities to form a Jewish volunteer regiment, the First Judeans, under Margolin, served as a unit within the armed British forces garrisoned in Palestine; it was of little use. But he managed to prevent further bloodshed by deploying armed men around the Arab villages. To calm one riot in Jaffa, where thirteen Jews were killed, Margolin, on his own initiative, supported by a group of militiamen, marched into the city, sending part of the regiment into action. Before the riots ended forty-seven Jews and forty-eight Arabs were killed, mainly by British police, with a total of around 200 injuries. The military authorities were horrified as they did not want a Jewish force fighting the Arabs, and in response the British disbanded the 'First Judeans'. Margolin was given the choice of being court martialled or returning to Australia. He chose the latter course.[3] Again, the Jewish community asked for military units to protect them. Again nothing happened.

'Mr Storrs lives in his uniform', wrote Janet Ashbee[4] in a letter to her husband who was temporarily back in England, 'and spends all his time walking about the old city propitiating and talking to Arabs and Beduins who have been pouring in.'

As the riots drew to a close, two ships were nearing Jaffa, one from New York, the other from England. One carried 23-year-old Golda Meir (then Myerson), who would become prime minister of Israel in 1969, with her husband, Morris. On board the other ship was Prince George, the fourth son of King George V. Golda's ship was diverted to Alexandria, as she, like other passengers, was not allowed to land because in an attempt to quieten the rebels, Samuel had introduced a temporary ban on Jewish immigration, which was another of the causes of the riots. The other, larger ship, appropriately called the *Iron Duke*, pulled to anchor as scheduled. Following the example of the eponymous Iron Duke, the Duke of Wellington, who had refused to cancel his ball in June 1815 in Brussels when he had heard that Napoleon's army was approaching, preparations continued in Jerusalem for the Prince's Ball. At Government House, the former German administration building, everything continued as if nothing had happened. Guards of honour were inspected, salutes taken, regimental bands played and the dapper prince smiled when presented to the Mayor of Jerusalem. The ploy of putting on a good face continued. Absent from among the guests were Deedes and his mother, Rosie: they had gone to London. Janet Ashbee described the evening:

> The old Germans must have turned in their graves to sniff the oil lamps blazing in blue and pink globes round the two storeys of the cloisters, and coyly hidden in banks of greenery; and to see the naked backs and breasts of Mrs Bramley [the wife of the head of police] and Co clasped to the blue and gold breasts of the Officers of the 'Iron Duke,' whirling to the jazziest Military band ever heard in Jerusalem . . . Mrs Storrs and I sat on the dais and tore everyone to shreds! . . .
>
> The food was bad, and I should say cheap; but you must save on something, and some people prefer spending it on the outside of their tummies (I cannot say backs in this case!). Mrs Heron [wife of the chief public health officer] was WONDERFUL in a creation of magenta satin!

Very abridged above and below, and very tight in the middle, with an 'overflow meeting in the front.'[5]

In the streets outside police guards were heavily armed and loaded Browning pistols were concealed in some of the trousers under the dinner-jackets. The round of social engagements continued, the Prince oblivious to the dangers in the streets. Another party at Government House followed. Janet Ashbee again described the occasion:

> On Saturday we had a terrible party at Government House, when we had to CURTSY to Prince George (Moi qui vous parle!), and we were all arranged around that enormous room like samples of coffee. Mr Cust [aide-de-camp to the High Commissioner] asked me if I would rather be a Notability of Jerusalem, or an Administration Wife, so I chose the latter! . . . It was boring, but fairly select, and NOT a Zoo, and quite nice things to eat. . . . Nothing amusing happened.
>
> On Friday Mr Storrs gave a VERY choice, short, and small party (about 45 of the best vintage only) for the Prince – a little music, and a one-act play, all very comfily and nicely done in the best manner. We are all amused and intrigued at Mrs Vester going straight down the Primrose Path, and frequently EVERY one of those worldly orgies, Anna-Grace in her train. . . .[6]

This was a far cry from Ben-Gurion's work with the Histadrut where he was trying to improve working conditions for artists, bricklayers, writers, miners, builders, truck drivers, scientists and other wage-earners, and at the same time forge a renaissance in Palestine. His aim was much more than opening up places with pioneer settlements. Anxious to lessen class differences within the Zionist movement he would later adopt the policy to fit the phrase he coined, 'From Class to Nation'.

Outnumbered and incapable of effectively resisting any onslaught, the Jews took steps to strengthen their position. First, they developed economic institutions that would make them less dependent on either Arab labour or the Arabs in any way. Secondly, they built up the Haganah by acquiring more arms and extending training sessions beyond the weekends.

TWENTY-FIVE

The Fall of Lloyd George

That walk to go down into Egypt,
And have not asked at my mouth;
To strengthen themselves in the strength of Pharaoh,
And to trust in the shadow of Egypt!

Isaiah 30:2

In London news of the riots provoked another debate. On 1 July 1922, what is known as the Churchill White Paper was issued, which restricted the expansion of the Jewish national home and limited immigration to what was considered the 'economic absorptive capacity of the country'. The paper stated that the government did not wish to see Palestine become 'as Jewish as England is English', but the founding of 'a centre in which Jewish people as a whole may take, on grounds of religion and race, an interest and a pride'. This coincided with the vote in the House of Commons on 4 July when Churchill made a speech in which he declared that Britain must honour her wartime pledges and promises. The House voted 292 to 35 to accept the League of Nations to administer the newly allocated mandate in Palestine.

An administrative system in Palestine was well entrenched by the time the mandate was ratified on 24 July 1922 by the fifty-two nations of the League of Nations. Mandates were also allotted to Britain for Mesopotamia and Jordan, and to France for Syria and the Lebanon. The United States was not a member of the League of Nations, but a joint resolution of the United States Congress on 30 June 1922 endorsed the concept of the Jewish National Home.

But the implementation of the mandate was soon to be followed by a change of government in London, which raised the issue of whether the Balfour Declaration was now so entrenched in international law that a new British government would find it difficult to abandon. In Britain the strains of the growing rift in the Liberal Party, the rise of Labour and the fear of Bolshevik subversion were all showing their mark. Within three months of the mandate's ratification Lloyd George, who had been prime minister for six years, was out of office after becoming the main player in the final act in the old 'Eastern Question' which was about to be replaced by the Middle Eastern Crisis.

In September and October of 1922, the British were on the verge of a new and unwanted war. For a second time in seven years the military might of Britain was asserting itself in Turkey. The Turks, led by Mustafa Kemal, were threatening to break the Versailles settlement by moving troops into a neutral zone ready to drive out the British occupying force based at Chanak, the main town in the Dardanelles area. Having won the war in the Middle East both Churchill and Lloyd George wanted to fight. Aware of a roll-on effect of the Turkish victory on the British imperial possessions in Iraq, Jordan and Palestine, a strong line was taken. If the neutral zone was violated the Turks would face war not just with the British, but the whole British Empire. Lloyd George also harboured personal feelings against Kemal whom he labelled 'an Oriental, a carpet-seller in a bazaar'.

Mustafa Kemal's armies, having almost driven invading Greek forces into the sea at Smyrna, were advancing in jubilation to the boundary of the neutral zone of the Dardanelles, which, under the 1920 Treaty of Sèvres, was occupied by Allied forces on both sides, at Chanak and Gallipoli. Turkish forces were determined to keep pressing forward until they re-conquered the Dardanelles and until Kemal forced the Allies to renegotiate the Versailles Treaty. Kemal insisted on the territories which had been occupied by Greek, French and British forces for nearly four years being restored to Turkey. Allied forces in Constantinople and the British High Commissioner there, Sir Horace Rumbold, were under threat.

British forces stationed along the Straits, under the command of Sir Charles 'Tim' Harington, the General Officer Commanding the British forces of occupation, were reinforced by an aircraft-carrier and troops from Cairo and Palestine. The British warned Kemal. Any violation of the neutral zones would not be tolerated, but he heeded not a word. He would march on Constantinople. Indeed, conscious of his strategic advantage he demanded that all the foreign forces evacuate the city. When he threatened the small Allied garrisons, Lloyd George appealed to the French and Italian governments. They almost laughed in his face.

Curzon, then Foreign Secretary in the coalition government, hastily visited Paris to persuade the French government to agree to a joint defence of Istanbul and Gallipoli Straits against the Turks. After their heavy losses at Gallipoli in 1915, the French President Poincaré was vehemently against any further fighting in Turkey. Not so the British. At a meeting on 15 September, they decided that an ultimatum should be served on Kemal against an eventual interference with what they called the buffer zone. When this message was sent to Ankara, however, Kemal replied that he did not know of the existence of any such zone. He showed that he was also a good diplomat. Like the sultans before him he was playing off France, Italy, Britain and Russia against one another. Instead of cooperating the French and Italians gave more help to Kemal by withdrawing their troops from the Asiatic shores. By now the French and the Italians realized that it would not be too long before a Turkish secular republic rose from the ashes with Kemal as a leader.

France and Italy abandoned the Treaty and made peace with Kemal. Russia followed. Only Lloyd George held out. Britain, alone, continued her armed resistance. It was Britain versus Kemal. The small British force of 7,600, stationed at Chanak and along the Straits, was expected to defend Constantinople. On 23 September, the Turkish soldiers gave up spitting at the British soldiers across the barbed wire at Chanak, and walked up to them, smoking and jeering. A disaster was only averted thanks to the wisdom and foresight of Harington and Kemal, who both managed restraint. Harington ignored instructions from London 'to hold Gallipoli at all costs'. Gallipoli had been Kemal's scene of victory in 1915, the first rung on his ladder to fame; now six years later it would be the scene of his ultimate victory – and Lloyd George's downfall.

In London most Conservatives felt that the coalition must end. A hurried meeting of Conservative MPs put an end to any invasion and instead an armistice was agreed at Mudanya and signed on 11 October. Constantinople with all the surrounding territory of Thrace up to the Maritza River and the area around Canakkale was restored to the Turks. Turkey was intact again – thanks to Kemal's iron will. After the Carlton Club vote, Austen Chamberlain sped straight to Downing Street and faced Lloyd George saying, 'We must resign LG . . . Baldwin has carried the meeting.' Lloyd George, though, already knew and lost no time in going to Buckingham Palace to hand his resignation to the king. However, he acted as prime minister for four more days because Andrew Bonar Law refused to take office until he had been elected leader by the Conservatives. On 29 October 1923, ten days after the fall of Lloyd George, the Turkish Republic was proclaimed with Kemal as its first president. Kemal proceeded to build, not a renewed Ottoman Empire, but a Turkish republic. Twenty days after the armistice, after over 400 years, the sultanate was abolished. At 6 a.m. on 17 November, the sultan was sped away in a British ambulance to a battleship waiting in the Bosphorus, which took him to comfortable exile on the Italian Riveria. Two years later, in March 1924, Kemal, now known as Ataturk, abolished the caliphate and began to transform the old cosmopolitan, dynastic empire into the secular republic of Turkey. Since the fall of the Caliphate there has been no counterpart to the Pope, as it were. Sherif Hussein in the Hejaz, as keeper of the holy places – Mecca and Medina – claimed some rights as spiritual leader of the Muslim world and briefly tried to fill the void by proclaiming himself caliph. But this was short-lived. Within a few months he was forced to abdicate – before the Wahhabis entered Mecca.

* * *

It had been seventeen years since the Conservatives had been in office. Now the Conservative Party turned to another child of the manse, to another Nonconformist and former member of the War Cabinet when they withdrew from the Lloyd George coalition. Balfour had been the last Conservative prime minister, the last of the old order, and now a 'New Look' Conservative was at the top, a man from a poor background. British society was class-orientated, but from Bonar Law onwards – with the four exceptions of Churchill, Anthony Eden, Harold Macmillan and Alec Douglas-Home – Conservative prime ministers no longer came exclusively from either the gentry or well-connected families.

Bonar Law, who disliked the free and easy ways of Lloyd George, reintroduced a new formality when he moved into 10 Downing Street on 23 October 1922. The 'Garden Suburb' was one of the first things to go. He also appointed a commission to interview officers, experts and staff from the administration in Palestine. The Arab nationalist movement was now well organized and so opposed to British rule that the continuation of the Jewish homeland under the British mandate was a matter of constant, intense and bitter debate.

In his maiden speech in the House of Lords a month before Lloyd George had fallen, Balfour had reminded the world of the historic importance of Palestine to the Jewish people:

> Here you have a small race, originally inhabiting a small country, I think about the size of Wales or Belgium . . . at no time in its history wielding anything that can be described as material power, sometimes crushed between great Oriental monarchies, its inhabitants deported, then scattered, then driven out of the country altogether into every part of the world, and yet maintaining continuity of religion and racial tradition of which we have no parallel elsewhere . . .

Earlier in the year, Lord Eustace Percy, who had been part of the administration in Palestine for four years, said in the House of Commons that, 'certain Englishmen . . . who do not like the Zionist policy . . . have inspired them [the Arabs] with certain ideas that they never dreamt of before, [and] have supplied this Arab Delegation with arguments'. He specifically referred to the English advisers of the Arab Delegation, who patronized the Arabs and were helping them in their agitation against the mandate.[1]

Lord Beaverbrook was among the growing number of politicians who were impatient for the British to pull out of Palestine. On 22 October 1922 the *Daily Express* asked its readers to 'try to bring public pressure to bear on the Conservative candidates in the constituencies to pledge themselves to the bag and baggage policy of evacuation in Mesopotamia, Palestine and Constantinople, not if or as commitments permit, but absolutely and at once'. The newspaper did not stop there. The following day its message was stronger: 'every [parliamentary] candidate must be pledged to evacuation' and every British taxpayer should 'insist [that] his Government should clear out "bag and baggage"'. The *Daily Mail* carried articles in a similar vein, but in milder language.[2]

Bonar Law's changes at 10 Downing Street were many, but, despite being bombarded with anti-Zionists demands, he stood by the decisions made at the old War Cabinet meetings. In referring to the press campaign urging the British to withdraw from Palestine and Mesopotamia, he told his audience at an election rally on 4 November at the Majestic Cinema in Leeds, 'all I can say is, we will examine it carefully, but in examining it we cannot, with our record as a nation behind us, consider merely what will pay us today. We must consider to what extent we are bound by obligation.'[3] It seems that Bonar Law was not alone in wanting Britain to keep Palestine, while being exasperated with the situation in Mesopotamia.

Other former members of the old War Cabinet and its Secretariat rallied to support Bonar Law. Austen Chamberlain wrote that acceptance of the Palestine Mandate had imposed 'obligations on this country which I am confident all British Governments will feel bound to fulfil'. His half-brother Neville expressed similar affirmative views. So did Leo Amery, Ormsby-Gore and others. After much delay a report was submitted which recommended continued British rule and rejected concessions to Arab demands. The report was adopted in the summer of 1923 by the British government and served as the basis for the continued British presence in the country. On his return to London from the Middle East, Churchill made a speech to the House of Commons about Palestine, 'I defy anybody after seeing work of this kind, achieved by so much labour, effort and skill, to say that the British Government, having taken up the position it has, could cast it all aside and leave it to be rudely and brutally overturned by the incursion of a fanatical attack by the Arab population from outside.'

Six months after moving into No. 10, Bonar Law's health was flagging and he took a holiday by the sea for health reasons at Le Touquet, returning in May 1923. He was suffering from throat cancer, and was the first of Lloyd George's War Cabinet to die. Baldwin and Beaverbrook were two of his pallbearers at Westminster Abbey. Asquith, referring to his reputation for pedestrianism, is believed to have said that it was appropriate that 'The Unknown Prime Minister should have been buried close to the Unknown Warrior.'[4] But Beaverbrook gave his fellow Canadian the greatest accolade, 'I have known one honest politician: Bonar Law. He was without guile.'[5]

* * *

When Baldwin became the third occupant at 10 Downing Street in three years, he inherited the new report on Palestine. Like Bonar Law, he had plenty of excuses to pull out of Palestine, but he refused to contemplate such an action. He had an affinity with the Holy Land that few men shared: his surname was the same as the first Crusader king of Jerusalem.

Photographs often showed Baldwin smoking his pipe, looking across the fields in a reflective manner, and this, together with his remarks about the rural idyll at the heart of Englishness, such as 'To me, England is the country and the country is England',[6] made him appear to be the quintessential inter-war English country gentleman; but he was, in fact, far from such pretensions. His grandfather had been a child of the manse. Nor did he have a very English background, being probably more Welsh than English. His father's family of Wesleyan Methodists in the north of England were circuit stewards, Sunday school superintendents, organists and general benefactors of the chapel in Stourport, Worcestershire. By the time he was born in 1867, his father's family's foundry at Stourport and wrought-iron-making forge at Wilden were making large sums of money. Unlike many others who had risen quickly in society, such as the Gladstones, during their early decades of success the family had made no attempt to break with the kirk or chapel to join the gentry in the Church. As if to stress the connection with the chapel, Baldwin was named after a great-grandfather, a Wesleyan minister in Stourport, but by then his parents had gone the way of many successful Nonconformists and become members of the Church of England. Baldwin's mother, Louisa, was one of the intelligent and strong-minded four daughters of the Revd George Browne MacDonald, the Wesleyan minister from Northern Ireland who was the incumbent at the chapel at Sloane Terrace in Chelsea. Baldwin's aunts were Georgiana, wife of the painter Edward Burne-Jones, Agnes, the wife of Sir Edward Poynter, President of the Royal Academy, and Alice, the mother of Rudyard Kipling.

In 1888, after Harrow and Cambridge, Baldwin joined the family firm, entering parliament twenty years later, in 1908. By 1923 he was prime minister. But his first term leading the country lasted only eight months. Announcing his policy of protection – to impose a high tax on foreign goods and a low tax, or no tax at all on colonial goods – he decided to hold an election in December on the matter. The Conservatives lost ninety seats and the Labour Party, with 191 seats, suddenly emerged as the leading opposition party. When, after a Commons defeat in January 1924, Baldwin felt he had to resign, George V called for the Leader of the Opposition, Ramsay MacDonald, to form a government, even though he did not have a majority in the Commons. With his twenty-year-old daughter Ishbel as official hostess at No. 10 and with J.H. Thomas, a former engine-driver, as Colonial Secretary the new government became the butt of jokes in the popular press. Beatrice Webb added another dimension by refusing to be called Lady Passfield when her husband Sidney was ennobled. What, it was asked, would cabinet ministers wear at royal levees? The good-natured king relaxed the dress rules. But the public still found the new party and MacDonald's excessively long moustaches, a source of amusement. However the jokes were superficial. Strikes continued and MacDonald, invoked the Emergency Powers Act.

With a new government in office, once again Palestine came under scrutiny. Lord Passfield, the new Foreign Secretary in the Labour government, indicated that he was not in favour of continuing the Jewish homeland. Although he did not get his way then, a future Labour Foreign Secretary would fulfil his ambition of separating Britain from the mandate.

In his *Whitehall Diary* Dr Thomas Jones, who had joined the cabinet Secretariat on its formation in 1916, described the second meeting of the imperial conference in which Smuts said, 'We should hold on to Palestine. There is no more subtle influence working in the world, I hope for good, than the influence of that international people (the Jews), full of brains and character, and dominating much bigger nations in many parts of the world through the filtration of their ideas and policies.'

Curzon, who had been the most vociferous opponent to the scheme in the War Cabinet, now supported the continued British presence:

> We cannot now recede. If we did the French would step in and then be on the threshold of Egypt and on the outskirts of the canal. Besides Palestine needed ports, electricity, and the Jews of America were rich and would subsidize such development. We must be fair and firm with the Arabs showing no invidious preference to the Zionists.

The MacDonald government lasted less than eleven months. By October 1924 Baldwin was back in No. 10, and the Conservatives were returned with a majority of 223. Amery, another survivor of the old War Cabinet Secretariat, now became Secretary of State for the Colonies. Ormsby-Gore was also back in office.

* * *

Another American president, Calvin Coolidge, supported the Jewish homeland in an unexpected way. Like Woodrow Wilson he was deeply religious. He joined the Congregational Church in the year he became president of the United States, having been Vice-President for two years. Under his direction the Anglo-American Convention was drawn up between the United States and Britain, which among other things gave equal commercial opportunities in Palestine to American nationals; this allowed American missionaries to maintain their educational, philanthropic and religious activities and included clauses to safeguard Palestine's antiquities. The Americans were especially keen to safeguard the excavation of biblical heritage sites. In London on 3 December 1924 the convention was signed by US Secretary of State Frank Kellogg and by Austen Chamberlain, and formally ratified in December 1925 by Coolidge in Washington.

One of the results of the convention was that the American School of Oriental Research in Jerusalem was revitalized by the appointment of the foremost of all Old Testament archaeologists, William Foxwell Albright. Just north of the old city an impressive octagonal building became the new Rockefeller Museum of Archaeology. Soon the tallest building in Jerusalem was the 'handsomest YMCA in the entire world', designed by Q.L. Harmon, architect of the Empire State Building in New York. With its heated swimming pool and other sports facilities it was a place where Jews and Christian Arabs were often seen together.

* * *

By the time Balfour made his first visit to the Jewish homeland in 1925, he was seventy-seven years old. So stormy and rough were the seas during his voyage on the *Esperia* that Balfour, like other passengers, was taken ill, but he recovered quickly once the ship docked in Egypt and he travelled by train to Jerusalem. He came for the opening ceremony of the Hebrew University on Mount Scopus, attended by 10,000 guests, including Allenby, Samuel and religious and academic dignitaries.

Jerusalem was *en fête*. The ceremony took place on an open site in a natural amphitheatre on Mount Scopus. When the recently ennobled Lord Balfour took his place on the platform, there was complete stillness, as the crowd listened to him saying, 'A great cultural effort within Palestine which came to an end many hundreds of years ago is going to be resumed in the ancient home of the people.' With tears rolling down his face he paid tribute to the importance of the Bible to the British: 'All of the English-speaking people have been brought up on a translation into English of the Hebrew Scripture, and that translation is one of the great literary treasures of all who speak the English tongue.' He concluded with a Hebrew prayer, 'Blessed art Thou, O Lord our God, King of the Universe, who hast kept us in life, and hast preserved us, and enabled us to reach this moment.'

The Arabs made sure that everyone knew about their one-day strike by backing it up with demonstrations. When Balfour continued his tour to Syria hostility increased. Riots in Damascus forced him to spend the last three days of his visit on a ship in the harbour at Beirut. This was all unexpected as, on the whole, since the 1921 riots hostilities had died down. For the Jews, Balfour appeared as a saviour; for the Arabs he was an insult to their religion and nationality. When asked about the rioting he replied, 'Oh, I wouldn't worry about that – nothing compared to what I went through in Ireland!'

The opening of the university coincided with the retirement of Sir Herbert Samuel. When he left in 1925 he felt that Palestine was 'the most peaceful place in the Middle East'.[7] Samuel was replaced by another Herbert, but one who had followed a military, not political, career. Field Marshal Herbert Plumer had earlier served in the Sudan and Rhodesia. Sir Hugh Foot compared the two administrations:

> So great had been the authority of Lord Plumer that all troops were withdrawn from the country. The Palestine Gendarmerie was disbanded and public security left to the civil police, of which most of the senior officers were British but nearly all the lower ranks Palestinians. When he left Palestine in 1928 there were some grounds for believing that the first two High Commissioners, the brilliant political administrator and the bluff, shrewd soldier, had in ten years established the British Mandate on a sound working basis.'[8]

* * *

By the time Plumer arrived, fired with Zionist hopes for building a utopia, pioneers, backed by capital from Jewish funds in America and Europe, had already introduced electricity and superb medical services, established new agricultural settlements and laid forests and networks of piped water. New wells were sunk and roads and railways spanned the land. The entire Jezreel Valley, purchased in 1921 with money from the Keren Hayesod (the Palestine Foundation Fund), the financial arm of the World Zionist Organization, set up ten new settlements on 17,500 acres in the valley. These included the first farms of the Moshav cooperative movement which, unlike the kibbutzim, allowed private farms. Immigrants also settled in towns. In March 1921 the American-Palestine Company was formed to undertake large-scale industrial development. Hastily constructed apartment blocks for workers changed the urban skylines. New suburbs outside the city walls sprang up in Jerusalem, as they did in Haifa and Tel Aviv, and between mid-1924 and the end of 1925 the population in Tel Aviv alone jumped from 21,500 to 40,000.

During the First World War the Jewish population had dropped to 66,000, the Muslims to 512,000 and the Christians to 61,000. In 1920 only 5,514 Jews entered the country, in 1921 just 9,140 and a year later they were nowhere near their pre-war total, still numbering only 83,794 as against 590,890 Muslim Arabs, 73,024 Christian Arabs and 9,478 Druzes. Immigration remained low and mostly male. An analysis of the newcomers in the Third Aliyah, which began with the end of the war and finished in 1923, was 36 per cent female and 64 per cent male, all mostly young people who were organized into collectives. But between 1924 and 1926 the numbers suddenly increased, with 63,000 Jewish immigrants arriving in Palestine. Then, in the year before the British celebrated their first decade of rule in Palestine, there was a reversal. By 1928 the figure totalled a mere 2,178.

This paucity of immigrants led to empty apartments, a collapse of the building sector and a rise in unemployment.[9] But the Histadrut had become almost a state within a state. It was the largest employer of Jews in Palestine, providing social and economic aid and setting up labour exchanges. Few trade unions in the world then could have been running so many diverse activities to benefit its members. There were cultural activities too – schools, a workers' bank, a workers' newspaper, a workers' sports association, pension funds and homes for old people. All Jewish labourers were entitled to belong and to obtain shares in the organization's assets. The Histadrut also set up Hevrat Ovdim (Society of Workers) to fund and manage large-scale agricultural and industrial enterprises. As early as 1921 it had boasted an agriculture marketing cooperative, a workers' bank and a construction firm. In contrast, Arab workers had no such framework to support them.

Among the idealistic new settlers was Koestler, who moved into a house in the Street of the Prophets, in the new Jewish quarter of Jerusalem, outside the old city. As a correspondent for a German newspaper he interviewed King Feisal in Iraq and others including Abdullah in Jordan (afterwards Ibn Sa'ud took over the Hejaz, and Hussein spent his last days as a refugee in one of his son's modest palaces); the Egyptian prime minister and the president of Lebanon. Koestler also wrote about the rivalry between the Husseini Jerusalem-based and Nashashibi Nablus-based clans as they struggled for leadership of the Arab national movement in Palestine.

In 1928 Jabotinsky returned to edit *Doar HaYom*, a daily newspaper which was also a vehicle for revisionism.[10] Koestler joined his staff and brightened it up with a weekend section and a crossword puzzle, and in just a few months circulation doubled to 2,000. But in July 1930 the British authorities, alarmed by the paper's right-wing politics, gave the publisher an ultimatum: Jabotinsky had to leave or the paper would be closed.

* * *

In September 1928 a screen erected by Jewish worshippers at the Western or Wailing Wall to segregate men from women became the cause of a bitter dispute as it was held to have changed a holy place. The president of the Muslim Council protested against the Jewish practice of bringing what were called 'appurtenances *of worship*' to the Wall which he specified as 'a wooden room covered with cloth, screens, mats, a large table in the middle and also the Ten Commandments placed on a chair which should not be there'. The wall is part of the Haram-al-Sharif which belongs to the Muslim community, as does the strip of pavement facing it. As said earlier, it is the remaining part of Herod's Temple it is also holy to Jews, and their custom of praying there dates back over a thousand years. The Muslims had earlier given them the right of prayer there but this right was limited. They could not interfere with its structure.

Muslims regarded the introduction of certain of these objects as an attempt to effect a permanent change at a holy site. Amid the tension, Arabs carried out a savage massacre in Hebron, Safed and Jerusalem. One hundred and forty Jews were killed, including women and children. In the subsequent inquiry the Arabs again voiced their fears that the fundamental aspiration of Zionism was to take possession of the whole Temple area and the Mosque of Omar, as a step towards driving the Arabs out of Palestine. Because of their shared heritage of the Old Testament, there were also problems over other sites, including the tomb of Jacob's wife Rachel near Bethlehem, to which the Jews held the keys.

On 16 August 1929 a crowd of several thousand Arabs pushed their way forward to the Wailing Wall where Jews were concluding the Tishah Be-Av ceremony. Worshippers were attacked, as were sacred objects. Prayer books were thrown into the air, and riots spread across the country. Martial law was not enough to stop the rebellion and extra troops were sent by the British administration. Despite the problems, in 1929 Jewish immigration increased and the economy picked up.

* * *

Weizmann no longer had access to the centres of power in Britain, as a few months before the riots, in May 1929, the Conservatives had been pushed out of office. Ramsay MacDonald yet again became Stanley Baldwin's successor. During his earlier brief tenure at No. 10 MacDonald had shown no sympathy to the position of the Jews in Palestine and this time his position remained unchanged. The Zionists anticipated that the new government would be swayed by the renewed Arab reaction to Jewish immigration and the recent Arab riots.

A commission of inquiry under the chairmanship of Sir Walter Shaw was dispatched to Palestine to investigate the causes of the riots. In March 1930 another Arab delegation, headed by Musa Kasim Pasha, went to London to lobby politicians. On 21 October 1930, the new Colonial Secretary, Lord Passfield, tried to repudiate the Balfour Declaration by publishing the commission report in the Passfield White Paper. It stated that Jewish immigration and land purchases should cease.[11]

Although Balfour and Lloyd George were out of office, they were still championing the cause of the Jewish homeland. Smuts, then Minister of Justice in South Africa, also stood by his earlier decisions. In December 1929 he arranged a meeting with Passfield and Henderson, Secretary of State for Foreign Affairs. He found Passfield 'a tired man who is overwhelmed with the problem' when it was pointed out that the White Paper was inconsistent with the mandate. But the seed of the idea was sown for a cabinet committee to be set up under Henderson, another former member of the War Cabinet.

The personal support of Lloyd George, Balfour and Smuts to Zionism was publicized in a solemn letter to *The Times* on 19 December 1929, drawing attention to the doubts which had arisen, and repeating, in unequivocal terms, the original intention of the Balfour Declaration. It was printed next to the leader, under the heading 'The Situation in Palestine. Working of the Mandate. Plea for Full Inquiry.'[12]

> To the Editor of *The Times*
>
> Sir – As members of the War Cabinet which was responsible for the Balfour Declaration 12 years ago, and for the policy of the National Home for the Jewish people which it foreshadowed, we view with deep anxiety the present situation in Palestine. On the events of last August, which are now the subject of inquiry by a special Commission, we forbear to comment. But it seems clear that, whatever the finding of that Commission may be the responsibility for the August outbreak, the work to which Britain set her hand at the close of the War is not proceeding satisfactorily.
>
> The Balfour Declaration pledged us to a policy: the Palestine Mandate entrusted us with vital administrative duties; but causes which are still obscure have impeded the task of administration, and consequently the full carrying out of the policy.
>
> In these circumstances we would urge on the Government the appointment of an authoritative Commission to investigate the whole working of the mandate. The Commission at present in Palestine was appointed with limited terms of reference to inquire into specific matters. This Commission, in our view, must, as soon as it has reported, be supplemented by a searching inquiry into the major questions of policy and administration. Our pledge is unequivocal, but, in order to fulfil it in the letter and the spirit, a considerable readjustment of the administrative machine may be desirable. Such a Commission would be an advertisement to the world that Britain has not weakened in a task to which her honour is pledged, and at the same time as assurance to Jews and Arabs alike that any proven defects in the present system of government will be made good.
>
> We are BALFOUR, D. LLOYD GEORGE, J.C. SMUTS

In the editorial, under the title 'Palestine Mandate', the editor commented on the situation:

> Lord Balfour and his fellow signatories ask for a deeper investigation, with wider terms of reference, into the whole working of the mandate, and, in view of the attacks that have been made upon it, there is something to be said for their view. But it will require rather closer definition. It is possible

> that the present Commission of Inquiry may find that the recent troubles have been chiefly caused by personal inadequacies either in Jerusalem or nearer home. . . .

By February 1931, as a result of Henderson's committee, which had modified Passfield's policy, a letter was issued from Ramsay MacDonald to Weizmann reaffirming that Jewish immigration would be limited only by Palestine's economic capacity to absorb new settlers. Again there was a reversal of policy.

* * *

Weizmann and Lloyd George owned houses in London within a hundred yards of each other, near Holland Park in Kensington. Weizmann had moved into 67 Addison Road in 1917; Lloyd George had acquired 2 Addison Road around 1923. Their casual meetings are not recorded, but Weizmann made three visits to see Lloyd George at Bron-y-de, the house he had built in 1921 at Churt, forty miles from London. Here, surrounded by a farm and orchards, he wrote his war memoirs. Lloyd George's nephew, Dr William George, remembers his uncle telling him of a visit by Weizmann[13] when a book was presented to Lloyd George inscribed, 'To the author of the Jewish homeland.'

TWENTY-SIX

Orde Wingate and the Haganah

Then were the horsehoofs broken by the means of the prancings
The prancings of their mighty ones.

The Song of Deborah, Judges 5:22

Orde Wingate's Bible was his most precious possession; his strongest belief was in the existence of a Judeo-Christian God, a Jehovah, a personal deity. Having rejected the dogma of the Christian Church he was sustained by the Old Testament, which he had begun studying as a small child. Born in India, in 1903, his parents were devout members of the Plymouth Brethren, a sect who believed in the literal interpretation of the Bible and the Second Coming of Christ. Unlike the writer Edmund Gosse, raised in another Plymouth Brethren home who had reacted against his strict childhood by writing a candid autobiography, *Father and Son*, religion remained the foundation stone of Wingate's life – although he did not uphold the beliefs of the Plymouth Brethren as deeply as Gosse's father. Gosse's description of the Sabbath shows how such Protestant sects often went back to the Jewish roots of their belief:

> My father objected very strongly to the expression Sabbath-day, as it is commonly used by Presbyterians and others. He said, quite justly, that it was an inaccurate modern innovation, that Sabbath was Saturday, the seventh day of the week, not the first, a Jewish festival and not a Christian commemoration. Yet his exaggerated view with regard to the observance of the First Day, namely, that it must be exclusively occupied with public and private exercises of divine worship, was based much more upon a Jewish than upon a Christian law. In fact, I do not remember that my Father ever produced a definite argument from the New Testament in support of his excessive passivity on the Lord's Day. He followed the early Puritan practice, except that he did not extend his observance, as I believe the old Puritans

> did, from sunset on Saturday to sunset on Sunday I was hotly and tightly dressed in black, all day long, as though ready at any moment to attend a funeral with decorum. . . .[1]

After an unsatisfactory education as a day boy at Charterhouse, Wingate followed in the footsteps of his father and his famous second cousin Sir Reginald Wingate (referred to in the family as 'Cousin Rex'), and entered the army. Then, after studying at the Royal Military Academy and the School of Oriental and African Studies at London University he spent five years with the Sudan Defence Force. At his wedding in Chelsea Old Church on 24 January 1935 to Lorna – so young that she had only recently left her Scottish boarding school – Wingate chose three pieces of music, as if he knew his next army posting would be the destination of his dreams, the Holy Land. The first was the hymn 'To be a Pilgrim', which begins with the words 'He who would valiant be . . . ' written by John Bunyan during his second prison term. The other two pieces of music were the Pilgrims' Chorus from *Tannhäuser* and C.H.H. Parry's popular adaptation of William Blake's poem, which evokes the image of England's 'green and pleasant Land' as the New Jerusalem. In September, the next year, this good-looking couple arrived in that very city. Wingate's post was as a Staff Intelligence Officer to Fifth Division headquarters in Haifa to organize raids against the Arab Terrorists. Problems in Palestine were unremitting and government policy continued to change with the changing governments in London.

Anxiety about the Arabs damaging Britain's vital pipeline carrying oil from Iraq to ships in the port of Haifa caused the British to speed up a system to protect it. In the late 1920s the British and French agreed on a compromise for the Iraq Petroleum Company, formerly the Anglo-Persian Oil Company, to construct two parallel pipelines from Kirkūk to Al Haditha in north-western Iraq. There these pipelines separated, the northern one being routed to the harbour of Tripoli, or Tarābulus, in Lebanon, then controlled by the French. The southern pipeline, which came into operation in 1934, was routed to Haifa where the British improved the harbour facilities. After six weeks of intensive training, Wingate launched his night-fighting operations, leading groups of Jews to raid camps swiftly so as to disable them before the Arabs set out on missions of terror and sabotage. He also showed troops how to locate the Arabs' arsenal and how to carry away their stores of weapons. After studying the Haganah's usually static responses to Arab attacks, he said,

'So long as you sit in your settlements and wait to fight and die, you will die before you have a chance to fight.'[2] The year after Wingate arrived, a crude oil stabilization plant was erected at the Haifa end of the pipeline (which would come into operation two years later, just in time for the Second World War).

Gideon's heroism and military victories in Chapter VII of the Book of Judges enthralled him. His Night Squads, which were punctuated with remarks about biblical landmarks, which he identified with enthusiasm were composed of a few British regulars and a larger number of young Haganah soldiers. Two of his pupils went on to become top commanders in the Israeli army. One was Yigal Allon, the other the 22-year-old Moshe Dayan, then dividing his time between studying, labouring in the fields of Nahalal, and working as a mounted policeman with the Jewish Settlement Police, who patrolled the area.

Dayan recalled Wingate saying that 'the very existence of mankind is justified when it is based on the moral foundation of the Bible. Whoever dares lift a hand against you and your enterprise here should be fought against.' On another occasion he told his soldiers, 'God give it to us to slay the enemies of the Jews, for the enemies of the Jews are the enemies of all mankind.'[3]

Wingate's report, 'Ways of Making His Majesty's Forces Operate at Night with the Objective of Putting an End to the Terror in Northern Palestine', introduced new attitudes and techniques in countering Arab guerrilla gangs. These were carried out from his headquarters at a kibbutz near Ein Harod, in the Jezreel Valley, in the very place where the warrior Gideon had once camped in biblical times. A typical soldier, Wingate believed that war was terrible, but he was pleased to be taking part in battles which for him were the fulfilment of a divine promise. Some people regarded him as something of a mystic[4] who considered Zionism as having been laid down by God himself. The Jewish people, he said, owed their existence to the Bible and the Holy Land. He always carried a copy of the Bible, even when fighting.

* * *

The continuing influx of Jewish refugees into Jaffa and Haifa, as they fled from Hitler's regime in Germany, led to more unrest. Persecution in Germany began after Hitler became Chancellor in January 1933. His death camps and experiments in eugenics were still in the future, as were his laws for the 'Protection of German Blood and Honour', but already laws were passed that excluded Jewish people from cultural life, stripped them of citizenship and forbade them to marry gentiles. Soon the Nuremberg Laws would stop them owning pets and radios, swimming in public pools or visiting cinemas or public parks. To work in journalism, law, medicine or education[5] was also forbidden. Their posts were filled by non-Jewish Germans.

In 1935 about 69,000 refugees arrived in Palestine – an increase of over 23,000 from the previous year. The Arabs reacted in April 1936 with violent rioting in Jaffa, which soon spread across the country. Sixteen people were killed in the first two days.[6] The Arabs made it clear that they were not going to tolerate either the Jews or British rule. The Arab General Strike, an all-out rebellion against the British followed and lasted 170 days. Outbursts of Arab violence in different parts of the country were engendered by a host of different leaders, from village chiefs or religious sheikhs with peasant followings, to urban gang leaders.

Despite the efficiency of the British army and the introduction of a unit of Jewish Settlement Police, adequate protection to the Jewish settlers, especially in country areas, was still lacking. Some authorities were ambivalent in their attitudes to the Haganah and sometimes they chose to look the other way, and at other times they imprisoned members for carrying illegal weapons. This inconsistency made life precarious, especially as settlers had to defend themselves. The Haganah had to smuggle in or secretly manufacture every weapon they used.

The British thought that the rioting, as previously in 1929, would wear itself out quickly. This time, though, it was going to take three years to suppress, and would result in the death of around 2,000 Arabs, 112 of whom were executed by the British. The Jewish death toll was much less. Koestler gave a sympathetic appraisal of the Arab situation in *Promise and Fulfilment*: 'On at least three occasions in thirty years, the Arabs had been promised the setting up of a legislative body, the cessation of Jewish immigration and a check on Jewish economic expansion.'[7]

Baldwin, who had been back in power since 1931, first as lord president of council in Ramsay MacDonald's National Government between 1931 and 1935, and then, in the June 1935 election, as prime minister for the third time, soon had to face a rebellion in the House of Commons over Palestine. With his Colonial Secretary, Ormsby-Gore, he managed to calm the situation. A Royal Commission under Lord Peel was set up and an extra 20,000 troops were sent out. When Peel arrived in Palestine the Mufti announced that *no*

Arabs would cooperate with an inquiry until immigration was suspended. In the end, though, when he saw the hundreds of British and Jews being interviewed, he himself gave evidence to support his case against continued Jewish migrants coming into the country. By the time the Peel Report was finished, there was a new king in Britain, George VI, and a new prime minister, Neville Chamberlain, and Ramsay MacDonald's son, Malcolm, was Colonial Secretary. This extract from the report summarizes the situation:

> Almost a million Arabs are in strife, open or latent, with some 400,000 Jews. There is no common ground between them. The Arab community is predominantly Asiatic in character, the Jewish community predominantly European. They differ in religion and language. Their cultural and social life, their ways of thought and conduct, are as incompatible as their national aspirations.

The report recommended the division of the country into Jewish and Arab states with national independence for both groups. While the Arabs responded by increased rioting, Ben-Gurion believed that it was a springboard to independence, but the Peel Report came to nothing.

At the time of the lavish spectacle of King George VI's coronation in England in May 1937, there was full-scale guerrilla warfare in Palestine. Telephone lines were cut, bridges made impassable, trains derailed, convoys ambushed, and there was fighting in the hills. Mufti-inspired Arab riots broke out in both in towns and countryside. Every day, people on both sides were killed.[8] To counter this situation the government in London adopted policies increasingly hostile to Zionism. These had become more extreme since Stanley Baldwin's resignation as prime minister over the abdication crisis. The general view then was that the mandate was unworkable. Little tolerance for the situation in Palestine was shown by the new Conservative government under Chamberlain, who felt that respect for the Arabs now had to be shown to prevent retaliation by the Muslims in India. In *The Long Weekend* Robert Graves summed up the situation:

> . . . the military were left to deal with well-organized marauding Arab bands as best they could, without either inflaming Arab feelings against British rule throughout the Near East or over-exciting the Jews. Before the outbreak of war the . . . Arab revolt had been quelled, but the problem was

> still unsolved: the Jews formed a prosperous, industrialized modern community, the Arabs – of whom there were twice as many – a poor, scattered, chiefly agricultural and labouring class. No cooperation between them seemed possible. Jewish farms were a standing annoyance to the Arab: tractors, artesian wells, nitrates, selected seeds, Zionist zeal, raised enormous crops from the same soil that he scratched with his plough for the sake of a few stunted sheaves. . . .[9]

* * *

Dayan wrote about Wingate with enormous affection.[10] He said that when he first met this slight stranger, he wondered how he would be able to advance in the dark over terrain unknown to him. When moving 'from the beaten path to clamber over rocks and through the bushes, I doubted that he would be able to keep up the brisk pace. He seemed so fragile. And what did he know of the Arabs, or of the slopes and gullies of the Nazareth hills which had been part of our lives since childhood?' But by dawn, as they climbed over barbed wire and bullets whipped up the sand in front of them, Dayan's doubts evaporated.

Wingate's tenacity also amazed the men. He never asked them to halt or rest. They just went on and on until they returned to base for breakfast. Dayan described how he sometimes would happily take off his clothes and sit in the room as the boys cooked:

> There we would fry omelette and potatoes on a primus stove and prepare a tomato salad. While all this was going on, Wingate would sit in a corner, stark naked, reading the Bible and munching raw onions as though they were the most luscious pears. Judged by ordinary standards he would not be regarded as normal. . . . He was a military genius and a wonderful man.[11]

But such was Wingate's charm and enthusiasm that the men never minded his odd habits or his tendency to pause to recite or read passages in the Bible, always relating any descriptions to their new whereabouts. Dayan explained, 'He would find testimony to our victory – the victory of God and the Jews.'

Wingate's uninhibited criticisms of British policy, coupled with the way he sought out Zionist leaders, including Weizmann, Ben-Gurion and various Haganah intelligence officers, emphasized his pro-Jewish stance. The military authorities were enraged by Wingate's unorthodox behaviour and considered his success with the Jews against the Arabs as a threat to any possible peace, and so in May 1939 he was sent to England to await another posting abroad. He saw his removal as just one more manifestation of Britain bowing to Arab demands. Whie staying at the Army and Navy Club in St James's Square in London he was distressed at the perceived injustice of the report written about him by his commanding officer:

> Captain Wingate possesses many exceptional qualities; however his ardent nature which gives him the power to pursue an objective enthusiastically often obscures his judgement and distorts his sense of proportion.
>
> He has a first-class brain, is exceptionally well read and has great mental energy but he is liable to employ these gifts for the furtherance of some idea which he has adopted because of its emotional appeal. While he has been in Palestine he has given his sympathy so wholeheartedly to the Jewish cause that his service to the intelligence branch has become valueless. . . .

This letter epitomizes the muddled attitude of the authorities in Palestine: in the previous year, 1938, he had been awarded the Distinguished Service Order for helping to clear Palestine of terrorists.

In London Wingate showed how he had embraced the Jewish cause by keeping up his contacts with the Zionists, including Victor Cazalet, a Member of Parliament, and Weizmann. Both men had suites at the Dorchester Hotel and each Wednesday hosted an informal Zionist meeting, followed by dinner with guests such as Balfour's niece, Blanche Dugdale, and Leo Amery. Wingate continued to promote the idea of the formation of another Jewish Legion. Although no longer present, Wingate was vividly remembered by the soldiers who had fought with him in Palestine. They referred to him as *hayedid*, 'the friend', and his name became a by-word for daring and courage among the thousands of young Jewish soldiers.

* * *

War with Germany was looming. Britain would not be able to keep large numbers of soldiers in Palestine for much longer. In an attempt to quell the Arab rebellion, a conference was held in London's St James's Palace in 1939. However, the Arabs refused to sit in the same room as the Jews, or enter by the same door. The British were therefore obliged to interview all sides separately, even Arabs from Egypt and Iraq. The Jewish delegation – all dressed like gentlemen in black morning-coats, striped trousers and silk ties – headed by Weizmann, included three former men of the Jewish Legion, Ben-Gurion, Katznelson and Ben-Zvi. Ben-Gurion insisted on the desperate need to open the door to Nazi-haunted migrants. Eventually British diplomatic skill brought both Arabs and Jews into one room. Six weeks later the delegates were still talking.

Britain, under pressure from Egypt, Saudi Arabia and Iraq, agreed that the Arabs in Palestine should remain in the majority, and increased restrictions on Jewish immigration and approved another White Paper – known by Jews in Palestine as the Black Paper. The British rationalized the need for keeping peace with the Muslims. Firstly there was the need of oil supplies from Arab countries. Secondly, there was the fear of a pan-Arab alliance siding with Hitler's Germany – if there was another world war Britain wanted the Arab nations as her own ally. Thirdly, there was pressure from Muslims in other parts of the British Empire. Rare were comments such as that by Major-General Bernard Montgomery, who had arrived in Palestine in 1938 to command a division, that the Arab nationalists were 'professional bandits'.

The British policy-setting White Paper, known as the 'White Book' of 17 May 1939, stated that 'To appease the Arabs, the Jewish immigration quota is to be drastically reduced to 75,000 for the next five years, and after that immigrants can only be allowed with the consent of the Arabs.' Land purchases by Jews were also stopped. At the end of ten years Palestine would be given independence; but there would be no Jewish state. One-third of the total population would consist of Jews who would take a proportionally smaller part in the administration of the country than the Arabs. Land could only be transferred to Jews in designated areas, equalling one-twentieth of the area of Palestine.

This policy was seen by many as a step back from the promises made by the Lloyd George government. The Balfour Declaration had been put on hold, so that at the time of the most urgent danger for European Jews the gates of the homeland were closed. The Arabs also rejected the new White Paper, demanding the immediate declaration of an Arab state and an end to Jewish immigration.

The severity of the new White Paper which committed the mandate to independence by 1949 came from the new Foreign Secretary, Lord Halifax, who appeared more anxious not to offend the Arabs than to honour British commitments to a Jewish homeland. He continued to stop land sales to Jews, denied them their own brigade, and took the official pro-Arab government line as laid down by his friend the Colonial Secretary, Malcolm MacDonald.[12] Vociferous opposition came from Amery and Churchill. Churchill denounced it as a breach of faith with the Jews and a violation of the Balfour Declaration itself and its ratification in 1922.

The Jewish Agency felt that because of Hitler's persecution they had no alternative but to help illegal immigrants. Daring schemes were hatched. Ben-Gurion, who foresaw a massive armed conflict between Arabs and Jews in Palestine, headed the effort to buy weapons and ordered the Haganah to stockpile. On 30 November 1939 Weizmann wrote to Halifax protesting that 'just at a time when almost two million Polish Jews are completely crushed under the Nazi occupation regime, Great Britain should impose an absolute bar on the entry into Palestine of even those of them who have managed to escape . . .'. This provoked a wimpish reply from Halifax. He said that Britain was putting her whole energy into a 'life-and-death struggle with Nazi Germany, the persecutor of Jewry in Central Europe and by ridding Europe of the present German regime we hope to render a supreme service to the Jewish people'.[13]

Weizmann received a considerable income from royalties on licences and patents from his synthetic acetone discoveries and other products. He used much of this to build the Weizmann Institute in Rehovot, between Tel Aviv and Jerusalem. It also allowed him to move in smart places[14] where he could lobby members of the government. The Dorchester became the hub of wartime London's political and social life, with people like Halifax and Duff and Diana Cooper maintaining suites there. The Turkish baths in the basement were considered to be one of the best bomb shelters in London.

On 25 November 1940 the refugee ship SS *Patria* was blown up by the Haganah in Haifa Harbour, to stop the British from turning ships back from where they had come to return to certain death, or to places like Mauritius where other Jewish refugees were being interned behind barbed wire. Inadvertently, 276 illegal Jewish immigrant passengers from Germany were killed. General Wavell had ordered the survivors to be shipped off so as not to antagonize the Arabs. Weizmann met Halifax at the Dorchester and appealed to him, on humanitarian rather than political grounds. 'As a special act of clemency' the survivors were permitted to remain.[15] Ben-Gurion would from then on be accused of advancing his aim of increasing the Jewish population because of his state-building schemes, even at the expense of exploiting a catastrophic situation. Not only had the Arab population of Palestine risen dramatically – from 663,000 in 1922 to just over a million in 1941, a rise of over 60 per cent – they had six times more land under citrus cultivation than they had had in 1920. But the paradox continued that although the Arabs were the only people who sold land to the Jews, the Arabs complained bitterly about the expanding Jewish agriculture. Despite limits imposed by the British, between 1933 and 1935, Arabs had sold land to the Jews to the value of £4,202,000.

Soon after the *Patria* incident, after reviewing setbacks to the Balfour Declaration and the sufferings of the Jews in Nazi Germany, Smuts made a broadcast:

> Can Christian Europe and America forget the people of the Book, the little people who gave them the greatest Book in the world, the Book in which the human soul has expressed itself as nowhere else in the world's literature? Dare we forget the People who gave us the noblest gift in history – the son of Man whose solitary figure still best expresses the world's desire for God, who still leads the slow and faltering advance of our race to its distant and spiritual goal?[16]

Now the Haganah would need to be more active. From being an illegal army equipped with a pistol here, a rifle there, it grew into a feared, but secret, fighting force following the techniques taught by Wingate.

TWENTY-SEVEN

The Second World War

If you have tears, prepare to shed them now.
Julius Caesar, III ii 171, William Shakespeare

Hitler invaded Poland, which was sandwiched between Nazi Germany and Soviet Russia. He then invaded Denmark and Norway. On 3 September 1939 Britain declared war. On 10 May 1940, the day on which Churchill replaced Neville Chamberlain as prime minister, Germany invaded France, Belgium and Holland. Holland and Belgium fell by the end of May, followed by Paris two weeks later. Battles raged back and forwards across Egypt's western borders while Syria and Lebanon passed under the control of pro-German Vichy French forces commanded by General Dentz, giving Germany a convenient base for intensified subversive activity. In Palestine the British defence system was similar to that used during the Crusades – a series of fortresses in strategic places, this time fifty concrete edifices known as 'Tegart forts'.[1] Although at war with the Vichy regime in France, Britain was not at war with Syria. Wavell made it clear that he did not want to become embroiled with the Vichy French in the Middle East, but at the same time he wanted to undermine them.

When Churchill set up his top secret service organization, the Special Operations Executive (SOE) in 1940, one of the first men he had recruited was Lawrence's brother Arnold, an archaeologist. Churchill sent him to Jerusalem in April 1940 as SOE liaison officer between the British and members of the Haganah. Arnold's job was to recruit members, mostly young European-born Jews, to undertake guerrilla activities against the Vichy French and Germans in Syria. Although many of the Haganah soldiers feared prison sentences being imposed on them by the British authorities because of their past guerrilla activities against Arabs, they were willing to enlist in the British army. Arnold, though, like his late brother, turned out to be pro-Arab, and he was not popular with the Jews. His time in Jerusalem only lasted six months.

Following Italy's entry into the war and France's capitulation, the focus of the war turned increasingly towards the Middle East. Wavell commanded some 36,000 troops in Egypt, 28,000 in Palestine, with another 22,000 garrisoned in the Sudan, Kenya, Aden, British Somaliland and Cyprus.

* * *

The situation was becoming desperate for the Jews in Europe, who were being marched off to concentration camps. Ben-Gurion, rugged and single-minded, determined not to be beaten by bureaucracy, was now asserting his control of the Haganah, which had taken on the responsibility for illegal immigration. As the plight of European Jews became their priority, the Haganah set up a network of complicated undercover arrangements, which included secret staging depots in Europe, methods of secretly boarding refugees on to boats, and the provision of tugboats to bring them to the shores of Palestine in defiance of the British naval blockade. Often hazardous disembarkation under cover of night, with signals made by flashing torches, was followed by perilous crawling along sand-dunes, hiding refugees from the police and then giving them false papers. The barren hills that rise so steeply out of the coastal plain, or the stony mountains with olives and fig trees in the corries, gave little cover. Military training for the Haganah took place at night, from crowded apartments in Tel Aviv to remote, cavernous places near the Dead Sea.[2] Wherever the Jews were training or smuggling people they had two enemies, the British and the Arabs.

From time to time many members of the Haganah were imprisoned in Acre's old Crusader fortress, the Akko, known as the toughest prison in the British penal system. Akko's infamous hangman, a sinister figure dressed in the traditional scarlet costume of a hangmen, always made sure that the gallows were in working order. Within four months of Wingate's departure, Dayan was one of the inmates. In mid-August 1939, just a few weeks before the outbreak of war, he had been sent on a Haganah Platoon Commanders' Course, disguised as a physical education course of the Jewish Sports Federation near the village of Yavniel in Lower Galilee. On 3 October, when British security officers appeared at his tent entrance, Dayan switched the subject of the lecture from tactics to training in track running. This, however, did not fool the officers who found a few rifles under mattresses. Dayan and about forty of his men were arrested, loaded on to two trucks and taken to the dreaded prison in Acre. He scribbled a note to his wife, 'Arrested, no need to worry', wrapped it around a small stone, and when the truck stopped, threw it towards a familiar face.

In his memoirs[3] Dayan related the horror of the iron gates clanging behind them, followed by the ordeal of standing in a dank detention room. Here their belongings were taken from them, and then they were led into a dark and narrow vaulted hall and directed to tattered and filthy mattresses on the floor. His friend Zvi Brenner was the first for interrogation. Dayan related hearing 'voices, then the sound of blows, followed by the moaning of someone in pain, then more talk and more groaning . . . later I heard from Zvi that he had been kicked and beaten, revived, and then beaten again because he had refused to give answers.'

Then it was Dayan's turn. When threatened with execution if he did not cooperate, he connived ways of giving limited replies. 'Two warders then came towards me with raised truncheons and were about to strike me when I uttered a warning. They stopped. I told them not to dare raise their hands against me or any of us. If they did, our friends on the outside would intervene, and those responsible would be punished . . .'. Dayan's trial opened on 25 October in an army camp near Acre with the 'exhibits' – grenades and ammunition found in their possession – on a bench, and their rifles lying on the ground beside them. Each man was sentenced to ten years in prison, and one of them was given a life sentence. Their heads were shaved and they were sent back to prison. At the end of November the sentence was reduced to five years. The daily routine was gruesome, with solitary confinement as a punishment for even minor offences. 'During my jail term, several condemned Arab prisoners were executed by hanging. The weeping and wailing of their relatives was heart-rending. After a hanging the entire prison would be gripped by an atmosphere of tension.'

After five months in Acre, early in 1941, Dayan and his forty-two companions were transferred to a camp at Mazra. He heard that the Jewish Agency and Zionist Organization leaders had persuaded the military in London to expand the ranks of Palestinian Jewish volunteers for service. On 17 February they were released, ready to volunteer in the British army. While Dayan had been in prison, Ben-Gurion had made an announcement that was used as a slogan: 'We must help the British army as if there was no White Paper and we must oppose the White Paper as if there was no Jewish Brigade.' During the next five years over 25,000 Jews in Palestine volunteered to join the British army, whereas the much larger Arab community furnished less than half that number.

* * *

In the dark and uncertain early days of 1941 the legendary General Irwin Rommel and his Afrika Korps were forcing the British army back towards Cairo and German tanks were heading towards the Suez Canal. Britain was facing defeat in the Middle East. The Germans had swept down through Greece and Yugoslavia and were leap-frogging south across the Mediterranean islands. In Iraq British troops were facing an uprising.

In May 1941 the 'Sea Lion' expedition was set up to blow up oil wells at Tripoli to prevent German aircraft from refuelling and bombing Cairo. This team comprised one English officer, the 26-year-old aristocratic Major Sir Anthony Palmer, and twenty-three members of the Haganah. Dayan had been chosen as one of the crew, but pulled out because he had become feverish and ill overnight. The use of these men by the British was a sensitive issue, as hundreds of Haganah soldiers were still imprisoned in Palestine and colonies in Africa.

On the morning of 18 May the police speed boat, *Sea Lion*, disguised as a pleasure boat, sailed from Haifa. Among the lifeboats were hidden explosives, a transmitter and food. The men had no certificates nor did they wear uniforms. They were never heard of again. Vague and contradictory reports began to emerge about their fate. Histories rarely mention the *Sea Lion* expedition.

Dayan ended up as one of the 'scouts' in the bloody invasion of Syria led by Wavell from Palestine under the codename 'Operation Exporter'. This lasted for three weeks, and terminated on 12 July 1941 with the surrender of the Vichy French forces. Eight weeks had passed from the date of the departure of the *Sea Lion*. Losing no time, the Haganah sent an officer to try to find out if any of the crew of the *Sea Lion* had been taken as prisoners-of-war. The officer heard that the men had landed near Tripoli but were caught by the French who had increased their security around the oil refinery due to a British air raid the night before. A French doctor in the hospital said that during the first week of June he had been called by the Vichy French military authorities to examine some decomposed bodies on the shore at Tripoli. But he had found only four bodies lying on the beach. One was wearing khaki trousers but was otherwise naked and there were eight machine-gun bullet holes in his chest. The other bodies were mangled by bullets or an explosion.

Nearby were the remnants of a life belt and a brown shoe. He was told that the bodies were then buried. When the agent tried to ask further questions he was warned off and told that the Vichy authorities had tried to keep the incident a secret. British papers connected with the expedition have never been released, not even to Palmer's wife and children.

* * *

By the following year the horror of the war had expanded, with the German invasion of the Union of Soviet Socialist Republics and the Japanese attack on Pearl Harbor in Hawaii in December 1941. Churchill then forged the Grand Alliance with Soviet leader Joseph Stalin and President Franklin D. Roosevelt against Germany, Italy and Japan.

As in the First World War, the Jews fought under their own banner, this time the Jewish Brigade, and once again such a unit was not formed until the penultimate year of the war. This comprised Jews recruited in Palestine who went to fight in Europe. Despite the tensions between the rulers and the ruled, despite the deep hostility created by the British immigration restrictions, the Jews put enormous energy into the British effort to defeat Hitler. Some volunteered to be parachuted behind German lines, as did the Jewish members of the army commandos, knowing as they did so that they only had a 50 per cent chance of survival. A large number of the commandos and paratroopers were recruited from the 4,000 Jewish refugees who had enlisted in Alien Pioneer companies, others were recruited directly from the Palmach, the strike arm of the Haganah. Among the most ambitious and mysterious were the Jewish commandos of the SIG, which stood for either 'Special Interrogation Group' or 'Special Intelligence Group' – nobody could agree on its meaning. These superbly trained men were used for infiltration behind enemy lines for special commando operations and sabotage.

Wingate's hopes of returning to Palestine to lead a Jewish army were squashed. When war broke out he had been sent to Ethiopia, where he found himself fighting Mussolini's army. While there he was briefly sent to Cairo, tentatively diagnosed with manic depression which he quickly overcame to win fame as the founder of the Chindit commandos in the jungles of Burma. Before he was killed in an air crash he was promoted to major-general.

* * *

In the winter of 1943/4 the British authorities, in an attempt to reduce anti-British sentiment in the Arab world, announced that more rigid limitations on the number of Jewish immigrants coming into Palestine were to be introduced. The bitterness caused by the restrictions, however, led to terrorist activities by two new rebel breakaway groups from the Haganah, the Irgun Zvai Leumi (with their war cry 'An eye for an eye!') and the Lehi (Stern Group). They would strike back, kill and terrorize. Unlike these two organizations, the Haganah, which remained the largest of the underground armies, did not at this stage initiate acts of aggression.

Irgun fanatics began their bloody battle to push the British out of Palestine, but their terrorist attacks started in earnest when Menahem Begin took over the command. Moderate Zionists were appalled when in November 1944 the Stern Gang assassinated the popular Lord Moyne (Walter Guinness), the most senior British minister for Middle Eastern Affairs in Cairo. International revulsion against this assassination meant that it was a turning-point for many, including Churchill, who had been Moyne's intimate friend. British security forces responded with the standard tactics of anti-colonial warfare, torture, collective punishment, detention without trial and military trials. Tension heightened. In Haifa, time-bombs blew up police cars – one set of mines destroyed the office of taxation. As the day for the near cessation of Jewish immigration grew close, violence intensified across the country. Cities were placed under curfew. Despite this, up and down the country, refugee cabaret singers from Berlin and Vienna sang their old numbers at various venues.

As the Second World War drew to a close, the troubles in Palestine intensified. The desperate plight of the refugees from the death camps was causing increasing problems; and one of the by-products of the war was accumulation of large arsenals of weapons that were to lead to an escalation of illicit arming by both Jews and Arabs.[4]

TWENTY-EIGHT

David and Goliath

And I John saw the Holy City, new Jerusalem, coming down from God out of heaven, prepared as a bride adorned for her husband

Revelation 21:2

Outside the King David Hotel in Jerusalem on VE Day, as flags were hoisted to the top of their mastheads[1] the High Commissioner for Palestine, Field Marshal Viscount Gort, saluted first the Union Jack and then the flags of the Allied nations. The band of the Palestine Police Force struck up 'God Save the King'. At the end of the afternoon Gort granted an amnesty to a number of Jewish and Arab political prisoners. But the Jewish Agency building was draped with the Zionist colours bordered in black in mourning for the Jews murdered in Europe. Among those marching in the Victory March were soldiers from both the First and Second World Wars carrying banners which demanded an end to the unjust and unfair immigration restrictions. By contrast, in another part of the city, near the Jaffa Gate, thousands of Arabs marched waving banners with nationalist slogans.

Meanwhile, in Syria, elections had been held during the war and a new government had been formed under the presidency of the Syrian nationalist Shukri al-Kuwatli, one of the leaders of earlier uprisings against the French occupation. The French were so slow in relinquishing control that rioting continued until the British army went north, on the side of the French. Syria then became a member of the newly formed United Nations and all French troops and administrative personnel departed. In Palestine, on the other hand, the situation was worsening every day. After the surrender of Germany, despite the Jews receiving warm praise from British military chiefs, their loyalty and heroic effort in the war now had no effect. Even the Haganah, no longer useful, was bitterly condemned by the administration. Hope was lost for a Jewish state being formed, and for an easing up of immigration restrictions on the desperate survivors of the concentration camps.

But abroad attitudes were changing. The deaths of some six million Jews in Hitler's concentration camps during the war focused the world's attention on the need to create a homeland for the Jews.

* * *

In July 1945 the Arab League, founded in Cairo by Egypt, Syria, Lebanon, Transjordan, Iraq and Saudi Arabia, threatened war if moves were made towards the creation of a Jewish State or if Jewish immigration to Palestine was increased. At the end of the same month, in Britain, the Labour Party won an electoral victory that astonished the world. Churchill and the Conservative Party were ousted and Labour, for the first time, commanded a majority in the House of Commons. But there were problems: Britain may have won the war, but she was insolvent for the first time in history. Despite bombed cities to rebuild and troops everywhere that had to be repatriated, Prime Minister Clement Attlee forged ahead with ambitious plans and included the foundation of the National Health Service, the nationalization of the coal mines, the railways, the iron and steel industries, electricity and gas services. Attlee also set in train ways to give independence to some of Britain's now costly colonial possessions.

At the age of sixty-four, Ernest Bevin, the trade union leader who did not mind being photographed with a cigarette hanging from the side of his mouth, became Lord Palmerston in a cloth cap. As the first Foreign Secretary who was unable to speak any foreign language, he brought an uncouth touch to that bastion of gentility and refinement, the Foreign Office, treating it as if it was his own Trade Union. Orphaned before he was seven years old, Bevin had started work at the age of thirteen, first as a van boy then as a van driver in Bristol. Here he was introduced to both the trade union movement and the Baptist chapel. Unlike Baptists such as Lloyd George or Truman, he had not been raised on the Bible – religion was something that he became interested in only when, as a teenager, he became a lay preacher. And he showed little interest in the Holy Land.

Bevin's opposition to the Jews was so extreme and his stance so pro-Arab that he was labelled an anti-Zionist. Despite the gas chambers and the concentration camps he showed no compassion for the plight of the Jews. In November 1945 he announced to the House of Commons what the Jews in Palestine had dreaded: the Labour Party would carry out the limitations imposed by the 1939 White Paper. There would be virtually no concessions for the hundreds of thousands of survivors of the death camps across Europe. Nor would there be any allowances for the thousands of Jewish soldiers who had fought on the side of Britain in the Middle East and lost their lives. Bevin's one concession was agreeing to an Anglo-American committee of inquiry. In April the committee announced that the old 1922 mandate should be changed into a trusteeship under the United Nations, and that the 1939 White Paper should be abandoned, along with restrictions on land sales (most of the total area of Palestine was still owned by Arab Palestinians). The committee also recommended that 100,000 Jewish immigrants should be allowed to enter the country immediately. Bevin was obdurate. He refused to hold any discussions with the Jews until they disarmed. This proved impossible, especially as the Palestinian Arabs were now being supplied with arms by the Russians. Bevin later expressed his personal feelings against the Jews in Palestine during a speech in parliament:

> over half a million Arabs have been turned by the Jewish immigrants into homeless refugees without employment or resources . . . [the ordinary young Arab] consider[s] that for the Arab population, which has been occupying Palestine for more than twenty centuries, to be turned out of their land and homes for another race is a profound injustice . . . I think that the driving of poor innocent people from their homes, whether it is in Germany by Hitler, or by anybody else, and making the ordinary working people of the place suffer, is a crime, and we really ought to join together to stop it if we can.[2]

More restrictions were introduced in Palestine. During this period Jews were not permitted to carry any type of weapon, making individual self-defence skills critical. On 29 June 1946, the 'Black Sabbath', the British raided the Jewish Agency Headquarters in Jerusalem and arrested some of its leaders. This was followed by a police swoop which began with night searches for arms and ended with the arrests of nearly 3,000 Jewish men and women.

Once again Churchill came to the rescue of the Jews. Defeated at the peak of his wartime fame, he was now a pugnacious Leader of the Opposition. In August 1946 he shouted across the floor that Labour had made 'strenuous pro-Zionist speeches and declarations' which had not been followed through.[3] Bevin's stance, he noted, was contrary to Labour's election promises.

At the Conservative Party Conference he took the opportunity of again attacking Bevin in a speech which was reported in *The Times*. Again he spoke of the Labour Party's 'lavish promises' that had excited 'passionate expectations' throughout the Jewish world and which 'were no sooner made than they were disregarded'.[4] Churchill might have considered Labour's policy a failure in fulfilling the terms of the mandate, but his views did not represent those of the Conservative Party.

* * *

A vote by the United Nations that Britain should withdraw from Palestine had coincided with the same decision by the new Labour government. Onerous night curfews were enforced and tension was high as more caches of arms were found and more members of the Haganah were being thrown into prison. Some officers complained that searching for weapons was the most unpleasant of tasks. Many arms were concealed under floorboards covered with filthy old clothes which emitted an odour described by one officer as 'worse than Mrs O'Riley's back privy on a bad day'.

A plan to arrest many top Jewish Agency leaders and a large number of the Haganah and Palmach high command was leaked to the Haganah by a British officer, thus allowing the men to go into hiding and escape. The officer, it is said, wished only to share a room with his Jewish girlfriend. In return for this room he turned over vital documents, including 600 pages describing detailed British plans for more raids and a wealth of material gathered on the Haganah by the British Intelligence Services from the early days of the mandate until 1946. As a result of this information, Jewish special commandos were built up for the fight against the British and the Arabs, and Ben-Gurion ordered the Haganah to take up armed struggle. On 22 July 1946 the anti-British attacks of the extremist Jewish military organization led to tragedy: explosives hidden in milk cans were smuggled into the basement kitchens of the King David Hotel, the headquarters of the British Forces, by members of the Irgun Zvai Leumi, and in the ensuing explosion more than ninety people were killed.

The restrictive British immigration policy in Palestine became even more tightly controlled, with a quota of just 2,000 Jews allowed each month. On one hand, agents of Britain and the United States were rounding up hundreds of Nazis who had gone into hiding, but on the other the surviving victims of the Nazis were still languishing in European displaced-persons camps. Only five of sixty-three illegal refugee ships got through the British naval blockades between 1945 and 1948. When the immigrant ship *Beauharnais* was towed into the harbour at Haifa, its passengers unfurled a banner from the deck and hung it over the side to be photographed so that European and American newspapers could display their words: 'We survived Hitler. Death is no stranger to us. Nothing can keep us from our Jewish homeland. The blood be on your head if you fire on this unarmed ship.'

The callousness of the postwar British Labour government in not allowing more of the hundreds of thousands of Jews from the Holocaust into Palestine was illustrated by their refusal to allow the *Exodus*, which had been purchased by the Sonneborn Institute, to land its 4,554 passengers. In Haifa, amazed members of a United Nations committee were moved to sympathy when, by chance, they saw from their hotel balconies the struggle between the refugees, the British army and the Haganah. The British were armed with rifles and tear gas, the Jews with cans of food and broomsticks. When the ship was brought to Haifa harbour the passengers were moved to three British ships and put in cages below decks, to be transported back to detention camps in Germany.[5] The dramatic *Exodus* tragedy was one of the events that would soon lead to the majority vote in the United Nations to divide Palestine into an Arab and a Jewish state.

Most refugees on dozens of illegal *Aliyah Bet* ships, risking mines, winter storms and the wrath of the British navy, never landed in Palestine. Few vessels escaped being intercepted at sea and most passengers were sent to internment camps either in Palestine or nearby Cyprus. But the sight of wretched Holocaust survivors being pulled back from reaching their homeland evoked worldwide sympathy and criticism of the British and contributed to the British decision to relinquish control of Palestine.

In February 1947 the British government decided to terminate its mandate in Palestine. At the United Nations Assembly, thirty years to the month since the Balfour Declaration had been announced, a vote came down thirty-three to thirteen in favour of partition in Palestine into two states, a Jewish territory and an Arab territory with Jerusalem as an international city administered by the UN. The Jewish state would be a narrow band along the coast, in the north reaching inland to the Sea of Galilee, and in the south encompassing the Negev Desert. The Arab state would comprise Gaza, the West Bank of the River Jordan and a piece of land to the north, bordering on

Lebanon. It was a mild November evening in 1947 when news of a United Nations agreement reached the people of Palestine. In Jerusalem and Tel Aviv, people cheered, danced the *hora* in the streets, waved blue and white flags and sang 'Hatikva'. While the Jews wanted to negotiate, the Arabs rejected the plan. There was no cheering in the Arab neighbourhoods. They denounced it with gunfire and promised to throw the Jews into the sea. There were around 40 million Arabs in the surrounding states who would support them. In Transjordan there was the British-trained and British-equipped Arab Legion which cost the British millions each year. Egypt was also well supplied with British arms.

Tel Aviv's outskirts were soon under sniper fire; Jerusalem's commercial centre was looted and set ablaze. Palestinian Arabs, aided by Arabs from nearby nations, commenced assaults on Jewish individuals and property. Britain announced that it would withdraw its forces from Palestine on 14 May 1948. The prospect loomed of the Jewish people being wiped out by Palestinian and Arab forces superior to the Jewish troops in numbers and equipment. Some of Ben-Gurion's advisers urged him to postpone declaring a Jewish state. In the United States, Assistant Secretary of State Dean Rusk even implied that if Ben-Gurion went ahead with statehood, the United States might prohibit donations by American Jews from being sent to the Jewish State. American officials also said that the United States government would not be receptive to a request to sell military equipment, even if the Arabs invaded the new state.

Before the British departure the fighting that had erupted was so fierce and so well organized that from the middle of April Palestine was effectively in a state of war. Jewish underground movements frequently obtained advance reports of planned actions and were thus able to hide Jewish underground leaders, let them escape or change plans before a British plan became operational. Curfews, searches and orders broadcast from megaphones on trucks by the British had little effect. In places portable barricades, huts and even dismantled watchtowers would be transported to settlements during the night. Hand-to-hand fighting went on until the last minute. Tens of thousands of rebel Arabs were in prisons, as were Jews. Offences ranged from being identified as a member of an underground military organization to smuggling in both migrants and arms. Arab wrath was also directed against the British: the Arabs resented the fact that the British had initially allowed the Jews protected entry into Palestine and made possible the growth of the

Jewish settlement. As the British began the massive task of dismantling thirty years of government, files were thrown on bonfires.

By this stage the Haganah had located a good supplier of illicit arms in Prague, but the effect of this find was countered by Prague sending supplies to the Arabs as well. And soon the Arabs had an extra advantage. On 12 January a Foreign Office spokesman in London announced that in conformity with treaty obligations, Egypt, Iraq and Transjordan would continue to be supplied with arms by Great Britain.[6]

TWENTY-NINE

The Culmination of 2,000 Years of Prayer and Longing

To my true king I offer'd free from stain
Courage and faith; vain faith, and courage vain.
For him I threw lands, honours, wealth, away,
And one dear hope, that was more prized than they.

From 'A Jacobite's Epitaph', Thomas Babington, Lord Macaulay

On Friday 14 May 1948, the year 5708 in the Hebrew calendar, when the state of Israel was proclaimed at a People's Council meeting, the setting took on the dimensions of a Verdi opera, with armies waiting in the wings. At the helm of the new state, as the provisional prime minister and defence minister, was David Ben-Gurion. As his voice rose, the armed might of five countries was gathering on three fronts, ready to destroy the Jews. They were waiting for the British to depart before they could surge in. The estimated numbers of Arab troops was around 80,000, some put it higher. To the north were the two new republics, Syria and Lebanon. To the south and the east were the three British puppet princedoms of King Ghazi's Iraq, King Farouk's Egypt and King Abdullah's Jordan. British guns were poised to make a mockery of Ben-Gurion's dramatic declaration to create an independent self-governing state. There had been much discussion about when this should take place. Technically it could not be until midnight on Friday. But late Friday afternoon was Shabbat, a time when the Orthodox Jews could not put pen to paper, travel by car or exert themselves. Finally it was agreed that as the ceremony would take no longer than an hour, it would be over before the setting of the sun.

The number of Jews in Palestine was still only around 600,000. Were there enough armed men and women, from the Negev to Galilee to the Jordan, to stand up against their hostile neighbours? And would the Jewish volunteers from the Diaspora be able to fly in safely or find a ship in time so they could aid them in battle? Short of weapons, short of manpower, how could they repulse the coming onslaught? But they had many advantages, including an elite strike force of Commandos and Saboteurs, the Palmach, and an intelligence-gathering operation which was the forerunner of the Israeli Secret Service, the Mossad, probably the best military intelligence organization in the world. With 45,000 men in the Haganah, effectiveness rested on speed, organization and the ability to get aeroplanes, guns, tanks and ammunition into the country. As noted in the previous chapter, for decades the armies of Jordan, Iraq and Egypt had been training under competent British officers, supplied with British weapons and financed by the British Treasury. Among the commanders and officers of the Arab armies were the first modern Arab army leaders, General Sir John Bagot Glubb Pasha, in charge of the Transjordan Arab Legion, and Captain Gamal Nasser of the Egyptian army.

* * *

British nerve had broken. Unable to quell the bloody violence between the Arabs and the Jews, or to sort out agreement on the proposed plan for partition, they were pulling out. British taxpayers surely had some tangible investments there in buildings, equipment and vehicles. Yet, although some assets were sold off cheaply, much was left. It was not in their authority, said the administration in Palestine, to hand the country over to either the Arabs or the Jews. So instead of transferring power, they forsook it. Eight hours before Ben-Gurion made his declaration, Sir Alan Cunningham, the last British High Commissioner, the seventh since Sir Herbert Samuel, wearing full general's uniform, had reviewed a small guard of honour at Government House in Jerusalem. Fifty men of the Highland Light Infantry played a bagpipe salute, 'Auld Lang Syne', and, as the flag was lowered for the last time, 'God Save the King'. Lorries, tanks and staff-cars, the hated symbols of British rule, drove down King George Avenue and into oblivion. Then the large armoured Daimler took Cunningham to Kalandia airfield north of Jerusalem to fly to Haifa where he boarded HMS *Euryalus*. In the long list of Palestine's thirty-eight conquerors, including King David, Nebuchadnezzar, Judah Maccabee, Pompey, Godfrey de Bouillon and Saladin, the British had occupied the land for the shortest time.

Thousands of offices and buildings were left in running order, but abandoned. Public utilities, such as the railways, the post offices and the veterinary services were left manned, but the reins of government, which had been held by the British for thirty-one years, were left in limbo. Just as the Arabs complained that during the mandate the British had favoured the Jews, while the Jews believed the reverse, the Arabs also say that the British left more Jews in public service positions than Arabs, while the Jews have claimed the opposite. Government policy in Palestine for the last few years had disastrous effects. Now that the British were hurrying towards Haifa, it was a finders-keepers game of Jew versus Arab. On the eve of departure, one startled journalist asked the Governor of Jerusalem, with whom the keys of office were being left. He said 'I'll leave them under the mat'. In London a horrified Conservative Opposition had censured the Labour Party for leaving not just a house but a whole country with no agreed transfer. Cunningham wrote that 'the British were blamed for not having handed over to anyone, whereas, in point of fact, there was nobody to whom to hand over'.[1] The veracity of this answer has been debated ever since.

As Ben-Gurion read the declaration in Tel Aviv, the United Nations in New York, who were moving into Government House in Jerusalem, was debating whether it would form a trusteeship and if it did so, what shape it would take. Meanwhile the *Euryalus* hovered on the edge of Palestinian waters. At midnight it would sail away, finishing what had been one of the least glorious episodes in the history of the British Empire. From the moment General Allenby had unfurled the Union Jack over the Holy Land on his arrival in Jerusalem in December 1917, to the time when British officers had lowered it that morning, the problem of Arab hostility had spiralled into unresolved conflict. Even so, British rule had given the Jews a durable platform for their return.

* * *

Speculation among the Arabs was not *about* victory, but about *how long* victory would take. There was an assumption that it would be a matter of days. Bloodthirsty rhetoric included the Secretary-General of the Arab League saying, 'This will be a war of extermination and a momentous massacre.' Only three years had passed since the end of the Holocaust and death of Hitler. The Jewish people appeared to be on the edge of yet another cataclysmic episode.

With their khaki uniforms relieved only by the red and white chequer of their headdresses, the Arab Legion was waiting to cross the Jordan into Palestine. The Iraqis were not far behind, surging westward to the banks of the Jordan where they would be deployed with the army of neighbouring Hashemite-ruled Iraq. One column of Egyptian troops was pushing up the hill country near the coast heading for Tel Aviv, a second crossing the Negev Desert via Beersheba and Hebron. They would soon be closing in on Jerusalem from the south. Two Egyptian Spitfires had flown low over Tel Aviv airport and punctured the planes on the ground with bullets, before gunning one down.

Ben-Gurion was steeling himself for a fight to the death. His hair had turned grey in his twenties, and now, at sixty-two, it was white. Despite being short – five foot three inches – with a disproportionately large head, a craggy face and a determined jaw, he had an immense physical presence. Persistent back pain did not hinder his almost youthful agility, which was no doubt helped by his daily five-mile constitutional walk. One of the rare occasions when Ben-Gurion was not wearing his usual khaki battledress was 14 May. Instead he wore collar, jacket and tie, just like Herzl in the portrait dominating the wall behind. It was fifty-one years since Herzl had organised the Zionist conference in Basle in 1897.

There were fears of assassination and the ceremony of the declaration being sabotaged, so the place and time of the announcement was kept secret until the last moment. But the military situation was not entirely unfavourable to the Jews. King Abdullah intended to extend his kingdom from Jordan, but he was still on the other side of the river, and it seemed unlikely that any local Palestinian leader would at that time also be holding a meeting to proclaim an Arab State. Apart from the Mufti of Jerusalem, there appeared to be no single Arab with enough popular political support locally to make him into an uncontested leader. The disunity that had allowed the Crusaders to take Jerusalem in 1099 and that had prevented the Palestinian Arabs from putting forward an effective case at the Paris Peace Conference in 1918 was again apparent.

Ben-Gurion's choice of ultra-modern Tel Aviv as the venue for his declaration was not just because it reflected his determination to build a new-style socialist state. Jerusalem, called by Isaiah the 'joy of many generations', was to be the capital, but it was then besieged. Neither food, nor people – nothing could get in or out. Water supplies had become critical. The new and the old would now forge ahead together. While antiquity was personified by Jerusalem, modernity was seen here in Tel Aviv, in the flashy, glitzy promenades, the cooperative housing on Ben-Yehuda Street and the nearby kibbutzim with their communal living quarters and productive farms. Just as Bauhaus architects had designed this city with its bright white angular modern buildings, so he wanted a new-look society, not just one rising out of national icons and religious relics.[2] Selecting the Tel Aviv Museum,[3] the former home of the city's first mayor, Meir Dizengoff, in Rothschild Boulevard, with its pottery shards and stone relics, rather than the Convention Centre, reinforced this ambition. Displayed near items from the past were the latest paintings, including some by Marc Chagall. Alongside Ben-Gurion's yearning for the new was a passionate interest in education and a pride in the long history of the Jews, which stretched back over five thousand years.

At precisely four o'clock Ben-Gurion began to read the Declaration of Independence of the new nation, 'Medinat Yisrael', the state of Israel, the name he had finally decided on the previous day. With much dignity he stood behind a draped table on the stage of the museum, and banged a walnut gavel on the table. Around and in front of him was a selected audience of 200 people, all of whom had earlier been notified by telephone. An atmosphere of solemnity, despite everything being makeshift, filled the room. Even the microphone had been borrowed from a radio shop around the corner. Chairs, too, had been lent from a nearby café. The audience included foreign guests, some old stalwarts of the Zionist movement, the press, plus the members of the Provisional State Council who sat at the T-shaped table. Airwaves took the words all around the world: '. . . Here they first attained to statehood, created cultural values of national and universal significance and gave to the world the eternal Book of Books . . .'. In mentioning the fact that it was the land where the Jewish people had written and given the Bible to the world was an acknowledgement of the support it had given Ben-Gurion and others in their fight to return. But he did not mention the actual word 'God'. Instead he concluded with the phrase, 'With trust in the Rock of Israel.'

The Bible played a large part in Ben-Gurion's life. A weekly Bible-study group met regularly in his home on Shabbat afternoon and he published a book on interpretations of the Old Testament. Included in the declaration was a reference to President Coolidge's earlier agreement to protect biblical antiquities, an undertaking to 'safeguard the sanctity and inviolability of the shrines and holy places of all religions'. This was to reassure the world's Christians and Muslims that Jerusalem would be open to all religions and all people. The thirty-seven signatories rose one by one to sign the parchment scroll. After 2,000 years of prayer and longing Israel was a self-governing nation, a triumph over unbelievable odds, a fulfilment of prophecy. It again had a Place on the Map. But it would only keep this place if its people could both withstand the Arab attacks and be recognized as an autonomous entity by other countries. Bevin in London was bringing pressure on British dominions and Western Europe to withhold recognition.

It took just thirty-seven minutes to deliver the 1,027 words of the declaration. As cameras flashed,[4] the Palestine Philharmonic played 'Hatikvah', the new national anthem. Outside, the flag of the world's youngest state was raised. Soon, however, all music would be drowned by the sound of machine-guns, bombs, tanks and the screams of the wounded. More corpses would lie in the gutters. More bodies would be buried under the desert sands.[5] Ben-Gurion, anticipating the battles ahead, wrote in his *War Diary* that he was 'a mourner among the joyful'.[6] Yet for a moment all seemed quiet. A cool sea breeze from the Mediterranean blew in across the sand dunes scented with eucalyptus and pine.

Like many of the men who made up the hierarchy in the new state, Ben-Gurion was a survivor of the First World War's Jewish Legion.[7] Another dozen men of the battalions which had made up the Jewish units in that war were also about to dominate the new government, the defence forces and newspapers. Absent from the stage but soon to be in power was another ex-Legionnaire, Levi Eshkol. Steadfast in their goal, the former members of the Jewish Legion had never lost sight of their ultimate aim, and since their days in the army, had also been part-time soldiers in the Haganah which was now about to defend the new nation.

The most prominent of them, excluding the two who became prime ministers, was the tall, gentle Ben-Zvi. In 1952 he would become the second president of Israel and serve for twelve years. Others were Jacob Dori, the future chief of staff of the Israel Defense Force; Dov Hos who would pioneer the Israel Air Force;[8] Gershon Agronsky, who became editor of the *Palestine Post* and mayor of Jerusalem; Berl Katznelson, the main spiritual leader of the labour movement; Eliyahu Golomb, who led the Haganah; and Pinchas Rutenberg, who later harnessed the Jordan for hydro-electricity. After the first Russian Revolution in February 1917 – during the short interval before the Bolshevik Revolution of October 1917 – Rutenberg had served under Kerensky as Chief of Police in Petrograd.

Like Ben-Gurion, most of these old comrades-in-arms were now over sixty. In contrast, Smuts was the only one of the British politicians in the War Cabinet still alive of those who had been responsible for creating both the Jewish homeland and the Jewish Legion. Bonar Law had died in 1922; both Milner and Curzon had followed him three years later in 1925; Carson and Henderson had both died in 1935; Austen Chamberlain and Geddes had died in 1937; Barnes in 1940 and Lloyd George in 1945. Nor could their old champion, Balfour, help the new state, since he had passed away in 1930.

The British Mandate was scheduled to finish at midnight on 14 May in Israel and 6.11 p.m. on 14 May in New York. It was a race against time. Everything hung not just on the countdown of the invasions by the surrounding armies, but on the men sitting in a large grey building, once home to an ice-skating rink, in Flushing Meadow, New York, now the headquarters of the United Nations General Assembly. Only if the United Nations failed to agree on an effective legal title would the administration set up by the Jewish inhabitants in their sector of Palestine continue. If enough countries voted for a trusteeship under the United Nations, Ben-Gurion's declaration would have been wasted time.

When Truman had been elevated to the presidency after Roosevelt's sudden death, many Jews were anxious about his stand towards the Jewish homeland. Both Truman's secretary of state and his secretary of defense were vehemently opposed to America recognizing Jewish independence and had argued that America would suffer reprisals if a Jewish state were to come into existence. Many reasons were put forward. America's most important oil concession in the region had been made with King Ibn Saud of Saudi Arabia in 1933. There was now a threat of that oil being cut off there by the Arabs, as it was in places such as Bahrain, Kuwait and Qatar. Similarly, the Soviets might intervene. Not to be forgotten were the millions of American dollars invested in military bases in Saudi Arabia, which could be jeopardized.

Cunningham's ship sailed out of Palestinian waters. At eleven minutes after the expiration of the British Mandate Truman made his declaration in Washington. Soon afterwards, in the hall of the United Nations, the American representative, who had earlier been urging the forming of a trusteeship, quietened the room. A message on ticker-tape had just been received from Truman:

> This Government has been informed that a Jewish State has been proclaimed in Palestine, and recognition has been requested by the Provisional Government itself. The United States recognizes the Provisional Government as the *de facto* authority of the new State of Israel.

This statement gave the new state of Israel legitimacy under international law. Ezekiel's prophecy was fulfilled. The wandering Jew had a home to return to. Israel's land and people were again united. Arab armies would now be fighting against a recognized state.[9] Truman's rapid action and recognition of the state and its provisional government nullified the proposal to place Palestine under a temporary United Nations trusteeship. A formal letter confirmed the *de facto* recognition a few days later, but the *de jure* recognition was not given until the following year. There was now no available time in which the UN could vote for a trusteeship. Two thousand years of prayer and longing was over. The Bible had triumphed. As Ben-Gurion said, 'From the Bible the Jewish people drew its faith in the return'. Jewish Palestine was ready for the onslaught.

Within an hour the Soviet Union added its recognition. Poland and Guatemala followed. New Zealand and Uruguay also voted. Despite discouragement from the British Foreign Secretary, Bevin, Australian support came from its foreign minister, Dr H.V. Evatt, who had been chairman of the UN *ad hoc* committee which had, during the previous year, devised the plan for the partition of Palestine.

Not all nations accepted the new state. Recognition for Israel from South Africa did not come for ten days. Smuts, despite being prime minister, had problems persuading his political colleagues to overlook their pro-British sensibilities. Whether it was a coincidence or not, he may have paid the price for his untiring devotion to Zionism. Two days after he accorded Israel the *de facto* recognition of South Africa, his government fell.[10] Canada, China and a number of Latin American states were appalled at America's sudden reversal of policy, and Britain did not recognize Israel's independence until 1949. All trade and diplomatic connections were cut. Soon oil stopped flowing to Haifa. In England Koestler had to cross the channel to France to obtain a visa and board a flight to Israel. Soon after he arrived Koestler noted the irony that it was two British foreign secretaries who had helped bring about the rebirth of Israel, Balfour and Bevin. 'The first gave the Jews their legal charter; the second, by refusing any compromise, forced them to fight it out and thus pass the test of nationhood.'

The old clashes and differences which had divided Ben-Gurion and Weizmann over the years now evaporated. Ben-Gurion and four other members of the new government sent him a telegram, 'On the occasion of the establishment of the Jewish State . . . you who have done more than any other living man towards its creation . . .'. This was followed by a message that Weizmann had been elected President of Israel, 'I doubt whether the Presidency is necessary to Dr Weizmann, but Dr Weizmann is a moral necessity for the state of Israel.'[11]

Two days later Weizmann travelled to Washington. He arrived to find that Truman had ordered Pennsylvania Avenue to be bedecked with the flags of the United States and Israel. At the White House he was received with the same pomp and formality as would be expected for the prime ministers of France or Britain. With Truman's handshake came the promise of a loan of 100 million dollars for the economic development of the fledgling nation.[12] Truman also reassured Weizmann that the United States would use its influence to ensure the defence of Israel and help Israel procure arms. Knowing Truman's devotion to the Old Testament, Weizmann presented him with a scroll of the Torah.

Although it is unlikely that we will ever be able to completely unravel the mystery of Truman's last minute intervention, the question must be asked, 'Did emotional factors anchored in his religious background come into play?' Like Lloyd George, Truman had grown up in a house where the study of the Bible had been a guiding force. His father and his four grandparents were chapel-going Southern Baptists. The large-print family Bible had been used by his devout mother to teach him how to read,[13] and its influence had never left him. The year in which he became president, 1945, he had written, 'I'm a Baptist, because I think that sect gives the common man the shortest and most direct approach to God.' In his memoirs he wrote, 'Palestine . . . has always interested me, partly because of its Biblical background. . . I've always done considerable reading of the Bible. I'd read it at least twice before I went to school. . . . I liked the stories in it. . . . The stories in the Bible, though, were to me stories about real people, and I felt I knew some of them better than actual people I knew.'

Despite his grandiose gesture and his reputation for being sympathetic towards the Jews, Truman, it seems, had an ambivalent attitude. In July 2003, when his handwritten diary of 1947 was found in the Truman Library, journalists, scholars and historians were amazed to read in his own words an outburst against the Jews which contradicts his image as a man with deep Zionist sympathies. On 21 July 1947 he used the diary to vent his anger at a request made to him by the former treasury secretary, Henry Morgenthau Jnr, who had pleaded for America to make a stand against the British who refused refugees on board the *Exodus* to land in Palestine. Truman wrote:

> He'd no business, whatever to call me. The Jews have no sense of proportion nor do they have any judgment on world affairs. . . The Jews, I find are very, very selfish. They care not how many Estonians, Latvians, Finns, Poles, Yugoslavs or Greeks get murdered or mistreated as D[isplaced] P[ersons] as long as the Jews get special treatment. Yet when they have power, physical, financial or political neither Hitler nor Stalin has anything on them for cruelty or mistreatment to the underdog. Put an underdog on top and it makes no difference whether his name is Russian, Jewish, Negro, Management, Labor, Mormon, Baptist he goes haywire. I've found very, very few who remember their past condition when prosperity comes.

Michael J. Devine, the director of the Truman Library, excused these extreme remarks: 'Truman frequently wrote from the gut and not the head, and there are numerous stories of him asking his secretary whether he had posted a letter so he could pull it out of the outbox.' The *Guardian* of 12 July 2003 quoted Robert Farrell, a Truman biographer who edited his private papers, as saying:

> There is a kind of rhetorical quality to that entry. He was irritated at the moment and as he wrote he sharpened everything. I would not want to assert that this is what he really meant. He was turned off by Morgenthau, whom he did not like. What he did think was that Morgenthau was getting into affairs that should not concern him.

The *Daily Telegraph* also reinforced the argument by quoting Michael Benson, the author of *Harry S. Truman and the Founding of Israel*, who wrote that Truman's motives for backing Israel were 'primarily humanitarian, moral and sentimental grounds, many of which are an outgrowth of the president's religious upbringing and his familiarity with the Bible.'

Five years after the independence of Israel, Truman expressed his enthusiasm for his pivotal rôle in the founding of Israel in unequivocal terms. When, with his old friend Eddie Jacobson, he visited the Jewish Theological Seminary in New York and was introduced as 'the man who helped create the state of Israel' he replied and corrected the remark, 'What do you mean, helped create? I was Cyrus, I am Cyrus' – evoking biblical imagery and referring to the Persian monarch who had permitted the Jewish exiles to return to Jerusalem.

THIRTY

The New Army

The thundering line of battle stands,
And in the air death moans and sings;
But Day shall clasp him with strong hands,
And night shall fold him in soft wings.

From 'Into Battle', Julian Grenfell

On 16 May 1948 the Arab Legion crossed the Jordan into Palestine. Other Arab forces entered at many points, claiming the occupation of Gaza in the south and Jericho in the east. Fighting was also reported on the Lebanese and Syrian fronts. The heaviest took place in Jerusalem, with both sides claiming the capture of key points on the road to Tel Aviv. Just as the vicar in St George's Cathedral outside the city wall of Jerusalem opened the second of three Whitsun services on Sunday 16 May the shouts of the Arabs rang through the air and a furious exchange of fire broke out on all sides. The Arabs had resumed their shelling of north Jerusalem. The Jews, using loudspeaker vans, urged the Arabs to yield.

As the bombs dropped Moshe Sharett set up a makeshift Foreign Office near Tel Aviv in a new suburb amid pine forests and the ubiquitous eucalyptus. Cables flashed out to Paris, Rome, Moravia, Sydney, Bangkok and other places, officially informing governments across the world of the new state and putting forward the case for immediate recognition. Office equipment was improvised in the old farmstead at Sarona, the suburb which had grown over the old German Templar village. Koestler might have bemoaned Sharett's table manners[1] but his efficiency was exemplary. Through air-raid alarms, sniping, the constant roar of gunfire in the distance, the cables continued. Sharett made do with one assistant and an old typewriter as the rest of the staff was isolated in Jerusalem, and travelling there from Tel Aviv required an armed convoy. Jerusalem was effectively shut off. Since Easter the Jewish population there had been isolated from the rest of the country in the longest siege since the Crusades. Encircled by a large Arab force, nobody and nothing could get in or out.[2] At that time around 100,000 Jews and 65,000 Arabs inhabited the city.

How long could independence last? Jews had stayed together as a nation and had outlived their old neighbours, the Assyrians. Disorganization accompanied the haste of the British departure. The majority of the 100,000 British troops who had been stationed in Palestine were still waiting impatiently to get away, jammed up near the docks in Haifa, the only port in Israel with a harbour deep enough to accommodate modern shipping. Most soldiers wanted to leave before the skirmishes led by the Arab guerrillas against the Jews expanded into full-scale battle.

While the British soldiers hastened to depart, ships crowded with new settlers, tanks and weapons were heading towards the coast. There were no longer any restrictions on the movement of people and weapons in and out of Israel, a situation that had not existed since 132 CE. Before guns and ammunition were smuggled in everything from sacks of potatoes to beehives, refrigerators and woollen sweaters. Now the only check on the flow of arms or people was Arab sabotage.

The first act of the provisional government in Tel Aviv was to revoke the British White Paper of 1939 which had limited immigration and land sales. Hundreds of thousands of would-be immigrants had never reached Palestine, but many of the 50,000 immigrants who had arrived during 1945–6, who had overcome the British-imposed controls,[3] would become soldiers. There could be no Jewish state without a Jewish army. It was a question of survival or annihilation.

Ben-Gurion was preparing to convert the underground character of the Haganah into a regular force. Overnight he had to mould it into battalions[4] and impose a clear chain of command. The escalation of violence had resulted in the majority of soldiers being dispersed all over the country. They were especially concentrated around Lake Galilee and in the Judean and Hebron Hills, guarding farms, orchards and vineyards, vegetable canning plants, perfume and soap factories against Arab Irregulars. Now the fight had to extend to the massive regular armies about to cross the borders. Another problem was discipline. Because of the secret nature of the Haganah, the men, exuberant and full of fighting spirit, had enjoyed more autonomy and informality than soldiers in traditional armies. The Jewish aversion to authoritarianism was noticeable in many ways. There was little 'sir-ing', no saluting and often not much spit and polish – tenacity and stamina were important, but was boot-polishing? The question was mooted as to whether the Jewish forces should imitate foreign armies. Many believed that there were better ways of showing respect than saluting, and continued the informal camaraderie that had already proved itself. But aware of the importance of appearances and propaganda in war, and in particular the need to show ranks of smartly clad soldiers on newsreels around the world to present an image of military preparedness, a compromise was reached. And so, like other armies, the Israeli forces now learned to march in step to the drums and trumpets of the military brass bands.

The army's organization was rapidly overhauled. Front-line commanders were commissioned and professional ex-officers, veterans from the British army, were hurriedly recruited. Orde Wingate remained a guiding spirit to the army and his tradition was carried on. Ben-Gurion explained his significance: 'The Haganah's best officers [including Moshe Dayan] were trained in the Special Night Squads, and Wingate's doctrines were taken over by the Israel Defence Force.'[5] Now other British officers helped the army, which was made up of Zionist pioneers, Holocaust survivors and new immigrants. The diversity of the origins of the soldiers, the majority immigrants, was also striking. Stocky men with brown faces and hawk-like noses contrasted with tall blonde freckled-faced refugees from Minsk, Cracow and Cologne, from England, Canada and South Africa.

The terrible scarcity of weapons continued. Parts of a tank which had been smuggled into Palestine in steamrollers was quickly assembled and a Mosquito fighter-bomber was flown to Israel straight off a film set in England by an ex-fighter pilot, Terry Farnfeld. (He set up a film company as a front. When he died there was a letter in his belongings from the Air Ministry in London wanting to know why a bomber which had been hired by him for a film had not been returned by the set date.) At least three other aircraft sent from Australia by private citizens, without government permission, were also used in these battles which were now referred to as the War of Independence. A mistress, too, played an interesting role in augmenting the military hardware. When the British were pulling out, a dozen or so tanks were left behind. One of the British commanders, who had a Jewish girlfriend and who had become pro-Zionist, secretly arranged for the tanks to be overlooked, and for the embryonic Israeli army to 'have the keys'. The tanks were decisive in the subsequent war in which Jewish frontiers were extended well beyond those authorized by the United Nations. Hundreds of thousands of Arabs were forced to leave their homes.

* * *

In the midst of the battle for independence, the provisional government of Israel declared that the Haganah was now the army of the new state, and its name was incorporated into the new title of the Israel Defense Forces (IDF), Zeva Haganah le-Israel. At the end of May, Ben-Gurion, in full battledress, paid a tribute to 'the vast debt' owed by the Jewish people to the Haganah and to the Jewish Legion. For the Jews, taking up arms as a people had been the first step towards nationhood. Now, for the first time since Roman days, a uniformed Jewish army under a Jewish government was fighting in Palestine.

Koestler described how Wingate's adored widow, Lorna, knowing the passion which Orde felt towards the Jews and Palestine, circled low in a small plane over a battle raging between Jews and Arabs, and 'to raise their spirits', she tossed from the sky the precious Bible of Orde Wingate. This story is often repeated, but, alas, it is only a myth. She had wanted to throw Orde's Bible out over Yemin Orde, a Galilean kibbutz named after her husband, but permission was refused as there were fears over her safety.[6] Back in London Wyndham Deedes immediately set up the Anglo-Israel Foundation. Youth scholarships to Israel were founded in his name.

* * *

By the time the fighting ceased early in 1949 half of Palestine's Arab population was displaced, outside their homeland, where their descendants remain today. A non-stop influx of Jews came to fill the vacuum. Israel was open to all Jewish immigrants (except criminals) despite the hardships this involved in providing housing, food, education and jobs. Israel's Jewish population jumped from 650,000 in May 1948 to two million in just over ten years. This was also due to the birth rate. Ben-Gurion awarded prizes to families with ten children or more. The 1949 Truce may have divided Jerusalem, but the new Jewish State united Jews everywhere.

When Leo Amery visited Israel in 1950 it was a single-chamber constitutional republic and a member of the United Nations. Amery's pride can be seen in his memoirs: 'I seem to have had my finger in the pie, not only of the Balfour Declaration, but of the genesis of the present Israeli Army.' He added that he had been personally instrumental in getting the Jewish Legion launched in those old War Cabinet days. But he has no place in popular histories of Israel, whereas Orde Wingate is still hailed as a hero of the Israeli army. A book published by the Israel Defense Force acknowledges Wingate as initiating the precepts and training which 'became the heritage of the Haganah, and it is to them, that the Israel Defense Force owes its success in times of war'.[7]

Attitudes are different now. Formidable as the Israeli army is, few now see it in a heroic mould; it is the same with Israel itself. But the determination of the early settlers and politicians – along with the help of the Baron de Rothschild – which led to them creating their own patch of earth in Palestine over a fifty-year period – was a remarkable achievement. Without the agricultural infrastructure that turned the deserts into green fields and orchards, it is unlikely that in the First World War Lloyd George would have established the Jewish homeland in the first place, and without Truman in power at the end of the Second World War it is doubtful that Israel would have survived. To add to the coincidental symmetry of the history, both men were brought up as Baptists. Had the influences of Protestant Nonconformism and the Old Testament had any effect on the decisions made by these politicians? If so there is an irony in Lloyd George's role, as the Liberals owed their support to the Nonconformists who in the nineteenth century campaigned for a separation between Church and State.

Epilogue

He loved the world that hated him: the tear
That dropped upon his Bible was sincere.
'Hope', William Cowper

Three years after Independence, the king of Jordan was assassinated in Jerusalem. The next year, 1952, King Farouk was deposed. Also in 1952 Weizmann died. At the institute named after him at Rehovot there is a small museum in his memory. On his desk the clock is stopped at the moment of his death. A Bible remains opened at the verse he was reading, prophesying the coming of Israel. He was buried in the grounds of the vast scientific research centre, the Weizmann Institute, which he had founded in 1934. It is now one of the most respected research centres for science in the world with a library that stays open twenty-four hours a day.

A year after Weizmann's death, Ben-Gurion stepped down as premier and retired to live in a wooden shack-like house in a small kibbutz, S'deh Boker, south of the Dead Sea, in his beloved Negev Desert – the land where Abraham had once wandered with his sheep, watering them at its ancient wells. But Ben-Gurion returned to live in Tel Aviv in February 1955, first as minister of defence and then nine months later as prime minister. The following year Golda Meir replaced Sharett as foreign minister, a role made more complicated by the coup in Iraq. The grandson of the first Feisal, King Feisal II, along with his Anglophile Prime Minister Nuri al-Said, were both hacked to death. While Abdel Karim Kassem embarked on an army-backed *coup d'état*, excited and frenzied crowds in Baghdad killed all the members of the royal family, smashed the statue of Sir Stanley Maude and invaded the British Embassy complex.

During Ben-Gurion's second term as prime minister, Israel celebrated its tenth anniversary. The population had more than doubled in just a decade and was now nearly two million, half of whom had come as immigrants since the British had left. Acre now had steel mills, Beersheba again manufactured ceramics and farms supplied three-quarters of the country's food. In this new prosperity the Bible was not forgotten. Ben-Gurion said that the 'most important of all' the events for the anniversary was the

International Bible Contest. At the semi-finals in the largest auditorium in Tel Aviv every seat was taken to hear the four hours of questions and answers. Fourteen runners-up from all over the world then arrived, including Baptists, Presbyterians and Methodists. Ben-Gurion, delighted by the response, said that 'this shows a revival of Bible-mindedness in Israel'.[1]

Just two months after the tenth anniversary of the state of Israel, in July 1958, a book was published in America that changed the public perception of Israel. The unforgettable novel *Exodus* by the Jewish US ex-marine Leon Uris became an international publishing phenomenon, the biggest best-seller in the United States since *Gone with the Wind*. Both the novel and the subsequent movie thrust Israel into the lives of millions, and with it a new sympathy for the young country. Portraying passionate Zionist pioneers struggling to wage a war for their independence against the British[2] oppressors, the novel told the story of the birth of a new nation through the romantic story of an American nurse and an Israeli freedom fighter. Translated into some fifty languages, it quickly sold over a million copies. According to the *New York Times Book Review*, Ben-Gurion said that 'As a piece of propaganda, it's the greatest thing ever written about Israel.' The film version, which was directed by Otto Preminger and starred Paul Newman, strengthened the *Exodus* story, turning it into a legend which attracted widespread sympathy for the founding of the state of Israel. Ben-Gurion praised it as 'the greatest film I have ever seen . . . people from around the world will come to visit us . . . it will make us new friends'.

The film of *Exodus* was followed in 1959 by the film of another book that promoted sympathy for the Jewish people, *The Diary of Anne Frank* starring Shelley Winters. Few things had such a profound or lasting impact on Israel as these two books and films. Fourteen-year-old Anne Frank's celebrated diary, which she kept between 1942 and 1944, was the first popular portrayal of the Holocaust on a personal level. It told the gripping account of Second World War refugees hiding in an attic in Nazi-occupied Amsterdam in the hope of avoiding being sent to concentration camps. But the book, first published two years after she had been killed in a gas chamber at the end of the war, did not gather momentum until the stage play and then the film appeared. Suddenly book sales soared and Anne Frank became one of the most memorable figures to emerge from the Second World War. After the Bible, *The Diary of Anne Frank* was to become the most widely read book in the world. In fifty years it would sell more than twenty-five million copies in fifty-four languages. The support given to the fledgling state of Israel, to a certain extent, symbolizes the power of a book. Indeed, no nation in the world owes more to books and to a book in particular.

In 1963 Ben-Gurion again retired and once more moved to the Negev Desert, this time for ten years. He died there at the age of eighty-seven, the last of the survivors of the Jewish Legion who had gone on to hold government office. He had outlived his old friend Ben-Zvi by nine years. Both Ben-Gurion's homes in the desert and in Tel Aviv became museums and libraries, as did Ben-Zvi's old home, which also became an institute for Jewish studies. Among Ben-Gurion's collection of 20,000 books in Tel Aviv is his Bible, the very one that he had taken into battle.

The legacy of the Bible is still alive today in the Israeli army. When taking the oath to join the army in the ceremonial parade, each recruit is presented with a personal Bible and a rifle or another personal weapon. These soldiers can trace their beginnings back to the Jewish Legion and the Haganah. Nothing epitomizes the merging of the religious, political and military elements more than the Beit Elayahu Military Museum[3] in Tel Aviv. Exhibits illustrate the five years of the Jewish Legion, the history of the clandestine Haganah army through the traumatic twenty-seven years of the British Mandate, and the nascent Israel Defense Force. On entering the museum visitors see a small glass showcase. Inside is a silver pistol lying on a black leather-bound Bible used in the secret oath-taking ceremony which initiated volunteers. These two items, symbolizing God and gunpowder, still lie on the same black cotton cloth on which they were kept when Jewish soldiers formed a clandestine army.

Dust thou art, and unto dust shalt thou return.

Genesis 3:19

APPENDIX 1

The Religion of Britain's Prime Ministers

Ten out of the nineteen UK prime ministers who came into office in the twentieth century were brought up in families who belonged to Nonconformist or Free Churches, that is either Congregationalist, Unitarian, Methodist, Baptist, Presbyterian or the Free Church of Scotland.

From the summer of 1902, when Lord Salisbury resigned, until Easter 1940, dissent transcended party allegiance. During that time Britain had eight different prime ministers, all but one of whom was Nonconformist. Arthur Balfour (Conservative) was christened in the Church of Scotland but brought up by his religious mother as a Presbyterian and became a practising spiritualist. Sir Henry Campbell-Bannerman (Liberal) was the son of a lowland Scot and Presbyterian; Herbert Asquith (Liberal) was a Congregationalist from Yorkshire; David Lloyd George (Liberal) was a Welsh Baptist and grandson of a Baptist minister. The distinguishing policies of the Liberals included free trade, low budgets, education and religious liberty. When Chancellor Lloyd George had laid the foundation of what later became the Welfare State, and levied income tax, he was often vociferous in speeches against the very rich. When curbing the powers of the House of Lords he attacked the Conservatives for trying to preserve a privileged elite. His actions enabled the Liberals to retain their working-class vote until the rise of the Labour Party. But he was the fifth and last Liberal prime minister. When the Conservative Scot, Andrew Bonar Law, the Canadian-born son of a Free Church [of Scotland] minister moved into No. 10 he became the first foreign-born prime minister and the first Conservative prime minister who was not a member of the Established Church. The Conservatives, like their Tory predecessors, were traditionally aristocratic and the defenders of the established Church of England. But the next Conservative to hold office, Stanley Baldwin in 1923, gave the appearance of being a traditional Conservative, although it was only a veneer. His mother's father was a Methodist minister and his father was the grandson of a Methodist minister, but both dropped Methodism and converted to the Church of England, endowed their local church and then changed their allegiance from being Liberal to Conservative supporters. A Worcestershire ironworks owner, Baldwin senior was typical of the middle-class Nonconformists who made money in manufacturing and who, although pious and sincere, were not indifferent to social distinctions. Ramsay MacDonald, who was prime minister in Britain's first but brief Labour government in 1924, was also accused of social climbing – but not because of changing churches. His driving ambition, moreover, should come as no surprise as he was the illegitimate son of a servant girl, who was deeply religious and a member of the Free Kirk in Lossiemouth, Scotland. His close friendship with the flamboyant Marchioness of Londonderry, famous for the tattoo of a curling snake up her right leg, led to criticisms in 1931, when he met Britain's disastrous financial crisis by forming what was called a 'National Government' with the Conservatives and Liberals (the election of 1924 had put him out of office, the 1929 election brought him in again). When Neville Chamberlain moved into 10 Downing Street in 1937 he was the eighth prime minister of the twentieth century and the seventh with a Nonconformist background. Like his famous father Joseph, he had been brought up a Unitarian.

In 1940 when power slipped from Chamberlain's hands and King George VI called Winston Churchill to form a coalition government, Churchill became the second prime minister in thirty-eight years who was a member of the Church of England. From then onwards there was a pattern of prime ministers being members of the Established Church. Churchill was followed by Clement Attlee (Labour), typical of the professional middle class, attending Church of England services on Sundays. In 1951 Churchill again became prime minister but stepped down after four years in favour of Sir Anthony Eden (Conservative). Eden, another member of the Church of England, was prime minister for only two years, since he resigned on grounds of failing health in 1957 after the Suez Crisis. His place at No. 10 was taken by Harold Macmillan, with his infectious enthusiasm and phrases such as 'You've never had it so good!' Macmillan's ancestors were Church of Scotland and Presbyterian, but he himself was an Anglican who had won a scholarship to Eton, a religious foundation which was based on the Established Church. After six years Macmillan became the third Tory in a row to suddenly cut short his term at No. 10. Sir Alec Douglas-Home's appointment as prime minister in November 1963 continued the pattern of Tory and Established Church at No. 10. But the trend away from Non-conformity ceased in 1964 when Harold Wilson, a Congregationalist, led the Labour Party to election victory. But it swung back to the Established Church at the next round when Edward Heath, the son of a carpenter from Broadstairs, whose first job had been as a sub-editor on the *Church Times*, beat him in 1970. Four years later he narrowly lost to Wilson, who was in office for only two years. In 1976 he stood down and 'Sunny Jim' Callaghan, a Baptist, took over. Margaret Thatcher, 'the iron lady', who followed him in 1979, was the prime minister to serve the longest without a break. Thatcher was a Methodist who later joined the Church of England. Her successors, John Major (Conservative) and Tony Blair (Labour) were both Anglican. The religions listed below are the faiths in which the prime ministers were brought up.

1. Arthur Balfour 1902–5 Conservative (Conservative) Presbyterian
2. Sir Henry Campbell-Bannerman 1905–8 Liberal (Liberal) Presbyterian
3. Herbert Asquith 1908–15 Liberal; 1915–16 Coalition (Liberal) Congregationalist
4. David Lloyd George 1916–22 Coalition (Liberal) Baptist
5. Andrew Bonar Law 1922–3 (Conservative) Free Church of Scotland
6. Stanley Baldwin 1923–4 (Conservative); Lord President of Coalition 1931–5; Anglican
7. James Ramsay MacDonald 1924; 1929–31 Labour; 1931–5; 1935–7 National Coalition (Labour) Presbyterian
8. Neville Chamberlain 1937–40 National Coalition (Conservative) Unitarian
9. Winston Churchill 1940–5 Coalition; 1945; 1951–5 (Conservative) Anglican
10. Clement Attlee 1945–51 (Labour) Anglican
11. Sir Anthony Eden 1955–7 (Conservative) Anglican
12. Harold Macmillan 1957–63 (Conservative) Anglican
13. Sir Alec Douglas-Home 1963–4 (Conservative)
14. Harold Wilson 1964–70; 1974–6 (Labour) Congregationalist
15. Edward Heath 1970–4 (Conservative) Anglican
16. James Callaghan 1976–9 (Labour) Baptist
17. Margaret Thatcher 1979–90 (Conservative) Methodist
18. John Major 1990–7 (Conservative) Anglican
19. Tony Blair 1997– (Labour) Anglican

APPENDIX 2

Jewish Immigration to Palestine and Demographics

The total Jewish population before the First World War in 1914 was estimated to be 80,000. This declined during the war to an estimated 50,000 in 1918. This figure increased thereafter with births and an increasing immigrant population, as the table below shows.

Year	Number of immigrants	Year	Number of immigrants
1919	1,806	1930	4,944
1920	8,223	1931	4,075
1921	8,294	1932	12,553
1922	8,685	1933	37,337
1923	8,175	1934	45,267
1924	13,892	1935	66,472
1925	34,386	1936	29,595
1926	13,855	1937	10,629
1927	3,034	1938	14,675
1928	2,178	1939	31,195
1929	5,249		

APPENDIX 3

Ben Gurion's Declaration, 14 May 1948

On Saturday 15 May 1948, the morning after Ben-Gurion's declaration in Tel Aviv, under the heading of 'End of Palestine Mandate New State of Israel Proclaimed', readers of *The Times* found the following on the third page:

> The British Mandate for Palestine ended at midnight. Some hours before, the Jewish National Council in Tel Aviv proclaimed a new Jewish state of Israel. The National Council is to act as a provisional Government, and Mr. Ben-Gurion has been made Prime Minister. President Truman later announced the *de facto* recognition of the provisional Government by the United States, while from Cairo Nokrashy Pasha broadcast that Egyptian armed forces had been ordered 'to enter Palestine . . .' by resolution of the General Assembly of the United Nations, hereby proclaim the establishment of a Jewish State in Palestine to be called 'Israel'.

* * *

David Ben-Gurion's declaration: ERETZ ISRAEL [(Hebrew) – The Land of Israel] was the birthplace of the Jewish people. Here their spiritual, religious and political identity was shaped. Here they first aspired to statehood, created cultural values of national and universal significance and gave to the world the eternal Book of Books. After being forcibly exiled from their land, the people remained faithful to it throughout their Diaspora and never ceased to pray and hope for their return to it and for the restoration in it of their political freedom. Impelled by this historic and traditional attachment, Jews strove in every successive generation to re-establish themselves in their ancient homeland. In recent decades they returned in their masses. Pioneers, ma'pilim [(Hebrew) – immigrants coming to Eretz-Israel in defiance of restrictive legislation] and defenders, they made deserts bloom, revived the Hebrew language, built villages and towns, and created a thriving community controlling its own economy and culture, loving peace but knowing how to defend itself, bringing the blessings of progress to all the country's inhabitants, and aspiring to independent nationhood. In the year 5657 (1897), at the summons of the spiritual father of the Jewish State, Theodor Herzl, the First Zionist Congress convened and proclaimed the right of the Jewish people to national rebirth in its own country. This right was recognized in the Balfour Declaration of 2 November 1917, and re-affirmed in the mandate of the League of Nations which, in particular, gave international sanction to the historic connection between the Jewish people and Eretz Israel and to the right of the Jewish people to rebuild its national home. The catastrophe which recently befell the Jewish people – the massacre of millions of Jews in Europe – was another clear demonstration of the urgency of solving the problem of its homelessness by re-establishing in Eretz Israel the Jewish State, which would open the gates of the homeland wide to every Jew and confer upon the Jewish people the status of a fully privileged member of the comity of nations. Survivors of the Nazi Holocaust in Europe, as well as Jews from other parts of the world, continued to migrate to Eretz Israel, undaunted by difficulties, restrictions and dangers, and never ceased to assert their right to a life of dignity, freedom and honest toil in their national homeland. In the Second World War, the Jewish community of this country contributed its full share to the struggle of the freedom- and peace-loving nations against the forces of Nazi wickedness and, by the blood of its soldiers and its war effort, gained the right to be reckoned among the peoples who founded the United Nations. On 29 November 1947, the United Nations General Assembly passed a resolution calling for the establishment of a Jewish State in Eretz Israel; the General Assembly required the inhabitants of Eretz Israel to take such steps as were necessary on their part for the implementation of that resolution. This recognition by the United Nations of the right of the Jewish people to establish their state is irrevocable. This right is the natural right of the Jewish people to be masters of their own fate, like all other nations, in their own sovereign state. ACCORDINGLY WE, MEMBERS OF THE PEOPLE'S COUNCIL, REPRESENTATIVES OF THE JEWISH COMMUNITY OF ERETZ ISRAEL AND OF THE ZIONIST MOVEMENT, ARE HERE ASSEMBLED ON THE DAY OF THE TERMINATION OF THE BRITISH MANDATE OVER ERETZ ISRAEL AND, BY VIRTUE OF OUR NATURAL AND HISTORIC RIGHT AND ON THE STRENGTH OF THE RESOLUTION OF THE UNITED NATIONS GENERAL ASSEMBLY, HEREBY DECLARE THE ESTABLISHMENT OF A JEWISH STATE IN ERETZ ISRAEL, TO BE KNOWN AS THE STATE OF ISRAEL. WE DECLARE that, with effect from the moment of the termination of the mandate being tonight, the eve of Sabbath, the 6th Iyar 5708 (15 May 1948), until the establishment of the elected, regular authorities of the State in accordance with the Constitution which shall be adopted by the Elected Constituent Assembly not later than 1 October 1948, the People's Council shall act as a Provisional Council of State, and its executive organ, the People's Administration, shall be the Provisional Government of the Jewish State, to be called 'Israel'. THE STATE OF ISRAEL will be open for Jewish immigration and for the Ingathering of the Exiles; it will foster the development of the country for the benefit of all its inhabitants; it will be based on freedom, justice and peace as envisaged by the prophets of Israel; it will ensure complete equality of social and political rights to all its inhabitants irrespective of religion, race or sex; it will guarantee freedom of religion, conscience, language, education and culture; it will safeguard the holy places of all religions; and it will be faithful to the principles of the Charter of the United Nations. THE STATE OF ISRAEL is prepared to cooperate with the agencies and representatives of the United Nations in implementing the resolution of the General Assembly of 29 November 1947, and will take steps to bring about the economic union of the whole of Eretz Israel. WE APPEAL to the United Nations to assist the Jewish people in the building-up of its State and to receive the state of Israel into the comity of nations. WE APPEAL – in the very midst of the onslaught launched against us now for months – to the Arab inhabitants of the state of Israel to preserve peace and participate in the upbuilding of the state on the basis of full and equal citizenship and due representation in all its provisional and permanent institutions. WE EXTEND our hand to all neighbouring states and their peoples in an offer of peace and good neighbourliness, and appeal to them to establish bonds of cooperation and mutual help with the sovereign Jewish people settled in its own land. The state of Israel is prepared to do its share in a common effort for the advancement of the entire Middle East. WE APPEAL to the Jewish people throughout the Diaspora to rally round the Jews of Eretz Israel in the tasks of immigration and upbuilding and to stand by them in the great struggle for the realization of the age-old dream – the redemption of Israel. PLACING OUR TRUST IN THE ALMIGHTY, WE AFFIX OUR SIGNATURES TO THIS PROCLAMATION AT THIS SESSION OF THE PROVISIONAL COUNCIL OF STATE, ON THE SOIL OF THE HOMELAND, IN THE CITY OF TEL AVIV, ON THIS SABBATH EVE, THE 5TH DAY OF IYAR 5708 (14 MAY 1958).

APPENDIX 4

Outline for a Jewish Colonization Scheme, drawn up by Lloyd George, 1903

The following is the draft of a little known document drawn up by David Lloyd George in 1903 (when he was a Member of Parliament and a partner in the solicitors' firm of Lloyd George, Roberts & Company) when he instructed by Leopold J. Greenberg (the London representative of Theodor Herzl, founder of the Zionist movement) to draw up papers for the first proposal for a Jewish homeland in the British Empire.

JEWISH COLONIZATION SCHEME
TERMS AND CONDITIONS
Of Concessions to be granted by His Majesty's Government to the Jewish Colonial Trust (Juedische Colonialbank) Limited for the establishment of a Jewish Settlement in British East Africa.
WHEREAS The Jewish Colonial Trust (Juedische Colonialbank) Limited is a Company incorporated under the Companies Acts with a Capital of £ 2,000,000 limited by shares and having for its objects amongst other things the promotion of colonization schemes which shall be to the interest of the Jewish race and the said Jewish Colonial Trust (Juedische Colonialbank) has represented to His Majesty's Government that its principal object is the settling of Jews under conditions favorable to their retention and encouragement of the Jewish National Idea,
AND WHEREAS it is desirable that for the furthering of the said object a settlement should be founded under laws and regulations adopted for the wellbeing of the Jewish people and whereby their social and physical status would be materially developed and improved,
AND WHEREAS a portion of His Majesty's dominions beyond the seas now included and contained in the Protectorate of British East Africa would be greatly enhanced in value by the foundation there of a Jewish Settlement and the creation and direction of public works and the promotion therein of commercial enterprises and the establishment of commercial relationship with neighboring districts,
AND WHEREAS it has been represented to His Majesty's Government that such territory suitable for the purposes aforesaid may be found in His Majesty's dominions in British East Africa and it is desirable that the Jewish Colonial Trust (Juedische Colonialbank) be empowered to search for and identify such territory with the view to the same after identification, delineation and approval being vested in the Jewish Colonial Trust (Juedische Colonialbank) with such rights powers and privileges as may be herein declared or may hereafter be approved for the purposes aforesaid:
NOW THEREFORE IT IS HEREBY DECLARED
1. That the Jewish Colonial Trust (Juedische Colonialbank) (hereinafter called "the Concessionaires") may and are hereby authorized to enter into and upon the lands comprised in His Majesty's dominions in British East Africa for the purpose of inspecting and examining the same and of ascertaining the condition thereof and the suitability of the same or any part thereof for the establishment of the Jewish Settlement or Colony (hereinafter called 'the Settlement') with full power to use for any of the purposes aforesaid any road or ways constructed therein and to plot out and survey the same to the intent that a portion thereof (hereinafter called 'the territory') if and when found suitable may be

identified and with the boundaries and abuttals thereof duly determined by the Concessionaires may be submitted to His Majesty's Secretary of State for the approval of His Majesty's Government.

2. THAT the Concessionaires shall bear and pay all necessary costs charges and expenses of and in connection with an expedition or survey party to and at British East Africa for the purpose of making and completing the said survey and identifying the said territory and submitting a full description and plan of the same to His Majesty's Government in accordance with Clause 1 hereof not being any costs or expenses of His Majesty's officials or servants or any persons in the employ of His Majesty whether they shall accompany or assist the Concessionaires or not.

3. THAT immediately upon the approval of the said territory by His Majesty's Government as being suitable and proper for the said settlement the entire management and control of the lands of the Crown in the said territory and of the proceeds of the sale letting and disposing thereof including all royalties mines and minerals shall be vested until the 31st December 1909 in the Concessionaires and thereafter in the administrators of the said territory formed in accordance with the Constitution hereinafter referred to.

4. THAT after the said approval as aforesaid and until the 31st December 1909 the Concessionaires shall hold and retain the said territory and all rights interests authorities and powers annexed or incident thereto UPON TRUST to allow the same to be used by Jews for settlement therein and the encouragement therein of the Jewish National Idea subject nevertheless to the supreme control as herein specified of His Majesty's Government for the purposes of government and preservation of public order AND UPON TRUST to hold the same for the purposes of the said settlement in accordance with the terms herein set out and now intended to be included in the Constitution hereinafter mentioned.

5. THAT at any time subsequent to the approval of the said lands and before the said 31st December 1909 the Concessionaires may submit to His Majesty's Government for approval by the said Government the terms of a Constitution for the regulations administration and good government of the Settlement whereby provision shall be made <I>inter alia<I> for the following matters and things: -

(a) FOR the introduction and establishment of a form of popular government in the territory which shall be Jewish in character and with a Jewish Governor to be appointed by His Majesty in Council.

(b) FOR granting to the settlement all necessary and proper powers to make ordinances and regulations for the internal administration and all matters necessary for the welfare and good government of the Jewish community and other persons in the said settlement.

(c) FOR the levying in and upon the said territory all such tax or taxes and assessments as the settlement may decide for the said purposes of administration and good government including police works and education and all such other purposes as may from time to time be exercised by His Majesty's Secretary of State but so that except with the previous consent of His Majesty's Secretary of State there shall be no differential treatment of the subjects of any State or Power as to trade or settlement or as to access to markets.

(d) FOR defining the relationship and status of the settlement and all persons therein with any other part or parts of His Majesty's dominions beyond the seas and with any Foreign State and with the Chief of independent tribes in British East Africa or any other Government community or persons but so that all persons domiciled in the territory shall be and become and always remain British and the subjects of His Majesty.

(e) FOR the compliance of the settlement with any requisition of His Majesty's Government with respect to any act or proceeding of the settlement with relation to any peoples or inhabitants of the territory other than resident Jews in respect of any matters of religion or the administration of Justice or otherwise howsoever.

(f) FOR the conformation by the Settlement with all restriction and provision (if any) with respect to import and export and other duties taxes or assessments which shall be contained in any treaty for the time being in force between His Majesty's Government and any other State or Power in relation to His Majesty's dominions in British East Africa.

(g) FOR restricting the settlement without the previous approval of His Majesty's Government from levying upon the subjects of any Foreign State or Power any duties taxes or assessments other than those authorized to be levied in the territory.
(h) FOR granting to the settlement power to exclude from the said territory any person or persons proposing to enter or settle in the same who shall or may be deemed to be opposed to the interests of the settlement or the government thereof or the dignity of His Majesty the King and the power (with the previous consent of His Majesty's Secretary of State) to expel from the territory without being liable for compensation or otherwise any person not fully and completely abiding by the ordinances rules and regulations for the time being in force in the territory or committing or conniving at a breach of the Constitution of the settlement.
(j) FOR the appointment of Judges and Officers for the administration of Justice and the provision of Courts of Justice for the administration of civil and criminal law in the territory so that the same may as far as practicable be in accordance with the law of England but subject to such alteration and amendments therein based upon Jewish law as shall from time to time be assented to and approved by the Secretary of State.
(k) FOR the preservation of the customs and laws of the native people of the territory with respect to the holding possession transfer and disposition of interests in lands and goods and the succession thereto and marriage divorce and legitimacy and other rights of property and personal rights.
(l) FOR the non-interference by the Settlement (except insofar as may be necessary in the interests of humanity and for the preservation of peace) with the religion of any class or tribe of the native peoples of the territory and all forms of religious worship and ordinances as heretofore exercised and practiced in the territory.
(m) FOR restricting the Settlement from granting any exclusive monopoly of trade to any person or corporation in the territory but so that no such restriction shall extend to any public works or undertakings usually or at any time heretofore authorized in England by Act of Parliament or otherwise to be carried out or undertaken by municipal corporations or other public authorities and the establishment of banks, railways, tramways, omnibus and motor conveyances, docks, telegraph, telephone, canals, irrigation works or other similar undertakings or works or in the event of any patent or protective rights for inventions or any literary, music, or dramatic copyright or any copyrights for works of art.
(n) FOR the calling or the said settlement by the name of 'New Palestine' or such other name as may from time to time be approved of and with the consent of His Majesty's Secretary of State and for the adoption and use in the territory of any distinctive or National flag which His Majesty's Secretary of State may from time to time approve.
(o) FOR the acquisition with the consent of His Majesty's Secretary of State of any other lands and premises in British East Africa and elsewhere whether abutting upon or contiguous to the said territory or not and the enlargement of the boundaries of the said territory and the extension to any new or additional lands of the rights powers and privileges vested in or exercised by the Settlement.
6. ALL settlers in and inhabitants of the territory shall so long as they conform to the provisions and terms of this concession of the said Constitution and the laws for the time in force in the said territory be free from molestation in respect to their persons and property and under the protection and control of His Majesty's Government.
7. ANY differences which may at any time hereafter arise between the Concessionaires or the Settlement and any State Government or person shall on the part of the Concessionaires or the Settlement as the case may be submitted to the arbitration or decision of His Majesty's Secretary of State whose award shall be final and binding upon them.

From Cohen, *The Rebirth of Israel* (Hyperion, Westport, Connecticut), p. 81.

APPENDIX 5

An Example of the Diminishing Support for Lloyd George by the Nonconformists

Letter from J.H. Shakespeare, Baptist Union of Great Britain, to the Rt Hon C. Addison, Ministry of Munitions, 1 May 1917, from the Lloyd George Archives at the House of Lords. This is one of the early letters indicating a shift in support for the Liberals by the Nonconformists.

> The Free churches, upon whose support Mr Lloyd George must depend so much in a general election, are, generally speaking, in a state of perplexity or suspicion towards him. Especially is this the case in the North of England. It is partly due to the necessary alliance with Carson and Milner and partly to lack of knowledge and false reports on what really happened when Mr. Asquith fell; partly also to such affairs as Lancashire and Cotton, etc. These strained relations have been getting a little worse lately. A War chest and a roll of supporters are of great value but the Free Churches are in the long run moved by nothing else than their traditional principles....

APPENDIX 6

Balfour's Plea for Zionism

In this seldom quoted document Balfour used the argument of attracting Jewish money, which could be used to develop the country, as a reason for supporting Zionism.

Mandate for Palestine: note by Mr Balfour, 5 November 1920
I had hoped to raise the question of the Mandate for Palestine at to-day's cabinet meeting. Unfortunately, I am confined to bed, and can only make a written appeal to my colleagues on a point which I think is of more importance than at first appears.

If the first version of the mandate is compared with the last in a strictly legal spirit, there is perhaps little difference between them; but I fear the difference is [in] effect will be great, and in a direction wholly unfavourable to Zionism.

Zionism is a new experiment, and one which depends for its success not merely upon the tact and judgment of the British administrators in Palestine, but upon Jewish sentiment throughout the world. If financial assistance is not forthcoming, and forthcoming on an immense scale, from the Jewish people outside Palestine, it is quite impossible that those economic developments can be undertaken and carried through on which the success of the whole experiment depends. Every legitimate effort should therefore be made to lighten the task of the Zionist leadeers who have got to make a world-wide appeal to their co-religionists.

Now all the changes made in the successive editions of the mandate are of a kind which will increase, rather than diminish, the difficulties of Dr Weizmann, Judge Brandeis, and their friends. They hold themsevels very strongly, and I am bound to say that I agree with them.

By watering down the phrases which appeal most to Zionist sentiment, you discourage your friends. Whom do you placate? Zionism has many enemies who would no doubt be gratified if Zionism were abandoned. But it is not abandoned; and the mandate in its latest form will give little comfort. Zionism has many friends whose ardour will be cooled, and whose suspicions will be roused by the change of tone and manner in the mandate even if unaccompanied by a change in its essential substance. These changes therefore will get you no new supporters, but will damp the ardour of many old ones; and it is on the ardour of the old ones that our hopes of success depend. The Zionist leaders, endeavouring on the one side, to deal with the masses of poverty-stricken and oppressed Jews, who wildly exaggerate what Zionism can do for their race, and, on the other, appealing for financial assistance from Jews throughout the world, have got a task of extraordinary difficulty before them. They may fail; but if they fail we are involved in their failure; and it is not only obviously right, but obviously prudent, to assist them in every way we can.

A.J.B. From the Lloyd George Archives at the House of Lords, F/200/6/1.

APPENDIX 7

Summary of the Rise of Arab Nationalism in Palestine until the time of the Mandate

In 1915, after the Turks' failed attack on Suez and their failure to incite the population in Egypt to revolt, British strategists in Cairo dreamt of an Arab uprising against the Turks. Turning the Hejaz, with its holy cities of Mecca and Medina, into a base friendly towards the British would diminish the threats to the Red Sea and bring the two most important Muslim holy cities back into the realm of the 100 million Muslim subjects in the British Empire. Since the outbreak of war, they had all been out of bounds. Medina, the birthplace of the Prophet, was 300 miles from Mecca, so strategically it was not a formidable task. British authorities wanted to be able to reassure the millions of Muslims throughout the world that the Holy Cities were inviolate and that pilgrimages were secure. Ideally, the caliphate would be separated from the Ottoman dynasty; the Sacred Places would be put under an independent ruler, and the title of 'Keeper of the Holy Places' would be transferred from the distant sultan to the local sherif of the Hejaz, Hussein Ibn Ali, who would become the caliph. The new problem of the conflict of loyalties for the Muslims was stressed by the Viceroy of India, who had tried to reassure Muslim subjects by explaining that the war was not inconsistent with their loyalty to King George and the British Empire. To complicate matters, the majority of men in the Indian army then, and the population of Egypt, were Muslim.

Hussein needed arms, money, a strong army, capable leaders, imported foodstuffs and the reassurance from the British that they would help the Arabs to independence. But the British saw Hussein only as a self-interested tribal chief, not as a Garibaldi or a Bolivar and initially they only wanted to stir up a limited Arab revolt and secure the holy places. Hussein, though, wanted much more that. Gilbert Clayton, the chief of the Arab Bureau, the centre of British Intelligence in the Middle East, asked Henry MacMahon, the High

Commissioner in Cairo, to obtain instructions from London. An agreement was needed urgently. Lord Kitchener sent authority to General Sir John Maxwell, 'empowering him in the name of the British government to deal with the Arabs and to try to ensure that their traditional loyalty to Britain would not be impaired'. The Arabs maintain that they constitute a promise from the British to virtually all Arabic-speaking countries in the Middle East, with the exception of Lebanon, that they would be free to choose their own political future. Hussein only rose against the Turks in June 1916 because he believed he had been given the word of the British government.

A comparison of MacMahon's first letter to Hussein (30 August) with his second (24 October) shows the extent that the British gave in to Arab demands. The first letter, full of ambiguities, with no commitment, suggested that decisions about frontiers should be postponed until the end of the war. Hussein, who saw through the charm and tricks of British diplomacy, said that he could not cooperate with the British on such vague terms. He replied asking for money, aid and assurances that all Arab lands under Ottoman control would be given self-rule. While it is often said that the sherif did not speak for the Arab world as a whole, Professor Eliezer Tauber of the Bar-Ilan University, in *The Arab Movements in World War I* (Frank Cass, London, 1993) says, 'The conditions that the leaders of al-Fatat and al-'Ahd submitted to Faysal [Feisal] [in Damascus] constituted the basis for the letter Husayn [Hussein] sent in July 1915 to the British high commissioner in Egypt.' He went on to say that the British flinched from Husayn's demands, '. . . however, the desertion to British lines of the Iraqi officer and member of al-'Ahd Muhammjad Sharif al-Faruqi, and the false information he gave to the British in Cairo concerning the strength and extent of the Arab movement, brought a complete turnabout in the British attitude . . .'

Suddenly, on 24 October, a letter written by MacMahon to Hussein met most of Hussein's demands. Known as 'the Hussein–MacMahon correspondence', these compromising letters were to be trawled out and discussed in parliaments and peace conferences for decades. The Arabs maintained that virtually all the Arabic-speaking countries in the Middle East, with the exception of Lebanon, would be free to choose their own political future. Below is the letter:

I have received your letter of the 29th Shawal, 1333, with much pleasure and your expression of friendliness and sincerity have given me the greatest satisfaction.

I regret that you should have received from my last letter the impression that I regarded the question of limits and boundaries with coldness and hesitation; such was not the case, but it appeared to me that the time had not yet come when that question could be discussed in a conclusive manner.

I have realised, however, from your last letter that you regard this question as one of vital and urgent importance. I have, therefore, lost no time in informing the Government of Great Britain of the contents of your letter, and it is with great pleasure that I communicate to you on their behalf the following statement, which I am confident you will receive with satisfaction.

The two districts of Mersina and Alexandretta and portions of Syria lying to the west of the districts of Damascus, Homs, Hama and Aleppo cannot be said to be purely Arab, and should be excluded from the limits demanded.

With the above modification, and without prejudice to our existing treaties with Arab chiefs, we accept those limits.

As for those regions within those frontiers wherein Great Britain is free to act without detriment to the interests of her ally, France, I am empowered in the name of the Government of Great Britain to give the following assurances and make the following reply to your letter:

(1) Subject to the above modifications, Great Britain is prepared to recognise and support the independence of the Arabs in all regions within the limits demanded by the sherif of Mecca.

(2) Great Britain will guarantee the holy places against all external aggression and will recognise their inviolability.

(3) When the situation admits, Great Britain will give to the Arabs her advice and will assist them to establish what may appear to be the most suitable forms of government in those various territories.

(4) On the other hand, it is understood that the Arabs have decided to seek the advice and guidance of Great Britain only, and that such European advisers and officials as may be required for the formation of a sound form of administration will be British.

(5) With regard to the vilayets of Baghdad and Basra, the Arabs will recognise that the established position and interests of Great Britain necessitate special administrative arrangements in order to secure these territories from foreign aggression to promote the welfare of the local population and to safeguard our mutual economic interests.

I am convinced that this declaration will assure you beyond all possible doubt of the sympathy of Great Britain towards the aspirations of her friends the Arabs and will result in a firm and lasting alliance, the immediate results of which will be the expulsion of the Turks from the Arab countries and the freeing of the Arab peoples from the Turkish yoke, which for so many years has pressed heavily upon them.

I have confined myself in this letter to the more vital and important questions. . . . It was with very great relief and satisfaction that I heard of the safe arrival of the Holy Carpet. . . . I am sending this letter by the hand of your trusted and excellent messengers, sheikh Mohammed ibn Arif ibn Uraifan. . . .

(signed) A. Henry MacMahon.

By the spring of 1916, messengers were continually plying between Hussein and Cairo. General Sir Reginald Wingate, who had earlier won fame in the Sudan, was given the title of General Officer Commanding Operations in the Hejaz – and the task of what was described as 'nourishing the revolt'. Six weeks after the first anniversary of the landing at Gallipoli, Sherif Hussein hoisted his flag. So began the Arab Revolt. By coincidence, on the very same day, 16 June 1916, Kitchener, one of the loudest advocates for the British to push the Arab Revolt, was drowned at sea.

The Turkish garrison was ready to overwhelm any opposition by the Arabs. Bringing British ammunition and support troops by sea seemed to be the sole route. Royal Navy warships already patrolled the Red Sea to stop any enemy vessels entering the Suez Roads. The pro-Arab British policy expanded quickly. In October, additional English officers, including Lawrence, arrived. Their job was to assist Hussein, keep the Arab Bureau in Cairo informed, urge the Arabs on to capture the Turkish stronghold at Medina, and disrupt and cut the Hejaz railway – the vital link between Syria and the Holy Cities.

* * *

In May 1916 the British and French governments then made another secret agreement. With optimism that they would eventually win the war, they divided up the Turkish provinces, even though, apart from Turkish losses to Russia around the Black Sea, there were no signs of Allied victory against the Turks. Sir Mark Sykes, who negotiated on behalf of Britain appeared to disregard the earlier arrangement with the Arabs. Secrecy surrounding the Sykes–Picot agreement meant that Sherif Hussein did not realise that the land he considered pledged to the Arabs was soon to be an issue. Attached to the Sykes–Picot agreement was a map with areas marked red for zones of British influence, blue for French influence. Palestine – the Holy Land, sacred to Muslim, Jew and Christian alike – was marked as a brown zone, with this explanation: 'Palestine, with the holy places, is separated from Turkish territory and subjected to special regime to be determined by agreement between Russia, France and Great Britain'.

It cannot be stressed too much that these two agreements were made when Asquith was prime minister of Britain and Grey Foreign Secretary. When Lloyd George came into power at the end of 1916 one of the first things he did was try to make peace with Turkey (see Chapter 16). While the new coalition government could not rescind these agreements, they could make others which, if circumstances changed – as they were all the time – could supersede them. For instance, the Russian Revolution had made the earlier Constantinople Agreement of March–April 1915, between Britain, Russia and France, null and void.

Although the last of the three famous conflicting agreement made by the British during the war, the Balfour Declaration in 1917 (see chapter sixteen) in November 1917, was very much a product of the Lloyd George War Cabinet, Sir Mark Sykes, was not only author of the Sykes–Picot Agreement, but, as a member of the new War Secretariat, closely involved in the wording of the Balfour Declaration. Christopher Sykes, the son of Sir Mark, better known as the biographer of Evelyn Waugh, gives a clear summary to the background of these documents in *Crossroads to Israel*. He also says how, towards the end of 1918, in anticipation of victory, Balfour asked the Foreign Office for a memorandum on the British pledges on the Arab lands. He hoped that the conflicting undertakings could somehow be reconciled without souring Britain's relationships. The controversy which resulted from these agreements is summarized in *The Emergence of Arab Nationalism*, by Frank Clements (Diploma Press, London, 1976), a bibliography of over 500 books, pamphlets and articles, which emphasises the many elements of alienation under three headings, 'The Struggle Between the Arabs and Turks'; 'The Peace Settlement and its Consequences'; 'The Fertile Crescent under the Mandate System' with authors ranging from Elie Kedourie and George Antonius to Martin Gilbert and Abdullah I, King of Jordan.

Notes

Prologue

1. The River Jordan rises in headstreams in Syria and Lebanon, and, flowing through the lake known as the Sea of Galilee, it then meanders south until it drops 1,286 feet below sea level. Finally it empties into the Dead Sea. The first mention of it is in the Old Testament when Abraham and Lot parted company. The name is derived from the Hebrew word meaning 'descender', since it runs its course from the heights of its sources to the lowest place on earth.
2. The Torah, also known as The Five Books of Moses or The Pentateuch (teachings or instruction), is the name of the first five books of the Bible (Genesis, Exodus, Leviticus, Numbers and Deuteronomy) and contains God's commandments.
3. When *The Times* described the meeting at the Opera House in Covent Garden, London, on 2 December following the announcement of the Balfour Declaration, it stressed that one of the themes of evening was the need for Arabs, Armenians and Jews to move towards harmony, and that one of the outstanding features was 'the Old Testament spirit which pervaded it . . . '.
4. He may have been inspired by Francis Bacon, who in his *Novum Organum* said that civilization was influenced by 'printing, gunpowder, and the magnet'.
5. David William Schmidt, MA thesis, 'Contribution of British Evangelical Thought to the Making of the Balfour Declaration' (Institute of Holy Land Studies, Jerusalem, 1995). Founded in 1957, this institute is now known as Jerusalem University College, an extension campus for more than a hundred accredited Christian universities, colleges and seminaries around the world as well as an independent, degree granting institution of higher education.

6. Ibid.

5. Ibid.

6. Chaim Weizmann, *Trial and Error* (Hamish Hamilton, 1949)
7. The rise of the Liberal Party is described by Trevor Wilson in his various books, including *The Downfall of the Liberal Party* (Collins, 1966) and J.A. Hamer, *Liberal Politics in the Age of Gladstone and Rosebery* (Clarendon Press, Oxford, 1972)
8. In the mid-1970s various developments helped the rise of Christian Zionism in the United States. While traditional Protestant denominations and the Roman Catholic Church were declining, evangelical movements became the fastest growing branches of Christianity.
9. Genesis 12: 17, Leviticus 26: 44–5 and Deuteronomy 7: 7–8 are often quoted to support Israel's biblical claim to the land.
10. Gershom Gorenberg, author of *The End of Days: Fundamentalism and the Struggle for the Temple Mount*, in an article in the *International Herald Tribune* on 14 October 2002 describes the relationship as 'strangely exploitative. . . . Accepting the embrace of Conservative evangelicals poses problems of principle for Jews and Israel, in return for a short-term pay-off. . . . The Christian right's view of Israel derives from a double-edged theological position. Following a classic anti-Jewish stance, it regards the Jewish people as spiritually blind for rejecting Jesus . . . it regards Israel's existence as proof that biblical prophecies are coming true – heralding an apocalypse in which Jews will either die or accept Jesus.'
11. Prime Minister Begin of Israel developed a unique relationship with Reagan and many fundamentalist leaders, especially Jerry Falwell, who, with his Moral Majority, had long supported Israel.

12. Dan Bahat *Carta's Historical Atlas of Jerusalem* (Carta, Jerusalem, 1986).
13. David Frum, *The Right Man: The Surprise Presidency of George W. Bush* (Random House, New York, 2002).
16. Review in the *Economist* 18 January 2003.

Chapter One

1. Dr Michael Lynch, *The Liberals and the Great War, 1914–18*, vol. 2, (University of Leicester, 1996).
2. A.J.P. Taylor, *English History 1914–45* (Oxford University Press, 1965).
3. Wellington had not been to university.
4. D. Lloyd George, *War Memoirs of David Lloyd George*, vol. 1 (Odhams Press, 1938).
5. Lloyd George, *War Memoirs*.
6. Asquith's second marriage had meant a withdrawal away from those Nonconformists who had earlier given him unwavering support.
7. John Grigg, in *Lloyd George, War Leader* (Allen Lane, 2002) describes the intimacy of the longstanding affair and is the subject of a brilliant essay in *The New York Review of Books*, 29 May 2003.
8. Frances Stephenson, who had come into his Lloyd George's life when governess to his daughter Megan had joined his staff in the Treasury in 1913.
9. His early childhood is covered by his brother, W. George, *My Brother and I* (Eyre & Spottiswood, 1958), Frank Owen's *Tempestuous Journey* (Hutchinson, 1954) and, of course, John Griff's *The Young Lloyd George* (Eyre, Methuen, 1973)
10. The Lloyd George Museum at Highgate, Lloyd George's home from 1863 to 1880, interprets his life and times and includes his uncle's shoemaker's workshop with its original benches and other items. Lloyd George Museum, Llanystumdwy, Criccieth, Gwynedd.
11. Grigg, Lloyd George.
12. Three hundred times in 1917.
13. The name was derived from the Garden Suburb movement which had been started at the turn of the century by Ebenezer Howard.
14. A.J.P. Taylor, *Beaverbrook* (Hamish Hamilton, 1972).
15. Roy Jenkins, *The Chancellors* (Macmillan, 1998).
16. Cliff Richards, the pop star, did likewise and became 'Richard'.
17. Edwin A. Jenkins, *From Foundry to Foreign Office* (Grayson & Grayson, 1933).
18. Gertrude Himmelfarb, *Poverty and Compassion, the Moral Imagination of the Late Victorians* (Knopf, New York 1991).
19. Kenneth Rose, *Superior Person* (Weidenfeld & Nicolson, 1969).
20. Taylor, *English History 1914–1945*.
21. Anthony Glyn, *Elinor Glyn* (Hutchinson, 1955).
22. Max Egremont in his much-acclaimed Balfour, *A Life of Arthur James Balfour* (Collins, 1980).
23. Ibid.
24. Nicolas Mosley in *Julian Grenfell* (Weidenfeld & Nicolson, 1976) described this exclusive group, 'The Souls met at dinners and parties in London; but their main centres of activity were country house weekends. Here they assembled and talked – mainly about ideas, books, personalities. They never referred to themselves as 'the Souls' but sometimes as 'the gang'. Their speciality was the games they played in the evenings – pencil-and-paper games, acting games, guessing games – Literary Consequences, Acrostics, Telegrams; Clumps, Charades ... The point of these games was to show off not just erudition but, as always wit ... It was accepted that Arthur Balfour was the leading member of 'the Souls...'.
25. Jean Balfour, 'The Palm Sunday Case', in *Proceedings of the Society for Psychical Research*, vol. 52, part 189, February 1960.
26. Rodney Goutman, Melbourne.
27. William Yale, *The Near East* (University of Michigan Press, 1958).
28. Laurence Evans, *United States Policy and the Partition of Turkey, 1914–1924* (Baltimore: John Hopkins, 1965), quoted in David Fromkin's *A Peace to End All Peace*.

29. Simon Schama, *Two Rothschilds and the Land of Israel* (Collins, London, 1978)
30. Cyril Falls, *Military Operations Egypt and Palestine*, History of the Great War, HMSO 1930.
31. Falls, *Military Operations*.
32. The land of Egypt played a major role in the story of both the Old and New Testament, the fame of its holy men drew pilgrims and Evangelicals to it early on, including Mark and Jerome.
33. Ironically, although Israel was the Promised Land, it is surrounded by countries which flow with some of the world's richest oil wells, but so far none has been found there.
34. Except in respect of scientific research – especially work on the Pyramids, the Sphinx, Luxor, Karnak and the Rosetta Stone – Napoleon's invasion of Egypt in 1798 was a disaster for the French. When the stone was discovered all knowledge of the ancient Egyptian language and writing had been lost for over a thousand years. Napoleon ordered copies and impressions to be made of it so work could commence on deciphering the ancient Egyptian scripts. In August 1799 Napoleon returned to France leaving his army – and the scientists – in Egypt. On his return one of the first things he did in Paris was attend meetings at the Institut de France. Aware of the importance of the Rosetta Stone and its three inscriptions – hieroglyphic, Coptic and Greek – he made the first speech to the world about its incredible discovery, as well as talking about Egypt's ancient monuments and the link which would be made between East and West if the ruins of the unfinished Ptolemaic Suez canal were excavated to connect the Red Sea and the Mediterranean. France was initially the major shareholder in the Suez Canal Company, the Compagnie Universelle du Canal Maritime de Suez, which had its head office in Paris
35. Arthur Balfour's long introduction to Nahum Solokow's *The History of Zionism*.
36. Peter Calvocoressi, *Who's Who in the Bible* (Penguin, 1990), p. xii.
37. Michael Keene, *The Bible* (Lion Access Guides, Oxford, 2002).
38. Werner Keller, *The Bible as History* (William Morrow, New York, 1981).

Chapter Two

1. Papers found at Hughenden. M.C.N. Salbstein, *The Emancipation of the Jews in Britain* (New Jersey, 1982), quoted by Paul Johnson in *A History of the Jews* (Weidenfeld & Nicolson, 1987).
2. Jocelyn Hellig, *The Holocaust and Anti-Semitism* (Oneworld, Oxford, 2003).
3. The Seven Deadly Sins of pride, greed, envy, wrath, lust, gluttony and sloth, though, have nothing to do with the Jewish faith. They were introduced in the fourth century by Saint Gregory.
4. David Ben-Gurion, *Ben-Gurion Looks at the Bible*, trans. Jonathan Kolatch (Jonathan David, New York, 1972).
5. Recently an ossuary excavated near Jerusalem was inscribed with words indicating that it had belonged to 'the brother of Jesus'. This naturally raised protests. Jesus could have no brother. His mother was the Virgin Mary. Was there an ambiguity about the translation of the word 'virgin' from the original Greek text? Did it just mean 'young girl'? Anyone searching for an exact quotation also meets a blank. Jesus himself left not even his signature in his own writing. In one of the Gospels he is described as sitting down and writing in the dust, but we do not even know if he could read or write (Mohammed, despite having a good knowledge of the Scriptures, could not). Another problem is the vagueness of the dates of the life of Jesus. No accurate chronology can be made. All we know is that his ministry – according to the synoptics, but not John – began when he was about thirty years old, after his cousin, John the Baptist, had baptized him in the River Jordan. One of the few firm dates is the execution of John himself. Salome, a Judean princess, seductively danced before her stepfather, Herod Antipas, who rashly promised her whatever she asked – John's head on a plate.

6. The status of Jesus as a saviour as foretold in the ancient Jewish scriptures could also have been told to make it fit in with Old Testament prophecies, such as those of David and Moses.
7. This point is covered in hundreds of books including A.N. Wilson's Paul, the Mind of the Apostle (Sinclair Stevenson, 1997) and Arthur Goldschmidt, Jr, A Concise History of the Middle East (Boulder and London, Westview, 1988).
8. John M. Allegro, The Chosen People (Hodder & Stoughton, 1971). Allegro goes on to say that the religious significance of the custom is probably simply that in removing the prepuce, one is preparing the organ for copulation, as on the erection of the penis of an uncircumcised man, the foreskin retracts to reveal the swollen glans. It is also said, but not proven, that cancer of the penis and the associated parts is seldom known when circumcision is carried out at birth, but that this does not apply when the procedure is undertaken in the early teens as is usually the case in the Arab world.
9. A.N. Wilson, Jesus (Harper Collins, 1992).
10. Raymond P. Scheindlin, A Short History of the Jewish People (Oxford University Press, New York, 2000).
11. Members of another Jewish sect, a monastic community, the Essenes, gathered the sacred scrolls of their library, and buried them in jars in caves above the Dead Sea.
12. In 55 BCE Julius Caesar successfully invaded Britain but promptly left, so that while the Britons were beaten no territory was added to Roman power and no garrison was left behind – nor were any prisoners taken. Britain was not mentioned in antiquity before the reference to Emperor Claudius' invasion of 43 CE in the second Book of Gallic War.
13. Colin Thubron, Jerusalem (Century Hutchinson, 1986). Thubron quotes Joseph Flavius.
14. The impact of Islam took on a new dimension with the Arab awakening from the middle of the nineteenth century; it became merged with Arab identity and unity.
15. The spirit of the revolt was vividly brought to life by discoveries in the twentieth century of caves around the Dead Sea. Among the documents found were copies of a proclamation signed by Bar Kochba, calling the Jews to arms, and giving orders to his lieutenants.
16. Denis Prager and Joseph Telushkin, Why the Jews? (Simon & Schuster, New York, 1983).
17. Scheindlin, A Short History.
18. David L. Edwards, A Concise History of English Christianity (Fount, 1998).
19. Cecil Roth expands on this in Jewish Contribution to Civilisation (Macmillan, 1938).
20. E.P. Sanders, The Historical Figure of Jesus (Penguin, 1995), Professor Sanders is America's most distinguished scholar in the field of historical research relating to Jesus.
21. 'Our Father who art in heaven, hallowed be thy name. They Kingdom come. Thy will be done in earth as in heaven. Give us our daily bread. And forgive us our trespasses, as we forgive them.'
22. Roth, Jewish Contribution.
23. There are many theories as to its original source, but one suggests that it is as formed by the initials of the Hebrew letters of 'El Melekh Ne'eman'.
24. Christians usually recite it before and sometimes afterwards as well, whereas the Jewish custom is to say it before eating.
25. Roth, Jewish Contribution.
26. Dan Bahat Carta's Historical Atlas of Jerusalem (Carta, Jerusalem).
27. There is often much debate about whether both priest and congregation should face east.
28. Many people assume that this orientation towards the east is because it is the direction of the rising sun – the soul looking toward the rising of the true light – but this is simply not the reason for the tradition.

29. Dating, it is said, from an old custom so they could stand up and start walking in that direction at the time of the Second Coming.
30. Since the eighteenth century these words have been set to the music of Handel.
31. The John Rylands Library in Manchester has a papyrus of Deuteronomy which was translated into Greek as early as the second century BCE.

Chapter Three

1. Helena's ex-husband Constantine was later killed at York while leading a campaign against the Picts and the Scots.
2. James Carroll *Constantine's Sword* (Houghton Mifflin, New York, 2001).
3. Eusebius Pamphilus of Caesarea, *The Life of the Blessed Emperor Constantine*, Bagster trans. Bagster, rev. Ernest Cushing Richardson (http://www.fordham.edu/halsall/basis/vita-constantine.html).
4. Paul J. Griffiths (ed.), *Christianity Through Non-Christian Eyes* (Orbis, New York, 1999).
5. H.V. Morton, *In the Steps of the Master* (Methuen, 1934).
6. Barbara Tuchman, *The Bible and the Sword* (New York University Press, 1956) asks whether Helena was British or not, but qualifies this doubt with, 'Perhaps the earliest Britons to go [to the Holy Land] may have been inspired by a sense of kinship with the popularizers of the Holy Land, Helena and Constantine, who had special associations for Britain. According to legend believed in the later Middle Ages Helena was of British birth, the daughter of a Welsh king . . .'
7. John Julius Norwich, *Byzantium* (Penguin, 1990).
8. Michael Avi-Yonah, *The Holy Land* (Thames & Hudson, 1972). This is one of the most useful books on the history of the Holy Land.
9. Palladius Galatea.
10. Tuchman, *Bible and Sword*.
11. Isaiah 57: 50: 'God said this shall be my eternal dwelling'. Joel 3:17 'I am the Lord your God my Holy Mountain'. Zachariah 8:3 'I will dwell in the midst of Jerusalem'.
12. He is not to be confused with the first Saint Augustine (354–430), also known as Aurelius Augustine of Hippo, the Algerian-born Roman intellectual. Whether he did much to poison the Catholic Church against the Jews is a subject often debated.
13. Paul J. Griffiths (ed.), *Christianity*.

Chapter Four

1. William Makepeace Thackeray, *Notes of a Journey from Cornhill to Grand Cairo, by way of Lisbon, Athens, Constantinople and Jerusalem* (Chapman & Hall, 1846).
2. Imad al-Din al-Isfahani.
3. Denis Prager and Joseph Telushkin, *Why the Jews?* (Simon & Schuster, 1983).
4. I am grateful to Neil Cohen, the rector of Christ Church in Jerusalem and author of *My Road Home* (Terra Nova, Bristol, 1997) for much background on Christianity which is included in this book.
5. Prager and Telushkin, *Why the Jews?*
6. Ivan G. Marcus, 'Jewish–Christian Symbiosis' in *Cultures of the Jews*, ed. David Biale (Schocken, New York, 2002).

Chapter Five

1. In line 463. 'The Wife of Bath's Prologue and Tale' is one of first of the twenty-four stories which make up *The Canterbury Tales*. The wife of Bath has travelled so much that she could be called a professional pilgrim.
2. Derek Brewer, *Chaucer and His World* (Longman, 1973).
3. John Gardner, *The Life and Times of Chaucer* (Alfred A. Knopf, New York, 1977).
4. Quoted in Maurice Keen, *English Society in the Later Middle Ages* (Allen Lane, Penguin, 1990).

Chapter Six

1. Howard M. Sachar, *A History of Israel* (Alfred A. Knopf, New York, 1982) – this and the other many books on the history of Israel by Sachar are highly recommended.

2. Scheindlin, *A Short History*.
3. Among the extensive range of books on the subject some of the most helpful are George Adam Smith, *Modern Criticism and the Preaching of the Old Testament to the Age* (Hodder & Stoughton,1899), Andrew Barrow, *The Flesh is Weak* (Hamish Hamilton, 1980), Tuchman, *The Bible and the Sword* and David L. Edwards, *A Concise History of English Christianity* (Fount, 1998), Alister McGrath, *In the Beginning* (Hodder & Stoughton, 2001), Paul Johnson's History of Christianity (Weidenfeld & Nicolson, 1976), *Dictionary of Christian Lore & Legend* (Thames & Hudson, 1983).
4. The Duke of Hamilton, *Maria R, Mary Queen of Scots, the Crucial Years* (Mainstream, Edinburgh, 1991).
5. Barrow, *The Flesh is Weak*.
6. James inherited through his great-grandmother, Margaret Tudor, Elizabeth's aunt.
7. McGrath, *In the Beginning*. Another factor was that when the early editions of the newly translated Bible had appeared there were officially no Jews living in England, so it was easy for people to romanticize about what they read about them.
8. Tuchman, *Bible and Sword*.
9. One of the most popular recent books on this subject is T*he Mayflower Pilgrims: Roots of Puritan, Presbyterian, Congregational and Baptist Heritage* by David Beale (Ambassador-International, 2000). Dr Beale is organizing a tour to the different sites associated with these religions in England in 2005.
10. Cecil Roth, *History of the Jews in England* (Clarendon Press, Oxford, 1941). It is difficult to find any other books covering the Jews in England which are as readable as Roth's.
11. Tuchman, *Bible and Sword*.
12. Among the many references to the Second Coming is Luke's account of the ascension, when the disciples ask Jesus, 'Lord, is this the time when you will restore the Kingdom to Israel?'
13. Paul Johnson's acclaimed and much reprinted *A History of the Jews*.

Chapter Seven

1. Both Cecil Roth, in *A History of the Jews in England* and Paul Johnson in his *History of the Jews* have masterly accounts of the how they eventually immigrated to England.
2. From literature from the John Bunyan Museum, Mill Street, Bedford, which displays the wooden flute he made out of stool leg while in prison.
3. Percy Ernst Schramm, *A History of the English Coronation* (Clarendon Press, Oxford, 1937).
4. In the nineteenth century the congregation at Bevis Marks included Benjamin Disraeli's family and Sir Moses Montefiore. It remains one of the few places of worship in England which is still lit with candles.
5. Roth, *History of the Jews*.
6. David L. Edwards, *A Concise History of English Christianity* (Fount, London, 1998).
7. George Chryssides, *The Elements of Unitarianism* (Element, Shaftesbury, 1998).
8. GCAH, The General Commission on Archives & History of the United Methodist Church has been the source of many new publications to celebrate the John Wesley Tercentennial in 2003.
9. Barrow, *The Flesh is Weak*.
10. Nahum Sokolow, *The History of Zionism*, with an introduction by A.J. Balfour (Longmans, Green & Co., 1919).

Chapter Eight

1. John Bierman and Colin Smith in *First in the Night* (Pan, 2001) give a detailed background of Orde Wingate's ancestry.
2. Prime Minister: 6 February 1855–19 February 1858; 12 June 1859–18 October 1865.
3. Jonathan Frankel, *The Damascus Affair* (Cambridge University Press, 1997).
4. William Yale, *The Near East* (University of Michigan Press, 1958).
5. A.N. Wilson, *The Victorians* (Hutchinson, 2002).
6. Quotes telling of the prophetic role at the end of time and the belief that the Messiah would only return *after* the

Jews had regained their own land are scattered through the Bible. One example is Luke's account of the ascension when the disciples ask Jesus, 'Lord, is this the time when you will restore the Kingdom to Israel?' Others are in the Book of Daniel, Zechariah 9–14, Ezekiel 38–9 and various Apocryphal books, as well as Matthew 24, the early Pauline letters xii and the Book of Revelation.

7. Jukka Nevakivi, *Britain, France and the Arab Middle East 1914–1920*.
8. Ashley's Diary quoted in Edwin Hodder's *The Life and Work of the Seventh Earl of Shaftesbury*, 3 vols (Cassell, 1886–7).
9. Public Record Office, FO 78/390, *The British Consulate in Jerusalem in Relation to the Jews of Palestine, 1838–1914*. [Extracts from Foreign Office records relating to the Consulate.] Ed. with an introduction and notes by Albert M. Hyamson (Jewish Historical Society of England, London, 1939 and 1941) in Hyamson, *The British Consulate in Jerusalem*, vol. 1.
10. In December 1838.
11. Michael Hennell, *Sons of the Prophets, Evangelical Leaders of the Victorian Church* (SPCK, 1979).
12. Howard M. Sachar, *A History of Israel* (Alfred A. Knopf, New York, 1982).
13. After the death of the third bishop in 1881, the bishopric was allowed to lapse and the treaty between Prussia and England that enabled it was dissolved in 1886.
14. Some of the most graphic descriptions of life in Jerusalem are in a series of books published by the Ben Zvi Press, including Mordechai Eliav, *Britain and the Holy Land* (Yad Izhak Ben-Zvi Press, Jerusalem, 1997).
15. William Makepeace Thackeray, *Notes of a Journey from Cornhill to Grand Cairo, by way of Lisbon, Athens, Constantinople and Jerusalem* (Chapman & Hall, 1846) gives a lively account of Jerusalem at the time and some of the tensions surrounding the bishopric.
16. Howard Sachar, *A History of Israel* (Alfred A. Knopf, New York, 1982).
17. Thackeray.
18. For instance when the English poet Robert Browning, a Congregationalist, (1812–89) briefly attended lectures at University College, London, students there included Nathaniel de Rothschild and James Joseph Sylvester. Later in life he counted amongst his friends many Jews in government, business, and the arts including members of the great families of Anglo-Jewry, such as the Rothschilds, Mocattas, and Goldsmids. The rise of the House of Rothschild in England in the banking world was paralleled with their rise into the highest aristocratic, literary, artistic and political circles.
19. A letter from Colonel Campbell to Viscount Palmerston dated 10 December 1838 (FP78/344, Consular 330) talks of the new consul's duties in Jerusalem which will 'not be merely commercial, but I should suppose that one great and perhaps the chief object of his duties, will be the protection of the Jewish nation in general'. From Mordechai Eliav, *Britain and the Holy Land*.
20. Attempts to link scientific discoveries in archaeology with literary and religious tradition and the quest to add to the knowledge of the Old Testament patriarchs, prophets and kings, led to the formation of many archaeological societies, one of the most famous being the Palestine Exploration Fund. The projects of this Fund included excavations in Jerusalem (1867–70) conducted by Charles Warren and Henry Birtles; the survey of western Palestine (1871–8) undertaken by Claude R. Conder and Horatio H. Kitchener (among others); excavations at Tell el-Hesi (1890–3) under the direction of Sir William Flinders Petrie, and Frederick J. Bliss; the Wilderness of Zin Archaeological Survey (1913–14) conducted by Sir Leonard Woolley and T.E. Lawrence.
21. Paul Kerr, *The Crimean War* (Boxtree, 1997). A letter from Finn to Palmerston (25 September 1850) says that the Franciscans complained about both the haughty attitude of the French and their inactivity.

22. Walter Zander, *Israel and the Holy Places of Christendom* (Weidenfeld & Nicolson, 1971)
23. Kerr, *Crimean War*.

Chapter Nine

1. Kerr, *Crimean War*.
2. Thackeray, *Notes of a Journey*.
3. The tensions between the churches can be seen by Thackeray's description of his visit to the church of the Holy Sepulchre. When he was there, 'he was in Russia, . . . under the protection of the Father of the Church and the Imperial Eagle! This butcher and tyrant, who sits on his throne only through the crime of those who held it before him – every step in whose pedigree is stained by some horrible mark of murder, parricide, adultery – this padded and whiskered pontiff – who rules in his jack-boots over a system of spies and soldiers, of deceit, ignorance, dissoluteness, and brute force, such as surely the history of the world never told of before – has a tender interest in the welfare of his spiritual children: . . . A pious exemplar of Christianity truly! . . . the Religion, of which the Emperor assumes to be the chief priest and defender!'
4. Norman Rich, *Why the Crimean War?* (Brown University Press of New England, 1985)
5. Ibid.
6. Wilson, *The Victorians*.
7. Ibid.
8. Zander, *Israel and the Holy Places of Christendom*.
9. Records at Christ Church, Jerusalem. Kelvin Crombie, the author of *For the Love of Zion* (Hodder & Stoughton, 1991), has extraordinary knowledge on this compli-cated subject and has worked at Christ Church in Jerusalem for over a decade.
10. Sir Martin Gilbert, 'Jerusalem: A Tale of One City' in *The New Republic*, 14 November 1994.
11. Many records of the Palestine Exploration Fund and of James Finn, are held by the Royal Geographical Society in London.

Chapter Ten

1. Cyril Alington and G. Lyttelton (eds), *An Eton Poetry Book* (Macmillan, 1938).
2. Sokolow, *History of Zionism*.
3. Herzl had seen the Kaiser twice and also put his case to the sultan in Constantinople, but had got nowhere with either. The first time things took a positive turn was during the Zionist Conference in London in 1900.
4. Leonard Stein, *The Balfour Declaration* (Valentine Mitchell, London, 1961).
5. Twenty-eight years earlier, in 1847, Rothschild and the house of Baring had raised 8 million pounds with no view to profit to deal with the miserable conditions in Ireland caused by the potato famine. Saul P. Colbi, *Christianity in the Holy Land Past & Present* (Am Hassefer, Tel Aviv, 1969).
6. Michael Jolles, *A Directory of Distinguished British Jews, 1830–1930* (Jolles, 2002).
7. One of the most comprehensive summaries of the Zionist side of the 'Uganda' scheme is the essay 'New Light on the East Africa Scheme' by Oskar K. Rabinowicz in Israel Cohen (ed.), *The Rebirth of Israel, A Memorial Tribute to Paul Goodman* (Hyperion Press, Connecticut, 1952; reprinted, 1976)
8. W.R.P. George, *The Making of Lloyd George* (Faber & Faber, 1976).
9. W.R.P. George, Lloyd George Backbencherv (Gomer, Wales, 1983).
10. The best biography of Weizmann is Jehuda Reinharz, *Chaim Weizmann, the Making of a Zionist Leader* (Oxford University Press, New York, 1985).
11. Like Herzl, Weizmann realized that commitment would achieve nothing without governmental cooperation. His initial contacts with Members of Parliament and ministers in London coincided with the time that hundreds of thousands of British troops were stationed in the Middle East in the First World War.
12. Blanche Dugdale, *Arthur James Balfour, First Earl of Balfour*, 2 vols (Hutchinson, 1936).
13. Ibid.

14. Again the Ben-Zvi Institute has provided access to seldom seen documents in Mordechai Eliav, *Britain and the Holy Land* (Yad Izhak Ben-Zvi Press, Jerusalem, 1997). Particularly relevant are the letters and information quoted here: FO 371/1794 – No. 218 (16925); FO 371/1794 – No. 218 (16925); and FO 371/1245–No. 146.

Chapter Eleven

1. W. George, *The Making of Lloyd George.*
2. Colbi, *Christianity in the Holy Land.* FO 78/2992 – No.10, quoted by Mordechai Eliav in Britain and the Holy Land, 1838–1914 (Yad Izhak Ben-Zvi Press, Jerusalem).
3. Moshe Aumann, *Land Ownership in Palestine 1880–1948* (Israel Academic Committee on the Middle East, Jerusalem, undated).
4. FO 78/1929 quoted by Eliav in Britain and the Holy Land. FO 78/2048.
5. Schama's *Two Rothschilds and the Land of Israel* gives a vivid description of the early development of Palestine.
6. Dunam = 1,000 square metres, the basic unit in Palestinian agriculture.
7. Doreen Warriner, 'Land Tenure in the Fertile Crescent,' in *The Economic History of the Middle East 1800–1914* ed. Charles Issawi (University of Chicago Press, Chicago, 1975), pp. 71–8. Quoted by Arnold Blumberg in *Zion before Zionism, 1838–1880* (Syracuse University Press, 1985).
8. Eliav, *Britain and the Holy Land.* In the Russian–Turkish war, the Russian troops reached the very gates of Constantinople at its famous suburb of San Stefano, where a Russian–Turkish treaty was signed in March 1878.
9 Leonard Stein, *The Balfour Declaration* (Valentine Mitchell, 1961).
10 Among the many very readable accounts of Ben-Gurion's life are his own memoirs and those by Shabtai Teveth, *Ben-Gurion, the Burning Ground* (Houghton Mifflin, Boston, 1987) and Robert St John, *Ben-Gurion* (Jarrolds, 1959).
11. Barnet Litvinoff, *Road to Jerusalem* (Weidenfeld & Nicolson, 1965).
12. From a display board at the Haganah Museum, 23 Rothschild Blvd, Tel Aviv, with a reference library and over four floors of exhibits this well established museum beside the home of Eliyahu Golomb, the former director of the Haganah is a landmark in Tel Aviv.
13. Letter from Lawrence to his mother, 2 August 1909, in David Garnett, *Selected Letters of T.E. Lawrence.*

Chapter Twelve

1. *The Times*, 10 November 1914. G.D. Clayton, *Britain and the Eastern Question: Missolonghi to Gallipoli* (University of London Press, 1971) gives an excellent account of the relationship between Britain and Turkey. Ironically, in 1917 Britain, who had remained Turkey's most loyal ally, was the country which gained most by the eventual collapse of the Ottoman Empire, and was to control Cyprus, Egypt, the Sudan, Aden, Palestine, Transjordan and Iraq.
2. Viscount Samuel, *Memoirs* (Cresset Press, 1945), pp. 139ff.
3. Leonard Stein, *The Balfour Declaration* (Vallentine Mitchell, 1961).
4. Henry Morgenthau, *Ambassador Morgenthau's Story* (Hodder & Stoughton, 1918) wrote 'on November 13th, when the Sultan issued his declaration of war; this declaration was really an appeal for a *jihad*, or a "Holy War" against the infidel. Soon afterward the Sheik-ul-Islam published his proclamation, summoning the whole Moslem world to arise and massacre their Christian oppressors. 'Oh, Moslems!' concluded this document. 'Ye who are smitten with happiness and are on the verge of sacrificing your life and your goods for the cause of right, and of braving perils, gather now around the Imperial throne, obey the commands of the Almighty, who, in the Koran, promises us bliss in this and in the next world; embrace ye the foot of the Caliph's throne and know ye that the state is at war with Russia, England, France, and their Allies, and that these are the

enemies of Islam. The Chief of the believers, the Caliph, invites you all as Moslems to join in the Holy War!'

5. John Freely has written extensively on the history of Turkey and among his many books, *Inside the Seraglio, Private Lives of the Sultans of Istanbul* (Viking, 1999) gives an illuminating background.
6. Liman von Sanders, *Five Years in Turkey* (The Battery Press, Nashville, Tennessee, in association with War & Peace Books, Fleet, 2000).
7. Morgenthau, *Morgenthau's Story*.
8. Frank E. Manuel, *The Realities of American–Palestine Relations* (Public Affairs Press, Washington, DC, 1949).
9. Ronald Sanders, *The High Walls of Jerusalem* (Holt, Rinehart & Winston, New York 1983).

Chapter Thirteen

1. Ronald Sanders, *The High Walls of Jerusalem* (Holt, Rinehart & Winston, New York 1983).
2. John Colvin, *Lions of Judah* (Quartet Books, 1977).
3. Sir Martin Gilbert, *From the Ends of the Earth, the Jews in the Twentieth Century* (Cassell & Co., 2001).
4. From papers at the Jewish Museum, Sydney.
5. Von Sanders, *Five Years in Turkey*.

Chapter Fourteen

1. The dichotomy over Jewish enlistment pushed many politicians to believe that the Jewish Legion would be a way of furthering recruitment. Roger Adelson in *Mark Sykes: Portrait of an Amateur* (Jonathan Cape, 1975) quotes Lloyd George as saying, 'The Jews might be able to render us more assistance than the Arabs' in the Palestine campaign. He gives the Weizmann archives at Rehovot as the source.
2. Christopher Sykes, *Cross Roads to Israel* (Collins, 1965).
3. The Mameluks ruled Palestine from 1250 to 1517.
4. George Adam Smith, *Historical Geography of the Holy Land* (Hodder and Stoughton, 1896).

Chapter Fifteen

1. Since 1816 the Gurkhas had been permitted to volunteer for service first in the East India Company's army, then in the Indian Army.
2. Fromkin points out in *A Peace to End All Peace* that the crux of the Zionist idea was that 'the renaissance of the Jewish nation should occur within the context of a political entity of its own'.

Chapter Sixteen

1. Lloyd George Archives in the House of Lords Record Office, London. This is also mentioned by David Fromkin in *A Peace to End All Peace*.
2. Richard Ellman, *Oscar Wilde* (Penguin, 1988).
3. *South African Jewish Chronicle* (SAJC), 22 September 1950, quoted in Richard P. Stevens, *Weizmann and Smuts* (The Institute for Palestine Studies, Beirut, 1975).
4. Ibid.
5. George N. Barnes, *From Workshop to War Cabinet* (Herbert Jenkins, 1924). After his trip to Egypt and Palestine he wrote *An Eastern Tour* (The Co-operative Printing Society, 1921). He is a remarkably obscure figure; he quit the Labour Party in 1920 and was not a minister in the early Labour governments.
6. Stevens, *Weizmann and Smuts*.
7. *Diaries of Lord Bertiev*, II, 122 (20 April 1917) quoted in Leonard Stein, *The Balfour Declaration* (Vallentine Mitchell, 1961).
8. Capitulations were special rights and privileges whereby foreigners were exempt from the jurisdiction of the Ottoman courts and from some forms of taxation. The expansion of westerners in the Middle East resulted in an expansion and extent of the capitulations. 'The millet system operated throughout the Ottoman Empire as a political organization that granted to non-Muslims the right to organize into communities possessing certain delegated powers under their own ecclesiastical heads. In time such communities or millets developed their own peculiar characteristics and

traditions, in this way becoming identified with the various nationalities.' From Kamel S. Abu-Jaber, *The Millet System in the Nineteenth-century Ottoman Empire* (1967).

9. William Yale, *The Near East* (University of Michigan Press, 1958).
10. Thomas Jones, *Whitehall Diary*, vol. I, 1916/1925, (Oxford University Press, 1969).
11. Mark Tessler, *A History of the Israeli–Palestinian Conflict* (Indiana University Press, 1994). One of the aims of his excellent book is to 'dispel the common misconception that the current struggle in Palestine is an extension of an ancient blood feud, fuelled by ethnic or religious antagonisms dating back hundreds of years . . . that it has in fact been less than a century since Jews and Arabs began to view one another as enemies.'
12. Robert D. Kaplan, *The Arabists* (The Free Press, New York, 1995).
13. J.R. Foster with George Handsley, *Two and a Half Years as a Prisoner-of-War in Turkey* (Jones & Hambly, Brisbane, 1919).
14. Johnson, *A History of the Jews*.

Chapter Seventeen

1. A.J. Sherman, *Mandate Days* (Thames & Hudson, 1997).
2. Cyril Falls, *Armageddon: 1918* (The Nautical and Aviation Publishing Company of America, 1964).
3. Robert John, *Behind the Balfour Declaration: the Hidden Origins of Today's Middle East Crisis* (Institute for Historical Review, 1988).
4. Arthur Koestler, *Promise and Fulfilment* (Macmillan, 1949).
5. Leo Amery, *The Leo Amery Diaries* (Hutchinson, 1980).
6. Stephen J. Whitefield, 'Declarations of Independence,' in *Cultures of the Jews*, ed. David Biale (Schocken, New York, 2002).
7. G.M. Trevelyan, *English Social History* (Longmans, 1944).
8. Until twenty-nine seats were gained in the House of Commons in 1926 the Labour Party was known as the Labour Representation Committee.
9. Quoted by Roy Jenkins in *Gladstone* (Pan, 1982). D.W. Bebbington, *The Nonconformist Conscience* (George Allen & Unwin, 1982) also covers the different aspects of Nonconformism in society and politics, as does Alan A. Jackson in *The Middle Classes 1900–1950* (David St John Thomas, Scotland, 1991).
10. Walter Bagehot, *Biographical Studies* quoted by Roy Jenkins in *Gladstone*.
11. Roy Jenkins, *Gladstone*.
12. Kenneth Baker, *The Prime Ministers* (Thames & Hudson, 1995).
13. W.E. Gladstone, *The Impregnable Rock of Holy Scripture* (Isbister, 1892).
14. Kelvin Crombie, *Anzacs, Empires and Israel's Restoration* (Vocational Education & Training Publications, Western Australia, 2000).
15. Fromkin, *A Peace to End All Peace* said that 'Palmerston's notion of restoring the Promised Land to the Jewish people...struck a responsive chord in British public opinion that harked back to Puritan enthusiasm.'
16. Ronald Storrs, *Zionism and Palestine in Lawrence of Arabia, Zionism and Palestine* (Penguin, 1940), originally published in *Orientations* (Ivor Nicholson and Watson, 1937). The full quote is: 'British espousal of the Hope of Israel would, it was hinted, serve triply our interest as well as our honour by ensuring the success of the Allied Loan in America, hitherto boycotted by anti-Russian Jewish Finance; by imparting to the Russian Revolution, of which the brains were assumed to be Jewish, a pro-British bias; and by sapping the loyalty of the Jews fighting in scores of thousands on and behind the front of Germany. We may record with relief that even if these material inducements had influenced the decision, the Balfour Declaration was on results utterly clean from such profit. The American Loan went much as had been anyhow expected; no sympathies for Britain accrued from the Soviets (which shortly denounced Zionism as a capitalist contrivance); and the loyalty of German Jewry remained unshaken . . .'.

Chapter Eighteen

1. Allenby in a letter to his wife quoted by Archibald Wavell in *Allenby* (Harrap & Co., 1940).
2. Brian Gardner *Allenby* (Cassell, 1965).
3. Crombie, *Anzacs.*
4. Eliahu Elath, (ed.), *Memories of Sir Wyndham Deedes* (Victor Gollancz in association with the Anglo–Israel Association, 1958).
5. John Presland (pseudonym for Gladys Skelton), *Deedes Bey: A Study of Sir Wyndham Deedes 1883–1923* (Macmillan, 1942).
6. Ibid.

Chapter Nineteen

1. Flora Solomon, *Baku to Baker Street* (Collins, 1984).
2. Martin Gilbert, *Jerusalem* (Pimlico, 1997).
3. Ibid.
4. Edward Keith-Roach, ed. Paul Eedle, *Pasha of Jerusalem: Memoirs of a District Commissioner under the British Mandate* (Radcliffe Press, 1994).
5. I am grateful to Patrick Streeter, who is presently writing a long overdue biography on John Patterson, for helping me with the background to his enigmatic character and analysing his books, such as *With the Judeans in the Palestine Campaign* (Hutchinson, London, 1922) and *Behind the Palestine Betrayal* (first published in the American Jewish Chronicle *c.*1940). Patterson's books and articles, together with Jabotinsky's book on the Jewish Legion and the Australian war histories of the area, give a good idea of the Jewish Legion's role in the First World War.
6. Zionist Archives, Jerusalem.

Chapter Twenty

1. Quoted by Ronald Storrs, *Orientations* (Ivor Nicholson and Watson, 1937) who writes extensively about the restoration of Jerusalem, as does Alan Crawford in *C.R. Ashbee* (Yale, London, 1985) and *Janet Ashbee, Love, Marriage and the Arts & Crafts Movement* by her daughter Felicity (Syracuse University Press, 2002).
2. J.H. Patterson, *With the Judeans.*
3. V. Jabotinsky, *The Jewish Legion* (Ackerman, New York, 1945).
4. Roosevelt Centre in Middleburg, Holland which has archives of Roosevelt correspondence.

Chapter Twenty-One

1. Shabtai Teveth, *Ben-Gurion, the Burning Ground* (Houghton Mifflin, Boston, 1987).
2. Sykes, *Cross Roads to Israel.*
3. Ibid.
4. Archibald Percival Wavell, *Allenby in Egypt*, vol. 2 of *Allenby: a Study in Greatness* (G.G. Harrap & Co., 1943).

Chapter Twenty-Two

1. John Terraine, *To Win a War, 1918, the Year of Victory* (Sidgwick & Jackson, 1978).
2. 'A History of the Peace Conference', vol. 6., ed. H.W.V. Temperley (Hodder & Stoughton, 1920).
3. FO 371 24565. Nicholas Bethell in *Palestine Triangle* (Futura, 1980) gives a balanced view of the British trying to cater to the needs of the Jews and the Arabs.
4. Sykes, *Cross Roads to Israel.*
5. Barnes, *Workshop to War Cabinet.*
6. Wyndham Deedes, *Palestine 1917–1944* (pamphlet issued by the British Association for the Jewish National Home in Palestine).
7. Roth, *Jewish Contribution.*
8 Janet Wallach, *Desert Queen* (Weidenfeld & Nicolson, 1996).

Chapter Twenty-Three

1. Eli Yassif, 'The "Other" Israel' in *Cultures of the Jews*, ed. David Biale (Schocken, New York, 2002).
2. A vivid picture of the early days under the British Mandate is given by Edward Keith-Roach in *Pasha of Jerusalem* (Radcliffe, 1994) whose family became friendly in Jerusalem with the Ashbee family; his son married one of the Ashbee's daughters
3. It might have been misleading but 'USA' were the first letters of three Yiddish words meaning 'our piece of work'.
4. Sir Hugh Foot, A Start in Freedom (Hodder & Stoughton, 1964).

5. Keith-Roach, *Pasha of Jerusalem.*
6. Solomon, *Baku to Baker Street.*
7. Ibid.
8. Among Sir Martin Gilbert's many books on the history of Israel which cover this subject are *Exile and Return* (Weidenfeld & Nicolson 1978), *From the Ends of the Earth: the Jews in the Twentieth Century* (Cassell, 2001); *Israel, a History* (Doubleday 1998), *Jerusalem in the Twentieth Century* (Chatto & Windus, 1996), and *Jerusalem, Illustrated History Atlas* (Valentine Mitchell, 1994.)

Chapter Twenty-Four

1. Sir Martin Gilbert, *Churchill, A Life* (William Heinemann, 1991).
2. Ibid.
3. He took a ship to Perth in Western Australia where he became an active member of a branch of the Returned Soldiers' League in Perth, rising to become a member of the state executive.
4. Felicity Ashbee, *Janet Ashbee, Love, Marriage and the Arts & Crafts Movement* (Syracuse University Press, 2002). Unfortunately, this book has not yet been published in Britain.
5. Ibid.
6. Ibid.

Chapter Twenty-Five

1. J.M. Machover, *Governing Palestine* (P.S. King & Son, 1936). He quotes 'Official Report, cols. 310–311'.
2. Harry Defries, *Conservative Party Attitudes to Jews 1900–1950* (Frank Cass, 2001).
3. *The Times*, 6 November 1922, quoted by Defries in *Conservative Party Attitude.*
4. Harold Wilson, *A Prime Minister on Prime Ministers* (Weidenfeld & Nicolson and Michael Joseph, 1977).
5. Ibid.
6. Stanley Baldwin, *On England and Other Addresses* (P. Allan & Co, 1926)
7. Quoted by Crombie in *Anzacs*. Crombie also quotes Yigal Lossin, *Pillar of Fire* (Shikmona, Jerusalem, 1983).
8. Sir Hugh Foot, *A Start in Freedom* (Hodder & Stoughton, 1964).
9. Ahron Bregman, *A History of Israel* (Palgrave, 2003).
10. David Cesarani, *Arthur Koestler, the Homeless Mind* (Heinemann, 1998).
11. Richard P. Stevens, *Weizmann and Smuts* (Institute for Palestine Studies, Beirut, 1975).
12. *The Times*, 20 December 1920, p. 15.
13. June 1934 – related by Dr William George.

Chapter Twenty-Six

1. Edmund Gosse, *Father and Son* (Heinemannn, 1907).
2. Moshe Dayan, *Story of My Life* (Weidenfeld & Nicolson, 1976).
3. Ibid.
4. Martin van Creveld, *The Sword and the Olive* (Public Affairs, New York, 1998). The term Nazi was a German slang expression for Adolf Hitler's National Sozialistische Deutsche Arbeiter Partei (National Socialist German Labour Party), abbreviated to NSDAP. From 1930 it was used in Germany by word of mouth as well as in the press to refer to Hitler, his colleagues and his storm-troopers (initially Hitler's bully-boys who attacked Communists and other opponents). After 1933, when the NSDAP and Hitler gained power in Germany, the international press increasingly used the term 'Nazi'.
5. Ben Wicks, *Dawn of the Promised Land* (Bloomsbury, 1997).
6. Crombie, *Anzacs.*
7. Koestler, *Promise and Fulfilment.*
8. Foot, *A Start in Freedom.*
9. Robert Graves and Alan Hodge, *The Long Week-End, a Social History of Great Britain 1918–1939* (Faber & Faber, 1940).
10. Dayan, *Story of My Life.*
11. Ibid.
12. Andrew Roberts, *The Holy Fox, A Life of Lord Halifax* (Weidenfeld & Nicolson, 1991).
13. John Harvey, ed., *The Diplomatic Diaries of Oliver Harvey 1937–40* (Collins, 1970), quoted by Roberts, *The Holy Fox.*
14. Most of Weizmann's royalties then came from the Terre Haute plant, Commercial Solvents Corporation, in America.
15. Roberts, *The Holy Fox.*
16. Radio address by Prime Minister Smuts, 2 November 1941, quoted by Richard P. Stevens in *Weizmann and Smuts.*

Chapter Twenty-Seven

1. Leon Uris, *In the Steps of Exodus* (Heinemannn, 1962).
2. Barnet Litvinoff, *Road to Jerusalem* (Weidenfeld & Nicolson, 1965).
3. Dayan, *Story of My Life.*
4. E.A. Speiser, *The United States and the Near East* (Harvard University Press, Cambridge, 1952).

Chapter Twenty-Eight

1. Martin Gilbert, *The Day the War Ended* (Harper Collins, 1995).
2. Parliamentary Debates, House of Commons, 26 January 1949.
3. Harry Defries, *Conservative Party Attitudes to Jews 1900–1950* (Frank Cass, 2001). Defries quotes the *Commons Debates*, 5th Series, vol. 426, col. 1251, 1 August 1946, and *The Times*, 7 October 1946 report on Churchill's address of the previous day to the Conservative Party Conference at Blackpool.
4. Ibid.
5. St John, *Ben-Gurion.*
6. Sykes, *Cross-Roads to Israel.*

Chapter Twenty-Nine

1. A.J. Sherman, *Mandate Days, British Lives in Palestine, 1918–1948* (Thames & Hudson, 1997).
2. Amos Elon, *Jerusalem* (Fontana, 1991), p. 239.
3. Once the home of Mayor Dizengoff.
4. 4,000 Jewish troops and 2,000 civilians were killed, tens of thousands were injured.
5. Ahron Bregman, *A History of Israel* (Palgrave, 2003) from David Ben-Gurion's *War Diary* (Tel Aviv, 1983), entry for 14 May 1948.
6. The 38th (London East End), the 39th (American volunteers), the 40th (Jewish Palestinians), the 41st (Reserve) and the 42nd battalions of the Royal Fusiliers, London Regiment.
7. The airfield at Tel Aviv was initially named after him.
8. Abba Eban, *My Country, the Story of Modern Israel* (Weidenfeld & Nicolson, London and Jerusalem, 1972), pp. 19–21.
9. Stevens, *Weizmann and Smuts.*
10. Weizmann, *Trial and Error.*
11. Martin Gilbert, *Israel: A History* (Doubleday, New York, 1998).
12. Stevens, *Weizmann and Smuts.*
13. Paper given by Glen Stassen at the Annual Meeting of the Southern Baptist Historical Society in the Truman Presidential Library in 1998.

Chapter Thirty

1. David Cesarani, *Arthur Koestler, The Homeless Mind* (Heinemann, 1998).
2. Walter Eytan, *The First Ten Years, Israel Between East & West a Diplomtic History of Israel* (Weidenfeld & Nicolson, 1958).
3. Elhannan Orren, 'The War of Independence', in *David Ben-Gurion*, ed. Ronald W. Zweig, – one of the many excellent books published by the Yad Izhak Ben-Zvi Institute, Jerusalem and by Frank Cass, London.
4. Yoav Gelber 'Ben-Gurion and the Formation of the Israel Defense Forces, 1947–48' in *David Ben-Gurion*, ed. Zweig.
5. Van Creveld, *The Sword and the Olive.* As a source in English he gives the article 'Our Friend: What Wingate Did for Us' (1963) in Khalidi, *From Haven to Conquest.*
6. Cesarani, *Koestler*. Wingate's subsequent reputation is analysed by Colin Smith and John Bierman in their much-praised biography of Wingate, *Fire in the Night* (Pan, 2001) – by far the best and most balanced account of his extraordinary life.
7. Eytan, *The First Ten Years.*

Epilogue

1. St John, *Ben-Gurion.*
2. Uris, *Exodus.*
3. Haganah Museum, 23 Rothschild Blvd, Tel Aviv, has a reference library and over four floors of exhibits. This well established museum, beside the home of Eliyahu Golomb, the former director of the Haganah, is a landmark in Tel Aviv.

References: Ain, *Well*. Jebel, *Mountain*. Jisr, *Bridge*. Khurbet, *Ruins*. Nahr, *River*
Ras, *Bluff or Cape*. Tell, *Mound*. Main Roads, ═══. Other Roads, -------

Acknowledgments

Writing this book has been a long journey made possible with the help of numerous people – from Britain and Israel, from Australia to Jordan and from America to Syria. Thanks go both to my sister, Margaret Morrissey, who gave daily assistance, from the inception of the book through to completion. And, of course, thanks are also extended to Dame Miriam Rothschild, to whom the book is dedicated. Apart from the inspiration of her own book, Dear Lord Rothschild, at Ashton she vividly brought much of the period alive with reminiscences about her uncle, the second Lord Rothschild (to whom the Balfour Declaration was addressed), her cousin Jimmy de Rothschild, Winston Churchill and David Ben-Gurion, who once stayed with her for two weeks in Oxford (and shared the upstairs bathroom with a pet bush baby). She also introduced me to dozens of people who gave fascinating insights, including Martin Gilbert, Miriam Balaban, Rina Samuel, Melanie Aspey at the Rothschild Archives (who supplied many of the photographs), Stephen Graubard and Michael Jolles. I am also grateful to David Lloyd George's nephew, Dr William George, now over ninety, who even remembered 'the Garden Suburb' at 10 Downing Street. An immense debt is owed to many academics including Muhammad Abdel Haleem, Professor of Islamic Studies at SOAS, Colin Shindler, Lecturer in Jewish Studies at SOAS, Bill Rubinstein, Professor of History at the University of Wales, Aberystwyth, and Peter Stanley, principal historian at the Australian War Memorial.

Thomas Carlyle acknowledged his debt to libraries when he told Queen Victoria that he lived in London because it had the 'best libraries in the world'. It would be difficult to find any other city with so many catalogued books on shelves, and I certainly would not have been able to carry out the extensive research for *God, Guns & Israel* without the resources of the SOAS Library, the British Library and the London Library, the invaluable archives at the Public Record Office at Kew and at the House of Lords Record Office. Not to be forgotten are the books from the old stacks at the University of Southampton Library, the Chelsea and Westminster Library or those at the Royal United Services Institute. I would like to thank the librarians and staff at these institutions, particularly Peter Salinger (SOAS), Guy Penman (the London Library) and John Montgommery (RUSI).

Abroad, libraries I consulted included the Central Zionist Archives in Jerusalem (where Naomi Niv did much to help) and the Ben-Zvi Archives. At the Dorot Jewish Library in New York Public Library librarian Michael Terry followed up his imaginative assistance with many emails and read through early versions; at the State Library of New South Wales the librarian, my old neighbour Dagmar Schmidmaer, produced her cousin Erhard Gohl, a former member of the German Templar community in Palestine. When on Magnetic Island in Queensland I used the James Cook University Library, and on the mainland the Townsville Library. Indeed, the happiest times while researching and writing this book have been in libraries or in bookshops such as Geraldine Waddington's in Oundle, the Worlds' End Bookshop in Chelsea, Tonnoir's in Townsville and Hatchard's Piccadilly. Of course, my greatest debt, is to the many authors of the countless articles, papers and books consulted: A.N. Wilson, Andrew Barrow, Andrew Roberts, Martin Gilbert, Kelvin Crombie and Felicity Ashbee. I am fortunate to know or to have met some of the above writers, but other key books, of course, were by people I have never met, including David Fromkin, Max Egremont, Leonard Stein, Nahum Sokolow, Mordechai Eliav, Elie Kedourie, David Schmitd, A.J.P. Taylor and Cyril Falls.

When I met HRH Prince El Hassan bin Talal of Jordan, grandson of King Abdullah, he stressed the need today for unity and pointed out the necessity to emphasize the fact that until the end of the First World War the lands which are now crossed with boundaries formed but one land, Syria, which stretched from Anatolia to Egypt.

I would like to extend a special word of thanks to my commissioning editor Christopher Feeney, who showed monumental patience and gave kind encouragement and let the initial concept expand; and to Elizabeth Stone who skilfully edited the book and pulled it into shape.

In London I received constant help from Jane Dorrell, and when on Magnetic Island from Maureen and Alan Sherriff, and Joelle Fleming who all read through different versions of the manuscript and, of course, my son, Jamie Page. I was fortunate to have the help of two priests, Kieth Turnbull, and Alexander Lucy Smith who helped with the religious sections, as did Don Gallagher and and my niece Jillian Smith. The saddest part of the research was looking up the Zionist Archives in Jerusalem in 2001 and giving the information to to my friend Antonia Thynne, whose father, Anthony Palmer, had been reported missing on the Sea Lion expedition that left Haifa in 1941 and whose father-in-law drew the watercolour of Gallipoli included in the plate section.

I also wish to thank Said Huendi in Amman for his extensive hospitality in April 2002 in showing me so much of Jordan, especially the Crusader castles and the religious sites near the Dead Sea; Neil Cohen, Kelvin Crombie and David Pileggi at Christ Church in the Old City of Jerusalem, who not only gave me a wonderful week in their vaulted rooms near the Tower of David in Autumn 2002, but put me in touch with the Ben-Zvi Archives and the thesis of David Schmidt; and John Flyer who checked my words on 'the Wife of Bath'. There is, alas, not room to list all the people who helped and guided me on this long trail, but further thanks go to Alan Crawford, who introduced me to Felicity Ashbee and kindly arranged the photograph of C.R. Ashbee, Jim Grant, George Haynes and Yigal Sheffy, who all read various early sections of the book and made helpful suggestions, and Michael Jolles, who not only researched many points but came week after week to help me in London and read through the first and final draft of the book. Michael Hickey, Anthony Mockler, Rodney Goutman, Maud Eime, George Sassoon for permission to quote from the works of his father, Siegfried Sassoon, the Seven Pillars of Wisdom Trust to quote from the works of T.E. Lawrence Captain Turker Erturk, Alan Ventress, Sir John Swire who shared his experiences as being ADC for the last British High Commissioner in Jerusalem, Carolyn Lockhart, Judith May, Ross Steele, Clive James, Neal Blewett, Patrick Streeter, Donald Palmer, Gary Davies, Elsa Klensch, Elizabeth Muirhead, Bernard Nevill, Patricia Dunkley, Arthur Wang, Eleanor Yadin, Faith Jones, Rafi Hanuka, Phillip Knightley, Paul Webb, Alison Kremer, Robert Ingle, Anne Arika, Dan Oren of the Jewish Legion Museum, Penny Hart and Barry Tobin who did my web pages.